LONDON: GEORGE BELL AND SONS
PORTUGAL ST. LINCOLN'S INN, W.C.
CAMBRIDGE: DEIGHTON, BELL & CO.
NEW YORK: THE MACMILLAN CO.
BOMBAY: A. H. WHEELER & CO.

BEDE'S ECCLESIASTICA

OF ENGLAN

BEDE'S
ECCLESIASTICAL HISTORY
OF ENGLAND

A REVISED TRANSLATION
WITH INTRODUCTION, LIFE, AND NOTES BY

A. M. SELLAR

LATE VICE-PRINCIPAL OF LADY MARGARET HALL, OXFORD

LONDON
GEORGE BELL AND SONS
1907

EDITOR'S PREFACE

THE English version of the "Ecclesiastical History" in the following pages is a revision of the translation of Dr. Giles, which is itself a revision of the earlier rendering of Stevens. In the present edition very considerable alterations have been made, but the work of Dr. Giles remains the basis of the translation. The Latin text used throughout is Mr. Plummer's. Since the edition of Dr. Giles appeared in 1842, so much fresh work on the subject has been done, and recent research has brought so many new facts to light, that it has been found necessary to rewrite the notes almost entirely, and to add a new introduction. After the appearance of Mr. Plummer's edition of the Historical Works of Bede, it might seem superfluous, for the present at least, to write any notes at all on the "Ecclesiastical History." The present volume, however, is intended to fulfil a different and much humbler function. There has been no attempt at any original work, and no new theories are advanced. The object of the book is merely to present in a short and convenient form the substance of the views held by trustworthy authorities, and it is hoped that it may be found useful by those students who have either no time or no inclination to deal with more important works.

Among the books of which most use has been made, are Mr. Plummer's edition of the "Ecclesiastical History,"

Messrs. Mayor and Lumby's edition of Books III and
IV, Dr. Bright's "Early English Church History," and
Dr. Hunt's "History of the English Church from its
foundation to the Norman Conquest." Many of the
articles in the "Dictionary of Christian Biography" and
the "Dictionary of Christian Antiquities," Dr. Mason's
"Mission of St. Augustine," Dr. Rhŷs's "Celtic Britain,"
and a number of other books, mentioned in the notes,
have been consulted.

For help received in different ways I wish to express
my gratitude to various correspondents and friends. I
am particularly indebted to Mr. Edward Bell, who has
kindly revised my proofs and made many valuable suggestions. For information on certain points I have to
thank the Rev. Charles Plummer, Fellow of Corpus
Christi College, Oxford, Professor Lindsay of St. Andrews University, Miss Wordsworth, Principal, and Miss
Lodge, Vice-Principal of Lady Margaret Hall, Oxford;
and in a very special sense I wish to ackowledge my
obligations to Miss Paterson, Assistant Librarian at the
University Library, St. Andrews, whose unfailing kindness in verifying references, and supplying me with
books, has greatly lightened my labours.

CONTENTS

ECCLESIASTICAL HISTORY

CONTENTS

CONTENTS

CONTENTS

CONTENTS

b

INTRODUCTION

THERE are, it has been estimated, in England and on the Continent, in all about 140 manuscripts of the "Ecclesiastical History." Of these, four date from the eighth century: the Moore MS. (Cambridge), so called, because, after being sold by auction in the reign of William III, it came into the possession of Bishop Moore, who bequeathed it to the University of Cambridge; Cotton, Tiberius A, xiv; Cotton, Tiberius C, ii; and the Namur MS. A detailed account of these, as well as of a great number of other manuscripts, will be found in Mr. Plummer's Introduction to his edition of Bede's Historical Works. He has been the first to collate the four oldest MSS., besides examining numerous others and collating them in certain passages. He has pointed out that two of the MSS. dating from the eighth century (the century in which Bede died), the Moore MS. and Cotton, Tiberius A, xiv, point to a common original which cannot be far removed from Bede's autograph. We are thus brought very near to our author, and may have more than in most cases the assurance that we have before us what he actually meant to say.

The earliest editions were printed on the Continent; the "editio princeps" is believed to date from 1475. A number of editions followed in the sixteenth and seventeenth centuries; the first in England was published by Abraham Whelock at Cambridge in 1643-4. Smith's

edition in 1722 marked a new era in the history of the
book. It was the first critical edition, the text being
based on the Moore MS. collated with three others, of
which two were eighth century MSS.; and succeeding
editors, Stevenson (1841), Giles (1842), Hussey (1846),
the editor in the "Monumenta Historica Britannica"
(1848), Moberly (1869), Holder (1882), base their work
mainly on Smith's. Mr. Mayor and Mr. Lumby together
edited Books III and IV with excellent notes in 1878.
Their text "reproduces exactly the Moore MS." which
they collated with some other Cambridge MSS. (cf.
Mayor and Lumby, Excursus II). In 1896 the Rev. C.
Plummer published his edition of Bede's Historical Works,
the first critical edition since Smith's, and "the very first
which exhibits in an *apparatus criticus* the various readings of the MSS. on which the text is based." For the
student of Bede this admirable book is of the highest
value, and the labours of all succeeding editors are made
comparatively light. Besides the most minute and accurate work on the text, it contains a copious and in-
teresting commentary and the fullest references to the
various sources upon which the editor has drawn.

The first translation of the "Ecclesiastical History" is
the Anglo-Saxon version, executed either by Alfred himself or under his immediate supervision. Of this version
Dr. Hodgkin says: "As this book had become a kind
of classic among churchmen, Alfred allowed himself here
less liberty than in some of his other translations. Some
letters, epitaphs, and similar documents are omitted,
and there is an almost complete erasure of the chapters
relating to the wearisome Paschal controversy. In other
respects the king's translation seems to be a fairly accurate reproduction of the original work." Mr. Plummer,
however, finds it "very rarely available for the settlement of minute differences of reading."

The first modern English translation is Thomas Stapleton's (1565), published at Antwerp. It is a controversial work, intended to point out to Queen Elizabeth "in how many and weighty pointes the pretended reformers of the Church . . . have departed from the patern of that sounde and Catholike faith planted first among Englishmen by holy S. Augustin, our Apostle, and his vertuous company, described truly and sincerely by Venerable Bede, so called in all Christendom for his passing vertues and rare lerning, the Author of this History." To save Elizabeth's time "in espying out the particulars," the translator has "gathered out of the whole History a number of diversities between the pretended religion of Protestants and the primitive faith of the english Church." If charm and appropriateness of style were the only qualities to be aimed at in a translation, we might well content ourselves with this rendering, which fills with despair the translator of to-day, debarred by his date from writing Elizabethan English.

The work was again translated by John Stevens (1723), and a third time (with some omissions) by W. Hurst in 1814. In 1840 Dr. Giles published a new edition of Stevens's translation with certain alterations; and a second edition of the same volume was published in 1842, and incorporated in the collected works of Bede, edited by Dr. Giles. In 1870 a literal translation by the Rev. L. Gidley was published. The present volume is a revision of the translation of Dr. Giles.

A brief analysis of the work may be of some use to the student in keeping distinct the different threads of the narrative, as owing to the variety of subjects introduced, and the want of strict chronological order, it is difficult to grasp the sequence of events as a coherent whole.

The sources from which Bede draws his material are

briefly indicated in the dedication to King Ceolwulf
which forms the Preface, and in it he acknowledges his
obligations to the friends and correspondents who have
helped and encouraged him. For the greater part of
Book I (cc. 1-22), which forms the introduction to his
real subject, he depends on earlier authors. Here he
does not specify his sources, but indicates them generally
as *priorum scripta*. These authors are mainly Pliny,
Solinus, Orosius, Eutropius, and the British historian
Gildas. In the story of Germanus and Lupus he follows
closely the Life of Germanus by Constantius of Lyons.
Prosper of Aquitaine also supplies him with some materials. When he comes to his main subject, the History
of the English Church, he appears to rely but little upon
books. Only a very few are referred to here and there,
e.g., The Life of St. Fursa, The Life of St. Ethelburg, Adamnan's work on the Holy Places, and the
Anonymous Life of St. Cuthbert. That some form of
annalistic records existed before his time, and that these
were consulted by him, we may infer from some of his
chronological references (cf. iii, 1, 9). Local information
with regard to provinces other than Northumbria he
obtains from his correspondents in various parts of England, and these are expressly mentioned in the Preface.

For the history of the Roman mission and of Kent
generally, as well as some particulars with regard to the
conversion of other provinces, his chief source is the
Church of Canterbury, which apparently possessed, besides oral tradition, written documents relating to the
first beginnings of the Church. Moreover, Nothelm, who
was the bearer of much important material, had been to
Rome and had permission to search the papal archives.
But it is in dealing with the history of Northumbria, as
is natural, that Bede's information is most varied and
copious. Much of it is apparently obtained directly from

eye-witnesses of the events, much would doubtless be preserved in the records of the Church of Lindisfarne, to which he had access, perhaps also in his own monastery. We know that the monasteries kept calendars in which the death-days of saints and others were entered, and other records of similar nature (cf. iv, 14), and that these were used as materials for history. | ·

Passing to the history itself, we may trace a division of subjects or periods roughly analogous to the division into books. Book I contains the long introduction, the sending of the Roman mission, and the foundation of the Church; Books II and III, the period of missionary activity and the establishment of Christianity throughout the land. Book IV may be said to describe the period of organization. In Book V the English Church itself becomes a missionary centre, planting the faith in Germany, and drawing the Celtic Churches into conformity with Rome.

BOOK I.—In Book I, cc. 1-22, Bede sketches the early history of Britain, describing the country and giving some account of the various races by whom it was inhabited. The story of the Roman occupation is narrated at some length, the invasions of the Picts and Scots and consequent miseries of the Britons, their appeals for help to the Romans, the final departure of their protectors, and the coming of the Saxons are described. We have some shadowy outlines of British Church History in the legendary account of the conversion of King Lucius, in the story of St. Alban, affording evidence of a great persecution of Christians during the Roman occupation, in the allusions to the Arian and Pelagian heresies, and in the mission of Germanus and Lupus. A brief allusion to the mission of Palladius is all that we hear of the Irish Church at this period.

These chapters are introductory to the main subject, the History of the English Church, which begins in

Chapter 23 with the mission of St. Augustine in 597 A.D.
The reception of the Christian faith in the kingdom of
Kent and the foundation of a national Church occupy the
remaining chapters of the book. Various letters of Pope
Gregory relating to the mission and his answers to the
questions of Augustine are given at length; and the
Book concludes with a piece of Northumbrian history,
Ethelfrid's conquests of the Britons and the defeat of
Aedan, king of the Dalriadic Scots, at Degsastan in
603 A.D.

BOOK II.—Book II opens with a biographical sketch
of Gregory the Great, the founder of the Mission. This
is followed by an account of Augustine's negotiations
with the leaders of the British Church with regard to the
Paschal question and some other matters, his failure to
win them over (a failure apparently largely due to his
own want of tact in dealing with the susceptible Celtic
temperament), his alleged prophecy of disaster and its
fulfilment some time after at the battle of Chester. Then
we have the consecration of Mellitus to London, as
Bishop of the East Saxons, and Justus to Rochester
(604 A.D.); the evangelization of the East Saxons by
Mellitus; the death of Augustine and succession of
Laurentius as Archbishop (no date is given; it may have
been in 605); fresh attempts at union with the Celtic
Churches, in which again we can perceive a failure of
courtesy on the one side met by an obstinate pride on the
other. The death of Ethelbert in Kent (616 A.D.) and
that of Sabert in Essex, soon after, lead to a pagan reaction in both provinces; Mellitus and Justus take refuge
on the Continent; Laurentius, intending to follow them,
is stopped by a vision which leads to the conversion of
King Eadbald and the recovery of Kent for Christianity.
Essex, however, continues to be pagan. On the death of
Laurentius (619 A.D.), Mellitus succeeds to Canterbury
and is himself succeeded by Justus (in 624). In Chapter 9
we enter upon a new development of the highest importance in the work of the mission. The marriage of Edwin,
king of Northumbria, and the Kentish princess, Ethelberg, brings about the conversion of Northumbria

through the preaching of Paulinus. The story is told in detail. Letters from Pope Boniface to Edwin and his consort are quoted at length, Edwin's early history with its bearing on the great crisis of his life is related; finally we have the decisive debate in the Witenagemot at Goodmanham and the baptism of the king at Easter, 627 A.D. Through the influence of Edwin on Earpwald, king of East Anglia, that province is next converted, but on the death of Earpwald the people lapse into paganism for three years, till Christianity is finally established by the labours of Bishop Felix, under the enlightened King Sigbert, who had himself been drawn to the faith in Gaul.

Meanwhile, peace and prosperity reign in Northumbria, and Paulinus extends his preaching to Lindsey. He re-receives the pall from Pope Honorius, in accordance with the original intention of Gregory that the Bishop of York should rank as a metropolitan. At Canterbury, Justus is succeeded by Archbishop Honorius. Parenthetically we have extracts from letters, probably of the year 640 A.D., addressed by the Roman see to the Irish clergy on the Paschal question and the Pelagian heresy.

In Chapter 20 we have a dramatic climax to the book in the overthrow and death of Edwin at the battle of Hatfield in 633 A.D.; the devastation of Northumbria by the British king, Caedwalla, and Penda of Mercia; and the flight of Paulinus, taking with him Ethelberg and Eanfled to Kent, where he ends his life in charge of the Church of Rochester. His work in Northumbria seems for the time, at least, wholly overthrown. Only James the Deacon remains heroically at his post to keep alive the smouldering embers of the faith.

Book III.—Book III opens with the story of the apostasy of the Northumbrian kings and the miseries of the "Hateful Year," terminated by the victory of Oswald at Heavenfield in 634 A.D. Christianity is brought again to Northumbria (635 A.D.) by the Celtic Mission, sent from Iona at the request of Oswald, who nobly co-operates with Aidan in the work of evangelization. Aidan fixes his see at Lindisfarne. The mention of Iona leads to a short account of the mission of St. Columba to the

The book ends with a fresh apostasy in Essex during the miseries of the great plague of 664. Mercia, so lately itself evangelized, becomes a new missionary centre, King Wulfhere sending Bishop Jaruman to recall the East Saxons to the faith.

Book IV.—In all but one of the kingdoms of England Christianity is now, at least in name, established, and the Church settles down to the work of organization. The man for this task is found in Theodore of Tarsus, consecrated Archbishop of the English in 668. He arrives at Canterbury in 669. We hear at once of the vigorous impulse given by him and Abbot Hadrian to the various departments of education there. Finding an irregularity in Ceadda's orders, he completes his ordination and makes him Bishop of the Mercians (probably in 669), with his see at Lichfield. Ceadda's death (672 A.D.), his character, and the miracles and visions connected with him are described. Parenthetically we get an account of Colman's activity in Ireland after his retirement, in consequence of the decision at Whitby. The most important political events at this time are the death of Oswy and succession of Egfrid in Northumbria in 670 or 671, and the death of Egbert and succession of Hlothere in Kent in 673.

In the same year the Council of Hertford, the first English provincial council, is held, and marks the strength and independence of the Church. Theodore proceeds with his reforms in the episcopate. Various events of ecclesiastical importance follow; the East Anglian diocese is divided about this time, and other changes are effected.

Essex, so long prone to lapses into paganism, becomes at this time a centre of religious life under its Bishop Earconwald and its king Sebbi. Earconwald, whose holiness is attested by many miraculous circumstances, was the founder of the monasteries of Chertsey and Barking, the latter of which was ruled by his sister, the saintly Ethelburg. Various miracles are related in connection with her and her monastery. The king of the East Saxons, Sebbi, is a man of unusual piety who resigns his kingdom and receives the tonsure.

After a brief allusion to West Saxon history, the devastation of Kent by Ethelred of Mercia in 676, and certain changes in the episcopate, we come to an important step in the organization of the Church taken by Theodore. In pursuance of his policy of increasing the number of bishops, he subdivides the great Northumbrian diocese. Wilfrid is expelled (678 A.D.). From these events we pass summarily to the evangelization of the South Saxons by Wilfrid, who extends his labours to the Isle of Wight, and thus the last of the English provinces is won for the faith.

In the Council of Hatfield (680 A.D.) the English Church asserts its orthodoxy and unites with the continental Churches in repudiating the heresy of the Monothelites. Turning to Northumbrian history, we have the story of Egfrid's queen, Ethelthryth, and a hymn composed in her honour by Bede. The war between Mercia and Northumbria in 679 is ended by the mediation of Theodore, and a miracle in connection with the battle of the Trent is related.

The remainder of the book is occupied mainly with Northumbrian history, the life and death of Hilda, Abbess of Whitby, the story of the poet Caedmon, the destruction of Coldingham, prophesied by the monk Adamnan, Egfrid's invasion of Ireland (684 A.D.) and of the country of the Picts (685 A.D.), his defeat and death in that year, the decline of Northumbria, the flight of Bishop Trumwine from Abercorn, and the succession of Aldfrid to the kingdom. The death of Hlothere of Kent (685 A.D.) is followed by anarchy in that province, till Wictred succeeds and restores peace.

In Chapters 27-32 we have an account of the life of St. Cuthbert and stories of the miracles wrought by his relics.

BOOK V.—Book V opens with the story of the holy Ethelwald, who succeeded Cuthbert as anchorite at Farne, and a miracle wrought through his intercession. This is followed (cc. 2-6) by an account of John of Beverley, Bishop of Hexham, and the miracles attributed to him. In Chapter 7 we have a piece of West Saxon history: Caedwalla, King of Wessex, after a life of war and bloodshed, goes to Rome to receive baptism there, and dies immediately after his admission into the Church (689 A.D.). He is succeeded by Ini, who in 725 likewise ended his days at Rome.

In 690 Theodore dies, after an episcopate of twenty-two years. Bertwald succeeds him at Canterbury in 693.

At this time Englishmen begin to extend their missionary enterprise abroad. Various missions are undertaken by men who have lived long in Ireland and caught the Celtic zeal for the work of evangelization. The story is told of the attempted mission of Egbert to Germany and the unsuccessful venture of Witbert. Wilbrord (in 690) and others plant the faith among the German tribes.

The vision of Drythelm in inserted here, probably on chronological grounds ("his temporibus"), and other visions of the future world follow.

Apparently about the same time a change is effected in the attitude of the greater part of the Celtic Church towards the Paschal question. The Northern Irish are converted to the Roman usages by Adamnan, Abbot of Iona, whose book on the "Holy Places" is here described (cc. 16-17).

The death of Aldfrid and succession of Osred in Northumbria in 705 are the next events narrated.

About this time the division of the West Saxon diocese is carried out, Aldhelm being appointed to Sherborne and Daniel to Winchester; the South Saxons receive a bishop of their own for the first time. In 709 A.D. Coenred of Mercia and Offa of Essex receive the tonsure at Rome, and in the same year Bishop Wilfrid dies. The story of his life is told.

Not long after, Hadrian dies and is succeeded by Albinus as Abbot of St. Augustine's. Bede's friend, Acca, succeeds Wilfrid as Bishop of Hexham. His services to the Church are enumerated.

An important step is taken at this time by the Northern Picts in the acceptance of the Roman rules with regard to Easter and the tonsure. The letter of Abbot Ceolfrid of Wearmouth and Jarrow to the Pictish king Naiton on this subject is quoted at length. Soon after, Iona yields to the preaching of Egbert, and receives the Catholic usages. Egbert dies in 729. In Chapter 23 a number of events are briefly mentioned; the death of Wictred of Kent in 725, and the succession of his sons, the death of the learned Tobias, Bishop of Rochester, in 726, the appearance of two comets in 729, followed by the devastation of Gaul by the Saracens, the death of the Northumbrian king Osric, and succession of Ceolwulf in 729; finally, the death of Archbishop Bertwald in 731 and the succession of Tatwine. Then follows an account of the state of the English episcopate in 731, the year in which Bede finished the History. The relations of the English with Picts, Scots, and Britons are described, and some allusion is made to the growth of monasticism in this time of external peace.

The book closes in Chapter 24 with a chronological summary of the whole work, an autobiographical sketch of the author, and a list of his works.

LIFE OF BEDE

FEW lives afford less material for the biographer than Bede's; few seem to possess a more irresistible fascination. Often as the simple story has been told, the desire to tell it afresh appears to be perennial. And yet it is perhaps as wholly devoid of incident as any life could be. The short autobiographical sketch at the end of the " Ecclesiastical History " tells us practically all: that he was born in the territory of the twin monastery of Wearmouth and Jarrow; that at the age of seven he was sent by his kinsfolk to be brought up, first under the Abbot Benedict, afterwards under Ceolfrid; that in his nineteenth year (the canonical age was twenty-five) he was admitted to the diaconate, and received priest's orders in his thirtieth year, in both instances at the hands of John, Bishop of Hexham, and by order of the Abbot Ceolfrid; that he spent his whole life in the monastery in learning, in teaching, and in writing, and in the observance of the monastic rule and attendance at the daily services of the Church. Of his family we know nothing; the name Beda appears to have been not uncommon. The fact that he was handed over by kinsmen (" cura propinquorum ") to Abbot Benedict would seem to imply that he was an orphan when he entered the monastery at the age of seven, but it was not unusual for parents to dedicate their infant children to the religious life, in many cases even at an earlier age than Bede's. We may compare the story of the little boy, Aesica, at Barking, related by Bede, and of Elfled, the daughter of Oswy, dedicated by her father before she was a year old.

c

The epithet "Venerable," commonly attached to his name, has given rise to more than one legend. It was apparently first applied to him in the ninth century, and is said to have been an appellation of priests. The best known of these legends is Fuller's story of a certain "dunce monk" who set about writing Bede's epitaph, and being unable to complete the verse, "Hic sunt in fossa Bedae . . . ossa," went to bed with his task unfinished. Returning to it in the morning, he found that an angel had filled the gap with the word "venerabilis." Another account tells how Bede, in his old age, when his eyes were dim, was induced by certain "mockers" to preach, under the mistaken belief that the people were assembled to hear him. As he ended his sermon with a solemn invocation of the Trinity, the angels (in one version it is the stones of a rocky valley) responded "Amen, very venerable Bede."

The land on which Bede was born was granted by Egfrid to Benedict Biscop for the foundation of the monasteries a short time after the birth of Bede. Wearmouth was founded in 674, Jarrow in 681 or 682. Bede was among those members of the community who were transferred to Jarrow under Abbot Ceolfrid, and under his rule and that of his successor, Huaetbert, he passed his life. With regard to the chief dates, the authorities differ, Simeon of Durham and others placing his birth as late as 677. Bede himself tells us that he was in his fifty-ninth year when he wrote the short autobiography at the end of the History. That work was finished in 731, and there seems to be no good reason to suppose that the autobiographical sketch was written at a later time. We may infer then that he was born in 673, that he was ordained deacon in 691 and priest in 702. For his death, 735, the date given in the "Continuation," seems to be supported by the evidence of the letter of Cuthbert to Cuthwin (*v. infra*). From this it appears that he died on a Wednesday, which nevertheless is called Ascension Day, implying, doubtless, that his death occurred on the eve, after the festival had begun, according to ecclesiastical reckoning. It is further explained

that Ascension Day was on the 26th of May ("VII
Kal. Junii "),[1] which was actually the case in the year
735.

Beyond the testimony borne to his exceptional diligence
as a student in a letter from Alcuin to the monks of
Wearmouth and Jarrow, we hear nothing of his childhood and early youth. One anecdote in the Anonymous
History of the Abbots may perhaps refer to him, though
no name is given. It tells how, when the plague of 686
devastated the monastery, the Abbot Ceolfrid, for lack
of fit persons to assist at the daily offices, decided to
recite the psalms without antiphons, except at vespers
and matins. But after a week's trial, unable to bear it
any longer, he restored the antiphons to their proper
place, and with the help of one little boy carried on the
services in the usual manner. This little boy is described
as being, at the time the History was written, a priest of
that monastery who "duly, both by his words and
writings, commends the Abbot's praiseworthy deeds to
all who seek to know them," and he has generally been
supposed to be Bede.

In the "Ecclesiastical History" (IV, 3) there is an
allusion to Bede's teachers, one of whom, Trumbert,
educated at Lastingham under Ceadda, is mentioned by
name. The monastery of Wearmouth and Jarrow must
have offered exceptional facilities for study. Benedict
had enriched it with many treasures which he brought
with him from his travels. Chief among these was the
famous library which he founded and which was enlarged
by Abbot Ceolfrid. Here Bede acquired that wide and
varied learning revealed in his historical, scientific, and
theological works. He studied with particular care and
reverence the patristic writings; his theological treatises
were, as he says, "compiled out of the works of the
venerable Fathers." He must have had a considerable

---

[1] The St. Gallen MS. (ninth century) has, however, "VII Id.
Mai." Messrs. Mayor and Lumby, adopting this reading, place
his death as late as 742, in which year the eve of Ascension Day
fell on May 9th. For their argument, v. Mayor and Lumby, pp.
401, 402.

knowledge of Greek, probably he knew some Hebrew. Though he is not wholly free from the mediaeval church-man's distrust of pagan authors, he constantly betrays his acquaintance with them, and the sense of form which must unconsciously influence the student of classical literature has passed into his own writings and preserved him from the barbarism of monkish Latin. His style is singularly clear, simple, and fluent, as free from obscurity as from affectation and bombast.

Thus was the foundation laid of that sound learning upon which his widespread influence both as a teacher and writer was reared. "I always took delight," he tells us, "in learning, or teaching, or writing." Prob-ably his writing was, as is so often the case, the out-come of his teaching; his object in both is to meet "the needs of the brethren." One of his pupils was Archbishop Egbert, the founder of the school of York, which gave a fresh impulse to learning, not only in England, but through Alcuin in France, at a time when a revival was most to be desired.

It was to Egbert that he paid one of the only two visits which he records. In the "Epistola ad Ecgbertum" he alludes to a short stay he had made with him the year before, and declines, on account of the illness which proved to be his last, an invitation to visit him again. He visited Lindisfarne in connection with his task of writing the life of Cuthbert. Otherwise we have no authentic record of any absence from the monastery. The story that he went to Rome at the request of Pope Sergius, founded on a statement of William of Malmes-bury, is now regarded as highly improbable. The oldest MS. of the letter of Sergius, requesting Ceolfrid to send one of his monks to Rome, has no mention of the name of Bede. If such an event had ever disturbed his ac-customed course of life, it is inconceivable that he should nowhere allude to it. Still less is the assertion that he lived and taught at Cambridge one which need be seriously debated by the present generation.

We may fairly assume that, except for a few short absences such as the visits to York and Lindisfarne, his whole life was spent in the monastery. It must have been a life of unremitting toil. His writings, numerous as they are, covering a wide range of subjects and involving the severest study, can only have been a part of his work; he had, besides, his duties as priest, teacher, and member of a religious community to fulfil. Even the manual labour of his literary work must have been considerable. He did not employ an amanuensis, and he had not the advantages with regard to copyists which a member of one of the larger monasteries might have had. "Ipse mihi dictator simul notarius (= shorthand writer) et librarius (= copyist)," he writes. Yet he never flags. Through all the outward monotony of his days his own interest remains fresh. He "takes delight" ("dulce habui") in it all. It is a life full of eager activity in intellectual things, of a keen and patriotic interest in the wider life beyond the monastery walls, which shows itself sadly enough in his reflections on the evils of the times, of the ardent charity which spends itself in labour for the brethren, and, pervading the whole, that spirit of quiet obedience and devotion which his own simple words describe as "the observance of monastic rule and the daily charge of singing in the Church." We can picture him, at the appointed hours, breaking off his absorbing occupations to take his place at the daily offices, lest, as he believed, he should fail to meet the angels there. Alcuin records a saying of his, "I know that angels visit the canonical hours and the congregations of the brethren. What if they do not find me among the brethren? May they not say, 'Where is Bede?'"

It is probably here, in this harmony of work and devotion, that we may find the secret of the fascination in the record of his uneventful days. It reconciles the sharp antithesis between the active and the contemplative life. It seems to attain to that ideal of "toil unsever'd from tranquillity" which haunts us all, but which we have almost ceased to associate with the life of man under present conditions. Balance, moderation, or rather, that rare quality which has been well called "the sanity of

saintliness," [1] these give a unity to the life of Bede and
preserve him from the exaggerations of the conventual
ideal. With all his admiration for the ascetic life, he
recognizes human limitations. It is cheering to find that
even he felt the need of a holiday. "Having completed,"
he writes, "the third book of the Commentary on
Samuel, I thought I would rest awhile, and, after recovering in that way my delight in study and writing,
proceed to take in hand the fourth." Intellectual power
commands his homage, but his mind is open to the ap-
preciation of all forms of excellence. It is the unlearned
brother, unfit for study and occupied in manual labour,
to whom, in his story, it is vouchsafed to hear the singing
of the angels who came to summon Ceadda to his rest.
The life of devotion ranks highest in his estimation, but
he records with approval how St. Cuthbert thought "that
to afford the weak brethren the help of his exhortation
stood in the stead of prayer, knowing that He Who said
'Thou shalt love the Lord thy God,' said likewise,
'Thou shalt love thy neighbour as thyself.'" He tells
us how St. Gregory bewailed his own loss in being
forced by his office to be entangled in worldly affairs.
"But," adds the human-hearted biographer, "it behoves us to believe that he lost nothing of his monastic
perfection by reason of his pastoral charge, but rather
that he gained greater profit through the labour of converting many, than by the former calm of his private
life." Yet he holds that this immunity from the evil influence of the world was chiefly due to Gregory's care in
organizing his house like a monastery and safeguarding
the opportunities for prayer and devotional study, even
while he was immersed in affairs at the court of Constantinople, and afterwards, when he held the most
onerous office in the Church.

This quality of sanity shows itself again in an unusual
degree of fairness to opponents. The Paschal error,
indeed, moves his indignation in a manner which is in-

[1] The phrase is the present Bishop of Oxford's in "Studies in
the Christian Character."

comprehensible and distasteful to the modern reader, but
even in the perverse and erring Celts he can recognize
"a zeal of God, though not according to knowledge."
Aidan's holiness of life wins from him a warm tribute of
admiration. In the monks of Iona, the stronghold of
the Celtic system, he can perceive the fruit of good
works and find an excuse for their error in their isolated
situation. In the British Church it is the lack of missionary zeal, rather than their attitude towards the Easter
question, which calls forth his strongest condemnation.

A characteristic akin to this is his love of truth. As a
historian, it shows itself in his scrupulous care in in-
vestigating evidence and in acknowledging the sources
from which he draws. Nowhere is his intellectual honesty
more apparent than in dealing with what he believes to
be the miraculous element in his history. In whatever
way we may regard these anecdotes, there can be no
doubt that Bede took the utmost pains to assure himself
of their authenticity. He is careful to acquire, if possible, first-hand evidence; where this cannot be obtained,
he scrupulously mentions the lack of it. He admits only
the testimony of witnesses of high character and generally quotes them by name.

These are but a few of the glimpses afforded us of the
personality of Bede, a personality never obtruded, but
everywhere unconsciously revealed in his work. Everywhere we find the impress of a mind of wide intellectual
grasp, a character of the highest saintliness, and a gentle
refinement of thought and feeling. The lofty spirituality
of Bede, his great learning and scholarly attainment are
the more striking when we reflect how recently his nation
had emerged from barbarism and received Christianity
and the culture which it brought with it to these shores.

The letter in which he declines Egbert's invitation on
the plea of illness is dated November, 734. If we may
assume that his death took place on the eve of Ascension
Day in 735, no long period of enfeebled health clouded
the close of his life, and weakness never interrupted his
work. His death has been described by his pupil, Cuthbert, who afterwards became Abbot of Wearmouth and

Jarrow in succession to Huaetbert, in the letter quoted
below. He was first buried at Jarrow but, according to
Simeon of Durham, his relics were stolen by the priest,
Elfred, and carried to Durham. In 1104, when the bones
of Cuthbert were translated to the new Cathedral, those
of Bede were found with them. Not long after, Hugh de
Puisac erected a shrine of gold and silver, adorned with
jewels, in which he placed them, along with the relics of
many other saints. The shrine disappeared at the Re-
formation, and only the stone on which it rested remains.[1]

Letter of Cuthbert to Cuthwin.

"To his fellow-lector, Cuthwin, beloved in Christ,
Cuthbert, his fellow-student, greeting and salvation for
ever in the Lord. I have very gladly received the gift
which thou sentest to me, and with much joy have read
thy devout and learned letter, wherein I found that which
I greatly desired, to wit, that masses and holy prayers
are diligently offered by you for our father and master
Bede, beloved of God. Wherefore I rejoice, rather for
love of him than from confidence in my own power, to
relate in few words after what manner he departed out
of this world, understanding also that thou hast desired
and asked this of me. He was troubled with weakness
and chiefly with difficulty in breathing, yet almost without pain, for about a fortnight before the day of our
Lord's Resurrection; and thus he afterwards passed his
time, cheerful and rejoicing, giving thanks to Almighty
God every day and night, nay, every hour, till the day of
our Lord's Ascension, to wit, the twenty-sixth day of May,
and daily gave lessons to us, his disciples; and whatsoever remained of the day he spent in singing psalms, as
far as he was able; he also strove to pass all the night
joyfully in prayer and thanksgiving to God, save only
when a short sleep prevented it; and then he no sooner
awoke than he straightway began again to repeat the
well-known sacred songs, and ceased not to give thanks

[1] Stevenson, "Church Historians," vol. i.

to God with uplifted hands. I declare with truth that
I have never seen with my eyes, or heard with my ears,
any man so earnest in giving thanks to the living God.
O truly blessed man! He repeated the words of St. Paul
the Apostle, ' It is a fearful thing to fall into the hands
of the living God,' and much more out of Holy Scripture;
wherein also he admonished us to think of our last hour,
and to arise out of the sleep of the soul; and being
learned in our native poetry, he said also in our tongue,
concerning the dread parting of souls from the body:

> Fore then neidfaerae
> naenig uiuurthit
> thonc suotturra
> than him tharf sie .
> to ymb hycgannae
> aer his hin iongae
> huaet his gastae
> godaes aeththa yflaes
> aefter deothdaege
> doemid uueorthae.

Which being interpreted is: ' Before the inevitable
journey hence, no man is wiser than is needful that he
may consider, ere the soul departs, what good or evil it
hath done and how it shall be judged after its departure.'
　　" He also sang antiphons for our comfort and his own.
One of these is, ' O King of Glory, Lord of all power,
Who, triumphing this day, didst ascend above all the
heavens, leave us not comfortless, but send to us the
promise of the Father, even the Spirit of Truth—Hallelujah.' And when he came to the words, ' leave us not
comfortless,' he burst into tears and wept much. And
an hour after, he fell to repeating what he had begun.
And this he did the whole day, and we, hearing it,
mourned with him and wept. Now we read and now we
lamented, nay, we wept even as we read. In such rapture
we passed the fifty days' festival ' till the aforesaid day;
and he rejoiced greatly and gave God thanks, because he
had been accounted worthy to suffer such weakness.
And he often said, ' God scourgeth every son whom He

---

¹ From Easter to Whitsuntide.

receiveth'; and the words of St. Ambrose, ' I have not
so lived as to be ashamed to live among you ; but neither
do I fear to die, because we have a merciful Lord.' And
during those days, besides the lessons we had daily from
him, and the singing of the Psalms, there were two
memorable works, which he strove to finish; to wit, his
translation of the Gospel of St. John, from the beginning,
as far as the words, ' But what are they among so
many?' into our own tongue, for the benefit of the
Church of God; and some selections from the books of
Bishop Isidore, saying, ' I would not have my boys read
a lie, nor labour herein without profit after my death.'

" When the Tuesday before the Ascension of our Lord
came, he began to suffer still more in his breathing, and
there was some swelling in his feet. But he went on
teaching all that day and dictating cheerfully, and now
and then said among other things, ' Learn quickly, I
know not how long I shall endure, and whether my
Maker will not soon take me away.' But to us it seemed
that haply he knew well the time of his departure; and
so he spent the night, awake, in giving of thanks. And
when the morning dawned, that is, on the Wednesday,
he bade us write with all speed what we had begun.
And this we did until the third hour. And from the third
hour we walked in procession with the relics of the
saints, according to the custom of that day.[1] And there
was one of us with him who said to him, ' There is still
one chapter wanting of the book which thou hast been
dictating, but I deem it burdensome for thee to be questioned any further.' He answered, ' Nay, it is light,
take thy pen and make ready, and write quickly.' And
this was done. But at the ninth hour he said to me,
' I have certain treasures in my coffer, some spices,
napkins and incense; run quickly and bring the priests
of our monastery to me, that I may distribute among
them the gifts which God has bestowed on me.' And
this I did trembling, and when they were come, he spoke
to every one of them, admonishing and entreating them

---

[1] Rogation Wednesday.

that they should diligently offer masses and prayers for him, and they promised readily. But they all mourned and wept, sorrowing most of all for the words which he spake, because they thought that they should see his face no long time in this world. But they rejoiced for that he said, 'It is time for me, if it be my Maker's will, to be set free from the flesh, and come to Him Who, when as yet I was not, formed me out of nothing. I have lived long; and well has my pitiful judge disposed my life for me; the time of my release is at hand; for my soul longs to see Christ my King in His beauty.' Having said this and much more for our profit and edification, he passed his last day in gladness till the evening; and the aforesaid boy, whose name was Wilbert, still said, 'Dear master, there is yet one sentence not written.' He answered, 'It is well, write it.' Soon after, the boy said, 'Now it is written.' And he said, 'It is well, thou hast said truly, it is finished. Take my head in thy hands, for I rejoice greatly to sit facing my holy place where I was wont to pray, that I too, sitting there, may call upon my Father.' And thus on the pavement of his little cell, chanting 'Glory be to the Father, and to the Son, and to the Holy Ghost,' and the rest, he breathed his last.

"And without doubt we must believe that inasmuch as he had always been devout and earnest on earth in the praise of God, his soul was carried by angels to the joys of Heaven which he desired. And all who heard him or beheld the death of our father Bede, said that they had never seen any other end his life in so great devotion and peace. For, as thou hast heard, so long as the soul abode in the body, he chanted the 'Gloria Patri' and other words to the glory of God, and with outstretched hands ceased not to give thanks to God.

"But know this, that much could be told and written concerning him, but my want of learning cuts short my words. Nevertheless, with the help of God, I purpose at leisure to write more fully concerning him, of those things which I saw with my own eyes and heard with my own ears."

THE ECCLESIASTICAL HISTORY OF
THE ENGLISH NATION

PREFACE

To the most glorious king Ceolwulf.[1] *Bede, the servant of Christ and Priest.*

I FORMERLY, at your request, most readily sent to you the Ecclesiastical History of the English Nation, which I had lately published, for you to read and judge; and I now send it again to be transcribed, and more fully studied at your leisure. And I rejoice greatly at the sincerity and zeal, with which you not only diligently give ear to hear the words of Holy Scripture, but also industriously take care to become acquainted with the actions and sayings of former men of renown, especially of our own nation. For if history relates good things of good men, the attentive hearer is excited to imitate that which is good; or if it recounts evil things of wicked persons, none the less the conscientious and devout hearer or reader, shunning that which is hurtful and wrong, is the

ERRATA

Page 9, headline, *for* '54 A.D.' *read* '54 B.C.'
Page 21, headline, *for* '394 A.D.' *read* '395 A.D.'
Page 214, note 4, *for* 'cc.' *read* 'pp.'
Page 215, note 1, *for* 'St. James "the Less"' *read* 'James, "the Lord's brother."'
Page 220, note 2, *for* 'Lumley' *read* 'Lumby.'
Page 254, note 1, line 4, *for* 'existence' *read* 'co-existence.'
Page 316, line 7, *for* 'Gedmund' *read* 'Gebmund.'
Page 346, note 6, *for* 'p. 56' *read* 'p. 356.'

THE ECCLESIASTICAL HISTORY OF
THE ENGLISH NATION

PREFACE

To the most glorious king Ceolwulf.[1] Bede, the servant of Christ and Priest.

I FORMERLY, at your request, most readily sent to you the Ecclesiastical History of the English Nation, which I had lately published, for you to read and judge; and I now send it again to be transcribed, and more fully studied at your leisure. And I rejoice greatly at the sincerity and zeal, with which you not only diligently give ear to hear the words of Holy Scripture, but also industriously take care to become acquainted with the actions and sayings of former men of renown, especially of our own nation. For if history relates good things of good men, the attentive hearer is excited to imitate that which is good; or if it recounts evil things of wicked persons, none the less the conscientious and devout hearer or reader, shunning that which is hurtful and wrong, is the more earnestly fired to perform those things which he knows to be good, and worthy of the service of God. And as you have carefully marked this, you are desirous that the said history should be more fully made known to yourself, and to those over whom the Divine Authority has appointed you governor, from your great regard to the common good. But to the end that I may remove all occasion of doubting what I have written, both from

---

[1] King of Northumbria, cf. V, 23. He succeeded Osric, 729 A.D. In a revolt he was forcibly tonsured, 731, but restored. He voluntarily became a monk in Lindisfarne in 737. The fact that Bede submitted the Ecclesiastical History to him for revision bears witness to his piety and learning.

B

yourself and other readers or hearers of this history, I
will take care briefly to show you from what authors I
chiefly learned the same.

My principal authority and aid in this work was the
most learned and reverend Abbot Albinus;[1] who, educated in the Church of Canterbury by those venerable
and learned men, Archbishop Theodore[2] of blessed
memory, and the Abbot Hadrian,[3] transmitted to me by
Nothelm,[4] the pious priest of the Church of London,
either in writing, or by word of mouth of the same
Nothelm, all that he thought worthy of memory that
had been done in the province of Kent, or the adjacent
parts, by the disciples of the blessed Pope Gregory,[5] as
he had learned the same either from written records, or
the traditions of his predecessors. The same Nothelm,
afterwards went to Rome, and having, with leave of
the present Pope Gregory,[6] searched into the archives of
the Holy Roman Church, found there some epistles of
the blessed Pope Gregory, and other popes; and, returning home, by the advice of the aforesaid most reverend
father Albinus, brought them to me, to be inserted in my
history. Thus, from the beginning of this volume to the
time when the English nation received the faith of Christ,
we have acquired matter from the writings of former men,

[1] Albinus, the first English abbot of the monastery of SS. Peter
and Paul at Canterbury, succeeded Hadrian in 709 or 710. On his
scholarship, cf. V, 20.

[2] Theodore, the great archbishop, noted for his organization of
the English Church and his services to education, consecrated in
668, at the age of sixty-five, by Pope Vitalian, on the recommendation of Hadrian, who had himself twice declined the office of archbishop. Theodore was a native of Tarsus, in Cilicia, a man of
great learning and scholarly attainments. Cf. IV, 1.

[3] Hadrian (v. previous note, cf. IV, 1), an African by birth, sent
to England by Pope Vitalian along with Theodore, became Abbot
of SS. Peter and Paul, Canterbury. He co-operated with Theodore
in his educational work.

[4] A presbyter of London, afterwards Archbishop of Canterbury,
735. Received the *pallium* (v. I, 27, p. 54, note) in 736.

[5] Gregory I (the Great), who sent the Roman mission to England.

[6] Gregory II, v. Plummer *ad loc.* for arguments showing con-
clusively that Gregory III cannot be meant.

gathered from various sources; but from that time till the present, what was transacted in the Church of Canterbury by the disciples of the blessed Pope Gregory or their successors, and under what kings the same happened, has been conveyed to us, as we have said, by Nothelm through the industry of the aforesaid Abbot Albinus. They also partly informed me by what bishops and under what kings the provinces of the East and West Saxons, as also of the East Angles, and of the Northumbrians, received the grace of the Gospel. In short, I was chiefly encouraged to undertake this work by the exhortations of the same Albinus. In like manner, Daniel,[1] the most reverend Bishop of the West Saxons, who is still living, communicated to me in writing some things relating to the Ecclesiastical History of that province, and the adjoining one of the South Saxons, as also of the Isle of Wight. But how, by the ministry of those holy priests of Christ, Cedd[2] and Ceadda,[3] the province of the Mercians was brought to the faith of Christ, which they knew not before, and how that of the East Saxons recovered the faith after having rejected it, and how those fathers lived and died, we learned from the brethren of the monastery, which was built by them, and is called Laestingaeu.[4] Further, what ecclesiastical matters took place in the province of the East Angles, was partly made known to us from the writings and tradition of former men, and partly by the account of the most reverend Abbot Esi.[5] What was done with regard to the faith of Christ, and what was the episcopal succession in the province of Lindsey,[6] we had either from the letters of the most reverend

[1] Cf. IV, 16, and V, 18. In V, 23 he is more accurately described as "Ventanus antistes." He was consecrated Bishop of Winchester when the West Saxon bishopric was divided in 705; and his diocese comprised only the smaller part of Wessex. He was the friend and counsellor of St. Boniface.
[2] Bishop of the East Saxons, cf. III, 21 foll.
[3] St. Chad, Bishop of the Northumbrians, afterwards of Lichfield; brother of Cedd: v. III, 23, 28; IV, 2, 3; V, 19.
[4] Lastingham, near Pickering in Yorkshire N.R., v. III, 23.
[5] Nothing further is known of him.
[6] The district to the north of the Wash.

prelate Cynibert,[1] or by word of mouth from other persons
of good credit. But what was done in the Church in the
different parts of the province of Northumbria from the
time when they received the faith of Christ till this present, I received not on the authority of any one man, but
by the faithful testimony of innumerable witnesses, who
might know or remember the same; besides what I had
of my own knowledge. Wherein it is to be observed,
that what I have written concerning our most holy father,
Bishop Cuthbert,[2] either in this volume, or in my account
of his life and actions, I partly took from what I found
written of him by the brethren of the Church of Lindisfarne,[3] accepting without reserve the statements I found
there; but at the same time took care to add such
things as I could myself have knowledge of by the faithful testimony of trustworthy informants. And I humbly
entreat the reader, that if he shall find in these our
writings anything not delivered according to the truth,
he will not lay the blame of it on me, for, as the true
rule of history requires, withholding nothing, I have laboured to commit to writing such things as I could gather
from common report, for the instruction of posterity.
   Moreover, I beseech all men who shall hear or read
this history of our nation, that for my infirmities both of
mind and body, they will offer up frequent intercessions
to the throne of Grace. And I further pray, that in recompense for the labour wherewith I have recorded in
the several provinces and more important places those
events which I considered worthy of note and of interest
to their inhabitants, I may for my reward have the benefit
of their pious prayers.

[1] Bishop of Sidnacester, in the province of Lindsey. He died
in 732: v. IV, 12; V, 23.
[2] The saint and hermit who was for two years Bishop of Lindisfarne, 685-687: v. IV, 26-32. Bede wrote his life both in prose and
verse.
[3] Holy Island, off the coast of Northumberland. Aidan chose
it as the place of his see and monastery in 635: v. III, 3.

BOOK I

CHAP. I. *Of the Situation of Britain and Ireland, and of their ancient inhabitants.*

BRITAIN, an island in the Atlantic, formerly called Albion, lies to the north-west, facing, though at a considerable distance, the coasts of Germany, France, and Spain, which form the greatest part of Europe. It extends 800 miles in length towards the north, and is 200 miles in breadth, except where several promontories extend further in breadth, by which its compass is made to be 4,875 miles.[1] To the south lies Belgic Gaul. To its nearest shore there is an easy passage from the city of Rutubi Portus, by the English now corrupted into Reptacaestir.[2] The distance from here across the sea to Gessoriacum,[3] the nearest shore in the territory of the Morini,[4] is fifty miles, or as some writers say, 450 furlongs. On the other side of the island, where it opens upon the boundless ocean, it has the islands called Orcades. Britain is rich in grain and trees, and is well adapted for feeding cattle and beasts of burden. It also produces vines in some places, and has plenty of land and water fowl of divers sorts; it is remarkable also for rivers abounding in fish, and plentiful springs. It has the greatest plenty of salmon and eels; seals are also frequently taken, and dolphins, as also whales; besides many sorts of shell-fish, such as mussels, in which are often found excellent pearls of all colours, red, purple, violet and green, but chiefly white. There is also a great abundance of snails, of which the scarlet dye is made, a most beautiful red, which never fades with the heat of the sun or exposure to rain, but the older it is, the more beautiful it becomes. It has both salt and hot

[1] This total varies in different authors. The first few pages of Bede are to a great extent copied out of Pliny, Solinus, Orosius, and Gildas.
[2] Richborough, Kent.   [3] Boulogne.
[4] Cf. Caes., B.G., *passim*; Verg., Aen., VIII, 727.

springs, and from them flow rivers which furnish hot
baths, proper for all ages and both sexes, in separate
places, according to their requirements. For water, as
St. Basil says,[1] receives the quality of heat, when it runs
along certain metals, and becomes not only hot but
scalding. Britain is rich also in veins of metals, as copper, iron, lead, and silver; it produces a great deal of
excellent jet, which is black and sparkling, and burns
when put to the fire, and when set on fire, drives away
serpents; being warmed with rubbing, it attracts whatever is applied to it, like amber. The island was formerly
distinguished by twenty-eight famous cities, besides innumerable forts, which were all strongly secured with
walls, towers, gates, and bars. And, because it lies
almost under the North Pole, the nights are light in
summer, so that at midnight the beholders are often in
doubt whether the evening twilight still continues, or
that of the morning has come; since the sun at night
returns to the east in the northern regions without passing far beneath the earth. For this reason the days are
of a great length in summer, and on the other hand, the
nights in winter are eighteen hours long, for the sun
then withdraws into southern parts. In like manner the
nights are very short in summer, and the days in winter,
that is, only six equinoctial hours. Whereas, in Armenia,
Macedonia, Italy, and other countries of the same latitude, the longest day or night extends but to fifteen
hours, and the shortest to nine.

There are in the island at present, following the number
of the books in which the Divine Law was written, five[2]
languages of different nations employed in the study and
confession of the one self-same knowledge, which is of
highest truth and true sublimity, to wit, English, British,
Scottish, Pictish, and Latin, the last having become
common to all by the study of the Scriptures. But at
first this island had no other inhabitants but the Britons,

[1] In his Hexameron.
[2] Latin is included as being the ecclesiastical language common
to all. Bede does not imply that there was a Latin-speaking race
still in the island.

from whom it derived its name, and who, coming over
into Britain, as is reported, from Armorica,[1] possessed
themselves of the southern parts thereof. Starting from
the south, they had occupied the greater part of the
island, when it happened, that the nation of the Picts,
putting to sea from Scythia,[2] as is reported, in a few
ships of war, and being driven by the winds beyond the
bounds of Britain, came to Ireland and landed on its
northern shores. There, finding the nation of the Scots,
they begged to be allowed to settle among them, but
could not succeed in obtaining their request. Ireland is
the largest island next to Britain, and lies to the west of
it; but as it is shorter than Britain to the north, so, on
the other hand, it runs out far beyond it to the south,
over against the northern part of Spain, though a wide
sea lies between them. The Picts then, as has been said,
arriving in this island by sea, desired to have a place
granted them in which they might settle. The Scots
answered that the island could not contain them both;
but " We can give you good counsel," said they, "whereby you may know what to do; we know there is another
island, not far from ours, to the eastward, which we often
see at a distance, when the days are clear. If you will go
thither, you can obtain settlements; or, if any should oppose you, we will help you." The Picts, accordingly, sailing over into Britain, began to inhabit the northern parts

[1] In Caesar's time, the whole district lying along the north-
western coast of Gaul, afterwards narrowed down to the modern
Brittany. That the Britons (or Brythons) came from Gaul is doubtless a fact. Another branch of the Celtic race, the Goidels or Gaels,
appears to have been in possession in Britain before them.
[2] By Scythia Bede means Scandinavia. He only mentions this
account as a tradition. The problem of the Picts has not been
solved yet. According to one view, they belonged to the pre-
Aryan inhabitants of Britain, pushed westward and northward by
the Celtic invaders. In Scotland they held their own for a considerable time in a wide tract of country, and they may have to
some extent amalgamated with the Celts who dispossessed them
(Rhŷs). Others regard them as Celts of the same branch as Welsh,
Cornish, and Britons, being probably nearest to Cornish. The
absence of all but the scantiest remains of their language makes
the question of their origin one of great difficulty.

thereof, for the Britons had possessed themselves of the southern. Now the Picts had no wives, and asked them of the Scots; who would not consent to grant them upon any other terms, than that when any question should arise, they should choose a king from the female royal race rather than from the male: which custom, as is well known, has been observed among the Picts to this day.[1] In process of time, Britain, besides the Britons and the Picts, received a third nation, the Scots, who, migrating from Ireland under their leader, Reuda, either by fair means, or by force of arms, secured to themselves those settlements among the Picts which they still possess. From the name of their commander, they are to this day called Dalreudini; for, in their language, Dal signifies a part.[2]

Ireland is broader than Britain and has a much healthier and milder climate; for the snow scarcely ever lies there above three days: no man makes hay in the summer for winter's provision, or builds stables for his beasts of burden. No reptiles are found there, and no snake can live there; for, though snakes are often carried thither out of Britain, as soon as the ship comes near the shore, and the scent of the air reaches them, they die. On the contrary, almost all things in the island are efficacious against poison. In truth, we have known that when men have been bitten by serpents, the scrapings of leaves of books that were brought out of Ireland, being put into water, and given them to drink, have immediately absorbed the spreading poison, and assuaged the swelling.

[1] The legend is an attempt to account for the law of Pictish succession, which was vested in the mother, v. Rhŷs, "Celtic Britain," pp. 170-171.

[2] "Dal," a division or part, is common in Irish names. Dalriada was a district in the north-eastern part of Ulster. From there, a tribe of Scots (a Celtic race who settled in Ireland at some unknown period) came to Kintyre and spread along the coasts of Argyll, which took from them the name of Dalriada (probably circ. 500 A.D.). They brought the Christian religion with them. Bede follows that version of the legend which makes Cairbre Riada, the eponymous hero of the Irish Dalriada (circ. 200 A.D.), himself found the colony in Scotland.

The island abounds in milk and honey, nor is there any lack of vines, fish, or fowl; and it is noted for the hunting of stags and roe-deer. It is properly the country of the Scots, who, migrating from thence, as has been said, formed the third nation in Britain in addition to the Britons and the Picts.

There is a very large gulf of the sea, which formerly divided the nation of the Britons from the Picts; it runs from the west far into the land, where, to this day, stands a strong city of the Britons, called Alcluith.[1] The Scots, arriving on the north side of this bay, settled themselves there.

CHAP. II. *How Caius Julius Caesar was the first Roman that came into Britain.*

Now Britain had never been visited by the Romans, and was entirely unknown to them before the time of Caius Julius Caesar, who, in the year 693 after the foundation of Rome, but the sixtieth year[2] before the Incarnation of our Lord, was consul with Lucius Bibulus. While he was making war upon the Germans and the Gauls, who were divided only by the river Rhine, he came into the province of the Morini, whence is the nearest and shortest passage into Britain. Here, having provided about eighty ships of burden and fast-sailing vessels, he sailed over into Britain; where, being first roughly handled in a battle, and then caught in a storm, he lost a considerable part of his fleet, no small number of foot-soldiers, and almost all his cavalry. Returning into Gaul, he put his legions into winter-quarters, and gave orders for building six hundred sail of both sorts. With these he again crossed over early in spring into Britain, but, whilst he was marching with the army against the enemy, the ships, riding at anchor, were caught in a storm and either dashed one against another, or driven upon the sands and wrecked. Forty of them were lost, the rest

[1] Dumbarton; *v. infra* c. 12, p. 24 and note.
[2] Caesar's invasion took place A.U.C. 699 and 700; B.C. 55 and 54.

were, with much difficulty, repaired. Caesar's cavalry was, at the first encounter, defeated by the Britons, and there Labienus, the tribune, was slain. In the second engagement, with great hazard to his men, he defeated the Britons and put them to flight. Thence he proceeded to the river Thames, where a great multitude of the enemy had posted themselves on the farther side of the river, under the command of Cassobellaunus,[1] and fenced the bank of the river and almost all the ford under water with sharp stakes: the remains of these are to be seen to this day, apparently about the thickness of a man's thigh, cased with lead, and fixed immovably in the bottom of the river. This being perceived and avoided by the Romans, the barbarians, not able to stand the charge of the legions, hid themselves in the woods, whence they grievously harassed the Romans with repeated sallies. In the meantime, the strong state of the Trinovantes,[2] with their commander Androgius,[3] surrendered to Caesar, giving him forty hostages. Many other cities, following their example, made a treaty with the Romans. Guided by them, Caesar at length, after severe fighting, took the town of Cassobellaunus,[4] situated between two marshes, fortified by sheltering woods, and plentifully furnished with all necessaries. After this, Caesar returned from Britain into Gaul, but he had no sooner put his legions into winter quarters, than he was suddenly beset and distracted with wars and sudden risings on every side.

[1] Cf. Caes., B.G., V, 11, 18 ff. A powerful British chief. His territory lay north and north-east of the Thames, roughly comprising Hertfordshire, Buckinghamshire, and Berkshire, but the exact limits are uncertain. His people were the Catuvellauni (the name is Gaulish in form).

[2] Cf. Caes., B.G., V, 20. The Trinovantes occupied Essex and part of Middlesex.

[3] Variations of this name given by ancient authors are Andragius and Androgorius. Caesar calls him Mandubracius.

[4] The position of this place is unknown.

CHAP. III. *How Claudius, the second of the Romans who came into Britain, brought the islands Orcades into subjection to the Roman empire; and Vespasian, sent by him, reduced the Isle of Wight under the dominion of the Romans.*

IN the year of Rome 798,[1] Claudius, fourth emperor from Augustus, being desirous to approve himself a prince beneficial to the republic, and eagerly bent upon war and conquest on every side, undertook an expedition into Britain, which as it appeared, was roused to rebellion by the refusal of the Romans to give up certain deserters. No one before or after Julius Caesar had dared to land upon the island. Claudius crossed over to it, and within a very few days, without any fighting or bloodshed, the greater part of the island was surrendered into his hands. He also added to the Roman empire the Orcades,[2] which lie in the ocean beyond Britain, and, returning to Rome in the sixth month after his departure, he gave his son the title of Britannicus. This war he concluded in the fourth year of his reign, which is the forty-sixth from the Incarnation of our Lord. In which year there came to pass a most grievous famine in Syria, which is recorded in the Acts of the Apostles to have been foretold by the prophet Agabus.

Vespasian,[3] who was emperor after Nero, being sent into Britain by the same Claudius, brought also under the Roman dominion the Isle of Wight, which is close to Britain on the south, and is about thirty miles in length from east to west, and twelve from north to south; being six miles distant from the southern coast of Britain at the east end, and three at the west. Nero, succeeding Claudius in the empire, undertook no wars at all; and, therefore, among countless other disasters brought by him upon the Roman state, he almost lost Britain; for

---

[1] Claudius came to Britain A.U.C. 796, 43 A.D.
[2] He can only have done so in name; it was probably Agricola who first conquered the Orkneys. Cf. Tac., Agric., 10.
[3] Cf. Tac., Agric., 13.

in his time two most notable towns were there taken and destroyed.

CHAP. IV. *How Lucius, king of Britain, writing to Pope Eleutherus, desired to be made a Christian.*

IN the year of our Lord 156, Marcus Antoninus Verus,[1] the fourteenth from Augustus, was made emperor, together with his brother, Aurelius Commodus. In their time, whilst the holy Eleutherus presided over the Roman Church, Lucius, king of Britain, sent a letter to him, entreating that by a mandate from him he might be made a Christian.[2] He soon obtained his pious request, and the Britons preserved the faith, which they had received, uncorrupted and entire, in peace and tranquillity until the time of the Emperor Diocletian.

CHAP. V. *How the Emperor Severus divided from the rest by a rampart that part of Britain which had been recovered.*

IN the year of our Lord 189, Severus, an African, born at Leptis, in the province of Tripolis, became emperor.[3] He was the seventeenth from Augustus, and reigned seventeen years. Being naturally of a harsh disposition, and engaged in many wars, he governed the state vigorously, but with much trouble. Having been victorious in all the grievous civil wars which happened in his time, he was drawn into Britain by the revolt of almost all the confederated tribes; and, after many great and severe battles, he thought fit to divide that part of the island, which he had recovered, from the other unconquered nations, not

---

[1] Marcus Antoninus Verus, commonly called Marcus Aurelius, succeeded in 161 A.D. His colleague in the empire was his adopted brother, Lucius Verus, whose full adoptive name was Lucius Aurelius Antoninus Verus Commodus. He died in 169. Eleutherus became Pope between 171 and 177. Bede's chronology is therefore wrong.

[2] Most modern authorities consider the story fabulous. But cf. Bright, "Early English Church History," pp. 3-5.

[3] Severus succeeded in 193 A.D. He died in 211.

with a wall, as some imagine, but with a rampart.[1] For a
wall is made of stones, but a rampart, with which camps
are fortified to repel the assaults of enemies, is made of
sods, cut out of the earth, and raised high above the
ground, like a wall, having in front of it the trench
whence the sods were taken, with strong stakes of wood
fixed above it. Thus Severus drew a great trench and
strong rampart, fortified with several towers, from sea
to sea. And there, at York, he fell sick afterwards and
died, leaving two sons, Bassianus and Geta;[2] of whom
Geta died, adjudged an enemy of the State; but Bassianus, having taken the surname of Antonius, obtained
the empire.

CHAP. VI. *Of the reign of Diocletian, and how he persecuted the Christians.*

In the year of our Lord 286,[3] Diocletian, the thirty-third
from Augustus, and chosen emperor by the army, reigned
twenty years, and created Maximian, surnamed Hercu-
lius, his colleague in the empire. In their time, one
Carausius,[4] of very mean birth, but a man of great ability
and energy, being appointed to guard the sea-coasts,
then infested by the Franks and Saxons, acted more to
the prejudice than to the advantage of the commonwealth,
by not restoring to its owners any of the booty taken

---

[1] This is the earthwork which runs parallel to the wall of Hadrian,
between the Solway and the Tyne, at an interval of from 30 to
1,300 yards from it. Its origin and purpose are doubtful. Ancient
authorities afford conflicting evidence with regard to the Roman
walls in Britain. Modern research seems to show that Severus
built no wall or rampart, though some ancient historians assert
that he did (*v.* Haverfield, quoted by Plummer, *ad loc.*; cf. *infra*
c. 12 and note).
[2] Bassianus Antoninus, surnamed Caracalla. Geta was murdered
by Caracalla.   [3] Diocletian succeeded in 284.
[4] Carausius was a native of Menapia, in Belgium, appointed to
command the Roman fleet stationed at Boulogne to guard the
coasts. He took the fleet with him when he usurped imperial
authority in Britain. Maximian, failing to reduce him, recognized
his authority and gave him the title of Augustus. He governed
vigorously and prosperously.

from the robbers, but keeping all to himself; thus giving
rise to the suspicion that by intentional neglect he suffered
the enemy to infest the frontiers. When, therefore, an
order was sent by Maximian that he should be put to
death, he took upon him the imperial purple, and possessed himself of Britain, and having most valiantly
conquered and held it for the space of seven years, he
was at length put to death by the treachery of his associate Allectus.[1] The usurper, having thus got the island
from Carausius, held it three years, and was then vanquished by Asclepiodotus,[2] the captain of the Praetorian
guards, who thus at the end of ten years restored Britain
to the Roman empire.

Meanwhile, Diocletian in the east, and Maximian Her-
culius in the west, commanded the churches to be destroyed, and the Christians to be persecuted and slain.
This persecution was the tenth since the reign of Nero,
and was more lasting and cruel than almost any before it;
for it was carried on incessantly for the space of ten years,
with burning of churches, proscription of innocent persons,
and the slaughter of martyrs. Finally, Britain also attained to the great glory of bearing faithful witness to God.

CHAP. VII. *The Passion of St. Alban and his companions, who at that time shed their blood for our Lord.*

At that time suffered St. Alban,[3] of whom the priest
Fortunatus,[4] in the Praise of Virgins, where he makes

[1] Allectus was a follower of Carausius. His revolt was apparently
supported by the independent tribes, probably Caledonians.
[2] Asclepiodotus was serving under Constantius Chlorus (one of
the reigning Caesars), who sailed to Britain and marched against
Allectus.
[3] The statement that the Diocletian persecution extended to
Britain rests on no trustworthy evidence at all. Yet though the
time assigned is probably wrong, there seems to be no reason to
doubt the existence of the British Protomartyr. The story rests
upon a local tradition traceable up to the visit of Germanus in
429 A.D., *v. infra* c. 18.
[4] Venantius Fortunatus, a Christian poet, Bishop of Poitiers,
b. 530 A.D. He was the last Latin poet of any note in Gaul.

mention of the blessed martyrs that came to the Lord
from all parts of the world, says:

And fruitful Britain noble Alban rears.

This Alban, being yet a pagan, at the time when at
the bidding of unbelieving rulers all manner of cruelty
was practised against the Christians, gave entertainment
in his house to a certain clerk,[1] flying from his persecutors.
This man he observed to be engaged in continual prayer
and watching day and night; when on a sudden the Divine
grace shining on him, he began to imitate the example
of faith and piety which was set before him, and being
gradually instructed by his wholesome admonitions, he
cast off the darkness of idolatry, and became a Christian
in all sincerity of heart. The aforesaid clerk having been
some days entertained by him, it came to the ears of the
impious prince, that a confessor of Christ, to whom a
martyr's place had not yet been assigned, was concealed
at Alban's house. Whereupon he sent some soldiers to
make a strict search after him. When they came to the
martyr's hut, St. Alban presently came forth to the
soldiers, instead of his guest and master, in the habit or
long coat which he wore, and was bound and led before
the judge.

It happened that the judge, at the time when Alban
was carried before him, was standing at the altar, and
offering sacrifice to devils. When he saw Alban, being
much enraged that he should thus, of his own accord,
dare to put himself into the hands of the soldiers, and
incur such danger on behalf of the guest whom he had
harboured, he commanded him to be dragged to the
images of the devils, before which he stood, saying,
"Because you have chosen to conceal a rebellious and
sacrilegious man, rather than to deliver him up to the
soldiers, that his contempt of the gods might meet with
the penalty due to such blasphemy, you shall undergo all

---

[1] In the lives of St. Alban (all later than Bede) this clerk is called
St. Amphibalus, a name probably invented from his cloak (*amphibalus*).

the punishment that was due to him, if you seek to abandon the worship of our religion." But St. Alban, who had voluntarily declared himself a Christian to the persecutors of the faith, was not at all daunted by the prince's threats, but putting on the armour of spiritual warfare, publicly declared that he would not obey his command. Then said the judge, " Of what family or race are you? "—" What does it concern you," answered Alban, " of what stock I am? If you desire to hear the truth of my religion, be it known to you, that I am now a Christian, and free to fulfil Christian duties."—" I ask your name," said the judge; " tell me it immediately."— " I am called Alban by my parents," replied he; " and I worship ever and adore the true and living God, Who created all things." Then the judge, filled with anger, said, " If you would enjoy the happiness of eternal life, do not delay to offer sacrifice to the great gods." Alban rejoined, "These sacrifices, which by you are offered to devils, neither can avail the worshippers, nor fulfil the desires and petitions of the suppliants. Rather, whosoever shall offer sacrifice to these images, shall receive the everlasting pains of hell for his reward."

The judge, hearing these words, and being much incensed, ordered this holy confessor of God to be scourged by the executioners, believing that he might by stripes shake that constancy of heart, on which he could not prevail by words. He, being most cruelly tortured, bore the same patiently, or rather joyfully, for our Lord's sake. When the judge perceived that he was not to be overcome by tortures, or withdrawn from the exercise of the Christian religion, he ordered him to be put to death. Being led to execution, he came to a river, which, with a most rapid course, ran between the wall of the town and the arena where he was to be executed.[1] He there saw a great multitude of persons of both sexes, and of divers ages and conditions, who were doubtless assembled by Divine inspiration, to attend the blessed confessor and martyr,

[1] The text of this passage is probably corrupt, but all the MSS. agree. I believe the above gives the intended meaning.

and had so filled the bridge over the river, that he could scarce pass over that evening. In truth, almost all had gone out, so that the judge remained in the city without attendance. St. Alban, therefore, urged by an ardent and devout wish to attain the sooner to martyrdom, drew near to the stream, and lifted up his eyes to heaven, whereupon the channel was immediately dried up, and he perceived that the water had given place and made way for him to pass. Among the rest, the executioner, who should have put him to death, observed this, and moved doubtless by Divine inspiration hastened to meet him at the appointed place of execution, and casting away the sword which he had carried ready drawn, fell at his feet, praying earnestly that he might rather be accounted worthy to suffer with the martyr, whom he was ordered to execute, or, if possible, instead of him.

Whilst he was thus changed from a persecutor into a companion in the faith and truth, and the other executioners rightly hesitated to take up the sword which was lying on the ground, the holy confessor, accompanied by the multitude, ascended a hill, about half a mile from the arena, beautiful, as was fitting, and of most pleasing appearance, adorned, or rather clothed, everywhere with flowers of many colours, nowhere steep or precipitous or of sheer descent, but with a long, smooth natural slope, like a plain, on its sides, a place altogether worthy from of old, by reason of its native beauty, to be consecrated by the blood of a blessed martyr. On the top of this hill, St. Alban prayed that God would give him water, and immediately a living spring, confined in its channel, sprang up at his feet, so that all men acknowledged that even the stream had yielded its service to the martyr. For it was impossible that the martyr, who had left no water remaining in the river, should desire it on the top of the hill, unless he thought it fitting. The river then having done service and fulfilled the pious duty, returned to its natural course, leaving a testimony of its obedience.[1] Here, therefore, the head of the undaunted martyr was

---

[1] There is again probably some confusion in the text.

C

struck off, and here he received the crown of life, which
God has promised to them that love him. But he who
laid impious hands on the holy man's neck was not permitted to rejoice over his dead body; for his eyes dropped
upon the ground at the same moment as the blessed
martyr's head fell.

At the same time was also beheaded the soldier, who
before, through the Divine admonition, refused to strike
the holy confessor. Of whom it is apparent, that though
he was not purified by the waters of baptism, yet he was
cleansed by the washing of his own blood, and rendered
worthy to enter the kingdom of heaven. Then the judge,
astonished at the unwonted sight of so many heavenly
miracles, ordered the persecution to cease immediately,
and began to honour the death of the saints, by which
he once thought that they might have been turned from
their zeal for the Christian faith. The blessed Alban
suffered death on the twenty-second day of June, near
the city of Verulam,[1] which is now by the English nation
called Verlamacaestir, or Vaeclingacaestir, where afterwards, when peaceable Christian times were restored, a
church of wonderful workmanship, and altogether worthy
to commemorate his martyrdom, was erected.[2] In which
place the cure of sick persons and the frequent working
of wonders cease not to this day.

At that time suffered Aaron and Julius,[3] citizens of
the City of Legions,[4] and many more of both sexes in
divers places; who, after that they had endured sundry
torments, and their limbs had been mangled after an un-

[1] Now St. Albans in Hertfordshire, on the Watling Street, hence
probably the name, Vaeclingacaestir.
[2] The place was afterwards called Holmhurst. The church
mentioned by Bede was superseded by the monastery of St.
Alban, the foundation of which is attributed to Offa, *circ.* 793 A.D.
Certain extraordinary privileges were granted to it, and its abbot
obtained a superiority over all other English abbots (Dugdale,
" Monasticon ").
[3] The evidence for their martyrdom is very doubtful.
[4] Caerleon-on-Usk, the headquarters of the Second legion, is
here meant (*v.* Merivale, H.R., vi, 248), though the name was also
applied to Chester, seat of the Twentieth legion (cf. II, 2, p. 87,
" civitas legionum ").

heard-of manner, when their warfare was accomplished, yielded their souls up to the joys of the heavenly city.

CHAP. VIII. *How, when the persecution ceased, the Church in Britain enjoyed peace till the time of the Arian heresy.*

WHEN the storm of persecution ceased, the faithful Christians, who, during the time of danger, had hidden themselves in woods and deserts and secret caves, came forth and rebuilt the churches which had been levelled to the ground; founded, erected, and finished the cathedrals raised in honour of the holy martyrs, and, as if displaying their conquering standards in all places, celebrated festivals and performed their sacred rites with pure hearts and lips. This peace continued in the Christian churches of Britain until the time of the Arian madness, which, having corrupted the whole world, infected this island also, so far removed from the rest of the world, with the poison of its error; and when once a way was opened across the sea for that plague, straightway all the taint of every heresy fell upon the island, ever desirous to hear some new thing, and never holding firm to any sure belief.

At this time Constantius, who, whilst Diocletian was alive, governed Gaul and Spain, a man of great clemency and urbanity, died in Britain. This man left his son Constantine,[1] born of Helena, his concubine, emperor of the Gauls. Eutropius writes that Constantine, being created emperor in Britain, succeeded his father in the sovereignty. In his time the Arian heresy broke out, and although it was exposed and condemned in the Council of Nicaea,[2] nevertheless, the deadly poison of its evil spread,

[1] Constantine the Great. For the legality of the marriage, *v.* Dict. of Christian Biography, article "Helena."
[2] The First General Council, 325 A.D. It asserted the doctrine of the ὁμοούσιον against Arius. For a short account of the heresy, *v.* Gore, Bampton Lectures, pp. 89-92. All the evidence goes to show that this heresy affected Britain much less than Bede, on the authority of Gildas, here implies.

CHAP. XI. *How during the reign of Honorius, Gratian and Constantine were created tyrants in Britain; and soon after the former was slain in Britain, and the latter in Gaul.*

IN the year of our Lord 407,[1] Honorius, the younger son of Theodosius, and the forty-fourth from Augustus, being emperor, two years before the invasion of Rome by Alaric, king of the Goths, when the nations of the Alani, Suevi, Vandals, and many others with them, having defeated the Franks and passed the Rhine, ravaged all Gaul, Gratianus, a citizen of the country, was set up as tyrant in Britain and killed. In his place, Constantine, one of the meanest soldiers, only for the hope afforded by his name, and without any worth to recommend him, was chosen emperor. As soon as he had taken upon him the command, he crossed over into Gaul, where being often imposed upon by the barbarians with untrustworthy treaties, he did more harm than good to the Commonwealth.[2] Whereupon Count Constantius,[3] by the command of Honorius, marching into Gaul with an army, besieged him in the city of Arles, took him prisoner, and put him to death. His son Constans, a monk, whom he had created Caesar, was also put to death by his own follower Count Gerontius,[4] at Vienne.

[1] The date of Honorius is correct, but the invasion of Alaric is put a year too late, if Bede refers to the first siege of Rome, in 408.

[2] The British army, alarmed by the inroads of barbarians, and actuated by a spirit of revolt against Roman authority, set up three local emperors in rapid succession: Marcus, Gratian, and Constantine. The first two they summarily deposed and killed, but Constantine by a great victory made himself master of Gaul and Britain and extorted from the Emperor Honorius a share in the Imperial authority. Meanwhile, the Britons expelled the few remaining Roman officials, and Honorius avenged himself on Constantine for the loss of Britain in the manner described in the text.

[3] A Roman general, afterwards associated with Honorius in the empire for a few months.

[4] Gerontius (Welsh *Geraint,* akin to Irish *Gerat* or *Gerait,* a champion), was a Briton, one of Constantine's generals. Turning against his master, he invited the Germans to invade Gaul and Britain, probably intending to secure Britain for himself. But his own men conspired against him and he died by his own hand.

Rome was taken by the Goths, in the year from its foundation, 1164.[1] Then the Romans ceased to rule in Britain, almost 470 years after Caius Julius Caesar came to the island. They dwelt within the rampart, which, as we have mentioned, Severus made across the island, on the south side of it, as the cities, watch-towers,[2] bridges, and paved roads there made testify to this day; but they had a right of dominion over the farther parts of Britain, as also over the islands that are beyond Britain.

CHAP. XII. *How the Britons, being ravaged by the Scots and Picts, sought succour from the Romans, who coming a second time, built a wall across the island; but when this was broken down at once by the aforesaid enemies, they were reduced to greater distress than before.*

FROM that time, the British part of Britain, destitute of armed soldiers, of all military stores, and of the whole flower of its active youth, who had been led away by the rashness of the tyrants never to return, was wholly exposed to rapine, the people being altogether ignorant of the use of weapons. Whereupon they suffered many years from the sudden invasions of two very savage nations from beyond the sea, the Scots from the west, and the Picts from the north. We call these nations from beyond the sea, not on account of their being seated out of Britain, but because they were separated from that part of it which was possessed by the Britons, two broad and long inlets of the sea lying between them, one of which runs into the interior of Britain, from the Eastern Sea, and the other from the Western, though they do not reach so far as to touch one another. The eastern has in the midst of it the city Giudi.[3] On the Western Sea, that is,

---

[1] Rome was taken 1163 A.U.C.; 410 A.D.
[2] Possibly "light-houses."
[3] Probably Inchkeith in the Forth. The Irish called the Firth of Forth the "Sea of Giudan" (*v.* Reeves' "Culdees," p. 124). But Professor Rhŷs is inclined to think that Bede has confused the

on its right shore, stands the city of Alcluith,[1] which in
their language signifies the Rock Cluith, for it is close by
the river of that name.

On account of the attacks of these nations, the Britons
sent messengers to Rome with letters piteously praying
for succour, and promising perpetual subjection, provided that the impending enemy should be driven away.
An armed legion was immediately sent them, which,
arriving in the island, and engaging the enemy, slew a
great multitude of them, drove the rest out of the territories of their allies, and having in the meanwhile delivered
them from their worst distress, advised them to build a
wall between the two seas across the island, that it
might secure them by keeping off the enemy. So they
returned home with great triumph. But the islanders
building the wall which they had been told to raise, not
of stone, since they had no workmen capable of such a
work, but of sods, made it of no use. Nevertheless, they
carried it for many miles between the two bays or inlets
of the sea of which we have spoken;[2] to the end that
where the protection of the water was wanting, they
might use the rampart to defend their borders from the
irruptions of the enemies. Of the work there erected,
that is, of a rampart of great breadth and height, there
are evident remains to be seen at this day. It begins at
about two miles' distance from the monastery of Aebbercurnig,[3] west of it, at a place called in the Pictish
language Peanfahel,[4] but in the English tongue, Pen-

island Giudi with Urbs Giudi, which may perhaps be identified
with the Urbs Iudeu of Nennius, probably either Carriden or Edinburgh (Rhŷs, " Celtic Britain ").

[1] Alcluith is the Welsh name (Ail=a rock). The Goidels called it
Dúnbrettan=the fortress of the Britons. Hence its modern name,
Dumbarton. The river is, of course, the Clyde.

[2] This is the earthen rampart, about thirty-five miles in length,
between the Clyde and the Forth, now attributed to Antoninus
Pius. Little is known about it, and it is probable that it was soon
abandoned.

[3] Abercorn, a village on the south bank of the Firth of Forth.

[4] The name is probably Celtic (Goidelic), though, if the view
which regards the Picts as a non-Celtic people be correct, it may
show traces of Pictish influence. It seems to be connected with

neltun, and running westward, ends near the city of Alcluith.

But the former enemies, when they perceived that the Roman soldiers were gone, immediately coming by sea, broke into the borders, trampled and overran all places, and like men mowing ripe corn, bore down all before them. Hereupon messengers were again sent to Rome miserably imploring aid, lest their wretched country should be utterly blotted out, and the name of a Roman province, so long renowned among them, overthrown by the cruelties of foreign races, might become utterly contemptible. A legion was accordingly sent again, and, arriving unexpectedly in autumn, made great slaughter of the enemy, obliging all those that could escape, to flee beyond the sea; whereas before, they were wont yearly to carry off their booty without any opposition. Then the Romans declared to the Britons, that they could not for the future undertake such troublesome expeditions for their sake, and advised them rather to take up arms and make an effort to engage their enemies, who could not prove too powerful for them, unless they themselves were enervated by cowardice. Moreover, thinking that it might be some help to the allies, whom they were forced to abandon, they constructed a strong stone wall from sea to sea, in a straight line between the towns that had been there built for fear of the enemy, where Severus also had formerly built a rampart.[1] This famous wall, which is still to be seen, was raised at public and private expense, the Britons also lending their assistance. It is eight feet in breadth, and twelve in height, in a straight line from east to west, as is still evident to

the Latin term "penna valli"=wing of (*i.e.,* pinnacle or turret at end of) the *vallum.* Readers of Scott's "Antiquary" will remember the celebrated dispute with regard to this word. The Anglian *Penneltun* is derived from the Goidelic name.

[1] This probably refers to the wall now attributed to Hadrian (*v.s.* c. 5 note). It ran for a distance of about eighty-five miles from Bowness-on-Solway to Wallsend-on-Tyne. Bede's authorities are Orosius and Gildas. The accounts he gives here and in c. 5 are an attempt to explain the difficulties and conflicting evidence with regard to these walls.

beholders. This being presently finished, they gave the
dispirited people good advice, and showed them how to
furnish themselves with arms. Besides, they built towers
to command a view of the sea, at intervals, on the
southern coast, where their ships lay, because there also
the invasions of the barbarians were apprehended, and
so took leave of their allies, never to return again.

After their departure to their own country, the Scots
and Picts, understanding that they had refused to return,
at once came back, and growing more confident than
they had been before, occupied all the northern and
farthest part of the island, driving out the natives, as far
as the wall. Hereupon a timorous guard was placed upon
the fortification, where, dazed with fear, they became
ever more dispirited day by day. On the other side, the
enemy constantly attacked them with barbed weapons,
by which the cowardly defenders were dragged in piteous
fashion from the wall, and dashed against the ground.
At last, the Britons, forsaking their cities and wall, took
to flight and were scattered. The enemy pursued, and
forthwith followed a massacre more grievous than ever
before; for the wretched natives were torn in pieces by
their enemies, as lambs are forn by wild beasts. Thus,
being expelled from their dwellings and lands, they saved
themselves from the immediate danger of starvation by
robbing and plundering one another, adding to the
calamities inflicted by the enemy their own domestic
broils, till the whole country was left destitute of food
except such as could be procured in the chase.

CHAP. XIII. *How in the reign of Theodosius the younger,
in whose time Palladius was sent to the Scots that believed
in Christ, the Britons begging assistance of Ætius, the
consul, could not obtain it.* [446 A.D.]

IN the year of our Lord 423, Theodosius, the younger,
the forty-fifth from Augustus, succeeded Honorius and
governed the Roman empire twenty-six years. In the

eighth year of his reign,[1] Palladius was sent by Celestinus, the Roman pontiff, to the Scots that believed in Christ, to be their first bishop. In the twenty-third year of his reign, Aetius,[2] a man of note and a patrician, discharged his third consulship with Symmachus for his colleague. To him the wretched remnant of the Britons sent a letter, which began thus :—" To Aetius, thrice Consul, the groans of the Britons." And in the sequel of the letter they thus unfolded their woes:—" The barbarians drive us to the sea; the sea drives us back to the barbarians: between them we are exposed to two sorts of death; we are either slaughtered or drowned." Yet, for all this, they could not obtain any help from him, as he was then engaged in most serious wars with Bledla and Attila, kings of the Huns. And though the year before this[3] Bledla had been murdered by the treachery of his own brother Attila, yet Attila himself remained so intolerable an enemy to the Republic, that he ravaged almost all Europe, attacking and destroying cities and castles. At the same time there was a famine at Constantinople, and soon after a plague followed; moreover, a great part of the wall of that city, with fifty-seven towers, fell to the ground. Many cities also went to ruin, and the famine and pestilential state of the air destroyed thousands of men and cattle.

[1] In 431 A.D. There is much confusion with regard to the mission of Palladius. According to later accounts, he was an unsuccessful forerunner of St. Patrick, but Bede here, following Prosper of Aquitaine, represents the Irish (Scotti) as in part already Christian. The origin of Irish Christianity is very obscure, and some have even doubted the existence of St. Patrick. Bede only mentions him once, viz., in the " Martyrology," which has been largely interpolated, and is, perhaps, not his genuine work. St. Patrick's latest biographer, Professor Bury, has, however, clearly established a certain amount of fact underlying much legendary matter. Some later authorities represent Palladius as preaching to the Scots (in the modern sense) and Patrick to the Irish.

[2] The great Roman general who preserved the Western Empire against the invasions of the barbarians for many years. He was assassinated by Valentinian in 454 A.D.

[3] Really two years before, 444 A.D.

CHAP. XIV. *How the Britons, compelled by the great famine, drove the barbarians out of their territories; and soon after there ensued, along with abundance of corn, decay of morals, pestilence, and the downfall of the nation.*

IN the meantime, the aforesaid famine distressing the Britons more and more, and leaving to posterity a lasting memory of its mischievous effects, obliged many of them to submit themselves to the depredators; though others still held out, putting their trust in God, when human help failed. These continually made raids from the mountains, caves, and woods, and, at length, began to inflict severe losses on their enemies, who had been for so many years plundering the country. The bold Irish robbers thereupon returned home, intending to come again before long. The Picts then settled down in the farthest part of the island and afterwards remained there, but they did not fail to plunder and harass the Britons from time to time.

Now, when the ravages of the enemy at length abated, the island began to abound with such plenty of grain as had never been known in any age before; along with plenty, evil living increased, and this was immediately attended by the taint of all manner of crime; in particular, cruelty, hatred of truth, and love of falsehood; insomuch, that if any one among them happened to be milder than the rest, and more inclined to truth, all the rest abhorred and persecuted him unrestrainedly, as if he had been the enemy of Britain. Nor were the laity only guilty of these things, but even our Lord's own flock, with its shepherds, casting off the easy yoke of Christ, gave themselves up to drunkenness, enmity, quarrels, strife, envy, and other such sins. In the meantime, on a sudden, a grievous plague fell upon that corrupt generation, which soon destroyed such numbers of them, that the living scarcely availed to bury the dead: yet, those that survived, could not be recalled from the spiritual death, which they had incurred through their sins, either by the death of their friends, or the fear of death. Whereupon, not long after, a more severe vengeance for their fearful crimes fell upon the sinful nation. They held a council to determine what was to be done, and where they should seek help to prevent or repel the cruel and frequent incursions of the northern nations; and in concert with their King Vortigern,[1] it was unanimously decided to call the Saxons to their aid from beyond the sea, which, as the event plainly showed, was brought about by the Lord's will, that evil might fall upon them for their wicked deeds.

CHAP. XV. *How the Angles, being invited into Britain, at first drove off the enemy; but not long after, making a league with them, turned their weapons against their allies.*

In the year of our Lord 449,[2] Marcian, the forty-sixth from Augustus, being made emperor with Valentinian, ruled the empire seven years. Then the nation of the Angles, or Saxons,[3] being invited by the aforesaid king,[4] arrived in Britain with three ships of war and had a place in which to settle assigned to them by the same king, in the eastern part of the island, on the pretext of fighting in defence of their country, whilst their real intentions were to conquer it. Accordingly they engaged with the enemy, who were come from the north to give battle, and the Saxons obtained the victory. When the news of their success and of the fertility of the country, and the cowardice of the Britons, reached their own home, a

---

[1] Though he is the subject of many legends, Vortigern is doubtless a historical figure, a ruler of south-eastern Britain. Bede's form of the name, Uurtigernus, is right. It is a British word, meaning "supreme lord" (Rhŷs).

[2] The date of Marcian's succession is 450.

[3] Bede only professes to give the date of the invasion approximately: cf. V, 24 ("quorum tempore"), I, 23; II, 14; V, 23 ("circiter"), calculating in round numbers apparently. He refers here to their first settlement, which, of course, does not preclude earlier attacks.

[4] *I.e.*, Vortigern.

more considerable fleet was quickly sent over, bringing
a greater number of men, and these, being added to the
former army, made up an invincible force. The new-
comers received of the Britons a place to inhabit among
them, upon condition that they should wage war against
their enemies for the peace and security of the country,
whilst the Britons agreed to furnish them with pay.
Those who came over were of the three most powerful
nations of Germany—Saxons, Angles, and Jutes. From
the Jutes are descended the people of Kent, and of the
Isle of Wight, including those in the province of the
West-Saxons who are to this day called Jutes, seated
opposite to the Isle of Wight. From the Saxons, that
is, the country which is now called Old Saxony, came
the East-Saxons, the South-Saxons, and the West-
Saxons. From the Angles, that is, the country which is
called Angulus,[1] and which is said, from that time, to
have remained desert to this day, between the provinces
of the Jutes and the Saxons, are descended the East-
Angles, the Midland-Angles, the Mercians, all the race of
the Northumbrians, that is, of those nations that dwell
on the north side of the river Humber, and the other
nations of the Angles. The first commanders are said
to have been the two brothers Hengist and Horsa.
Of these Horsa was afterwards slain in battle by the
Britons,[2] and a monument, bearing his name, is still
in existence in the eastern parts of Kent. They were
the sons of Victgilsus, whose father was Vitta, son of
Vecta, son of Woden; from whose stock the royal
race of many provinces trace their descent. In a short
time, swarms of the aforesaid nations came over into the
island, and the foreigners began to increase so much,
that they became a source of terror to the natives them-

[1] *Anglia* was believed to be derived from *Angulus*. The country
is the modern Schleswig, which the Angles appear to have almost
entirely evacuated. For the Continental Saxons, cf. V, 9. It has
been supposed that the Jutes came from Jutland, where, at a later
period, they mingled with the Danes (*ibid.*), but this is now regarded as doubtful.

[2] At Aylesford, in Kent. Horsted is the traditional burial-place
of Horsa.

selves who had invited them. Then, having on a sudden
entered into league with the Picts, whom they had by
this time repelled by force of arms, they began to turn
their weapons against their allies. At first, they obliged
them to furnish a greater quantity of provisions; and,
seeking an occasion of quarrel, protested, that unless
more plentiful supplies were brought them, they would
break the league, and ravage all the island; nor were
they backward in putting their threats into execution.
In short, the fire kindled by the hands of the pagans,
proved God's just vengeance for the crimes of the people;
not unlike that which, being of old lighted by the Chal-
deans, consumed the walls and all the buildings of Jerusalem. For here, too, through the agency of the pitiless
conqueror, yet by the disposal of the just Judge, it
ravaged all the neighbouring cities and country, spread
the conflagration from the eastern to the western sea,
without any opposition, and overran the whole face of
the doomed island. Public as well as private buildings
were overturned; the priests were everywhere slain
before the altars; no respect was shown for office, the
prelates with the people were destroyed with fire and
sword; nor were there any left to bury those who had been
thus cruelly slaughtered. Some of the miserable remnant,
being taken in the mountains, were butchered in heaps.
Others, spent with hunger, came forth and submitted
themselves to the enemy, to undergo for the sake of food
perpetual servitude, if they were not killed upon the
spot. Some, with sorrowful hearts, fled beyond the seas.
Others, remaining in their own country, led a miserable
life of terror and anxiety of mind among the mountains,
woods and crags.

CHAP. XVI. *How the Britons obtained their first victory
over the Angles, under the command of Ambrosius, a
Roman.*

WHEN the army of the enemy, having destroyed and dispersed the natives, had returned home to their own

settlements,[1] the Britons began by degrees to take heart, and gather strength, sallying out of the lurking places where they had concealed themselves, and with one accord imploring the Divine help, that they might not utterly be destroyed. They had at that time for their leader, Ambrosius Aurelianus,[2] a man of worth, who alone, by chance, of the Roman nation had survived the storm, in which his parents, who were of the royal race, had perished. Under him the Britons revived, and offering battle to the victors, by the help of God, gained the victory. From that day, sometimes the natives, and sometimes their enemies, prevailed, till the year of the siege of Badon-hill,[3] when they made no small slaughter of those enemies, about forty-four years after their arrival in England. But of this hereafter.

CHAP. XVII. *How Germanus the Bishop, sailing into Britain with Lupus, first quelled the tempest of the sea, and afterwards that of the Pelagians, by Divine power.* [429 A.D.]

SOME few years before their arrival, the Pelagian heresy, brought over by Agricola, the son of Severianus,[4] a Pelagian bishop, had corrupted with its foul taint the faith of the Britons. But whereas they absolutely refused to embrace that perverse doctrine, and blaspheme the grace of Christ, yet were not able of themselves to confute the subtilty of the unholy belief by force of argu-

---

[1] *I.e.*, in Thanet.
[2] The most probable view is that he was the last of those Romans who usurped imperial authority in Britain (*v.s.* cc. 6, 9).
[3] The identification of this place with Badbury, in Dorsetshire (Guest, followed by Freeman and Green) seems to be disproved (W. H. Stevenson, in the "English Historical Review," xvii, pp. 633, 634). The locality is quite uncertain; Skene actually places it near Linlithgow. According to Bede's reckoning the date of the battle would be 493 approximately. The "Annales Cambriae" give 516. For a full discussion of the question, *v.* Plummer, *ad loc.* Cf. also Mr. Stevenson's article.
[4] Nothing more is known of them. Pelagius left Britain in early life and did not himself spread his heresy there.

ment, they bethought them of wholesome counsels and
determined to crave aid of the Gallican prelates in that
spiritual warfare. Hereupon, these, having assembled a
great synod, consulted together to determine what persons should be sent thither to sustain the faith, and by
unanimous consent, choice was made of the apostolic
prelates, Germanus, Bishop of Auxerre, and Lupus of
Troyes,[1] to go into Britain to confirm the people's faith
in the grace of God. With ready zeal they complied with
the request and commands of the Holy Church, and put
to sea. The ship sped safely with favouring winds till
they were halfway between the coast of Gaul and Britain.
There on a sudden they were obstructed by the male-
volence of demons, who were jealous that men of such
eminence and piety should be sent to bring back the
people to salvation. They raised storms, and darkened
the sky with clouds. The sails could not support the
fury of the winds, the sailors' skill was forced to give
way, the ship was sustained by prayer, not by strength,
and as it happened, their spiritual leader and bishop,
being spent with weariness, had fallen asleep. Then,
as if because resistance flagged, the tempest gathered
strength, and the ship, overwhelmed by the waves, was
ready to sink. Then the blessed Lupus and all the rest,
greatly troubled, awakened their elder, that he might
oppose the raging elements. He, showing himself the
more resolute in proportion to the greatness of the
danger, called upon Christ, and having, in the name
of the Holy Trinity, taken and sprinkled a little water,
quelled the raging waves, admonished his companion,
encouraged all, and all with one consent uplifted their

[1] The life of Germanus was written by Constantius, a priest of
Lyons, who is Bede's authority for cc. 17-21. According to him,
these bishops were sent to Britain by a Gallican Synod. Prosper of
Aquitaine attributes the origin of the mission to Pope Celestine,
"acting on the advice of the deacon Palladius" (probably the
missionary to the Irish mentioned c. 13). The two statements are
not irreconcilable (cf. Bright, p. 18). There are churches dedicated
to SS. Germanus and Lupus in Wales and Cornwall. Both had
been trained in the school of Lérins, a monastery in the group of
islands off the coast at Cannes.

voices in prayer. Divine help was granted, the enemies
were put to flight, a cloudless calm ensued, the winds
veering about set themselves again to forward their
voyage, the sea was soon traversed, and they reached
the quiet of the wished-for shore. A multitude flock-
ing thither from all parts, received the bishops, whose
coming had been foretold by the predictions even of
their adversaries. For the evil spirits declared their fear,
and when the bishops expelled them from the bodies of
the possessed, they made known the nature of the
tempest, and the dangers they had occasioned, and confessed that they had been overcome by the merits and
authority of these men.

In the meantime the bishops speedily filled the island
of Britain with the fame of their preaching and miracles;
and the Word of God was by them daily preached, not
only in the churches, but even in the streets and fields,
so that the faithful and Catholic were everywhere confirmed, and those who had been perverted accepted the
way of amendment. Like the Apostles, they acquired
honour and authority through a good conscience, learning through the study of letters, and the power of working miracles through their merits. Thus the whole
country readily came over to their way of thinking; the
authors of the erroneous belief kept themselves in hiding,
and, like evil spirits, grieved for the loss of the people
that were rescued from them. At length, after long
deliberation, they had the boldness to enter the lists.[1]
They came forward in all the splendour of their wealth,
with gorgeous apparel, and supported by a numerous
following; choosing rather to hazard the contest, than
to undergo among the people whom they had led astray,
the reproach of having been silenced, lest they should
seem by saying nothing to condemn themselves. An
immense multitude had been attracted thither with their
wives and children. The people were present as spectators
and judges; the two parties stood there in very different
case; on the one side was Divine faith, on the other

---

[1] This conference is said to have been held at Verulam.

human presumption; on the one side piety, on the other pride; on the one side Pelagius, the founder of their faith, on the other Christ. The blessed bishops permitted their adversaries to speak first, and their empty speech long took up the time and filled the ears with meaningless words. Then the venerable prelates poured forth the torrent of their eloquence and showered upon them the words of Apostles and Evangelists, mingling the Scriptures with their own discourse and supporting their strongest assertions by the testimony of the written Word. Vainglory was vanquished and unbelief refuted; and the heretics, at every argument put before them, not being able to reply, confessed their errors. The people, giving judgement, could scarce refrain from violence, and signified their verdict by their acclamations.

CHAP. XVIII. *How the same holy man gave sight to the blind daughter of a tribune, and then coming to St. Alban, there received of his relics, and left other relics of the blessed Apostles and other martyrs.* [429 A.D.]

AFTER this, a certain man, who held the office of tribune, came forward with his wife, and brought his blind daughter, a child of ten years of age, to be healed of the bishops. They ordered her to be brought to their adversaries, who, being rebuked by their own conscience, joined their entreaties to those of the child's parents, and besought the bishops that she might be healed. They, therefore, perceiving their adversaries to yield, poured forth a short prayer, and then Germanus, full of the Holy Ghost, invoking the Trinity, at once drew from his side a casket which hung about his neck, containing relics of the saints, and, taking it in his hands, applied it in the sight of all to the girl's eyes, which were immediately delivered from darkness and filled with the light of truth. The parents rejoiced, and the people were filled with awe at the miracle; and after that day, the heretical beliefs were so fully obliterated from the minds of all, that they thirsted for and sought after the doctrine of the bishops.

This damnable heresy being thus suppressed, and the authors thereof confuted, and all the people settled in the purity of the faith, the bishops went to the tomb of the martyr, the blessed Alban, to give thanks to God through him. There Germanus, having with him relics of all the Apostles, and of divers martyrs, after offering up his prayers, commanded the tomb to be opened, that he might lay therein the precious gifts; judging it fitting, that the limbs of saints brought together from divers countries, as their equal merits had procured them admission into heaven, should find shelter in one tomb. These being honourably bestowed, and laid together, he took up a handful of dust from the place where the blessed martyr's blood had been shed, to carry away with him. In this dust the blood had been preserved, showing that the slaughter of the martyrs was red, though the persecutor was pale in death.[1] In consequence of these things, an innumerable multitude of people was that day converted to the Lord.

CHAP. XIX. *How the same holy man, being detained there by sickness, by his prayers quenched a fire that had broken out among the houses, and was himself cured of his infirmity by a vision.* [429 A.D.]

As they were returning thence, the treacherous enemy, having, as it chanced, prepared a snare, caused Germanus to bruise his foot by a fall, not knowing that, as it was with the blessed Job, his merits would be but increased by bodily affliction. Whilst he was thus detained some time in the same place by his infirmity, a fire broke out in a cottage neighbouring to that in which he was; and having burned down the other houses which were thatched

---

[1] Bede's authority, Constantius, shows here the first trace of any acquaintance of early historians with the story of St. Alban. The last sentence is somewhat obscure. Probably the idea is that the blood of the martyrs continues to cry aloud for vengeance.

with reed, fanned by the wind, was carried on to the dwelling in which he lay. The people all flocked to the prelate, entreating that they might lift him in their arms, and save him from the impending danger. But he rebuked them, and in the assurance of his faith, would not suffer himself to be removed. The whole multitude, in terror and despair, ran to oppose the conflagration; but, for the greater manifestation of the Divine power, whatsoever the crowd endeavoured to save, was destroyed; and what the sick and helpless man defended, the flame avoided and passed by, though the house that sheltered the holy man lay open to it,[1] and while the fire raged on every side, the place in which he lay appeared untouched, amid the general conflagration. The multitude rejoiced at the miracle, and was gladly vanquished by the power of God. A great crowd of people watched day and night before the humble cottage; some to have their souls healed, and some their bodies. All that Christ wrought in the person of his servant, all the wonders the sick man performed cannot be told. Moreover, he would suffer no medicines to be applied to his infirmity; but one night he saw one clad in garments as white as snow, standing by him, who reaching out his hand, seemed to raise him up, and ordered him to stand firm upon his feet; from which time his pain ceased, and he was so perfectly restored, that when the day came, with good courage he set forth upon his journey.

CHAP. XX. *How the same Bishops brought help from Heaven to the Britons in a battle, and then returned home.* [430 A.D.]

IN the meantime, the Saxons and Picts, with their united forces, made war upon the Britons, who in these straits were compelled to take up arms. In their terror thinking themselves unequal to their enemies, they implored the

---

[1] Reading " reserato." The reading " reservato " is perhaps easier and has some MS. authority.

assistance of the holy bishops; who, hastening to them
as they had promised, inspired so much confidence into
these fearful people, that one would have thought they
had been joined by a mighty army. Thus, by these apostolic leaders, Christ Himself commanded in their camp.
The holy days of Lent were also at hand, and were
rendered more sacred by the presence of the bishops, insomuch that the people being instructed by daily sermons,
came together eagerly to receive the grace of baptism.
For a great multitude of the army desired admission to
the saving waters, and a wattled church was constructed
for the Feast of the Resurrection of our Lord, and so
fitted up for the army in the field as if it were in a city.
Still wet with the baptismal water the troops set forth;
the faith of the people was fired; and where arms had
been deemed of no avail, they looked to the help of God.
News reached the enemy of the manner and method of
their purification,[1] who, assured of success, as if they
had to deal with an unarmed host, hastened forward
with renewed eagerness. But their approach was made
known by scouts. When, after the celebration of Easter,
the greater part of the army, fresh from the font, began
to take up arms and prepare for war, Germanus offered
to be their leader. He picked out the most active, ex-
plored the country round about, and observed, in the
way by which the enemy was expected, a valley encompassed by hills[2] of moderate height. In that place he
drew up his untried troops, himself acting as their
general. And now a formidable host of foes drew near,
visible, as they approached, to his men lying in ambush.
Then, on a sudden, Germanus, bearing the standard,
exhorted his men, and bade them all in a loud voice re-

[1] Reading "castitatis," from which it is difficult to extract any
meaning. The above strains the Latin unduly. Constantius has
'castrorum," which gives a better sense.

[2] Maes-y-Garmon ("The Field of Germanus"), near Mold, in
Flintshire, has been fixed upon as the scene of the Hallelujah
Victory, and the river in which the army was baptized is said to be
the Alyn (Ussher, "Antiqq."). The story is generally regarded
as legendary.

peat his words. As the enemy advanced in all security, thinking to take them by surprise, the bishops three times cried, "Hallelujah." A universal shout of the same word followed, and the echoes from the surrounding hills gave back the cry on all sides, the enemy was panic-stricken, fearing, not only the neighbouring rocks, but even the very frame of heaven above them; and such was their terror, that their feet were not swift enough to save them. They fled in disorder, casting away their arms, and well satisfied if, even with unprotected bodies, they could escape the danger; many of them, flying head-long in their fear, were engulfed by the river which they had crossed. The Britons, without a blow, inactive spectators of the victory they had gained, beheld their vengeance complete. The scattered spoils were gathered up, and the devout soldiers rejoiced in the success which Heaven had granted them. The prelates thus triumphed over the enemy without bloodshed, and gained a victory by faith, without the aid of human force. Thus, having settled the affairs of the island, and restored tranquillity by the defeat of the invisible foes, as well as of enemies in the flesh, they prepared to return home. Their own merits, and the intercession of the blessed martyr Alban, obtained for them a calm passage, and the happy vessel restored them in peace to the desires of their people.

CHAP. XXI. *How, when the Pelagian heresy began to spring up afresh, Germanus, returning to Britain with Severus, first restored bodily strength to a lame youth, then spiritual health to the people of God, having con-demned or converted the Heretics.* [447 A.D.]

NOT long after, news was brought from the same island, that certain persons were again attempting to teach and spread abroad the Pelagian heresy, and again the holy Germanus was entreated by all the priests, that he would defend the cause of God, which he had before maintained. He speedily complied with their request; and taking

with him Severus,[1] a man of singular sanctity, who was
disciple to the blessed father, Lupus, bishop of Troyes,
and at that time, having been ordained bishop of the
Treveri, was preaching the Word of God to the tribes of
Upper Germany, put to sea, and with favouring winds
and calm waters sailed to Britain.[2]

In the meantime, the evil spirits, speeding through the
whole island, were constrained against their will to foretell that Germanus was coming, insomuch, that one
Elafius, a chief of that region, without tidings from any
visible messenger, hastened to meet the holy men, carrying with him his son, who in the very flower of his youth
laboured under a grievous infirmity; for the sinews of
the knee were wasted and shrunk, so that the withered
limb was denied the power to walk. All the country
followed this Elafius. The bishops arrived, and were
met by the ignorant multitude, whom they blessed, and
preached the Word of God to them. They found the
people constant in the faith as they had left them; and
learning that but few had gone astray, they sought out
the authors of the evil and condemned them. Then
suddenly Elafius cast himself at the feet of the bishops,
presenting his son, whose distress was visible and needed
no words to express it. All were grieved, but especially
the bishops, who, filled with pity, invoked the mercy of
God; and straightway the blessed Germanus, causing
the youth to sit down, touched the bent and feeble knee
and passed his healing hand over all the diseased part.
At once health was restored by the power of his touch,
the withered limb regained its vigour, the sinews resumed
their task, and the youth was, in the presence of all the
people, delivered whole to his father. The multitude was
amazed at the miracle, and the Catholic faith was firmly
established in the hearts of all; after which, they were,
in a sermon, exhorted to amend their error. By the judgement of all, the exponents of the heresy, who had been

---

[1] Thirteenth bishop of Trèves. This account sums up nearly all
that is known of him.

[2] This second voyage of St. Germanus is supposed to have taken
place about eighteen years after the first, i.e., in 447.

banished from the island, were brought before the bishops, to be conveyed into the continent, that the country might be rid of them, and they corrected of their errors. So it came to pass that the faith in those parts continued long after pure and untainted. Thus when they had settled all things, the blessed prelates returned home as prosperously as they had come.

But Germanus, after this, went to Ravenna to intercede for the tranquillity of the Armoricans,[1] where, after being very honourably received by Valentinian and his mother, Placidia, he departed hence to Christ; his body was conveyed to his own city with a splendid retinue, and mighty works attended his passage to the grave. Not long after, Valentinian was murdered by the followers of Aetius, the patrician, whom he had put to death, in the sixth[2] year of the reign of Marcian, and with him ended the empire of the West.

CHAP. XXII. *How the Britons, being for a time at rest from foreign invasions, wore themselves out by civil wars, and at the same time gave themselves up to more heinous crimes.*

IN the meantime, in Britain, there was some respite from foreign, but not from civil war. The cities destroyed by the enemy and abandoned remained in ruins; and the natives, who had escaped the enemy, now fought against each other. Nevertheless, the kings, priests, private men, and the nobility, still remembering the late calamities and slaughters, in some measure kept within bounds; but when these died, and another generation succeeded, which knew nothing of those times, and was only acquainted with the existing peaceable state of things, all

[1] The Armoricans had revolted, and Aetius (*v.s.* c. 13 and note) had enlisted the services of the Alani against them. Germanus, who had at one time been duke of the Armoricans, went to the Imperial Court at Ravenna to intercede for them.
[2] Really the fifth (16th March, 455 A.D.). Romulus Augustulus is usually regarded as the last emperor of the west. He was overthrown in 476 A.D.

the bonds of truth and justice were so entirely broken, that there was not only no trace of them remaining, but only very few persons seemed to retain any memory of them at all. To other crimes beyond description, which their own historian, Gildas,[1] mournfully relates, they added this—that they never preached the faith to the Saxons, or English, who dwelt amongst them. Nevertheless, the goodness of God did not forsake his people, whom he foreknew, but sent to the aforesaid nation much more worthy heralds of the truth, to bring it to the faith.

CHAP. XXIII. *How the holy Pope Gregory sent Augustine, with other monks, to preach to the English nation, and encouraged them by a letter of exhortation, not to desist from their labour.* [596 A.D.]

IN the year of our Lord 582, Maurice, the fifty-fourth from Augustus, ascended the throne, and reigned twenty-one years. In the tenth year of his reign, Gregory,[2] a man eminent in learning and the conduct of affairs, was promoted to the Apostolic see of Rome, and presided over it thirteen years, six months and ten days. He, being moved by Divine inspiration, in the fourteenth year of the same emperor, and about the one hundred and fiftieth after the coming of the English into Britain, sent the servant of God, Augustine,[3] and with him divers other monks, who feared the Lord, to preach the Word of God to the English nation. They having, in obedience

[1] The British historian, author of the " De Excidio Liber Querulus," so called from the historian's denunciations of the sins of the Britons. He himself tells us that he was born in the year of the battle of Badon Hill (Mons Badonicus), and that he wrote his History forty-four years after that date. According to Bede (cf. c. 15, *ad init.*, and c. 16, *ad fin.*) this would place his birth approximately in the year 493, but see note on c. 16.

[2] Gregory the Great. Cf. Preface. Bede places the date of his accession a year too late as well as that of his death (*v*, II, 1, *ad init.,* but in the same chapter he rightly places his death in the second year of Phocas, *i.e.*, 604).

[3] Augustine was prior of St. Gregory's Monastery dedicated to St. Andrew in Rome.

to the pope's commands, undertaken that work, when they had gone but a little way on their journey, were seized with craven terror, and began to think of returning home, rather than proceed to a barbarous, fierce, and unbelieving nation, to whose very language they were strangers; and by common consent they decided that this was the safer course. At once Augustine, who had been appointed to be consecrated bishop, if they should be received by the English, was sent back, that he might, by humble entreaty, obtain of the blessed Gregory, that they should not be compelled to undertake so dangerous, toilsome, and uncertain a journey. The pope, in reply, sent them a letter of exhortation, persuading them to set forth to the work of the Divine Word, and rely on the help of God. The purport of which letter was as follows:

"*Gregory, the servant of the servants of God, to the servants of our Lord.* Forasmuch as it had been better not to begin a good work, than to think of desisting from one which has been begun, it behoves you, my beloved sons, to fulfil with all diligence the good work, which, by the help of the Lord, you have undertaken. Let not, therefore, the toil of the journey, nor the tongues of evil-speaking men, discourage you; but with all earnestness and zeal perform, by God's guidance, that which you have set about; being assured, that great labour is followed by the greater glory of an eternal reward. When Augustine, your Superior, returns, whom we also constitute your abbot, humbly obey him in all things; knowing, that whatsoever you shall do by his direction, will, in all respects, be profitable to your souls. Almighty God protect you with His grace, and grant that I may, in the heavenly country, see the fruits of your labour, inasmuch as, though I cannot labour with you, I shall partake in the joy of the reward, because I am willing to labour. God keep you in safety, my most beloved sons. Given the 23rd of July, in the fourteenth year of the reign of our most religious lord, Mauritius Tiberius Augustus, the thirteenth year after the consulship of our lord aforesaid, and the fourteenth indiction."[1]

[1] Cf. IV, 5, p. 227, note.

CHAP. XXIV. *How he wrote to the bishop of Arles to entertain them.* [596 A.D.]

THE same venerable pope also sent at the same time a letter to Aetherius, archbishop of Arles,[1] exhorting him to give favourable entertainment to Augustine on his way to Britain; which letter was in these words:

"*To his most reverend and holy brother and fellow bishop Aetherius, Gregory, the servant of the servants of God.* Although religious men stand in need of no recommendation with priests who have the charity which is pleasing to God; yet because an opportunity of writing has occurred, we have thought fit to send this letter to you, Brother, to inform you, that with the help of God we have directed thither, for the good of souls, the bearer of these presents, Augustine, the servant of God, of whose zeal we are assured, with other servants of God, whom it is requisite that your Holiness readily assist with priestly zeal, affording him all the comfort in your power. And to the end that you may be the more ready in your help, we have enjoined him to inform you particularly of the occasion of his coming; knowing, that when you are acquainted with it, you will, as the matter requires, for the sake of God, dutifully dispose yourself to give him comfort. We also in all things recommend to your charity, Candidus,[2] the priest, our common son, whom we have transferred to the administration of a small patrimony in our Church. God keep you in safety, most reverend brother. Given the 23rd day of July, in the fourteenth year of the reign of our most religious lord, Mauritius Tiberius Augustus, the

---

[1] This is a mistake. Aetherius was archbishop of Lyons. Vergilius was archbishop of Arles. The letter given here, however, is the letter sent to Aetherius. Similar letters were despatched to other bishops at this time; among them one to Vergilius of Arles.

[2] A presbyter sent into Gaul by Gregory in 595 A.D. to administer the little patrimony of St. Peter in Gaul, to collect its revenues and to invest them in raiment for the poor, or in English slave lads to serve in the monasteries and receive a Christian education.

thirteenth year after the consulship of our lord aforesaid, and the fourteenth indiction."

CHAP. XXV. *How Augustine, coming into Britain, first preached in the Isle of Thanet to the King of Kent, and having obtained licence from him, went into Kent, in order to preach therein.* [597 A.D.]

AUGUSTINE, thus strengthened by the encouragement of the blessed Father Gregory, returned to the work of the Word of God, with the servants of Christ who were with him, and arrived in Britain. The powerful Ethelbert was at that time king of Kent;[1] he had extended his dominions as far as the boundary formed by the great river Humber, by which the Southern Saxons are divided from the Northern. On the east of Kent is the large Isle of Thanet, containing, according to the English way of reckoning, 600 families,[2] divided from the mainland by the river Wantsum,[3] which is about three furlongs in breadth, and which can be crossed only in two places; for at both ends it runs into the sea. On this island landed[4] the servant of the Lord, Augustine, and his companions, being, as is reported, nearly forty men. They had obtained, by order of the blessed Pope Gregory, interpreters of the nation of the Franks,[5] and sending to Ethelbert, signified that they

[1] Ethelbert was the third Bretwalda or dominant king. He had established a practical hegemony over the East Anglians, the Mercians of the Trent Valley, the South Saxons, East Saxons, and even the West Saxons (cf. II, 5, p. 94).

[2] Families, *i.e., hides*. The hide, probably, was as much land as would support a family, hence the extent must have varied with the different conditions in different parts of the country.

[3] In Bede's time Thanet was divided from the rest of Kent by a broad channel called the Wantsum, now partly represented by the River Stour.

[4] The conjecture that they landed at Ebbsfleet, which is also traditionally regarded as the landing-place of Hengist, has been generally adopted. Other possible landing-places are Stonar and Richborough. For a full discussion of the question, *v.* "The Mission of St. Augustine," ed. Rev. A. T. Mason, D.D.

[5] It has been supposed, on the strength of this passage, that the speech of the Franks and the English was still mutually intelligible.

were come from Rome, and brought a joyful message, which most undoubtedly assured to those that hearkened to it everlasting joys in heaven, and a kingdom that would never end, with the living and true God. The king hearing this, gave orders that they should stay in the island where they had landed, and be furnished with necessaries, till he should consider what to do with them. For he had before heard of the Christian religion, having a Christian wife of the royal family of the Franks, called Bertha;[1] whom he had received from her parents, upon condition that she should be permitted to preserve inviolate the rites of her religion with the Bishop Liudhard,[2] who was sent with her to support her in the faith. Some days after, the king came into the island, and sitting in the open air, ordered Augustine and his companions to come and hold a conference with him. For he had taken precaution that they should not come to him in any house, lest, by so coming, according to an ancient superstition, if they practised any magical arts, they might impose upon him, and so get the better of him. But they came endued with Divine, not with magic power, bearing a silver cross for their banner, and the image of our Lord and Saviour painted on a board; and chanting litanies, they offered up their prayers to the Lord for the eternal salvation both of themselves and of those to whom and for whom they had come. When they had sat down, in obedience to the king's commands, and preached to him and his attendants there present

This is supported by a statement of Gregory (letter to Theoderic and Theodebert) that he had desired Augustine to take some Frankish priests with him. It is assumed that these priests were the interpreters. On the other hand, in view of the fact that only fifty years later we find the language of the Franks regarded in England as a "barbara loquella" (III, 7), it has been inferred that the interpreters were men who had acquired a knowledge of the dialect of Kent through commerce or otherwise.

[1] Daughter of Charibert, king of Paris.

[2] Said (on doubtful authority) to have been bishop of Senlis. He acted as the queen's private chaplain. There is nothing to show that either he or Bertha attempted to spread their religion in England, though probably their influence may not have been without effect on Ethelbert.

the Word of life, the king answered thus: " Your words and promises are fair, but because they are new to us, and of uncertain import, I cannot consent to them so far as to forsake that which I have so long observed with the whole English nation. But because you are come from far as strangers into my kingdom, and, as I conceive, are desirous to impart to us those things which you believe to be true, and most beneficial, we desire not to harm you, but will give you favourable entertainment, and take care to supply you with all things necessary to your sustenance; nor do we forbid you to preach and gain as many as you can to your religion." Accordingly he gave them an abode in the city of Canterbury,[1] which was the metropolis of all his dominions, and, as he had promised, besides supplying them with sustenance, did not refuse them liberty to preach. It is told that, as they drew near to the city, after their manner, with the holy cross, and the image of our sovereign Lord and King, Jesus Christ, they sang in concert this litany: " We beseech thee, O Lord, for Thy great mercy, that Thy wrath and anger be turned away from this city, and from Thy holy house, for we have sinned. Hallelujah."

CHAP. XXVI. *How St. Augustine in Kent followed the doctrine and manner of life of the primitive Church, and settled his episcopal see in the royal city.* [597 A.D.]

As soon as they entered the dwelling-place assigned to them, they began to imitate the Apostolic manner of life in the primitive Church; applying themselves to constant prayer, watchings, and fastings; preaching the Word of life to as many as they could; despising all worldly things, as in nowise concerning them; receiving only their necessary food from those they taught; living themselves in all respects conformably to what they taught, and being always ready to suffer any adversity, and even

[1] The old Roman town of Doruvernis, which is the name Bede gives to it throughout the History.

to die for that truth which they preached. In brief, some
believed and were baptized, admiring the simplicity of
their blameless life, and the sweetness of their heavenly
doctrine. There was on the east side of the city, a church
dedicated of old to the honour of St. Martin,[1] built whilst
the Romans were still in the island, wherein the queen,
who, as has been said before, was a Christian, was wont
to pray. In this they also first began to come together,
to chant the Psalms, to pray, to celebrate Mass, to
preach, and to baptize, till when the king had been converted to the faith, they obtained greater liberty to preach
everywhere and build or repair churches.

When he, among the rest, believed and was baptized,
attracted by the pure life of these holy men and their
gracious promises, the truth of which they established
by many miracles, greater numbers began daily to flock
together to hear the Word, and, forsaking their heathen
rites, to have fellowship, through faith, in the unity of
Christ's Holy Church. It is told that the king, while he
rejoiced at their conversion and their faith, yet compelled
none to embrace Christianity, but only showed more
affection to the believers, as to his fellow citizens in the
kingdom of Heaven. For he had learned from those who
had instructed him and guided him to salvation, that the
service of Christ ought to be voluntary, not by compul-
sion. Nor was it long before he gave his teachers a
settled residence suited to their degree in his metropolis
of Canterbury, with such possessions of divers sorts as
were necessary for them.

[1] St. Martin was regarded with special reverence in Britain and
Ireland. Possibly some of the earliest missionaries may have been
his disciples, *e.g.*, St. Ninian and St. Patrick. The Roman church
of St. Martin at Canterbury has been frequently altered and partly
rebuilt, so that " small portions only of the Roman walls remain.
Roman bricks are used as old materials in the parts rebuilt "
(Parker).

CHAP. XXVII. *How St. Augustine, being made a bishop, sent to acquaint Pope Gregory with what had been done in Britain, and asked and received replies, of which he stood in need.* [597-601 A.D.]

In the meantime, Augustine, the man of God, went to Arles, and, according to the orders received from the holy Father Gregory, was ordained archbishop of the English nation,[1] by Aetherius,[2] archbishop of that city. Then returning into Britain, he sent Laurentius the the priest[3] and Peter the monk[4] to Rome, to acquaint Pope Gregory, that the English nation had received the faith of Christ, and that he was himself made their bishop. At the same time, he desired his solution of some doubts which seemed urgent to him. He soon received fitting answers to his questions, which we have also thought meet to insert in this our history:

The First Question of the blessed Augustine, Bishop of the Church of Canterbury.—Concerning bishops, what should be their manner of conversation towards their clergy? or into how many portions the offerings of the faithful at the altar are to be divided? and how the bishop is to act in the Church?

Gregory, Pope of the City of Rome, answers.—Holy

---

[1] Augustine was not consecrated as archbishop either of London or Canterbury, but by the general title of "Archbishop of the English." According to Gregory's original scheme, London, not Canterbury, was to have been the seat of the primacy of southern England (cf. c. 29), London and York being doubtless the most important cities of south and north known to him from their history during the Roman occupation. But Christianity was not permanently established in London till it was too late to remove the see from Canterbury, which would obviously commend itself to Augustine as the most suitable place to be the metropolitan city.

[2] For Aetherius read Vergilius (v. c. 24, note). "The occupant of the see of Arles was in some sense primate of France at this time, and, as such, Vergilius received the *pallium* and the papal vice-gerentship in the kingdom of Childebert" (Dict. Christ. Biog.).

[3] He succeeded Augustine as archbishop. For his history, v. II, 6, 7.

[4] Cf. *infra* c. 33.

E

Scripture, in which we doubt not you are well versed, testifies to this, and in particular the Epistles of the Blessed Paul to Timothy, wherein he endeavours to show him what should be his manner of conversation in the house of God; but it is the custom of the Apostolic see to prescribe these rules to bishops when they are ordained: that all emoluments which accrue, are to be divided into four portions;—one for the bishop and his household, for hospitality and entertainment of guests; another for the clergy; a third for the poor; and the fourth for the repair of churches. But in that you, my brother, having been instructed in monastic rules, must not live apart from your clergy in the Church of the English, which has been lately, by the will of God, converted to the faith, you must establish the manner of conversation of our fathers in the primitive Church, among whom, none said that aught of the things which they possessed was his own, but they had all things common.

But if there are any clerks not received into holy orders,[1] who cannot live continent, they are to take wives, and receive their stipends outside of the community; because we know that it is written concerning the same fathers of whom we have spoken that a distribution was made unto every man according as he had need. Care is also to be taken of their stipends, and provision to be made, and they are to be kept under ecclesiastical rule, that they may live orderly, and attend to singing of psalms, and, by the help of God, preserve their hearts and tongues and bodies from all that is unlawful. But as for those that live in common, there is no need to say any-thing of assigning portions, or dispensing hospitality and showing mercy; inasmuch as all that they have over is to be spent in pious and religious works, according to the teaching of Him who is the Lord and Master of all, "Give alms of such things as ye have over, and behold all things are clean unto you."[2]

[1] *I.e.*, those in minor orders; all below the subdiaconate.
[2] St. Luke, xi, 41. *Quod superest* (Vulgate) = πλήν (R.V., "How-beit"; A.V., "But rather"), adverbial. Gregory takes it to mean "what is over."

Augustine's Second Question.—Whereas the faith is one and the same, are there different customs in different Churches? and is one custom of Masses observed in the holy Roman Church, and another in the Church of Gaul?[1]

Pope Gregory answers.—You know, my brother, the custom of the Roman Church in which you remember that you were bred up. But my will is, that if you have found anything, either in the Roman, or the Gallican, or any other Church, which may be more acceptable to Almighty God, you should carefully make choice of the same, and sedulously teach the Church of the English, which as yet is new in the faith, whatsoever you can gather from the several Churches. For things are not to be loved for the sake of places, but places for the sake of good things. Choose, therefore, from every Church those things that are pious, religious, and right, and when you have, as it were, made them up into one bundle, let the minds of the English be accustomed thereto.

Augustine's Third Question.—I beseech you, what punishment must be inflicted on one who steals anything from a church?

Gregory answers.—You may judge, my brother, by the condition of the thief, in what manner he is to be corrected. For there are some, who, having substance, commit theft; and there are others, who transgress in this matter through want. Wherefore it is requisite, that some be punished with fines, others with stripes; some with more severity, and some more mildly. And when the severity is greater, it is to proceed from charity, not from anger; because this is done for the sake of him who is corrected, that he may not be delivered up to the fires of Hell. For it behoves us to maintain discipline among the faithful, as good parents do with their children according to the flesh, whom they punish with stripes for their faults, and yet they design to make those whom they chastise their heirs, and preserve their possessions

---

[1] Augustine must have observed these differences of ritual as he travelled through Gaul. Presumably also he found the Gallic use adopted at St. Martin's, Canterbury, by Liudhard. Dr. Bright summarizes these differences, "Early English Church History," p. 64.

for those whom they seem to visit in wrath. This charity
is, therefore, to be kept in mind, and it dictates the
measure of the punishment, so that the mind may do
nothing beyond the rule prescribed by reason. You will
add to this, how men are to restore those things which
they have stolen from the church. But let not the Church
take more than it has lost of its worldly possessions, or
seek gain from vanities.

Augustine's Fourth Question. — Whether two full
brothers may marry two sisters, who are of a family far
removed from them?

Gregory answers.—Most assuredly this may lawfully be
done; for nothing is found in Holy Writ on this matter
that seems to contradict it.

Augustine's Fifth Question.—To what degree may the
faithful marry with their kindred? and is it lawful to
marry a stepmother or a brother's wife?

Gregory answers.—A certain secular law in the Roman
commonwealth allows, that the son and daughter of a
brother and sister,[1] or of two full brothers, or two sisters,
may be joined in matrimony; but we have found, by experience, that the offspring of such wedlock cannot grow
up; and the Divine law forbids a man to "uncover the
nakedness of his kindred." Hence of necessity it must
be the third or fourth generation of the faithful, that can
be lawfully joined in matrimony; for the second, which
we have mentioned, must altogether abstain from one
another. To marry with one's stepmother is a heinous
crime, because it is written in the Law, "Thou shalt not
uncover the nakedness of thy father:" now the son, indeed, cannot uncover his father's nakedness; but in
regard that it is written, "They twain shall be one flesh,"
he that presumes to uncover the nakedness of his stepmother, who was one flesh with his father, certainly un-
covers the nakedness of his father. It is also prohibited
to marry with a sister-in-law, because by the former
union she is become the brother's flesh. For which thing

. [1] Reading "fratris et sororis" (for "frater et soror"), as the
sense requires, but there is no MS. authority for the change.

also John the Baptist was beheaded, and obtained the crown of holy martyrdom. For, though he was not ordered to deny Christ, and it was not for confessing Christ that he was killed, yet inasmuch as the same Jesus Christ, our Lord, said, "I am the Truth," because John was killed for the truth, he also shed his blood for Christ.

But forasmuch as there are many of the English, who, whilst they were still heathens, are said to have been joined in this unholy union, when they attain to the faith they are to be admonished to abstain, and be made to know that this is a grievous sin. Let them fear the dread judgement of God, lest, for the gratification of their carnal desires, they incur the torments of eternal punishment. Yet they are not on this account to be deprived of the Communion of the Body and Blood of Christ, lest they should seem to be punished for those things which they did through ignorance before they had received Baptism. For in these times the Holy Church chastises some things with zeal, and tolerates some in mercy, and is blind to some in her wisdom, and so, by forbearance and blindness often suppresses the evil that stands in her way. But all that come to the faith are to be admonished not to presume to do such things. And if any shall be guilty of them, they are to be excluded from the Communion of the Body and Blood of Christ. For as the offence is, in some measure, to be tolerated in those who did it through ignorance, so it is to be rigorously punished in those who do not fear to sin knowingly.

Augustine's Sixth Question.—Whether a bishop may be consecrated without other bishops being present, if there be so great a distance between them, that they cannot easily come together?

Gregory answers.—In the Church of England, of which you are as yet the only bishop, you cannot otherwise ordain a bishop than in the absence of other bishops. For when do bishops come over from Gaul, that they may be present as witnesses to you in ordaining a bishop? But we would have you, my brother, to ordain bishops in such a manner, that the said bishops may not be far

washed with water? Or approach to receive the Mystery of the Holy Communion? All which things are requisite to be known by the ignorant nation of the English.

Gregory answers.—I do not doubt but that these questions have been put to you, my brother, and I think I have already answered you therein. But I believe you would wish the opinion which you yourself might give and hold to be confirmed by my reply also. Why should not a woman with child be baptized, since the fruitfulness of the flesh is no offence in the eyes of Almighty God? For when our first parents sinned in Paradise, they forfeited the immortality which they had received, by the just judgement of God. Because, therefore, Almighty God would not for their fault wholly destroy the human race, he both deprived man of immortality for his sin, and, at the same time, of his great goodness and loving-kindness, reserved to him the power of propagating his race after him. On what ground, then, can that which is preserved to human nature by the free gift of Almighty God, be excluded from the privilege of Holy Baptism? For it is very foolish to imagine that the gift can be opposed to grace in that Mystery in which all sin is blotted out. When a woman is delivered, after how many days she may come into the church, you have learnt from the teaching of the Old Testament, to wit, that she is to abstain for a male child thirty-three days, and sixty-six for a female. Now you must know that this is to be received in a mystery; for if she enters the church the very hour that she is delivered, to return thanks, she is not guilty of any sin; because the pleasure of the flesh is a fault, and not the pain; but the pleasure is in the copulation of the flesh, whereas there is pain in bringing forth the child. Wherefore it is said to the first mother of all, "In sorrow thou shalt bring forth children." If, therefore, we forbid a woman that has brought forth, to enter the church, we make a crime of her very punishment. To baptize either a woman who has brought forth, if there be danger of death, even the very hour that she brings forth, or that which she has brought forth the very hour it is born, is in no way prohibited, because, as the grace of the Holy Mystery is to be with much discretion provided for those who are in full life and capable of understanding, so is it to be without any delay administered to the dying; lest, while a further time is sought to confer the Mystery of redemption, if a small delay intervene, the person that is to be redeemed be dead and gone.

Her husband is not to approach her, till the infant born be weaned. An evil custom is sprung up in the lives of married people, in that women disdain to suckle the children whom they bring forth, and give them to other women to suckle; which seems to have been invented on no other account but incontinency; because, as they will not be continent, they will not suckle the children whom they bear. Those women, therefore, who, from evil custom, give their children to others to bring up, must not approach their husbands till the time of purification is past. For even when there has been no child-birth, women are forbidden to do so, whilst they have their courses, insomuch that the Law condemns to death any man that shall approach unto a woman during her uncleanness. Yet the woman, nevertheless, must not be forbidden to come into the church whilst she has her courses; because the superfluity of nature cannot be imputed to her as a crime; and it is not just that she should be refused admittance into the church, for that which she suffers against her will. For we know, that the woman who had the issue of blood, humbly approaching behind our Lord's back, touched the hem of his garment, and her infirmity immediately departed from her. If, therefore, she that had an issue of blood might commendably touch the garment of our Lord, why may not she, who has her courses, lawfully enter into the church of God? But you may say, Her infirmity compelled her, whereas these we speak of are bound by custom. Consider, then, most dear brother, that all we suffer in this mortal flesh, through the infirmity of our nature, is ordained by the just judgement of God after the fall; for to hunger, to thirst, to be hot, to be cold, to be weary, is from the

infirmity of our nature; and what else is it to seek food
against hunger, drink against thirst, air against heat,
clothes against cold, rest against weariness, than to procure a remedy against distempers? Thus to a woman
her courses are a distemper. If, therefore, it was a commendable boldness in her, who in her disease touched
our Lord's garment, why may not that which is allowed
to one infirm person, be granted to all women, who,
through the fault of their nature, are rendered infirm?

She must not, therefore, be forbidden to receive the
Mystery of the Holy Communion during those days.
But if any one out of profound respect does not presume
to do it, she is to be commended; yet if she receives it, she
is not to be judged. For it is the part of noble minds in
some manner to acknowledge their faults, even when
there is no fault; because very often that is done without
a fault, which, nevertheless, proceeded from a fault.
Thus, when we are hungry, it is no sin to eat; yet our
being hungry proceeds from the sin of the first man.
The courses are no sin in women, because they happen
naturally; yet, because our nature itself is so depraved,
that it appears to be defiled even without the concur-
rence of the will, a defect arises from sin, and thereby
human nature may itself know what it is become by
judgement. And let man, who wilfully committed the
offence, bear the guilt of that offence against his will.
And, therefore, let women consider with themselves, and
if they do not presume, during their courses, to approach
the Sacrament of the Body and Blood of our Lord, they
are to be commended for their praiseworthy considera-
tion; but when they are carried away with love of the
same Mystery to receive it according to the custom of
the religious life, they are not to be restrained, as we
said before. For as in the Old Testament the outward
works are observed, so in the New Testament, that
which is outwardly done, is not so diligently regarded as
that which is inwardly thought, that the punishment may
be with discernment. For whereas the Law forbids the
eating of many things as unclean, yet our Lord says in
the Gospel, " Not that which goeth into the mouth de-

fileth a man; but that which cometh out of the mouth, this defileth a man." And afterwards he added, expounding the same, "Out of the heart proceed evil thoughts." Where it is abundantly shown, that that is declared by Almighty God to be polluted in deed, which springs from the root of a polluted thought. Whence also Paul the Apostle says, "Unto the pure all things are pure, but unto them that are defiled and unbelieving, nothing is pure." And presently, declaring the cause of that defilement, he adds, "For even their mind and conscience is defiled." If, therefore, meat is not unclean to him whose mind is not unclean, why shall that which a woman suffers according to nature, with a clean mind, be imputed to her as uncleanness?

A man who has approached his own wife is not to enter the church unless washed with water, nor is he to enter immediately although washed. The Law prescribed to the ancient people, that a man in such cases should be washed with water, and not enter into the church before the setting of the sun. Which, nevertheless, may be understood spiritually, because a man acts so when the mind is led by the imagination to unlawful concupiscence; for unless the fire of concupiscence be first driven from his mind, he is not to think himself worthy of the congregation of the brethren, while he sees himself burdened by the iniquity of a perverted will. For though divers nations have divers opinions concerning this affair, and seem to observe different rules, it was always the custom of the Romans, from ancient times, for such an one to seek to be cleansed by washing, and for some time reverently to forbear entering the church. Nor do we, in so saying, assign matrimony to be a fault; but forasmuch as lawful intercourse cannot be had without the pleasure of the flesh, it is proper to forbear entering the holy place, because the pleasure itself cannot be without a fault. For he was not born of adultery or fornication, but of lawful marriage, who said, "Behold I was conceived in iniquity, and in sin my mother brought me forth." For he who knew himself to have been conceived in iniquity, lamented that he

was born from sin, because he bears the defect, as a tree
bears in its bough the sap it drew from the root. In
which words, however, he does not call the union of the
married couple iniquity, but the will itself. For there are
many things which are lawful and permitted, and yet we
are somewhat defiled in doing them. As very often by
being angry we correct faults, and at the same time disturb our own peace of mind; and though that which we
do is right, yet it is not to be approved that our mind
should be disturbed. For he who said, "My eye was
disturbed with anger," had been angry at the vices of
sinners. Now, seeing that only a calm mind can rest
in the light of contemplation, he grieved that his eye was
disturbed with anger; because, whilst he was correcting
evil actions below, he was obliged to be confused and
disturbed with regard to the contemplation of the highest
things. Anger against vice is, therefore, commendable,
and yet painful to a man, because he thinks that by his
mind being agitated, he has incurred some guilt. Lawful
commerce, therefore, must be for the sake of children,
not of pleasure; and must be to procure offspring, not to
satisfy vices. But if any man is led not by the desire of
pleasure, but only for the sake of getting children, such
a man is certainly to be left to his own judgement, either
as to entering the church, or as to receiving the Mystery
of the Body and Blood of our Lord, which he, who being
placed in the fire cannot burn, is not to be forbidden by
us to receive. But when, not the love of getting children,
but of pleasure prevails, the pair have cause to lament
their deed. For this the holy preaching concedes to them,
and yet fills the mind with dread of the very concession.
For when Paul the Apostle said, "Let him that cannot
contain have his own wife;" he presently took care to
subjoin, "But this I say by way of permission, not of
commandment." For that is not granted by way of permission which is lawful, because it is just; and, therefore, that which he said he permitted, he showed to be
an offence.

It is seriously to be considered, that when God was
about to speak to the people on Mount Sinai, He first

601 A.D.] GREGORY ANSWERS AUGUSTINE 61

commanded them to abstain from women. And if purity
of body was there so carefully required, where God spoke
to the people by the means of a creature as His representative, that those who were to hear the words of God
should abstain; how much more ought women, who
receive the Body of Almighty God, to preserve themselves
in purity of flesh, lest they be burdened with the very
greatness of that inestimable Mystery? For this reason
also, it was said to David, concerning his men, by the
priest, that if they were clean in this particular, they
should receive the shewbread, which they would not have
received at all, had not David first declared them to be
clean. Then the man, who, afterwards, has been washed
with water, is also capable of receiving the Mystery of
the Holy Communion, when it is lawful for him, according to what has been before declared, to enter the
church.

Augustine's Ninth Question.—Whether after an illusion, such as is wont to happen in a dream, any man may
receive the Body of our Lord, or if he be a priest, celebrate the Divine Mysteries?

Gregory answers.—The Testament of the Old Law, as
has been said already in the article above, calls such a
man polluted, and allows him not to enter into the church
till the evening, after being washed with water. Which,
nevertheless, a spiritual people, taking in another sense,
will understand in the same manner as above; because
he is imposed upon as it were in a dream, who, being
tempted with uncleanness, is defiled by real representa-
tions in thought, and he is to be washed with water,
that he may cleanse away the sins of thought with tears;
and unless the fire of temptation depart before, may know
himself to be in a manner guilty until the evening. But
a distinction is very necessary in that illusion, and one
must carefully consider what causes it to arise in the
mind of the person sleeping; for sometimes it proceeds
from excess of eating or drinking; sometimes from the
superfluity or infirmity of nature, and sometimes from
the thoughts. And when it happens either through
superfluity or infirmity of nature, such an illusion is not

to be feared at all, because it is to be lamented, that
the mind of the person, who knew nothing of it, suffers
the same, rather than that he occasioned it. But when
the appetite of gluttony commits excess in food, and
thereupon the receptacles of the humours are oppressed,
the mind thence contracts some guilt; yet not so much
as to hinder the receiving of the Holy Mystery, or celebrating Mass, when a holy day requires it, or necessity
obliges the Mystery to be shown forth, because there is
no other priest in the place; for if there be others who
can perform the ministry, the illusion proceeding from
over-eating ought not to exclude a man from receiving the
sacred Mystery; but I am of opinion he ought humbly to
abstain from offering the sacrifice of the Mystery, but
not from receiving it, unless the mind of the person
sleeping has been disturbed with some foul imagination.
For there are some, who for the most part so suffer the
illusion, that their mind, even during the sleep of the
body, is not defiled with filthy thoughts. In which case,
one thing is evident, that the mind is guilty, not being
acquitted even in its own judgement; for though it does
not remember to have seen anything whilst the body was
sleeping, yet it calls to mind that, when the body was
awake, it fell into gluttony. But if the illusion of the sleeper
proceeds from evil thoughts when he was awake, then
its guilt is manifest to the mind; for the man perceives
from what root that defilement sprang, because what he
had consciously thought of, that he afterwards unconsciously endured. But it is to be considered, whether
that thought was no more than a suggestion, or proceeded to delight, or, what is worse, consented to sin.
For all sin is committed in three ways, viz., by suggestion, by delight, and by consent. Suggestion comes
from the Devil, delight from the flesh, and consent from
the spirit. For the serpent suggested the first offence,
and Eve, as flesh, took delight in it, but Adam, as the
spirit, consented. And when the mind sits in judgement
on itself, it must clearly distinguish between suggestion
and delight, and between delight and consent. For when
the evil spirit suggests a sin to the mind, if there ensue

no delight in the sin, the sin is in no way committed; but when the flesh begins to take delight in it, then sin begins to arise. But if it deliberately consents, then the sin is known to be full-grown. The seed, therefore, of sin is in the suggestion, the nourishment of it in delight, its maturity in the consent. And it often happens that what the evil spirit sows in the thought, in that the flesh begins to find delight, and yet the soul does not consent to that delight. And whereas the flesh cannot be delighted without the mind, yet the mind struggling against the pleasures of the flesh, is after a manner unwillingly bound by the carnal delight, so that through reason it opposes it, and does not consent, yet being bound by delight, it grievously laments being so bound. Wherefore that great soldier of our Lord's host, groaned and said, " I see another law in my members warring against the law of my mind, and bringing me into captivity to the law of sin, which is in my members." Now if he was a captive, he did not fight; but he did fight; wherefore he was a captive and at the same time therefore fought against the law of the mind, which the law that is in the members opposed; but if he fought, he was no captive. Thus, then, man is, as I may say, a captive and yet free. Free on account of justice, which he loves, a captive by the delight which he unwillingly bears within him.

CHAP. XXVIII. *How Pope Gregory wrote to the bishop of Arles to help Augustine in the work of God.* [601 A.D.]

THUS far the answers of the holy Pope Gregory, to the questions of the most reverend prelate, Augustine. Now the letter, which he says he had written to the bishop of Arles, was directed to Vergilius, successor to Aetherius,[1] and was in the following words:

" *To his most reverend and holy brother and fellow bishop, Vergilius; Gregory, servant of the servants of God.*

[1] This is Bede's attempt to reconcile the discrepancy created by his mistake in cc. 24 and 27.

With how much kindness brethren, coming of their own
accord, are to be entertained, is shown by this, that they
are for the most part invited for the sake of brotherly
love. Therefore, if our common brother, Bishop Augustine, shall happen to come to you, let your love, as is becoming, receive him with so great kindness and affection,
that it may refresh him by the benefit of its consolation
and show to others how brotherly charity is to be cul-
tivated. And, since it often happens that those who are
at a distance first learn from others the things that need
correction, if he bring before you, my brother, any sins
of bishops or others, do you, in conjunction with him,
carefully inquire into the same, and show yourself so
strict and earnest with regard to those things which
offend God and provoke His wrath, that for the amendment of others, the punishment may fall upon the guilty,
and the innocent may not suffer under false report. God
keep you in safety, most reverend brother. Given the
22nd day of June, in the nineteenth year of the reign of
our most religious lord, Mauritius Tiberius Augustus, the
eighteenth year after the consulship of our said lord, and
the fourth indiction."

CHAP. XXIX. *How the same Pope sent to Augustine
the Pall and a letter, along with several ministers of
the Word.* [601 A.D.]

MOREOVER, the same Pope Gregory, hearing from Bishop
Augustine, that the harvest which he had was great and
the labourers but few, sent to him, together with his
aforesaid envoys, certain fellow labourers and ministers
of the Word, of whom the chief and foremost were Mellitus, Justus, Paulinus, and Rufinianus,[1] and by them all

---

[1] Mellitus was consecrated Bishop of London in 604, and succeeded Laurentius in the see of Canterbury in 619. Justus was
consecrated Bishop of Rochester in 604, and succeeded Mellitus as
Primate in 624 (*v.* II, 3, foll.). Paulinus was the great missionary
bishop of the Northumbrians (*v.* II, 9, foll.). Rufinianus was the
third abbot of St. Augustine's monastery (SS. Peter and Paul).

things in general that were necessary for the worship and service of the Church, to wit, sacred vessels and altar-cloths, also church-furniture, and vestments for the bishops and clerks, as likewise relics of the holy Apostles and martyrs; besides many manuscripts. He also sent a letter, wherein he signified that he had despatched the pall to him, and at the same time directed how he should constitute bishops in Britain. The letter was in these words:

"*To his most reverend and holy 'brother and fellow bishop, Augustine; Gregory, the servant of the servants of God.* Though it be certain, that the unspeakable rewards of the eternal kingdom are reserved for those who labour for Almighty God, yet it is requisite that we bestow on them the benefit of honours, to the end that they may by this recompense be encouraged the more vigorously to apply themselves to the care of their spiritual work. And, seeing that the new Church of the English is, through the bounty of the Lord, and your labours, brought to the grace of God, we grant you the use of the pall in the same, only for the celebration of the solemn service of the Mass; that so you may ordain twelve bishops in different places, who shall be subject to your jurisdiction. But the bishop of London shall, for the future, be always consecrated by his own synod, and receive the pall, which is the token of his office, from this holy and Apostolic see, which I, by the grace of God, now serve. But we would have you send to the city of York such a bishop as you shall think fit to ordain; yet so, that if that city, with the places adjoining, shall receive the Word of God, that bishop shall also ordain twelve bishops, and enjoy the honour of a metropolitan; for we design, if we live, by the help of God, to bestow on him also the pall; and yet we would have him to be subject to your authority, my brother; but after your decease, he shall so preside over the bishops he shall have ordained, as to be in no way subject to the jurisdiction of the bishop of London. But for the future let there be this distinction as regards honour between the bishops of the cities of London and York, that he who has been

F

first ordained have the precedence.[1] But let them take
counsel and act in concert and with one mind dispose
whatsoever is to be done for zeal of Christ; let them
judge rightly, and carry out their judgement without
dissension.

"But to you, my brother, shall, by the authority of
our God and Lord Jesus Christ, be subject not only
those bishops whom you shall ordain, and those that
shall be ordained by the bishop of York, but also all the
prelates in Britain; to the end that from the words and
manner of life of your Holiness they may learn the rule of
a right belief and a good life, and fulfilling their office in
faith and righteousness, they may, when it shall please
the Lord, attain to the kingdom of Heaven. God preserve you in safety, most reverend brother.

"Given the 22nd of June, in the nineteenth year of the
reign of our most religious lord, Mauritius Tiberius
Augustus, the eighteenth year after the consulship of our
said lord, and the fourth indiction."

CHAP. XXX. *A copy of the letter which Pope Gregory
sent to the Abbot Mellitus, then going into Britain.*
[601 A.D.]

THE aforesaid envoys having departed, the blessed Father
Gregory sent after them a letter worthy to be recorded,
wherein he plainly shows how carefully he watched over
the salvation of our country. The letter was as follows:

"*To his most beloved son, the Abbot Mellitus; Gregory,
the servant of the servants of God.* We have been much
concerned, since the departure of our people that are
with you, because we have received no account of the
success of your journey. Howbeit, when Almighty God
has led you to the most reverend Bishop Augustine,
our brother, tell him what I have long been considering

---

[1] Cf. c. 27 *ad init.,* note. Gregory's symmetrical scheme was
never carried out, and it was not till 735 that York became a
metropolitan see.

in my own mind concerning the matter of the English people; to wit, that the temples of the idols in that nation ought not to be destroyed; but let the idols that are in them be destroyed; let water be consecrated and sprinkled in the said temples, let altars be erected, and relics placed there. For if those temples are well built, it is requisite that they be converted from the worship of devils to the service of the true God; that the nation, seeing that their temples are not destroyed, may remove error from their hearts, and knowing and adoring the true God, may the more freely resort to the places to which they have been accustomed. And because they are used to slaughter many oxen in sacrifice to devils, some solemnity must be given them in exchange for this, as that on the day of the dedication, or the nativities of the holy martyrs, whose relics are there deposited, they should build themselves huts of the boughs of trees about those churches which have been turned to that use from being temples, and celebrate the solemnity with religious feasting, and no more offer animals to the Devil, but kill cattle and glorify God in their feast, and return thanks to the Giver of all things for their abundance; to the end that, whilst some outward gratifications are retained, they may the more easily consent to the inward joys. For there is no doubt that it is impossible to cut off every thing at once from their rude natures; because he who endeavours to ascend to the highest place rises by degrees or steps, and not by leaps. Thus the Lord made Himself known to the people of Israel in Egypt; and yet He allowed them the use, in His own worship, of the sacrifices which they were wont to offer to the Devil, commanding them in His sacrifice to kill animals, to the end that, with changed hearts, they might lay aside one part of the sacrifice, whilst they retained another; and although the animals were the same as those which they were wont to offer, they should offer them to the true God, and not to idols; and thus they would no longer be the same sacrifices. This then, dearly beloved, it behoves you to communicate to our aforesaid brother, that he, being placed where he is at present, may consider how he is to order all things. God preserve you in safety, most beloved son.

"Given the 17th of June,[1] in the nineteenth year of the reign of our most religious lord, Mauritius Tiberius Augustus, the eighteenth year after the consulship of our said lord, and the fourth indiction."

CHAP. XXXI. *How Pope Gregory, by letter, exhorted Augustine not to glory in his miracles.* [601 A.D.]

AT which time he also sent Augustine a letter concerning the miracles that he had heard had been wrought by him; wherein he admonishes him not to incur the danger of being puffed up by the number of them. The letter was in these words:

"I know, dearly beloved brother, that Almighty God, by means of you, shows forth great miracles to the nation which it was His will to choose. Wherefore you must needs rejoice with fear, and fear with joy concerning that heavenly gift; for you will rejoice because the souls of the English are by outward miracles drawn to inward grace; but you will fear, lest, amidst the wonders that are wrought, the weak mind may be puffed up with self-esteem, and that whereby it is outwardly raised to honour cause it inwardly to fall through vain-glory. For we must call to mind, that when the disciples returned with joy from preaching, and said to their Heavenly Master, ' Lord, even the devils are subject to us through Thy Name;' forthwith they received the reply, ' In this rejoice not; but rather rejoice, because your names are written in heaven.'[2] For their minds were set on private and temporal joys, when they rejoiced in miracles; but they are recalled from the private to the common

---

[1] The date is obviously wrong, as it makes this letter earlier than that in c. 29. The name of the month is omitted in two of the oldest MSS. A satisfactory emendation (*v.* Plummer, *ad loc.*) is *Augustarum* (for *Juliarum*), the last month in Maurice's reign (XV Kal. Aug., *i.e.* 18th July).

[2] St. Luke, x, 17-20.

joy, and from the temporal to the eternal, when it is said to them, ' Rejoice in this, because your names are written in heaven.' For all the elect do not work miracles, and yet the names of all are written in heaven. For those who are disciples of the truth ought not to rejoice, save for that good thing which all men enjoy as well as they, and in which their joy shall be without end.

" It remains, therefore, most dear brother, that amidst those outward actions, which you perform through the power of the Lord, you should always carefully judge yourself in your heart, and carefully understand both what you are yourself, and how much grace is bestowed upon that same nation, for the conversion of which you have received even the gift of working miracles. And if you remember that you have at any time sinned against our Creator, either by word or deed, always call it to mind, to the end that the remembrance of your guilt may crush the vanity which rises in your heart. And whatsoever gift of working miracles you either shall receive, or have received, consider the same, not as conferred on you, but on those for whose salvation it has been given you."

CHAP. XXXII. *How Pope Gregory sent letters and gifts to King Ethelbert.* [601 A.D.]

THE same blessed Pope Gregory, at the same time, sent a letter to King Ethelbert, with many gifts of divers sorts; being desirous to glorify the king with temporal honours, at the same time that he rejoiced that through his own labour and zeal he had attained to the knowledge of heavenly glory. The copy of the said letter is as follows:

" *To the most glorious lord, and his most excellent son, Ethelbert, king of the English, Bishop Gregory.* Almighty God advances good men to the government of nations, that He may by their means bestow the gifts of His loving-kindness on those over whom they are placed. This we know to have come to pass in the English nation, over whom your Highness was placed, to the end, that by

means of the blessings which are granted to you, heavenly
benefits might also be conferred on your subjects. Therefore, my illustrious son, do you carefully guard the grace
which you have received from the Divine goodness, and
be eager to spread the Christian faith among the people
under your rule; in all uprightness increase your zeal
for their conversion; suppress the worship of idols;
overthrow the structures of the temples; establish the
manners of your subjects by much cleanness of life, exhorting, terrifying, winning, correcting, and showing
forth an example of good works, that you may obtain
your reward in Heaven from Him, Whose Name and the
knowledge of Whom you have spread abroad upon earth.
For He, Whose honour you seek and maintain among
the nations, will also render your Majesty's name more
glorious even to posterity.

"For even so the most pious emperor, Constantine, of
old, recovering the Roman commonwealth from the false
worship of idols, brought it with himself into subjection to
Almighty God, our Lord Jesus Christ, and turned to Him
with his whole mind, together with the nations under his
rule. Whence it followed, that his praises transcended
the fame of former princes; and he excelled his predecessors in renown as much as in good works. Now,
therefore, let your Highness hasten to impart to the
kings and peoples that are subject to you, the knowledge
of one God, Father, Son, and Holy Ghost; that you may
surpass the ancient kings of your nation in praise and
merit, and while you cause the sins of others among
your own subjects to be blotted out, become the more
free from anxiety with regard to your own sins before
the dread judgement of Almighty God.

"Willingly hear, devoutly perform, and studiously
retain in your memory, whatsoever counsel shall be given
you by our most reverend brother, Bishop Augustine,
who is trained up in the monastic rule, full of the knowledge of Holy Scripture, and, by the help of God, endued
with good works; for if you give ear to him when he
speaks on behalf of Almighty God, the sooner will Almighty God hear his prayers for you. But if (which God

forbid!) you slight his words, how shall Almighty God hear him on your behalf, when you neglect to hear him on behalf of God? Unite yourself, therefore, to him with all your mind, in the fervour of faith, and further his endeavours, by that virtue which God has given you, that He may make you partaker of His kingdom, Whose faith you cause to be received and maintained in your own.

"Besides, we would have your Highness know that, as we find in Holy Scripture from the words of the Almighty Lord, the end of this present world, and the kingdom of the saints, which will never come to an end, is at hand. But as the end of the world draws near, many things are about to come upon us which were not before, to wit, changes in the air, and terrors from heaven, and tempests out of the order of the seasons, wars, famines, pestilences, earthquakes in divers places; which things will not, nevertheless, all happen in our days, but will all follow after our days. If, therefore, you perceive that any of these things come to pass in your country, let not your mind be in any way disturbed; for these signs of the end of the world are sent before, for this reason, that we may take heed to our souls, and be watchful for the hour of death, and may be found prepared with good works to meet our Judge. Thus much, my illustrious son, I have said in few words, with intent that when the Christian faith is spread abroad in your kingdom, our discourse to you may also be more copious, and we may desire to say the more, as joy for the full conversion of your nation is increased in our mind.

"I have sent you some small gifts, which will not appear small to you, when received by you with the blessing of the blessed Apostle, Peter. May Almighty God, therefore, perfect in you His grace which He has begun, and prolong your life here through a course of many years, and in the fulness of time receive you into the congregation of the heavenly country. May the grace of God preserve you in safety, my most excellent lord and son.

"Given the 22nd day of June, in the nineteenth year of the reign of our most religious lord, Mauritius

Tiberius Augustus, in the eighteenth year after his consulship, and the fourth indiction."

CHAP. XXXIII. *How Augustine repaired the church of our Saviour, and built the monastery of the blessed Peter the Apostle; and concerning Peter the first abbot of the same.*

AUGUSTINE having had his episcopal see granted him in the royal city, as has been said, recovered therein, with the support of the king, a church, which he was informed had been built of old by the faithful among the Romans, and consecrated it in the name of the Holy Saviour, our Divine Lord Jesus Christ, and there established a residence for himself and all his successors.[1] He also built a monastery not far from the city to the eastward, in which, by his advice, Ethelbert erected from the foundation the church of the blessed Apostles, Peter and Paul,[2] and enriched it with divers gifts; wherein the bodies of the same Augustine, and of all the bishops of Canterbury, and of the kings of Kent, might be buried. Nevertheless, it was not Augustine himself who consecrated that church, but Laurentius, his successor.

The first abbot of that monastery was the priest Peter,[3] who, being sent on a mission into Gaul, was drowned in a bay of the sea, which is called Amfleat,[4] and committed to a humble tomb by the inhabitants of the place; but since it was the will of Almighty God to reveal his

[1] The Cathedral: Christchurch, Canterbury; but the original structure was destroyed by fire about 1067. It was rebuilt by Lanfranc, and enlarged under his successor, St. Anselm. Prior Conrad finished and decorated the chancel, and the Church was dedicated in 1130. The choir was again burnt down in 1174, but at once rebuilt. It was completed in 1184. A new nave and transept were built between 1378 and 1410, and the great central tower was carried up to its present height by the end of the fifteenth century.

[2] Afterwards called St. Augustine's Abbey.

[3] Cf. c. 27 *ad init.*

[4] Ambleteuse, a small sea-port, about six miles to the north of Boulogne.

merits, a light from Heaven was seen over his grave every night; till the neighbouring people who saw it, perceiving that he had been a holy man that was buried there, and inquiring who and whence he was, carried away the body, and interred it in the church, in the city of Boulogne, with the honour due to so great a person.

CHAP. XXXIV. *How Ethelfrid, king of the Northumbrians, having vanquished the nations of the Scots, expelled them from the territories of the English.* [603 A.D.]

AT this time, the brave and ambitious king, Ethelfrid,[1] governed the kingdom of the Northumbrians, and ravaged the Britons more than all the chiefs of the English, insomuch that he might be compared to Saul of old, king of the Israelites, save only in this, that he was ignorant of Divine religion. For he conquered more territories from the Britons than any other chieftain or king, either subduing the inhabitants and making them tributary, or driving them out and planting the English in their places. To him might justly be applied the saying of the patriarch blessing his son in the person of Saul, " Benjamin shall ravin as a wolf; in the morning he shall devour the prey, and at night he shall divide the spoil." [2] Hereupon, Aedan, king of the Scots that dwell in Britain,[3] being alarmed by his success, came against him with a great and mighty army, but was defeated and fled with a few followers; for almost all his army was cut to pieces at a famous place, called Degsastan, that is, Degsa Stone.[4] In which battle also Theodbald, brother to Ethelfrid,

---

[1] II, 2, 12; III, 1. He was the grandson of Ida, first king of Bernicia (V, 24, and note). His father, Ethelric, seized Deira on the death of Aelli (II, 1, p. 83), and Ethelfrid ruled over both the Northumbrian kingdoms from 593 to 617.

[2] Gen., xlix, 27.

[3] *I.e.*, the Dalriadic Scots, *v.s.* c. 1, and note. For Aedan and his wars, *v.* Rhŷs, "Celtic Britain," pp. 157-159.

[4] Perhaps Dalston, near Carlisle; more probably, on philological grounds, Dawstane Rig in Liddesdale; *v.* Skene, "Celtic Scotland," I, p. 162.

was killed, with almost all the forces he commanded. This war Ethelfrid brought to an end in the year of our Lord 603, the eleventh of his own reign, which lasted twenty-four years, and the first year of the reign of Phocas, who then was at the head of the Roman empire. From that time, no king of the Scots durst come into Britain to make war on the English to this day.

BOOK II

CHAP. I. *Of the death of the blessed Pope Gregory.*[1]
[604 A.D.]

AT this time, that is, in the year of our Lord 605,[2] the blessed Pope Gregory, after having most gloriously governed the Roman Apostolic see thirteen years, six months, and ten days, died, and was translated to an eternal abode in the kingdom of Heaven. Of whom, seeing that by his zeal he converted our nation, the English, from the power of Satan to the faith of Christ, it behoves us to discourse more at large in our Ecclesiastical History, for we may rightly, nay, we must, call him our apostle; because, as soon as he began to wield the pontifical power over all the world, and was placed over the Churches long before converted to the true faith, he made our nation, till then enslaved to idols, the Church of Christ, so that concerning him we may use those words of the Apostle; "if he be not an apostle to others, yet doubtless he is to us; for the seal of his apostleship are we in the Lord."[3]

He was by nation a Roman, son of Gordianus, tracing his descent from ancestors that were not only noble, but religious. Moreover Felix, once bishop of the same Apostolic see, a man of great honour in Christ and in the Church, was his forefather.[4] Nor did he show his

---

[1] For a detailed study of St. Gregory, *v.* "Gregory the Great, his place in History and Thought," by F. Homes Dudden, B.D. (1905). The oldest biographies are: (1) a Life of Gregory, written by a monk of Whitby, probably about 713 A.D., recently discovered in a MS. belonging to the Monastery of St. Gallen; (2) the Life by Paul the Deacon, written towards the end of the eighth century; (3) the Life by John the Deacon, written about the end of the ninth century.

[2] Cf. I, 23. Gregory's pontificate extended from 590 to 604.

[3] 1 Cor., ix, 2.

[4] We cannot be certain which Felix is meant. The choice seems to lie between Felix III, Bishop of Rome, 483-492, and Felix IV,

nobility in religion by less strength of devotion than his
parents and kindred. But that nobility of this world which
was seen in him, by the help of the Divine Grace, he used
only to gain the glory of eternal dignity; for soon quitting his secular habit, he entered a monastery, wherein
he began to live with so much grace of perfection that
(as he was wont afterwards with tears to testify) his
mind was above all transitory things; that he rose
superior to all that is subject to change; that he used to
think of nothing but what was heavenly; that, whilst detained by the body, he broke through the bonds of the
flesh by contemplation; and that he even loved death,
which is a penalty to almost all men, as the entrance into
life, and the reward of his labours. This he used to say
of himself, not to boast of his progress in virtue, but
rather to bewail the falling off which he imagined he
had sustained through his pastoral charge. Indeed, once
in a private conversation with his deacon, Peter, after
having enumerated the former virtues of his soul, he
added sorrowfully, " But now, on account of the pastoral
charge, it is entangled with the affairs of laymen, and,
after so fair an appearance of inward peace, is defiled with
the dust of earthly action. And having wasted itself on
outward things, by turning aside to the affairs of many
men, even when it desires the inward things, it returns to
them undoubtedly impaired. I therefore consider what I
endure, I consider what I have lost, and when I behold
what I have thrown away, that which I bear appears the
more grievous."

So spake the holy man constrained by his great
humility. But it behoves us to believe that he lost nothing
of his monastic perfection by reason of his pastoral
charge, but rather that he gained greater profit through
the labour of converting many, than by the former calm
of his private life, and chiefly because, whilst holding the
pontifical office, he set about organizing his house like a
monastery. And when first drawn from the monastery,

526-530. Mr. Homes Dudden decides in favour of the latter, on the
authority of John the Deacon. In either case, the word *atavus*
cannot be used in its strict sense.

ordained to the ministry of the altar, and sent to Constantinople as representative[1] of the Apostolic see, though he now took part in the secular affairs of the palace, yet he did not abandon the fixed course of his heavenly life; for some of the brethren of his monastery, who had followed him to the royal city in their brotherly love, he employed for the better observance of monastic rule, to the end that at all times, by their example, as he writes himself, he might be held fast to the calm shore of prayer, as it were, with the cable of an anchor, whilst he should be tossed up and down by the ceaseless waves of worldly affairs; and daily in the intercourse of studious reading with them, strengthen his mind shaken with temporal concerns. By their company he was not only guarded against the assaults of the world, but more and more roused to the exercises of a heavenly life.

For they persuaded him to interpret by a mystical exposition the book of the blessed Job,[2] which is involved in great obscurity; nor could he refuse to undertake that work, which brotherly affection imposed on him for the future benefit of many; but in a wonderful manner, in five and thirty books of exposition, he taught how that same book is to be understood literally; how to be referred to

---

[1] *Apocrisiarius*, official representative of the see of Rome at the Imperial Court of Constantinople (Latin: *responsalis*). Ducange explains the word as: "nomen inditum legatis, quod ἀποκρίσεις seu responsa principum deferrent."

[2] His "Moralia," a commentary on the Book of Job, expounding it historically, allegorically, and in its practical bearing on morals. His other undoubtedly genuine works are those mentioned in the text: Twenty-two homilies on Ezekiel; forty homilies on the Gospels for the day, preached by himself at various times; the "Liber Regulae Pastoralis," on the duties and responsibilities of the pastoral office, a very widely studied book; four books of Dialogues, "De vita et miraculis patrum Italicorum et de aeternitate animae," also one of his most famous works; and fourteen books of letters to various persons on many subjects. There are also some doubtful works. Of these, the "Liber Sacramentorum" (*v. infra*), the "Liber Antiphonarius" (a collection of Antiphons for Mass), and the Hymns have been generally regarded as genuine, but recent research seems to show that they cannot be attributed to Gregory. That he introduced the "Cantus Gregorianus" can also probably be no longer maintained; *v. infra* c. 20, *ad fin*. note.

the mysteries of Christ and the Church; and in what
sense it is to be adapted to every one of the faithful.
This work he began as papal representative in the royal
city, but finished it at Rome after being made pope.
Whilst he was still in the royal city, by the help of the
grace of Catholic truth, he crushed in its first rise a new
heresy which sprang up there, concerning the state of our
resurrection. For Eutychius,[1] bishop of that city, taught,
that our body, in the glory of resurrection, would be
impalpable, and more subtile than wind and air. The
blessed Gregory hearing this, proved by force of truth,
and by the instance of the Resurrection of our Lord, that
this doctrine was every way opposed to the orthodox
faith. For the Catholic faith holds that our body, raised
by the glory of immortality, is indeed rendered subtile by
the effect of spiritual power, but is palpable by the reality
of nature; according to the example of our Lord's Body,
concerning which, when risen from the dead, He Himself
says to His disciples, "Handle Me and see, for a spirit
hath not flesh and bones, as ye see Me have.[2] In main-
taining this faith, the venerable Father Gregory so
earnestly strove against the rising heresy, and with the
help of the most pious emperor, Tiberius Constantine,[3]
so fully suppressed it, that none has been since found to
revive it.

He likewise composed another notable book, the
"Liber Pastoralis," wherein he clearly showed what sort
of persons ought to be preferred to rule the Church; how
such rulers ought to live; with how much discrimination
they ought to instruct the different classes of their hearers,

[1] Patriarch of Constantinople, celebrated as a saint by the
Greeks. He was born at Theium in Phrygia, *circ.* 512 A.D. Towards the end of his life he maintained the above theory in a book
on the Resurrection. He was opposed by Gregory, and the book
was burnt by order of the Emperor Tiberius, who, however, visited
him when he fell ill soon after, and received his blessing. He died
on Easter Day, 582, and the "heresy" was suffered to rest. (He
is, of course, not to be confused with Eutyches, author of the
heresy known as "Eutychianism," *v.* IV, 17.)
[2] St. Luke, xxiv, 39.
[3] Tiberius II, emperor of the East, 578-582 A.D.

and how seriously to reflect every day on their own frailty. He also wrote forty homilies on the Gospel, which he divided equally into two volumes; and composed four books of Dialogues, in which, at the request of his deacon, Peter, he recounted the virtues of the more renowned saints of Italy, whom he had either known or heard of, as a pattern of life for posterity; to the end that, as he taught in his books of Expositions what virtues men ought to strive after, so by describing the miracles of saints, he might make known the glory of those virtues. Further, in twenty-two homilies, he showed how much light is latent in the first and last parts of the prophet Ezekiel, which seemed the most obscure. Besides which, he wrote the " Book of Answers,"[1] to the questions of the holy Augustine, the first bishop of the English nation, as we have shown above, inserting the same book entire in this history; and the useful little " Synodical Book,"[2] which he composed with the bishops of Italy on necessary matters of the Church; as well as private letters to certain persons. And it is the more wonderful that he could write so many lengthy works, seeing that almost all the time of his youth, to use his own words, he was frequently tormented with internal pain, constantly enfeebled by the weakness of his digestion, and oppressed by a low but persistent fever. But in all these troubles, forasmuch as he carefully reflected that, as the Scripture testifies,[3] " He scourgeth every son whom He receiveth," the more severely he suffered under those present evils, the more he assured himself of his eternal hope.

Thus much may be said of his immortal genius, which could not be crushed by such severe bodily pains. Other popes applied themselves to building churches or adorning them with gold and silver, but Gregory was wholly intent upon gaining souls. Whatsoever money he had,

[1] I, 27.
[2] A Synodical epistle, such as newly-elected bishops were in the habit of sending to other bishops. The subject-matter is the same as that of the " Pastoral Care."
[3] Heb., xii, 6.

he took care to distribute diligently and give to the poor,
that his righteousness might endure for ever, and his
horn be exalted with honour; so that the words of the
blessed Job might be truly said of him,[1] "When the ear
heard me, then it blessed me; and when the eye saw me,
it gave witness to me: because I delivered the poor that
cried, and the fatherless, and him that had none to help
him. The blessing of him that was ready to perish came
upon me, and I caused the widow's heart to sing for joy.
I put on righteousness, and it clothed me; my judgement
was as a robe and a diadem. I was eyes to the blind, and
feet was I to the lame. I was a father to the poor; and
the cause which I knew not, I searched out. And I brake
the jaws of the wicked, and plucked the spoil out of his
teeth." And a little after: "If I have withheld," says
he, "the poor from their desire; or have caused the eyes
of the widow to fail; or have eaten my morsel myself
alone, and the fatherless hath not eaten thereof: (for
from my youth compassion grew up with me, and from
my mother's womb it came forth with me."[2])

To his works of piety and righteousness this also may
be added, that he saved our nation, by the preachers he
sent hither, from the teeth of the old enemy, and made it
partaker of eternal liberty. Rejoicing in the faith and
salvation of our race, and worthily commending it with
praise, he says, in his exposition of the blessed Job,
"Behold, the tongue of Britain, which only knew how
to utter barbarous cries, has long since begun to raise
the Hebrew Hallelujah to the praise of God! Behold, the
once swelling ocean now serves prostrate at the feet of
the saints; and its wild upheavals, which earthly princes
could not subdue with the sword, are now, through the
fear of God, bound by the lips of priests with words
alone; and the heathen that stood not in awe of troops
of warriors, now believes and fears the tongues of the
humble! For he has received a message from on high

---

[1] Job, xxix, 11-17.
[2] The quotation is from the Vulgate (Job, xxxi, 16-18). The
sentence is finished in v. 22: "Then let mine arm fall from my
shoulder blade . . ."

and mighty works are revealed; the strength of the
knowledge of God is given him, and restrained by the
fear of the Lord, he dreads to do evil, and with all his
heart desires to attain to everlasting grace." In which
words the blessed Gregory shows us this also, that St.
Augustine and his companions brought the English to
receive the truth, not only by the preaching of words,
but also by showing forth heavenly signs.

The blessed Pope Gregory, among other things, caused
Masses to be celebrated in the churches of the holy
Apostles, Peter and Paul, over their bodies. And in the
celebration of Masses, he added three petitions of the
utmost perfection : "And dispose our days in thy peace,
and bid us to be preserved from eternal damnation, and
to be numbered in the flock of thine elect."[1]

He governed the Church in the days of the Emperors
Mauritius and Phocas, and passing out of this life in the
second year of the same Phocas,[2] he departed to the true
life which is in Heaven. His body was buried in the
church of the blessed Apostle Peter before the sacristy,
on the 12th day of March, to rise one day in the same
body in glory with the rest of the holy pastors of the
Church. On his tomb was written this epitaph :

Receive, O Earth, his body taken from thine own; thou canst
restore it, when God calls to life. His spirit rises to the stars; the
claims of death shall not avail against him, for death itself is but
the way to new life. In this tomb are laid the limbs of a great
pontiff, who yet lives for ever in all places in countless deeds of
mercy. Hunger and cold he overcame with food and raiment, and
shielded souls from the enemy by his holy teaching. And whatsoever he taught in word, that he fulfilled in deed, that he might be
a pattern, even as he spake words of mystic meaning. By his

---

[1] John the Deacon attributes to Gregory the "Liber Sacramentorum," or Gregorian Sacramentary, a revision of the Gelasian
Sacramentary. It seems probable, however, that it is of much later
date. Only a few alterations in the Liturgy and in the ceremonial
of the Mass are proved to have been effected by Gregory. In the
Canon of the Mass he introduced two changes, viz.: (1) he inserted
the words here quoted; (2) he altered the position of the Lord's
Prayer (v. Homes Dudden, pp. 264-271).

[2] I.e., 604 A.D., cf. I, 23; II, 1, ad init., note.

guiding love he brought the Angles to Christ, gaining armies for the Faith from a new people. This was thy toil, thy task, thy care, thy aim as shepherd, to offer to thy Lord abundant increase of the flock. So, Consul of God, rejoice in this thy triumph, for now thou hast the reward of thy works for evermore.

Nor must we pass by in silence the story of the blessed Gregory, handed down to us by the tradition of our ancestors, which explains his earnest care for the salvation of our nation. It is said that one day, when some merchants had lately arrived at Rome, many things were exposed for sale in the market place, and much people resorted thither to buy: Gregory himself went with the rest, and saw among other wares some boys put up for sale, of fair complexion, with pleasing countenances, and very beautiful hair. When he beheld them, he asked, it is said, from what region or country they were brought? and was told, from the island of Britain, and that the inhabitants were like that in appearance. He again inquired whether those islanders were Christians, or still involved in the errors of paganism, and was informed that they were pagans. Then fetching a deep sigh from the bottom of his heart, "Alas! what pity," said he, "that the author of darkness should own men of such fair countenances; and that with such grace of outward form, their minds should be void of inward grace. He therefore again asked, what was the name of that nation? and was answered, that they were called Angles. "Right," said he, "for they have an angelic face, and it is meet that such should be co-heirs with the Angels in heaven. What is the name of the province from which they are brought?" It was replied, that the natives of that province were called Deiri.[1] "Truly are they *De ira*," said he, "saved from wrath, and called to the mercy of Christ. How is the king of that province

[1] Deira was the southern part of the province of Northumbria, the northern part being Bernicia. Deira was bounded on the south by the Humber; on the north, according to some authorities, by the Tyne, according to others, by the Tees. The discrepancy doubtless arose from the fact that the part between the two latter rivers was a desert subject to no authority. To the west lay the British kingdoms.

called?" They told him his name was Aelli;[1] and he, playing upon the name, said, "Allelujah, the praise of God the Creator must be sung in those parts."

Then he went to the bishop of the Roman Apostolic see[2] (for he was not himself then made pope), and entreated him to send some ministers of the Word into Britain to the nation of the English, that it might be converted to Christ by them; declaring himself ready to carry out that work with the help of God, if the Apostolic Pope should think fit to have it done. But not being then able to perform this task, because, though the Pope was willing to grant his request, yet the citizens of Rome could not be brought to consent that he should depart so far from the city, as soon as he was himself made Pope, he carried out the long-desired work, sending, indeed, other preachers, but himself by his exhortations and prayers helping the preaching to bear fruit. This account, which we have received from a past generation, we have thought fit to insert in our Ecclesiastical History.

CHAP. II. *How Augustine admonished the bishops of the Britons on behalf of Catholic peace, and to that end wrought a heavenly miracle in their presence; and of the vengeance that pursued them for their contempt.* [*Circ.* 603 A.D.]

In the meantime, Augustine, with the help of King Ethelbert, drew together to a conference the bishops and doctors of the nearest province of the Britons, at a place

[1] The son of Yffi, the first king of Deira. The ancient pedigrees trace the descent of the royal houses of Deira and Bernicia from two sons of Woden.

[2] This pope was either Benedict I (574-578) or Pelagius II (578-590), the immediate predecessor of Gregory. The oldest extant life of Gregory (*v.s.* p. 75, note) makes him Benedict, and is followed by John the Deacon. If this is right, the incident related in the text must be placed before Gregory's departure to Constantinople in 579. Paul the Deacon places it after his return in 585 or 586, and asserts that the pope was Pelagius II.

which is to this day called, in the English language,
Augustine's Ác, that is, Augustine's Oak,[1] on the borders
of the Hwiccas[2] and West Saxons; and began by
brotherly admonitions to persuade them to preserve
Catholic peace with him, and undertake the common
labour of preaching the Gospel to the heathen for the
Lord's sake. For they did not keep Easter Sunday at
the proper time, but from the fourteenth to the twentieth
moon; which computation is contained in a cycle of
eighty-four years.[3] Besides, they did many other things

---

[1] The date of the synod is uncertain. It was probably about
602 or 603 A.D., after the arrival of Gregory's "Responsa." The
"nearest province" must mean what we call South Wales, though it
is possible that the Britons of Cornwall were also represented. The
scene of the conference has been generally supposed to be Aust,
on the Severn, opposite Chepstow, and the name may possibly
preserve the memory of Augustine, though more probably it is
derived from "Trajectus Augusti" (Haddan and Stubbs). Other
possible sites are Malmesbury (Green, "Making of England"),
and a spot called "the Oak," near Cricklade, on the Upper
Thames, which would be on the borders of the Hwiccas and West
Saxons (v. Plummer, ad loc.).
[2] The Hwiccas were in the present Gloucestershire and Worcestershire, north-west of Wessex.
[3] Cf. especially III, 25, and V, 21. (Other references are: II, 4,
19; III, 3, 4, 26, 29; V, 15, 22.)
A full discussion of this involved question is beyond our scope.
Readers are referred to Plummer (Excursus on Paschal Controversy), Bright, or Hunt. Here, the point at issue may be briefly
stated. It was regarded as essential by the Roman Church that
Easter Day should be kept on a Sunday, in the third week of the
first month, i.e., the month in which the full moon occurred on or
after the vernal equinox. The Celts observed the Feast on Sunday,
and were, therefore, not rightly called "Quartodecimans" (the
name given to those who observed it on the 14th of the month
Nisan, the day of the Jewish Passover, without regard to the day
of the week). They differed from the Romans in fixing the vernal
equinox at March 25th, instead of March 21st, and in their reckoning of the third week, holding it to be from the 14th to the 20th
of the moon inclusive. The Roman Church originally reckoned
it from the 16th to the 22nd, but ultimately fixed it from the 15th
to the 21st (cf. V, 21, p. 365).
There was a further divergence in the "cycles" adopted to
ascertain the day in each year on which the Paschal moon would
fall. The Celts retained an old cycle of eighty-four years, while
the Romans had finally adopted one of nineteen. It is obvious that

which were opposed to the unity of the church.[1] When, after a long disputation, they did not comply with the entreaties, exhortations, or rebukes of Augustine and his companions, but preferred their own traditions before all the Churches which are united in Christ throughout the world, the holy father, Augustine, put an end to this troublesome and tedious contention, saying, "Let us entreat God, who maketh men to be of one mind in His Father's house, to vouchsafe, by signs from Heaven, to declare to us which tradition is to be followed; and by what path we are to strive to enter His kingdom. Let some sick man be brought, and let the faith and practice of him, by whose prayers he shall be healed, be looked upon as hallowed in God's sight and such as should be adopted by all." His adversaries unwillingly consenting, a blind man of the English race was brought, who having been presented to the British bishops, found no benefit or healing from their ministry; at length, Augustine, compelled by strict necessity, bowed his knees to the Father of our Lord Jesus Christ, praying that He would restore his lost sight to the blind man, and by the bodily enlightenment of one kindle the grace of spiritual light in the hearts of many of the faithful. Immediately the blind man received sight, and Augustine was proclaimed by all to be a true herald of the light from Heaven. The Britons then confessed that they perceived that it was the

these differences must necessarily lead to great divergence in practice and consequently serious inconvenience. The real importance of this and the other points of difference, settled afterwards at the Synod of Whitby, lay in the question whether England was to conform to the practice of the Catholic Church, or to isolate herself from it by local peculiarities (cf. the reply of the British to Augustine: "They would do none of those things nor receive him as their archbishop ").

[1] E.g., Consecration of bishops by a single bishop, certain differences of ritual (Gregory's "Responsa" admit of some latitude in these matters), and the tonsure, which was a more controversial point (cf. III, 26, and V, 21). The Romans shaved only the top of the head, letting the hair grow in the form of a crown. The Celts shaved the whole front of the head from ear to ear, leaving the hair at the back. A third method was the Oriental, which consisted in shaving the whole head (cf. IV, 1).

true way of righteousness which Augustine taught; but
that they could not depart from their ancient customs
without the consent and sanction of their people. They
therefore desired that a second time a synod might be appointed, at which more of their number should be present.

This being decreed, there came, it is said, seven
bishops of the Britons,[1] and many men of great learning,
particularly from their most celebrated monastery, which
is called, in the English tongue, Bancornaburg,[2] and over
which the Abbot Dinoot[3] is said to have presided at that
time. They that were to go to the aforesaid council, betook themselves first to a certain holy and discreet man,
who was wont to lead the life of a hermit among them,
to consult with him, whether they ought, at the preaching of Augustine, to forsake their traditions. He
answered, "If he is a man of God, follow him."—
"How shall we know that?" said they. He replied,
"Our Lord saith, Take My yoke upon you, and learn of
Me, for I am meek and lowly in heart; if therefore,
Augustine is meek and lowly of heart, it is to be believed
that he bears the yoke of Christ himself, and offers it to
you to bear. But, if he is harsh and proud, it is plain
that he is not of God, nor are we to regard his words."
They said again, "And how shall we discern even this?"
—"Do you contrive," said the anchorite, "that he first
arrive with his company at the place where the synod is
to be held; and if at your approach he rises up to you,
hear him submissively, being assured that he is the servant of Christ; but if he despises you, and does not rise
up to you, whereas you are more in number, let him also
be despised by you."

[1] The place of the second conference is not mentioned. It is
generally assumed that it was the same as that of the first. All
attempts to determine the names and sees of these bishops rest
pon the most uncertain evidence.

[2] Probably Bangor-is-Coed, in Flintshire, from which it appears
that North Wales was represented at the second conference. The
size and importance of the monastery are inferred by William of
Malmesbury, writing in the twelfth century, from the extent of the
ruins, which were all that was left of it in his time.

[3] Dunawd, or Dunod; Latin: Donatus (Rhŷs).

They did as he directed; and it happened, that as they approached, Augustine was sitting on a chair. When they perceived it, they were angry, and charging him with pride, set themselves to contradict all he said. He said to them, "Many things ye do which are contrary to our custom, or rather the custom of the universal Church, and yet, if you will comply with me in these three matters, to wit, to keep Easter at the due time; to fulfil the ministry of Baptism, by which we are born again to God, according to the custom of the holy Roman Apostolic Church;[1] and to join with us in preaching the Word of God to the English nation, we will gladly suffer all the other things you do, though contrary to our customs." They answered that they would do none of those things, nor receive him as their archbishop; for they said among themselves, "if he would not rise up to us now, how much more will he despise us, as of no account, if we begin to be under his subjection?" Then the man of God, Augustine, is said to have threatened them, that if they would not accept peace with their brethren, they should have war from their enemies; and, if they would not preach the way of life to the English nation, they should suffer at their hands the vengeance of death. All which, through the dispensation of the Divine judgement, fell out exactly as he had predicted.

For afterwards the warlike king of the English, Ethelfrid,[2] of whom we have spoken, having raised a mighty army, made a very great slaughter of that heretical nation, at the city of Legions,[3] which by the English is

---

[1] It is not known in what way the practice of the British Church differed from that of the Romans in the rite of Baptism. It may have been by the neglect of Confirmation as the completion of Baptism (cf. "compleatis" in the text). Other suggestions are: single immersion (but this was permitted in Spain); the omission of chrism, an omission which was affirmed of the Irish at a later period; some defect in the invocation of the Trinity. This conjecture rests on a canon respecting Baptism established in the English Church from the time of Augustine (quoted by Haddan and Stubbs from a letter of Pope Zacharias to Boniface), which enforces the full invocation.   [2] I, 34.

[3] Chester, the seat of the Twentieth legion. "Legionum civitas,

called Legacaestir, but by the Britons more rightly Car-
legion. Being about to give battle, he observed their
priests, who were come together to offer up their prayers
to God for the combatants, standing apart in a place of
greater safety; he inquired who they were, and what
they came together to do in that place. Most of them
were of the monastery of Bangor,[1] in which, it is said,
there was so great a number of monks, that the monastery being divided into seven parts, with a superior set
over each, none of those parts contained less than three
hundred men, who all lived by the labour of their hands.
Many of these, having observed a fast of three days, had
come together along with others to pray at the aforesaid
battle, having one Brocmail[2] for their protector, to defend
them, whilst they were intent upon their prayers, against
the swords of the barbarians. King Ethelfrid being informed of the occasion of their coming, said, "If then
they cry to their God against us, in truth, though they
do not bear arms, yet they fight against us, because they
assail us with their curses." He, therefore, commanded
them to be attacked first, and then destroyed the rest of
the impious army, not without great loss of his own
forces. About twelve hundred of those that came to pray
are said to have been killed, and only fifty to have
escaped by flight. Brocmail, turning his back with his
men, at the first approach of the enemy, left those whom
he ought to have defended unarmed and exposed to the
swords of the assailants. Thus was fulfilled the prophecy
of the holy Bishop Augustine, though he himself had
been long before taken up into the heavenly kingdom,
that the heretics should feel the vengeance of temporal
death also, because they had despised the offer of eternal
salvation.

quae nunc simpliciter Cestra vocatur." (William of Malmesbury.)
Cf. note on I, 7, p. 18. The date of the battle cannot be accurately
fixed. The "Annales Cambriae" give 613, but it may have been
a few years later. Bede only tells us that it was a considerable time
after Augustine's death, which was probably in 604 or 605.
    [1] Cf. *supra* p. 86, note 2.
    [2] Nothing certain is known of this Welsh prince.

CHAP. III. *How St. Augustine made Mellitus and Justus bishops; and of his death.* [604 A.D.]

In the year of our Lord 604, Augustine, Archbishop of Britain, ordained two bishops, to wit, Mellitus and Justus;[1] Mellitus to preach to the province of the East-Saxons, who are divided from Kent by the river Thames, and border on the Eastern sea. Their metropolis is the city of London, which is situated on the bank of the aforesaid river, and is the mart of many nations resorting to it by sea and land. At that time, Sabert, nephew to Ethelbert through his sister Ricula, reigned over the nation, though he was under subjection to Ethelbert, who, as has been said above, had command over all the nations of the English as far as the river Humber. But when this province also received the word of truth, by the preaching of Mellitus, King Ethelbert built the church of St. Paul the Apostle,[2] in the city of London, where he and his successors should have their episcopal see. As for Justus, Augustine ordained him bishop in Kent, at the city of Dorubrevis, which the English call Hrofaes-caestrae,[3] from one that was formerly the chief man of it, called Hrof. It is about twenty-four miles distant from the city of Canterbury to the westward, and in it King Ethelbert dedicated a church to the blessed Apostle Andrew,[4] and bestowed many gifts on the bishops of both those churches, as well as on the Bishop of Canterbury, adding lands and possessions for the use of those who were associated with the bishops.

After this, the beloved of God, our father Augustine,

[1] I, 29, and note.
[2] The site is covered by the present cathedral.
[3] Rochester. The new see was closely dependent on Canterbury, and till 1148 the archbishop had the appointment to this bishopric.
[4] Probably in memory of his monastery on the Coelian (cf. I, 23). According to Rochester tradition, Ethelbert gave to the church some land called Priestfield to the south of the city, and other lands to the north. There exists a charter of Ethelbert to the city of Rochester, believed to be genuine.

died,[1] and his body was laid outside, close by the church of the blessed Apostles, Peter and Paul, above spoken of, because it was not yet finished, nor consecrated, but as soon as it was consecrated,[2] the body was brought in, and fittingly buried in the north chapel [3] thereof; wherein also were interred the bodies of all the succeeding archbishops, except two only, Theodore and Bertwald, whose bodies are in the church itself, because the aforesaid chapel could contain no more.[4] Almost in the midst of this chapel is an altar dedicated in honour of the blessed Pope Gregory, at which every Saturday memorial Masses are celebrated for the archbishops by a priest of that place. On the tomb of Augustine is inscribed this epitaph:

"Here rests the Lord Augustine, first Archbishop of Canterbury, who, being of old sent hither by the blessed Gregory, Bishop of the city of Rome, and supported by God in the working of miracles, led King Ethelbert and his nation from the worship of idols to the faith of Christ, and having ended the days of his office in peace, died the 26th day of May, in the reign of the same king."

[1] The year is not given, and is not certainly known. It is generally assumed to have been 604 or 605.
[2] This was in 613, by Laurentius. St. Augustine's body was translated on September 13th. It was moved again in the twelfth century and placed under the high altar.
[3] "Porticus"; variously translated: "porch," "aisle," "transept," and "chapel." Ducange explains it as "aedis sacrae propylaeum in porticus formam exstructum," and says it was also used improperly for the sanctuary. Plummer (ad loc.) says it means side chapel, as often. The mention of the altar just below seems to support this meaning (if, indeed, haec refers to the "porticus," and not to the church itself, as is assumed in the A.S. version).
[4] For Theodore v. Preface, p. 2, note 2; IV, 1; V, 8, et saep.; and for Bertwald, V, 8. Cuthbert (740-758) was the first archbishop buried in Christ Church, Canterbury, instead of at St. Augustine's.

CHAP. IV. *How Laurentius and his bishops admonished the Scots to observe the unity of the Holy Church, particularly in keeping of Easter; and how Mellitus went to Rome.*

LAURENTIUS [1] succeeded Augustine in the bishopric, having been ordained thereto by the latter, in his lifetime, lest, upon his death, the Church, as yet in so unsettled a state, might begin to falter, if it should be destitute of a pastor, though but for one hour. Wherein he also followed the example of the first pastor of the Church, that is, of the most blessed Peter, chief of the Apostles, who, having founded the Church of Christ at Rome, is said to have consecrated Clement to help him in preaching the Gospel, and at the same time to be his successor. Laurentius, being advanced to the rank of archbishop, laboured indefatigably, both by frequent words of holy exhortation and constant example of good works to strengthen the foundations of the Church, which had been so nobly laid, and to carry it on to the fitting height of perfection. In short, he not only took charge of the new Church formed among the English, but endeavoured also to bestow his pastoral care upon the tribes of the ancient inhabitants of Britain, as also of the Scots, who inhabit the island of Ireland,[2] which is next to Britain. For when he understood that the life and profession of the Scots in their aforesaid country, as well as of the Britons in Britain, was not truly in accordance with the practice of the Church in many matters, especially that they did not celebrate the festival of Easter at the due time, but thought that the day of the Resurrection of our Lord ought, as has been said above, to be observed between the 14th and 20th of the moon; he wrote, jointly with his fellow bishops, a hortatory epistle, entreating and conjuring them to keep the unity of peace and Catholic observance with the Church of

[1] Cf. I, 27, *ad init.*
[2] Bede thus distinguishes them from the colony in Scotland. Cf. I, 1, and note.

Christ spread throughout the world. The beginning of
which epistle is as follows:

"*To our most dear brethren, the Lords Bishops and
Abbots throughout all the country of the Scots,*[1] *Laurentius,
Mellitus, and Justus, Bishops, servants of the servants of
God.* When the Apostolic see, according to the universal
custom which it has followed elsewhere, sent us to these
western parts to preach to pagan nations, and it was our
lot to come into this island, which is called Britain, before
we knew them, we held both the Britons and Scots in
great esteem for sanctity, believing that they walked
according to the custom of the universal Church; but
becoming acquainted with the Britons, we thought that
the Scots had been better. Now we have learnt from
Bishop Dagan,[2] who came into this aforesaid island, and
the Abbot Columban,[3] in Gaul, that the Scots in no way
differ from the Britons in their walk; for when Bishop
Dagan came to us, not only did he refuse to eat at the
same table, but even to eat in the same house where we
were entertained."

Also Laurentius with his fellow bishops wrote a letter
to the bishops of the Britons, suitable to his degree, by
which he endeavoured to confirm them in Catholic unity;
but what he gained by so doing the present times still show.

About this time, Mellitus, bishop of London, went to
Rome, to confer with the Apostolic Pope Boniface about
the necessary affairs of the English Church. And the
same most reverend pope, assembling a synod of the

[1] Ireland. Iona may be included, as may be inferred from a
comparison of III, 21 ("reversus est ad insulam Hii") with III, 24
("ad Scottiam rediit"). But Bede does not use "Scottia" for
Scotland.
[2] Bishop of Inver Daeile (Ennereilly) in Wicklow.
[3] The most famous of the great Irish missionaries who laboured
on the Continent. He was born in Leinster about 540, went to
Gaul about 574, founded three monasteries (Annegray, Luxeuil, and
Fontaines), worked for twenty years among the Franks and Bur-
gundians, afterwards among the Suevi and Alemanni, and finally
in Italy, where he founded a monastery at Bobbio and died there
in 615. He was a vigorous supporter of the Celtic usages and an
active opponent of Arianism. He instituted a monastic rule of
great severity.

bishops of Italy,[1] to prescribe rules for the life and peace of the monks, Mellitus also sat among them, in the eighth year of the reign of the Emperor Phocas, the thirteenth indiction, on the 27th of February,[2] to the end that he also might sign and confirm by his authority whatsoever should be regularly decreed, and on his return into Britain might carry the decrees to the Churches of the English, to be committed to them and observed; together with letters which the same pope sent to the beloved of God, Archbishop Laurentius, and to all the clergy; as likewise to King Ethelbert and the English nation. This pope was Boniface, the fourth after the blessed Gregory, bishop of the city of Rome. He obtained for the Church of Christ from the Emperor Phocas the gift of the temple at Rome called by the ancients Pantheon, as representing all the gods; wherein he, having purified it from all defilement, dedicated a church to the holy Mother of God, and to all Christ's martyrs, to the end that, the company of devils being expelled, the blessed company of the saints might have therein a perpetual memorial.[3]

CHAP. V. *How, after the death of the kings Ethelbert and Sabert, their successors restored idolatry; for which reason, both Mellitus and Justus departed out of Britain.* [616 A.D.]

In the year of our Lord 616, which is the twenty-first year after Augustine and his company were sent to preach to the English nation, Ethelbert, king of Kent, having most gloriously governed his temporal kingdom fifty-six years, entered into the eternal joys of the king-

---

[1] Nothing more is known of this council. The pope was Boniface IV, 608-615.

[2] 610 A.D.

[3] To commemorate the dedication the pope introduced into the Western Church the Festival of All Saints, celebrated at first probably on 13th May. The Eastern Church had from early times observed a Festival of All Martyrs, which became later the Festival of All Saints, kept by them on the Sunday after Whitsunday.

dom of Heaven. He was the third of the English kings
who ruled over all the southern provinces that are divided
from the northern by the river Humber and the borders
contiguous to it;[1] but the first of all that ascended to the
heavenly kingdom. The first who had the like sovereignty
was Aelli, king of the South-Saxons; the second, Caelin,
king of the West-Saxons, who, in their own language,
is called Ceaulin; the third, as has been said, was Ethelbert, king of Kent; the fourth was Redwald, king of the
East-Angles, who, even in the life-time of Ethelbert, had
been acquiring the leadership for his own race. The fifth
was Edwin, king of the Northumbrian nation, that is, of
those who live in the district to the north of the river
Humber; his power was greater; he had the over-
lordship over all the nations who inhabit Britain, both
English and British, except only the people of Kent;
and he reduced also under the dominion of the English,
the Mevanian Islands[2] of the Britons, lying between
Ireland and Britain; the sixth was Oswald, the most
Christian king of the Northumbrians, whose kingdom
was within the same bounds ; the seventh, his brother
Oswy, ruled over a kingdom of like extent for a time,
and for the most part subdued and made tributary the
nations of the Picts and Scots, who occupy the northern
parts of Britain : but of that hereafter.

King Ethelbert died on the 24th day of the month of
February, twenty-one years after he had received the
faith,[3] and was buried in St. Martin's chapel within the
church of the blessed Apostles Peter and Paul, where also
lies his queen, Bertha. Among other benefits which he

[1] As Bretwalda, or paramount sovereign (*v.* Stubbs, "Constitutional History," I, pp. 162-163). Aelli and Ceaulin are not elsewhere mentioned in this work. For Redwald, *v. infra* c. 12;
for Edwin, c. 9, foll. ; for Oswald, III, 1, foll.; and for Oswy, III,
14, foll.

[2] Anglesea and Man.

[3] This is inaccurate and inconsistent with Bede's own statement
in V. 24. Augustine did not arrive in Britain till 597. The dates
given above, at the beginning of this chapter, are, however, probably correct, if he means that Ethelbert died twenty-one years
after the dispatch of the mission from Rome.

conferred upon his nation in his care for them, he established, with the help of his council of wise men,[1] judicial decisions, after the Roman model; which are written in the language of the English, and are still kept and observed by them. Among which, he set down first what satisfaction should be given by any one who should steal anything belonging to the Church, the bishop, or the other clergy, for he was resolved to give protection to those whom he had received along with their doctrine.

This Ethelbert was the son of Irminric, whose father was Octa, whose father was Oeric, surnamed Oisc, from whom the kings of Kent are wont to be called Oiscings.[2] His father was Hengist, who, being invited by Vortigern, first came into Britain, with his son Oisc, as has been said above.

But after the death of Ethelbert, the accession of his son Eadbald proved very harmful to the still tender growth of the new Church; for he not only refused to accept the faith of Christ, but was also defiled with such fornication, as the Apostle testifies, as is not so much as named among the Gentiles, that one should have his father's wife.[3] By both which crimes he gave occasion to those to return to their former uncleanness, who, under his father, had, either for favour or fear of the king, submitted to the laws of the faith and of a pure life. Nor did the unbelieving king escape without the scourge of Divine severity in chastisement and correction; for he was troubled with frequent fits of madness, and possessed by an unclean spirit. The storm of this disturbance was increased by the death of Sabert, king of the East Saxons, who departing to the heavenly kingdom, left three sons, still pagans, to inherit his temporal crown. They immediately began openly to give themselves up to idolatry, which, during their father's lifetime, they had seemed

---

[1] The Witenagemot, the supreme assembly. This is the first recorded instance of its legislative action. The "decisions" are the so-called "dooms."

[2] "—ing" is a Saxon patronymic.

[3] It was Ethelbert's second wife. Bertha had died before him.

somewhat to abandon, and they granted free licence to
their subjects to serve idols. And when they saw the
bishop, whilst celebrating Mass in the church, give the
Eucharist to the people, filled, as they were, with folly
and ignorance, they said to him, as is commonly reported, "Why do you not give us also that white bread,
which you used to give to our father Saba (for so they
were wont to call him), and which you still continue to
give to the people in the church?" To whom he answered,
"If you will be washed in that font of salvation, in which
your father was washed, you may also partake of the
holy Bread of which he partook; but if you despise the
laver of life, you can in no wise receive the Bread of
life." They replied, "We will not enter into that font,
because we know that we do not stand in need of it, and
yet we will be refreshed by that bread." And being
often earnestly admonished by him, that this could by
no means be done, nor would any one be admitted to partake of the sacred Oblation without the holy cleansing, at
last, they said, filled with rage, "If you will not comply
with us in so small a matter as that which we require,
you shall not stay in our province." And they drove
him out and bade him and his company depart from
their kingdom. Being driven thence, he came into Kent,
to take counsel with his fellow bishops, Laurentius and
Justus, and learn what was to be done in that case;
and with one consent they determined that it was better
for them all to return to their own country, where they
might serve God in freedom of mind, than to continue to
no purpose among barbarians, who had revolted from
the faith. Mellitus and Justus accordingly went away
first, and withdrew into the parts of Gaul, intending
there to await the event. But the kings, who had driven
from them the herald of the truth, did not continue long
unpunished in their worship of devils. For marching
out to battle against the nation of the Gewissi,[1] they
were all slain with their army. Nevertheless, the people,

[1] Or Gewissae. The West Saxons, an antiquated term for them.
Cf. III, 7: "Occidentalium Saxonum, qui antiquitus Gewissae
vocabantur" (cf. "visi"=west, in "Visigoth").

having been once turned to wickedness, though the authors of it were destroyed, would not be corrected, nor return to the unity of faith and charity which is in Christ.

CHAP. VI. *How Laurentius, being reproved by the Apostle Peter, converted King Eadbald to Christ; and how the king soon recalled Mellitus and Justus to preach the Word.* [617-618 A.D.]

LAURENTIUS, being about to follow Mellitus and Justus, and to quit Britain, ordered his bed to be laid that night in the church of the blessed Apostles, Peter and Paul, which has been often mentioned before; wherein having laid himself to rest, after he had with tears poured forth many prayers to God for the state of the Church, he fell asleep; in the dead of night, the blessed chief of the Apostles appeared to him, and scourging him grievously a long time, asked of him with apostolic severity, why he was forsaking the flock which he had committed to him? or to what shepherd he was leaving, by his flight, Christ's sheep that were in the midst of wolves? "Hast thou," he said, "forgotten my example, who, for the sake of those little ones, whom Christ commended to me in token of His affection, underwent at the hands of infidels and enemies of Christ, bonds, stripes, imprisonment, afflictions, and lastly, death itself, even the death of the cross, that I might at last be crowned with Him?" Laurentius, the servant of Christ, roused by the scourging of the blessed Peter and his words of exhortation, went to the king as soon as morning broke, and laying aside his garment, showed the scars of the stripes which he had received. The king, astonished, asked who had presumed to inflict such stripes on so great a man. And when he heard that for the sake of his salvation the bishop had suffered these cruel blows at the hands of the Apostle of Christ, he was greatly afraid; and abjuring the worship of idols, and renouncing his unlawful marriage, he received the faith of Christ,

H

blessed chief of the Apostles, in the year of our Lord 624, on the 24th day of April.

CHAP. VIII. *How Pope Boniface sent the Pall and a letter to Justus, successor to Mellitus.* [624 A.D.]

JUSTUS, bishop of the church of Rochester, immediately succeeded Mellitus in the archbishopric. He consecrated Romanus bishop of that see in his own stead, having obtained authority to ordain bishops from Pope Boniface, whom we mentioned above as successor to Deusdedit: of which licence this is the form:

"*Boniface, to his most beloved brother Justus.* We have learnt not only from the contents of your letter addressed to us, but from the fulfilment granted to your work, how faithfully and vigilantly you have laboured, my brother, for the Gospel of Christ; for Almighty God has not forsaken either the mystery of His Name, or the fruit of your labours, having Himself faithfully promised to the preachers of the Gospel, 'Lo! I am with you alway, even unto the end of the world';[1] which promise His mercy has particularly manifested in this ministry imposed upon you, opening the hearts of the nations to receive the wondrous mystery of your preaching. For He has blessed with a rich reward your Eminence's acceptable course, by the support of His loving kindness; granting a plentiful increase to your labours in the faithful management of the talents committed to you, and bestowing it on that which you might confirm to many generations.[2] This is conferred on you by that recompense whereby, constantly persevering in the ministry imposed upon you, you have awaited with praiseworthy patience the redemption of that nation, and that they might profit by your merits, salvation has been bestowed

[1] St. Matt., xxviii, 20.
[2] *I.e.*, the reward is bestowed on that gift of faithful and successful service which he might hand on in its results to posterity. But the text is probably corrupt, and it is difficult to extract sense from it.

on them. For our Lord Himself says, ' He that endureth
to the end shall be saved.' [1] You are, therefore, saved by
the hope of patience, and the virtue of endurance, to the
end that the hearts of unbelievers, being cleansed from
their natural disease of superstition, might obtain the
mercy of their Saviour: for having received letters from
our son Adulwald,[2] we perceive with how much knowledge of the Sacred Word you, my brother, have brought
his mind to the belief in true conversion and the certainty
of the faith. Therefore, firmly confiding in the long-
suffering of the Divine clemency, we believe that, through
the ministry of your preaching, there will ensue most
full salvation not only of the nations subject to him, but
also of their neighbours; to the end, that as it is written,
the recompense of a perfect work may be conferred on
you by the Lord, the Rewarder of all the just; and that
the universal confession of all nations, having received
the mystery of the Christian faith, may declare, that in
truth ' Their sound is gone out into all the earth, and
their words unto the end of the world.' [3]

" We have also, my brother, moved by the warmth of
our goodwill, sent you by the bearer of these presents,
the pall, giving you authority to use it only in the celebration of the Sacred Mysteries; granting to you likewise
to ordain bishops when there shall be occasion, through
the Lord's mercy; that so the Gospel of Christ, by the
preaching of many, may be spread abroad in all the
nations that are not yet converted. You must, therefore,
endeavour, my brother, to preserve with unblemished
sincerity of mind that which you have received through
the kindness of the Apostolic see, bearing in mind what
it is that is represented by the honourable vestment which
you have obtained to be borne on your shoulders. And
imploring the Divine mercy, study to show yourself such
that you may present before the tribunal of the Supreme
Judge that is to come, the rewards of the favour granted
to you, not with guiltiness, but with the benefit of souls.

" God preserve you in safety, most dear brother! "

[1] St. Matt., x, 22.   [2] He means Eadbald.
                    [3] Ps. xix, 4.

CHAP. IX. *Of the reign of King Edwin, and how Paulinus, coming to preach the Gospel, first converted his daughter and others to the mysteries of the faith of Christ.* [625-626 A.D.]

AT this time the nation of the Northumbrians, that is, the English tribe dwelling on the north side of the river Humber, with their king, Edwin,[1] received the Word of faith through the preaching of Paulinus,[2] of whom we have before spoken. This king, as an earnest of his reception of the faith, and his share in the heavenly kingdom, received an increase also of his temporal realm, for he reduced under his dominion all the parts of Britain[3] that were provinces either of the English, or of the Britons, a thing which no English king had ever done before; and he even subjected to the English the Mevanian islands, as has been said above.[4] The more important of these, which is to the southward, is the larger in extent, and more fruitful, containing nine hundred and sixty families, according to the English computation; the other contains above three hundred.

The occasion of this nation's reception of the faith was the alliance by marriage of their aforesaid king with the kings of Kent, for he had taken to wife Ethelberg, otherwise called Tata,[5] daughter to King Ethelbert. When he first sent ambassadors to ask her in marriage of her brother Eadbald, who then reigned in Kent, he received the answer, "That it was not lawful to give a Christian maiden in marriage to a pagan husband, lest the faith and the mysteries of the heavenly King should be profaned by her union with a king that was altogether a stranger to the worship of the true God." This answer being brought to Edwin by his messengers, he promised that he would in no manner act in opposition to the Christian faith, which the maiden professed; but would give leave to her, and all that went with her, men and

[1] Cf. c. 5, p. 94.
[2] I, 29.
[3] Except Kent. Cf. *supra*, c. 5.
[4] *Ibid.*
[5] A term of endearment.

women, bishops and clergy, to follow their faith and worship after the custom of the Christians. Nor did he refuse to accept that religion himself, if, being examined by wise men, it should be found more holy and more worthy of God.

So the maiden was promised, and sent to Edwin, and in accordance with the agreement, Paulinus, a man beloved of God, was ordained bishop, to go with her, and by daily exhortations, and celebrating the heavenly Mysteries, to confirm her and her company, lest they should be corrupted by intercourse with the pagans. Paulinus was ordained bishop by the Archbishop Justus, on the 21st day of July, in the year of our Lord 625, and so came to King Edwin with the aforesaid maiden as an attendant on their union in the flesh. But his mind was wholly bent upon calling the nation to which he was sent to the knowledge of truth; according to the words of the Apostle, "To espouse her to the one true Husband, that he might present her as a chaste virgin to Christ."[1] Being come into that province, he laboured much, not only to retain those that went with him, by the help of God, that they should not abandon the faith, but, if haply he might, to convert some of the pagans to the grace of the faith by his preaching. But, as the Apostle says, though he laboured long in the Word, "The god of this world blinded the minds of them that believed not, lest the light of the glorious Gospel of Christ should shine unto them."[2]

The next year there came into the province one called Eumer, sent by the king of the West-Saxons, whose name was Cuichelm,[3] to lie in wait for King Edwin, in hopes at once to deprive him of his kingdom and his life. He had a two-edged dagger, dipped in poison, to the end that, if the wound inflicted by the weapon did not avail to kill the king, it might be aided by the deadly venom. He came to the king on the first day of the Easter

[1] 2 Cor., xi, 2.   [2] 2 Cor., iv, 4.
[3] Apparently joint king with his father, Cynegils (III, 7). The hegemony which the West-Saxon Ceaulin had possessed (*v.s.* c. 5) had passed to Northumbria.

festival,¹ at the river Derwent, where there was then a
royal township,² and being admitted as if to deliver a
message from his master, whilst unfolding in cunning
words his pretended embassy, he started up on a sudden,
and unsheathing the dagger under his garment, assaulted
the king. When Lilla, the king's most devoted servant,
saw this, having no buckler at hand to protect the king
from death, he at once interposed his own body to receive
the blow; but the enemy struck home with such force,
that he wounded the king through the body of the
slaughtered thegn. Being then attacked on all sides with
swords, in the confusion he also slew impiously with
his dagger another of the thegns, whose name was
Forthhere.

On that same holy Easter night, the queen had brought
forth to the king a daughter, called Eanfled. The king,
in the presence of Bishop Paulinus, gave thanks to his
gods for the birth of his daughter; and the bishop, on
his part, began to give thanks to Christ, and to tell the
king, that by his prayers to Him he had obtained that
the queen should bring forth the child in safety, and
without grievous pain. The king, delighted with his
words, promised, that if God would grant him life and
victory over the king by whom the murderer who had
wounded him had been sent, he would renounce his
idols, and serve Christ; and as a pledge that he would
perform his promise, he delivered up that same daughter
to Bishop Paulinus, to be consecrated to Christ. She
was the first to be baptized of the nation of the Northumbrians, and she received Baptism on the holy day of
Pentecost, along with eleven others of her house.³ At
that time, the king, being recovered of the wound which
he had received, raised an army and marched against

¹ *I.e.*, Easter Eve, April 19th, 626.
² Supposed to be at Aldby, near Stamford Bridge, but other
conjectures have been advanced.
³ Twelve in some MSS. and in V, 24. The baptism was on the
Eve of Whitsunday (cf. V. 24, " in Sabbato Pentecostes "). The
Eves of Easter and Whitsunday were usual days for baptisms; the
Roman Church tried to limit them to these seasons, but Christmas
and Epiphany were also favourite times.

the nation of the West-Saxons; and engaging in war, either slew or received in surrender all those of whom he learned that they had conspired to murder him. So he returned victorious into his own country, but he would not immediately and unadvisedly embrace the mysteries of the Christian faith, though he no longer worshipped idols, ever since he made the promise that he would serve Christ; but first took heed earnestly to be instructed at leisure by the venerable Paulinus, in the knowledge of faith, and to confer with such as he knew to be the wisest of his chief men, inquiring what they thought was fittest to be done in that case. And being a man of great natural sagacity, he often sat alone by himself a long time in silence, deliberating in the depths of his heart how he should proceed, and to which religion he should adhere.

CHAP. X. *How Pope Boniface, by letter, exhorted the same king to embrace the faith.* [*Circ.* 625 A.D.]

AT this time he received a letter from Pope Boniface[1] exhorting him to embrace the faith, which was as follows:

COPY OF THE LETTER OF THE MOST BLESSED AND APOSTOLIC POPE OF THE CHURCH OF THE CITY OF ROME, BONIFACE, ADDRESSED TO THE ILLUSTRIOUS EDWIN, KING OF THE ENGLISH.

" *To the illustrious Edwin, king of the English, Bishop Boniface, the servant of the servants of God.* Although the power of the Supreme Deity cannot be expressed by

[1] Boniface V, unless, as Dr. Bright suggests, the name is a scribe's error for Honorius, his successor. Boniface V died in October, 625. Paulinus had only been consecrated in the preceding July, so it is impossible that Boniface could have heard of Edwin's delay in receiving the faith; *v.* following letter (c. 11). But there is a reference in the same letter to Eadbald's conversion, the news of which must have come in the time of Boniface rather than of Honorius. The difficulty is not cleared up.

the function of human speech, seeing that, by its own
greatness, it so consists in invisible and unsearchable
eternity, that no keenness of wit can comprehend or express how great it is; yet inasmuch as His Humanity,
having opened the doors of the heart to receive Himself,
mercifully, by secret inspiration, puts into the minds of
men such things as It reveals concerning Itself,[1] we have
thought fit to extend our episcopal care so far as to make
known to you the fulness of the Christian faith; to the end
that, bringing to your knowledge the Gospel of Christ,
which our Saviour commanded should be preached to all
nations, we might offer to you the cup of the means of
salvation.[2]

"Thus the goodness of the Supreme Majesty, which,
by the word alone of His command, made and created all
things, the heaven, the earth, the sea, and all that in them
is, disposing the order by which they should subsist, hath,
ordaining all things, with the counsel of His co-eternal
Word, and the unity of the Holy Spirit, made man after
His own image and likeness, forming him out of the mire
of the earth; and granted him such high privilege of distinction, as to place him above all else; so that, preserving the bounds of the law of his being, his substance
should be established to eternity. This God,—Father,
Son, and Holy Ghost, the undivided Trinity,—from the
east unto the west, through faith by confession to the
saving of their souls, men worship and adore as the
Creator of all things, and their own Maker; to Whom
also the heights of empire and the powers of the world
are subject, because the pre-eminence of all kingdoms is
granted by His disposition. It hath pleased Him, therefore, in the mercy of His loving kindness, and for the
greater benefit of all His creatures,[3] by the fire of His
Holy Spirit wonderfully to kindle the cold hearts even of

[1] Reading " profert " for the impossible " proferetur." The style
of this letter is very involved and there seems to be a good deal of
corruption in the text.
[2] Adopting the conjecture " propinemus."
[3] The MSS. reading ("totius creaturae suae dilatandi subdi")
yields no sense here, but no satisfactory conjecture has been made.

the nations seated at the extremities of the earth in the knowledge of Himself.

"For we suppose, since the two countries are near together, that your Highness has fully understood what the clemency of our Redeemer has effected in the enlightenment of our illustrious son, King Eadbald, and the nations under his rule; we therefore trust, with assured confidence that, through the long-suffering of Heaven, His wonderful gift will be also conferred on you; since, indeed, we have learnt that your illustrious consort, who is discerned to be one flesh with you, has been blessed with the reward of eternity, through the regeneration of Holy Baptism. We have, therefore, taken care by this letter, with all the goodwill of heartfelt love, to exhort your Highness, that, abhorring idols and their worship, and despising the foolishness of temples, and the deceitful flatteries of auguries, you believe in God the Father Almighty, and His Son Jesus Christ, and the Holy Ghost, to the end that, believing and being released from the bonds of captivity to the Devil, you may, through the co-operating power of the Holy and undivided Trinity, be partaker of the eternal life.

"How great guilt they lie under, who adhere in their worship to the pernicious superstition of idolatry, appears by the examples of the perishing of those whom they worship. Wherefore it is said of them by the Psalmist, 'All the gods of the nations are devils,[1] but the Lord made the heavens.' And again, 'Eyes have they, but they see not; they have ears, but they hear not; noses have they, but they smell not; they have hands, but they handle not; feet have they, but they walk not. Therefore they are made like unto those that place the hope of their confidence in them.'[2] For how can they have power to help any man, that are made out of corruptible matter, by the hands of your inferiors and subjects, and on which, by employing human art, you have bestowed a lifeless similitude of members? which, moreover, unless they

---

[1] From the Vulgate, Ps. xcv, 5 (Ps. xcvi, 5 in our Psalter).
[2] Ps. cxiii, 5-8 (cxv in our Psalter).

be moved by you, will not be able to walk; but, like a
stone fixed in one place, being so formed, and having no
understanding, sunk in insensibility, have no power of
doing harm or good. We cannot, therefore, by any
manner of discernment conceive how you come to be so
deceived as to follow and worship those gods, to whom
you yourselves have given the likeness of a body.

"It behoves you, therefore, by taking upon you the
sign of the Holy Cross, by which the human race has been
redeemed, to root out of your hearts all the accursed
deceitfulness of the snares of the Devil, who is ever the
jealous foe of the works of the Divine Goodness, and to
put forth your hands and with all your might set to work
to break in pieces and destroy those which you have
hitherto fashioned of wood or stone to be your gods.
For the very destruction and decay of these, which never
had the breath of life in them, nor could in any wise
receive feeling from their makers, may plainly teach
you how worthless that was which you hitherto worshipped. For you yourselves, who have received the
breath of life from the Lord, are certainly better than
these which are wrought with hands, seeing that Almighty God has appointed you to be descended, after
many ages and through many generations, from the first
man whom he formed. Draw near, then, to the knowledge of Him Who created you, Who breathed the breath
of life into you, Who sent His only-begotten Son for
your redemption, to save you from original sin, that
being delivered from the power of the Devil's perversity
and wickedness, He might bestow on you a heavenly
reward.

"Hearken to the words of the preachers, and the
Gospel of God, which they declare to you, to the end
that, believing, as has been said before more than once,
in God the Father Almighty, and in Jesus Christ His Son,
and the Holy Ghost, and the indivisible Trinity, having
put to flight the thoughts of devils, and driven from you
the temptations of the venomous and deceitful enemy,
and being born again of water and the Holy Ghost, you
may, through the aid of His bounty, dwell in the bright-

ness of eternal glory with Him in Whom you shall have believed.

We have, moreover, sent you the blessing of your protector, the blessed Peter, chief of the Apostles, to wit, a shirt of proof with one gold ornament, and one cloak of Ancyra, which we pray your Highness to accept with all the goodwill with which it is sent by us."

CHAP. XI. *How Pope Boniface advised the king's consort to use her best endeavours for his salvation.* [*Circ.* 625 A.D.]

THE same pope also wrote to King Edwin's consort, Ethelberg, to this effect:

THE COPY OF THE LETTER OF THE MOST BLESSED AND APOSTOLIC BONIFACE, POPE OF THE CITY OF ROME, TO ETHELBERG, KING EDWIN'S QUEEN.

"*To the illustrious lady his daughter, Queen Ethelberg, Boniface, bishop, servant of the servants of God.* The goodness of our Redeemer has in His abundant Providence offered the means of salvation to the human race, which He rescued, by the shedding of His precious Blood, from the bonds of captivity to the Devil; to the end that, when He had made known His name in divers ways to the nations, they might acknowledge their Creator by embracing the mystery of the Christian faith. And this the mystical purification of your regeneration plainly shows to have been bestowed upon the mind of your Highness by God's gift. Our heart, therefore, has greatly rejoiced in the benefit bestowed by the bounty of the Lord, for that He has vouchsafed, in your confession, to kindle a spark of the orthodox religion, by which He might the more easily inflame with the love of Himself the understanding, not only of your illustrious consort, but also of all the nation that is subject to you.

"For we have been informed by those, who came to acquaint us with the laudable conversion of our illustrious

CHAP. XII. *How Edwin was persuaded to believe by a vision which he had once seen when he was in exile.* [*Circ.* 616 A.D.]

THUS wrote the aforesaid Pope Boniface for the salvation of King Edwin and his nation. But a heavenly vision, which the Divine Goodness was pleased once to reveal to this king, when he was in banishment at the court of Redwald, king of the Angles,[1] was of no little use in urging him to receive and understand the doctrines of salvation. For when Paulinus perceived that it was a difficult task to incline the king's proud mind to the humility of the way of salvation and the reception of the mystery of the life-giving Cross, and at the same time was employing the word of exhortation with men, and prayer to the Divine Goodness, for the salvation of Edwin and his subjects; at length, as we may suppose, it was shown him in spirit what the nature of the vision was that had been formerly revealed from Heaven to the king. Then he lost no time, but immediately admonished the king to perform the vow which he had made, when he received the vision, promising to fulfil it, if he should be delivered from the troubles of that time, and advanced to the throne.

The vision was this. When Ethelfrid,[2] his predecessor, was persecuting him, he wandered for many years as an exile, hiding in divers places and kingdoms, and at last came to Redwald, beseeching him to give him protection against the snares of his powerful persecutor. Redwald willingly received him, and promised to perform what was asked of him. But when Ethelfrid understood that he had appeared in that province, and that he and his companions were hospitably entertained by Redwald, he sent messengers to bribe that king with a great sum of money to murder him, but without effect. He sent a second and a third time, offering a greater bribe each

[1] *I.e.*, of East Anglia (Norfolk, Suffolk, and Cambridgeshire). Cf. c. 5, *ad init.*   [2] I, 34, and note.

time, and, moreover, threatening to make war on him if
his offer should be despised. Redwald, whether terrified
by his threats, or won over by his gifts, complied with this
request, and promised either to kill Edwin, or to deliver
him up to the envoys. A faithful friend of his, hearing of
this, went into his chamber, where he was going to bed,
for it was the first hour of the night; and calling him out,
told him what the king had promised to do with him, adding, "If, therefore, you are willing, I will this very hour
conduct you out of this province, and lead you to a place
where neither Redwald nor Ethelfrid shall ever find you."
He answered, "I thank you for your good will, yet I
cannot do what you propose, and be guilty of being the
first to break the compact I have made with so great a
king, when he has done me no harm, nor shown any
enmity to me; but, on the contrary, if I must die, let it
rather be by his hand than by that of any meaner man.
For whither shall I now fly, when I have for so many
long years been a vagabond through all the provinces of
Britain, to escape the snares of my enemies?" His
friend went away; Edwin remained alone without, and
sitting with a heavy heart before the palace, began to be
overwhelmed with many thoughts, not knowing what to
do, or which way to turn.

When he had remained a long time in silent anguish
of mind, consumed with inward fire,[1] on a sudden in
the stillness of the dead of night he saw approaching a
person, whose face and habit were strange to him, at
sight of whom, seeing that he was unknown and un-
looked for, he was not a little startled. The stranger
coming close up, saluted him, and asked why he sat
there in solitude on a stone troubled and wakeful at that
time, when all others were taking their rest, and were
fast asleep. Edwin, in his turn, asked, what it was to
him, whether he spent the night within doors or abroad.
The stranger, in reply, said, "Do not think that I am
ignorant of the cause of your grief, your watching, and
sitting alone without. For I know of a surety who you

---

[1] Cf. Verg. Aen., IV, 2, "caeco carpitur igni."

I

are, and why you grieve, and the evils which you fear
will soon fall upon you. But tell me, what reward you
would give the man who should deliver you out of these
troubles, and persuade Redwald neither to do you any
harm himself, nor to deliver you up to be murdered
by your enemies." Edwin replied, that he would give
such an one all that he could in return for so great a
benefit. The other further added, "What if he should
also assure you, that your enemies should be destroyed,
and you should be a king surpassing in power, not only
all your own ancestors, but even all that have reigned
before you in the English nation?" Edwin, encouraged
by these questions, did not hesitate to promise that he
would make a fitting return to him who should confer
such benefits upon him. Then the other spoke a third
time and said, "But if he who should truly foretell that
all these great blessings are about to befall you, could
also give you better and more profitable counsel for your
life and salvation than any of your fathers or kindred ever
heard, do you consent to submit to him, and to follow
his wholesome guidance?" Edwin at once promised that
he would in all things follow the teaching of that man
who should deliver him from so many great calamities,
and raise him to a throne.

Having received this answer, the man who talked to
him laid his right hand on his head saying, "When this
sign shall be given you, remember this present discourse
that has passed between us, and do not delay the performance of what you now promise." Having uttered
these words, he is said to have immediately vanished.
So the king perceived that it was not a man, but a spirit,
that had appeared to him.

Whilst the royal youth still sat there alone, glad of the
comfort he had received, but still troubled and earnestly
pondering who he was, and whence he came, that had so
talked to him, his aforesaid friend came to him, and
greeting him with a glad countenance, "Rise," said he,
"go in; calm and put away your anxious cares, and
compose yourself in body and mind to sleep; for the
king's resolution is altered, and he designs to do you no

harm, but rather to keep his pledged faith; for when he had privately made known to the queen his intention of doing what I told you before, she dissuaded him from it, reminding him that it was altogether unworthy of so great a king to sell his good friend in such distress for gold, and to sacrifice his honour, which is more valuable than all other adornments, for the love of money." In short, the king did as has been said, and not only refused to deliver up the banished man to his enemy's messengers, but helped him to recover his kingdom. For as soon as the messengers had returned home, he raised a mighty army to subdue Ethelfrid; who, meeting him with much inferior forces, (for Redwald had not given him time to gather and unite all his power,) was slain on the borders of the kingdom of Mercia, on the east side of the river that is called Idle.[1] In this battle, Redwald's son, called Raegenheri, was killed. Thus Edwin, in accordance with the prophecy he had received, not only escaped the danger from his enemy, but, by his death, succeeded the king on the throne.

King Edwin, therefore, delaying to receive the Word of God at the preaching of Paulinus, and being wont for some time, as has been said, to sit many hours alone, and seriously to ponder with himself what he was to do, and what religion he was to follow, the man of God came to him one day, laid his right hand on his head, and asked, whether he knew that sign? The king, trembling, was ready to fall down at his feet, but he raised him up, and speaking to him with the voice of a friend, said, " Behold, by the gift of God you have escaped the hands of the enemies whom you feared. Behold, you have obtained of His bounty the kingdom which you desired. Take heed not to delay to perform your third promise; accept the faith, and keep the precepts of Him Who, delivering you from temporal adversity, has raised you to the honour of a temporal kingdom; and if, from this time

[1] A tributary of the Trent. The battle is supposed to have been fought near Retford, in Nottinghamshire, before April 12th, 617. Cf. Bede's statement that Edwin was baptized on April 12th, 627, in the eleventh year of his reign (c. 14).

forward, you shall be obedient to His will, which through me He signifies to you, He will also deliver you from the everlasting torments of the wicked, and make you partaker with Him of His eternal kingdom in heaven."

CHAP. XIII. *Of the Council he held with his chief men concerning their reception of the faith of Christ, and how the high priest profaned his own altars.* [627 A.D.]

THE king, hearing these words, answered, that he was both willing and bound to receive the faith which Paulinus taught; but that he would confer about it with his chief friends and counsellors, to the end that if they also were of his opinion, they might all together be consecrated to Christ in the font of life. Paulinus consenting, the king did as he said; for, holding a council with the wise men,[1] he asked of every one in particular what he thought of this doctrine hitherto unknown to them, and the new worship of God that was preached? The chief of his own priests, Coifi, immediately answered him, "O king, consider what this is which is now preached to us; for I verily declare to you what I have learnt beyond doubt, that the religion which we have hitherto professed has no virtue in it and no profit. For none of your people has applied himself more diligently to the worship of our gods than I; and yet there are many who receive greater favours from you, and are more preferred than I, and are more prosperous in all that they undertake to do or to get. Now if the gods were good for any thing, they would rather forward me, who have been careful to serve them with greater zeal. It remains, therefore, that if upon examination you find those new doctrines, which are now preached to us, better and more efficacious, we hasten to receive them without any delay."

Another of the king's chief men, approving of his wise words and exhortations, added thereafter: "The present

---

[1] The Witenagemot.

life of man upon earth, O king, seems to me, in comparison with that time which is unknown to us, like to the swift flight of a sparrow through the house wherein you sit at supper in winter, with your ealdormen and thegns, while the fire blazes in the midst, and the hall is warmed, but the wintry storms of rain or snow are raging abroad. The sparrow, flying in at one door and immediately out at another, whilst he is within, is safe from the wintry tempest; but after a short space of fair weather, he immediately vanishes out of your sight, passing from winter into winter again. So this life of man appears for a little while, but of what is to follow or what went before we know nothing at all. If, therefore, this new doctrine tells us something more certain, it seems justly to deserve to be followed." The other elders and king's counsellors, by Divine prompting, spoke to the same effect.

But Coifi added, that he wished more attentively to hear Paulinus discourse concerning the God Whom he preached. When he did so, at the king's command, Coifi, hearing his words, cried out, " This long time I have perceived that what we worshipped was naught; because the more diligently I sought after truth in that worship, the less I found it. But now I freely confess, that such truth evidently appears in this preaching as can confer on us the gifts of life, of salvation, and of eternal happiness. For which reason my counsel is, O king, that we instantly give up to ban and fire those temples and altars which we have consecrated without reaping any benefit from them." In brief, the king openly assented to the preaching of the Gospel by Paulinus, and renouncing idolatry, declared that he received the faith of Christ: and when he inquired of the aforesaid high priest of his religion, who should first desecrate the altars and temples of their idols, with the precincts that were about them, he answered, " I; for who can more fittingly than myself destroy those things which I worshipped in my folly, for an example to all others, through the wisdom which has been given me by the true God?" Then immediately, in contempt of his vain superstitions,

he desired the king to furnish him with arms and a
stallion, that he might mount and go forth to destroy the
idols; for it was not lawful before for the high priest either
to carry ams, or to ride on anything but a mare. Having,
therefore, girt a sword about him, with a spear in his
hand, he mounted the king's stallion, and went his way
to the idols. The multitude, beholding it, thought that
he was mad; but as soon as he drew near the temple he
did not delay to desecrate it by casting into it the spear
which he held; and rejoicing in the knowledge of the
worship of the true God, he commanded his companions
to tear down and set on fire the temple, with all its precincts. This place where the idols once stood is still
shown, not far from York, to the eastward, beyond the
river Derwent, and is now called Godmunddingaham,[1]
where the high priest, by the inspiration of the true God,
profaned and destroyed the altars which he had himself
consecrated.[2]

CHAP. XIV. *How King Edwin and his nation became
Christians; and where Paulinus baptized them.* [627
A.D.]

KING EDWIN, therefore, with all the nobility of the nation,
and a large number of the common sort, received the
faith, and the washing of holy regeneration, in the
eleventh year of his reign, which is the year of our Lord
627, and about one hundred and eighty after the coming
of the English into Britain. He was baptized at York,
on the holy day of Easter,[3] being the 12th of April, in the
church of St. Peter the Apostle, which he himself had
built of timber there in haste, whilst he was a catechumen
receiving instruction in order to be admitted to baptism.
In that city also he bestowed upon his instructor and
bishop, Paulinus, his episcopal see. But as soon as he
was baptized, he set about building, by the direction of

[1] Goodmanham, near Market Weighton, in the East Riding of
Yorkshire.   [2] Cf. Verg. Aen., II. 502.
[3] *I.e.*, Easter Eve. Cf. c. 9, p. 104, note 3.

Paulinus, in the same place a larger and nobler church of stone, in the midst whereof the oratory which he had first erected should be enclosed.[1] Having, therefore, laid the foundation, he began to build the church square, encompassing the former oratory. But before the walls were raised to their full height, the cruel death[2] of the king left that work to be finished by Oswald his successor. Paulinus, for the space of six years from this time, that is, till the end of the king's reign, with his consent and favour, preached the Word of God in that country, and as many as were foreordained to eternal life believed and were baptized. Among them were Osfrid and Eadfrid, King Edwin's sons who were both born to him, whilst he was in banishment, of Quenburga, the daughter of Cearl, king of the Mercians.

Afterwards other children of his, by Queen Ethelberg, were baptized, Ethelhun and his daughter Ethelthryth, and another, Wuscfrea, a son; the first two were snatched out of this life whilst they were still in the white garments of the newly-baptized,[3] and buried in the church at York. Yffi,[4] the son of Osfrid, was also baptized, and many other noble and royal persons. So great was then the fervour of the faith, as is reported, and the desire for the laver of salvation among the nation of the Northumbrians, that Paulinus at a certain time coming with the king and queen to the royal township, which is called Adgefrin,[5] stayed there with them thirty-six days, fully occupied in catechizing and baptizing; during which

[1] On the site now covered by York Cathedral. The little wooden oratory was carefully preserved and adorned with gifts. The church has been repeatedly rebuilt, and of the Saxon building nothing remains but the central wall of the crypt.

[2] Cf. *infra* c. 20.

[3] The newly-baptized wore white garments till the octave of the day of their baptism, and appeared in church daily with lighted tapers and accompanied by their sponsors.

[4] For Wuscfrea and Yffi, *v. infra* c. 20, p. 132.

[5] Yeavering in Glendale, near Wooler in Northumberland. The name, Adgefrin, is one of those (common in Anglo-Saxon) in which the preposition is prefixed. "Æt" (Latin *ad*) and "in" are so used. The idiom is preserved in the Latin. Cf. Ad Murum, Ad Caprae Caput (III, 21), Infeppingum (*ibid.*), *et saep.*

days, from morning till night, he did nothing else but instruct the people resorting from all villages and places, in Christ's saving Word; and when they were instructed, he washed them with the water of absolution in the river Glen,[1] which is close by. This township, under the following kings, was abandoned, and another was built instead of it, at the place called Maelmin.[2]

These things happened in the province of the Bernicians; but in that of the Deiri also, where he was wont often to be with the king, he baptized in the river Swale, which runs by the village of Cataract;[3] for as yet oratories, or baptisteries, could not be built in the early infancy of the Church in those parts. But in Campodonum,[4] where there was then a royal township, he built a church which the pagans, by whom King Edwin was slain, afterwards burnt, together with all the place. Instead of this royal seat the later kings built themselves a township in the country called Loidis.[5] But the altar, being of stone, escaped the fire and is still preserved in the monastery of the most reverend abbot and priest, Thrydwulf, which is in the forest of Elmet.[6]

CHAP. XV. *How the province of the East Angles received the faith of Christ.* [627-628 A.D.]

EDWIN was so zealous for the true worship, that he likewise persuaded Earpwald, king of the East Angles, and son of Redwald, to abandon his idolatrous superstitions,

---

[1] The stream, in its upper reaches called the Bowmont Water, is still called the Glen at Yeavering. It is a tributary of the Till. Pallinsburn, in the neighbourhood of Coldstream, preserves by its name the memory of similar baptisms by Paulinus.

[2] Perhaps Millfield, near Wooler; but Mindrum and Kirknewton in the same district have also been suggested.

[3] Catterick Bridge (the Roman station Cataractonium, on the Watling Street), near Richmond in the North Riding of Yorkshire.

[4] Perhaps Doncaster. Other suggestions are Slack, near Huddersfield, and Tanfield, near Ripon. The Anglo-Saxon version has Donafeld.

[5] Leeds. The royal township (*villa*) is said to have been at Oswinthorp.   [6] Elmet Wood, near Leeds.

and with his whole province to receive the faith and mysteries of Christ. And indeed his father Redwald had long before been initiated into the mysteries of the Christian faith in Kent, but in vain; for on his return home, he was seduced by his wife and certain perverse teachers, and turned aside from the sincerity of the faith; and thus his latter state was worse than the former; so that, like the Samaritans of old, he seemed at the same time to serve Christ and the gods whom he served before; and in the same temple he had an altar for the Christian Sacrifice, and another small one at which to offer victims to devils. Aldwulf,[1] king of that same province, who lived in our time, testifies that this temple had stood until his time, and that he had seen it when he was a boy. The aforesaid King Redwald was noble by birth, though ignoble in his actions, being the son of Tytilus, whose father was Uuffa, from whom the kings of the East Angles are called Uuffings.[2]

Earpwald, not long after he had embraced the Christian faith, was slain by one Ricbert, a pagan; and from that time the province was in error for three years, till Sigbert succeeded to the kingdom,[3] brother to the same Earpwald, a most Christian and learned man, who was banished, and went to live in Gaul during his brother's life, and was there initiated into the mysteries of the faith, whereof he made it his business to cause all his province to partake as soon as he came to the throne. His exertions were nobly promoted by Bishop Felix,[4]

[1] Cf. IV, 17, 23. His father was Ethelhere, King of East Anglia (III, 24).

[2] For the patronymic, cf. *supra* c. 5, p. 95, and note.

[3] Cf. III, 18. He was Earpwald's half-brother, and had been driven into exile by his step-father, Redwald. Besides becoming a Christian, he had acquired a taste for secular learning in the ecclesiastical schools of Gaul.

[4] Cf. III, 18, 20. "An important feature of this mission, as it was of the Kentish, was the combination of education with religion, by means of a school such as Sigbert had seen abroad, and as by this time existed at Canterbury in connection with the house of SS. Peter and Paul" (Bright, p. 143). The name of Felix is preserved in Felixstowe, on the coast of Suffolk, and in Feliskirk, a Yorkshire village.

who, coming to Honorius, the archbishop,[1] from the parts of Burgundy, where he had been born and ordained, and having told him what he desired, was sent by him to preach the Word of life to the aforesaid nation of the Angles. Nor were his good wishes in vain; for the pious labourer in the spiritual field reaped therein a great harvest of believers, delivering all that province (according to the inner signification of his name) from long iniquity and unhappiness, and bringing it to the faith and works of righteousness, and the gifts of everlasting happiness. He had the see of his bishopric appointed him in the city Dommoc,[2] and having presided over the same province with pontifical authority seventeen years, he ended his days there in peace.

CHAP. XVI. *How Paulinus preached in the province of Lindsey; and of the character of the reign of Edwin.* [*Circ.* 628 A.D.]

PAULINUS also preached the Word to the province of Lindsey,[3] which is the first on the south side of the river Humber, stretching as far as the sea; and he first converted to the Lord the reeve of the city of Lincoln, whose name was Blaecca, with his whole house. He likewise built, in that city, a stone church of beautiful workmanship; the roof of which has either fallen through long neglect, or been thrown down by enemies, but the walls are still to be seen standing, and every year miraculous cures are wrought in that place, for the benefit of those who have faith to seek them. In that church, when

[1] *Infra* cc. 16, 18, *et saep.* He was a disciple of Pope Gregory, "vir in rebus ecclesiasticis sublimiter institutus" (V, 19).

[2] Dunwich, on the coast of Suffolk, once an important town, afterwards partially submerged. The diocese was divided into two by Theodore, and both sees became extinct during the Danish invasions. After various vicissitudes, the seat of the East Anglian bishopric was established at Norwich. Cf. IV, 5, p. 231, note 1.

[3] Lindsey, the largest of the three divisions of Lincolnshire, was at times Mercian, at times Northumbrian. At this time it appears to have been dependent on Northumbria; cf. IV, 12, note.

Justus had departed to Christ, Paulinus consecrated
Honorius bishop in his stead, as will be hereafter mentioned in its proper place.[1] A certain priest and abbot
of the monastery of Peartaneu,[2] a man of singular veracity, whose name was Deda, told me concerning the
faith of this province that an old man had informed
him that he himself had been baptized at noon-day, by
Bishop Paulinus, in the presence of King Edwin, and
with him a great multitude of the people, in the river
Trent, near the city, which in the English tongue is
called Tiouulfingacaestir;[3] and he was also wont to
describe the person of the same Paulinus, saying that he
was tall of stature, stooping somewhat, his hair black,
his visage thin, his nose slender and aquiline, his aspect
both venerable and awe-inspiring. He had also with him
in the ministry, James, the deacon,[4] a man of zeal and
great fame in Christ and in the church, who lived even
to our days.

It is told that there was then such perfect peace in
Britain, wheresoever the dominion of King Edwin extended, that, as is still proverbially said, a woman with
her new-born babe might walk throughout the island,
from sea to sea, without receiving any harm. That king
took such care for the good of his nation, that in several
places where he had seen clear springs near the high-
ways, he caused stakes to be fixed, with copper drink-
ing-vessels hanging on them, for the refreshment of
travellers; nor durst any man touch them for any other
purpose than that for which they were designed, either
through the great dread they had of the king, or for the
affection which they bore him. His dignity was so great
throughout his dominions, that not only were his banners

[1] Cf. *infra* c. 18, *ad init.* The church which stands on the probable site of this church is called St. Paul's. The name has been supposed to be a corruption of "Paulinus."

[2] Partney, in Lincolnshire; afterwards it became a cell of Bardney Abbey.

[3] The place cannot be identified with certainty. Torksey, South-
well, Newark, Fiskerton, and Littleborough have all been suggested.

[4] Cf. *infra* c. 20, *ad fin.*

borne before him in battle, but even in time of peace, when he rode about his cities, townships, or provinces, with his thegns, the standard-bearer was always wont to go before him. Also, when he walked anywhere along the streets, that sort of banner which the Romans call Tufa,[1] and the English, Thuuf, was in like manner borne before him.

CHAP. XVII. *How Edwin received letters of exhortation from Pope Honorius, who also sent the pall to Paulinus.* [634 A.D.]

AT that time Honorius, successor to Boniface, was Bishop of the Apostolic see. When he learned that the nation of the Northumbrians, with their king, had been, by the preaching of Paulinus, converted to the faith and confession of Christ, he sent the pall to the said Paulinus, and with it letters of exhortation to King Edwin, with fatherly love inflaming his zeal, to the end that he and his people should persist in belief of the truth which they had received. The contents of which letter were as follow:

" *To his most noble son, and excellent lord, Edwin king of the Angles, Bishop Honorius, servant of the servants of God, greeting.* The wholeheartedness of your Christian Majesty, in the worship of your Creator, is so inflamed with the fire of faith, that it shines out far and wide, and, being reported throughout the world, brings forth plentiful fruits of your labours. For the terms of your kingship you know to be this, that taught by orthodox preaching the knowledge of your King and Creator, you believe and worship God, and as far as man is able, pay Him the sincere devotion of your mind. For what else are we able to offer to our God, but our readiness to worship Him and to pay Him our vows, persisting in good actions, and confesssing Him the Creator of mankind? And, therefore, most excellent son, we exhort you with

[1] A form of standard adopted from the Romans. It was made of feathers attached to a spear.

such fatherly love as is meet, to labour to preserve this gift in every way, by earnest striving and constant prayer, in that the Divine Mercy has vouchsafed to call you to His grace; to the end that He, Who has been pleased to deliver you from all errors, and bring you to the knowledge of His name in this present world, may likewise prepare a place for you in the heavenly country. Employing yourself, therefore, in reading frequently the works of my lord Gregory, your Evangelist, of apostolic memory, keep before your eyes that love of his doctrine, which he zealously bestowed for the sake of your souls; that his prayers may exalt your kingdom and people, and present you faultless before Almighty God. We are preparing with a willing mind immediately to grant those things which you hoped would be by us ordained for your bishops, and this we do on account of the sincerity of your faith, which has been made known to us abundantly in terms of praise by the bearers of these presents. We have sent two palls to the two metropolitans, Honorius and Paulinus;[1] to the intent, that when either of them shall be called out of this world to his Creator, the other may, by this authority of ours, substitute another bishop in his place; which privilege we are induced to grant by the warmth of our love for you, as well as by reason of the great extent of the provinces which lie between us and you; that we may in all things support your devotion and likewise satisfy your desires. May God's grace preserve your Highness in safety!"

CHAP. XVIII. *How Honorius, who succeeded Justus in the bishopric of Canterbury, received the pall and letters from Pope Honorius.* [634 A.D.]

IN the meantime, Archbishop Justus was taken up to the heavenly kingdom, on the 10th of November,[2] and

---

[1] Cf. the instructions of Gregory: I, 29.
[2] Bede does not mention the year of his death. The Saxon Chronicle places it in 627, and this is supported by William of Malmesbury. Smith places it in 630.

Honorius, who was elected to the see in his stead, came
to Paulinus to be ordained, and meeting him at Lincoln
was there consecrated the fifth prelate of the Church of
Canterbury from Augustine. To him also the aforesaid
Pope Honorius sent the pall, and a letter, wherein he
ordains the same that he had before ordained in his
epistle to King Edwin, to wit, that when either the
Archbishop of Canterbury or of York shall depart this
life, the survivor, being of the same degree, shall have
power to ordain another bishop in the room of him that
is departed; that it might not be necessary always to
undertake the toilsome journey to Rome, at so great a
distance by sea and land, to ordain an archbishop.
Which letter we have also thought fit to insert in this
our history:

"*Honorius to his most beloved brother Honorius*: Among
the many good gifts which the mercy of our Redeemer is
pleased to bestow on His servants He grants to us in
His bounty, graciously conferred on us by His goodness,
the special blessing of realizing by brotherly intercourse,
as it were face to face, our mutual love. For which gift
we continually render thanks to His Majesty; and we
humbly beseech Him, that He will ever confirm your
labour, beloved, in preaching the Gospel, and bringing
forth fruit, and following the rule of your master and
head, the holy Gregory; and that, for the advancement
of His Church, He may by your means raise up further
increase; to the end, that through faith and works, in
the fear and love of God, what you and your predecessors
have already gained from the seed sown by our lord
Gregory, may grow strong and be further extended; that
so the promises spoken by our Lord may hereafter be
brought to pass in you; and that these words may summon you to everlasting happiness: 'Come unto Me all
ye that labour and are heavy laden, and I will refresh
you.'[1] And again, 'Well done, good and faithful servant;
thou hast been faithful over a few things, I will make
thee ruler over many things; enter thou into the joy of

[1] St. Matt., xi, 28.

thy Lord.'[1] And we, most beloved brothers, sending you first these words of exhortation out of our enduring charity, do not fail further to grant those things which we perceive may be suitable for the privileges of your Churches.

"Wherefore, in accordance with your request, and that of the kings our sons,[2] we do hereby in the name of the blessed Peter, chief of the Apostles, grant you authority, that when the Divine Grace shall call either of you to Himself, the survivor shall ordain a bishop in the room of him that is deceased. To which end also we have sent a pall to each of you, beloved, for celebrating the said ordination; that by the authority which we hereby commit to you, you may make an ordination acceptable to God; because the long distance of sea and land that lies between us and you, has obliged us to grant you this, that no loss may happen to your Church in any way, on any pretext whatever, but that the devotion of the people committed to you may increase the more. God preserve you in safety, most dear brother! Given the 11th day of June, in the reign of these our lords and emperors, in the twenty-fourth year of the reign of Heraclius, and the twenty-third after his consulship; and in the twenty-third of his son Constantine, and the third after his consulship; and in the third year of the most prosperous Caesar, his son Heraclius,[3] the seventh indiction; that is, in the year of our Lord, 634."

[1] St. Matt., xxv, 21.
[2] *I.e.*, the kings of Northumbria and Kent. For similar combined action on the part of a Northumbrian and a Kentish king, cf. III, 29.
[3] *I.e.*, Heracleonas, son of Heraclius and half-brother of Constantine III; associated with them in the Empire.

CHAP. XIX. *How the aforesaid Honorius first, and afterwards John, wrote letters to the nation of the Scots, concerning the observance of Easter, and the Pelagian heresy.* [640 A.D.]

THE same Pope Honorius also wrote to the Scots,[1] whom he had found to err in the observance of the holy Festival of Easter, as has been shown above, with subtlety of argument exhorting them not to think themselves, few as they were, and placed in the utmost borders of the earth, wiser than all the ancient and modern Churches of Christ, throughout the world; and not to celebrate a different Easter, contrary to the Paschal calculation and the decrees of all the bishops upon earth sitting in synod. Likewise John,[2] who succeeded Severinus, successor to the same Honorius, being yet but Pope elect, sent to them letters of great authority and erudition for the purpose of correcting the same error; evidently showing, that Easter Sunday is to be found between the fifteenth of the moon and the twenty-first, as was approved in the Council of Nicaea.[3] He also in the same epistle admonished them to guard against the Pelagian heresy,[4] and reject it, for he had been informed that it was again springing up among them. The beginning of the epistle was as follows:

"*To our most beloved and most holy Tomianus, Columbanus, Cromanus, Dinnaus, and Baithanus, bishops; to*

[1] *I.e.*, Irish. For their error with regard to Easter, *v.s.* c. 4.
[2] John IV, consecrated December 25th, 640. Severinus was Pope for a few months only. Apparently (cf. *infra*) the Irish ecclesiastics had consulted him about the Easter question.
[3] Cf. *supra* c. 2, p. 84, note. On the Paschal question the Council of Nicaea passed no canon, but the understanding was established that "all the brethren in the East, who formerly celebrated Easter with the Jews, will henceforth keep it agreeably with the Romans and ourselves and all who from ancient time have kept Easter as we"; *i.e.*, that they should all keep Easter on the first day of the week, but never on the 14th of the month Nisan, even when it fell on a Sunday. The object of the rule was to avoid the day of the Jewish Passover.   [4] Cf. I, 10, note.

Cromanus, Ernianus, Laistranus, Scellanus, and Segenus, priests; to Saranus and the rest of the Scottish doctors and abbots, Hilarus, the arch-presbyter, and vice-gerent of the holy Apostolic See; John, the deacon, and elect in the name of God; likewise John, the chief of the notaries and vice-gerent of the holy Apostolic See, and John, the servant of God, and counsellor of the same Apostolic See.[1] The writings which were brought by the bearers to Pope Severinus, of holy memory, were left, when he departed from the light of this world, without an answer to the questions contained in them. Lest any obscurity should long remain undispelled in a matter of so great moment, we opened the same, and found that some in your province, endeavouring to revive a new heresy out of an old one, contrary to the orthodox faith, do through the darkness of their minds reject our Easter, when Christ was sacrificed; and contend that the same should be kept with the Hebrews on the fourteenth of the moon."[2]

By this beginning of the epistle it evidently appears that this heresy arose among them in very late times, and that not all their nation, but only some of them, were involved in the same.

After having laid down the manner of keeping Easter, they add this concerning the Pelagians in the same epistle:

"And we have also learnt that the poison of the Pelagian heresy again springs up among you; we,

---

[1] These bishops have been identified as follows: Tomianus is Tomene, Abbot and Bishop of Armagh; Columbanus is Colman, Abbot of Clonard (also a bishop); Cromanus is Cronan, Bishop of Nendrum, or Inishmahee; Dinnaus is probably Dima, Bishop of Connor; Baithanus has not been identified with any certainty. With regard to the priests the proposed identifications are more conjectural. Saranus is a certain Saran Ua Critain. Two vice-gerents of the Papal see are associated with the Pope elect in writing this letter. The arch-presbyter and the "primicerius notariorum," with the archdeacon, acted as vice-gerents during a vacancy, or in the absence of the Pope (cf. Plummer *ad loc.*).

[2] This is not fairly stated. The Irish were not "Quartodecimans," *i.e.*, did not insist on the celebration of Easter being on the fourteenth of the moon. They only included that day as a possible one for Easter (cf. *supra* c. 2, p. 84, note 3).

therefore, exhort you, that you put away from your thoughts all such venomous and superstitious wickedness. For you cannot be ignorant how that execrable heresy has been condemned; for it has not only been abolished these two hundred years, but it is also daily condemned by us and buried under our perpetual ban; and we exhort you not to rake up the ashes of those whose weapons have been burnt. For who would not detest that insolent and impious assertion, ' That man can live without sin of his own free will, and not through the grace of God?' And in the first place, it is blasphemous folly to say that man is without sin, which none can be, but only the one Mediator between God and men, the Man Christ Jesus, Who was conceived and born without sin; for all other men, being born in original sin, are known to bear the mark of Adam's transgression, even whilst they are without actual sin, according to the saying of the prophet, ' For behold, I was conceived in iniquity; and in sin did my mother give birth to me.' "[1]

CHAP. XX. *How Edwin being slain, Paulinus returned into Kent, and had the bishopric of Rochester conferred upon him.* [633 A.D.]

EDWIN reigned most gloriously seventeen years over the nations of the English and the Britons, six whereof, as has been said, he also was a soldier in the kingdom of Christ. Caedwalla,[2] king of the Britons, rebelled against him, being supported by the vigorous Penda, of the royal race of the Mercians, who from that time governed that nation for twenty-two years with varying success.

---

[1] Ps. li, 5, in our Psalter. The quotation is partly from the Vulgate, partly from the " Roman " Psalter, *i.e.*, Jerome's revision of the old Italic version.

[2] Or Cadwallon, King of Gwynedd, in North Wales. His father Cadvan, had sheltered Edwin during his first exile. Afterwards, when Cadwallon invaded Northumbria, Edwin defeated him and drove him from his kingdom. Having regained it, Cadwallon now allied himself with Penda, king of the Mercians (626- or 627-655) in a successful attempt to shake off the Northumbrian supremacy.

A great battle being fought in the plain that is called Haethfelth,[1] Edwin was killed on the 12th of October, in the year of our Lord 633, being then forty-eight years of age, and all his army was either slain or dispersed. In the same war also, Osfrid,[2] one of his sons, a warlike youth, fell before him; Eadfrid,[3] another of them, compelled by necessity, went over to King Penda, and was by him afterwards slain in the reign of Oswald, contrary to his oath. At this time a great slaughter was made in the Church and nation of the Northumbrians; chiefly because one of the chiefs, by whom it was carried on, was a pagan, and the other a barbarian, more cruel than a pagan; for Penda, with all the nation of the Mercians, was an idolater, and a stranger to the name of Christ; but Caedwalla, though he professed and called himself a Christian, was so barbarous in his disposition and manner of living, that he did not even spare women and innocent children, but with bestial cruelty put all alike to death by torture, and overran all their country in his fury for a long time, intending to cut off all the race of the English within the borders of Britain. Nor did he pay any respect to the Christian religion which had sprung up among them; it being to this day the custom of the Britons to despise the faith and religion of the English, and to have no part with them in anything any more than with pagans. King Edwin's head was brought to York, and afterwards taken into the church of the blessed Peter the Apostle, which he had begun, but which his successor Oswald finished, as has been said before. It was laid in the chapel of the holy Pope Gregory, from whose disciples he had received the word of life.[4]

The affairs of the Northumbrians being thrown into confusion at the moment of this disaster, when there seemed to be no prospect of safety except in flight, Paulinus, taking with him Queen Ethelberg, whom he had before brought thither, returned into Kent by sea,

[1] Generally identified with Hatfield Chase, north-east of Doncaster.   [2] C. 14, p. 119.   [3] *Ibid.*
[4] His body was ultimately buried at Whitby; cf. III, 24, p. 190, and note.

and was very honourably received by the Archbishop
Honorius and King Eadbald. He came thither under the
conduct of Bassus, a most valiant thegn of King Edwin,
having with him Eanfled, the daughter, and Wuscfrea,
the son of Edwin, as well as Yffi, the son of Osfrid,
Edwin's son.[1] Afterwards Ethelberg, for fear of the
kings Eadbald and Oswald,[2] sent Wuscfrea and Yffi over
into Gaul to be bred up by King Dagobert,[3] who was
her friend; and there they both died in infancy, and
were buried in the church with the honour due to royal
children and to Christ's innocents. He also brought with
him many rich goods of King Edwin, among which were
a large gold cross, and a golden chalice, consecrated to
the service of the altar, which are still preserved, and
shown in the church of Canterbury.

At that time the church of Rochester had no pastor,
for Romanus,[4] the bishop thereof, being sent on a
mission to Pope Honorius by Archbishop Justus, was
drowned in the Italian Sea; and thus Paulinus, at the
request of Archbishop Honorius and King Eadbald, took
upon him the charge of the same, and held it until he
too, in his own time, departed to heaven, with the fruits
of his glorious labours; and, dying in that Church, he left
there the pall which he had received from the Pope of
Rome. He had left behind him in his Church at York,
James, the deacon, a true churchman and a holy man,
who continuing long after in that Church, by teaching
and baptizing, rescued much prey from the ancient
enemy; and from him the village, where he chiefly dwelt,
near Cataract,[6] has its name to this day. He had great
skill in singing in church, and when the province was
afterwards restored to peace, and the number of the

[1] For Eanfled, *v.s.* c. 9. For Yffi and Wuscfrea, c. 14.
[2] Cf. c. 5.
[3] He was a kinsman. Ethelberg's mother, Bertha, was a
daughter of Charibert, King of Paris (cf. I, 25, note). His brother,
Chilperic, was Dagobert's grandfather.
[4] Cf. c. 8.   [5] C. 16, and III, 25.
[6] Cf. c. 14. The village cannot be identified. Akeburgh has
been suggested, the name being regarded as a corruption of
"Jacobsburgh."

faithful increased, he began to teach church music to
many, according to the custom of the Romans, or of the
Cantuarians.[1] And being old and full of days, as the
Scripture says, he went the way of his fathers.

patrum viam secutus est

[1] The "Cantus Romanus," brought to England by the Roman
mission; *i.e.,* the style of Church music according to the use of
Rome. The theory that Gregory the Great was the founder of
Gregorian music, which superseded the old "Cantus Ambrosianus"
everywhere in the West except at Milan, must in all probability be
abandoned. It seems to be established that no change of any importance was made till nearly a hundred years after Gregory's
time, and "the terms 'Gregorianus,' 'Ambrosianus Cantus,' probably mean nothing more than the style of singing according to the
respective uses of Rome and Milan." (F. Homes Dudden, "Gregory
the Great," I, p. 274.)

BOOK III

CHAP. I. *How King Edwin's next successors lost both the faith of their nation and the kingdom; but the most Christian King Oswald retrieved both.* [633 A.D.]

EDWIN being slain in battle, the kingdom of the Deiri, to which province his family belonged, and where he first began to reign, passed to Osric, the son of his uncle Aelfric, who, through the preaching of Paulinus, had also received the mysteries of the faith. But the kingdom of the Bernicians—for into these two provinces the nation of the Northumbrians was formerly divided[1]—passed to Eanfrid, the son of Ethelfrid,[2] who derived his origin from the royal family of that province. For all the time that Edwin reigned, the sons of the aforesaid Ethelfrid, who had reigned before him, with many of the younger nobility, lived in banishment among the Scots or Picts, and were there instructed according to the doctrine of the Scots, and were renewed with the grace of Baptism. Upon the death of the king, their enemy, they were allowed to return home, and the aforesaid Eanfrid, as the eldest of them, became king of the Bernicians. Both those kings,[3] as soon as they obtained the government of their earthly kingdoms, abjured and betrayed the mysteries of the heavenly kingdom to which they had been admitted, and again delivered themselves up to defilement and perdition through the abominations of their former idolatry.

But soon after, the king of the Britons, Caedwalla,[4] the unrighteous instrument of rightful vengeance, slew them both. First, in the following summer, he put Osric to death; for, being rashly besieged by him in the municipal

---

[1] Cf. II, I, p. 82, note.
[2] I, 34; II, 2, 12.
[3] *I.e.*, Osric and Eanfrid.
[4] Cf. II, 20, *ad init.*

town,[1] he sallied out on a sudden with all his forces, took him by surprise, and destroyed him and all his army. Then, when he had occupied the provinces of the Northumbrians for a whole year,[2] not ruling them like a victorious king, but ravaging them like a furious tyrant, he at length put an end to Eanfrid, in like manner, when he unadvisedly came to·him with only twelve chosen soldiers, to sue for peace. To this day, that year is looked upon as ill-omened, and hateful to all good men; as well on account of the apostacy of the English kings, who had renounced the mysteries of the faith, as of the outrageous tyranny of the British king. Hence it has been generally agreed, in reckoning the dates of the kings, to abolish the memory of those faithless monarchs, and to assign that year to the reign of the following king, Oswald, a man beloved of God. This king, after the death of his brother Eanfrid,[3] advanced with an army, small, indeed, in number, but strengthened with the faith of Christ; and the impious commander of the Britons, in spite of his vast forces, which he boasted nothing could withstand, was slain at a place called in the English tongue Denisesburna, that is, the brook of Denis.[4]

---

[1] "In oppido municipio." Commentators are agreed that Bede means York. It was a Roman "Colonia," and is called a "municipium" by Aurelius Victor, though whether Bede attaches any definitely Roman meaning to the term seems doubtful. Ducange explains "municipium" as "castrum," "castellum muris cinctum."

[2] From the death of Edwin (October 12th, 633), for Oswald's reign is reckoned as lasting nine years, including the "hateful year," and he was killed August 5th, 642. Cf. *infra* c. 9.·

[3] *I.e.*, probably before the end of 634.

[4] Not identified with any certainty, but probably the Rowley Water or a tributary of it. It cannot be, as has been suggested, the Devil's Water, which is clearly distinguished from it in a charter of the thirteenth century. Caedwalla must have fled southwards for eight or nine miles after the battle (cf. next note).

CHAP. II. *How, among innumerable other miracles of healing wrought by the wood of the cross, which King Oswald, being ready to engage against the barbarians, erected, a certain man had his injured arm healed.* [634 A.D.]

THE place is shown to this day, and held in much veneration, where Oswald, being about to engage in this battle, erected the symbol of the Holy Cross, and knelt down and prayed to God that he would send help from Heaven to his worshippers in their sore need. Then, we are told, that the cross being made in haste, and the hole dug in which it was to be set up, the king himself, in the ardour of his faith, laid hold of it and held it upright with both his hands, till the earth was heaped up by the soldiers and it was fixed. Thereupon, uplifting his voice, he cried to his whole army, "Let us all kneel, and together beseech the true and living God Almighty in His mercy to defend us from the proud and cruel enemy; for He knows that we have undertaken a just war for the safety of our nation." All did as he had commanded, and accordingly advancing towards the enemy with the first dawn of day, they obtained the victory, as their faith deserved. In the place where they prayed very many miracles of healing are known to have been wrought, as a token and memorial of the king's faith; for even to this day, many are wont to cut off small splinters from the wood of the holy cross, and put them into water, which they give to sick men or cattle to drink, or they sprinkle them therewith, and these are presently restored to health.

The place is called in the English tongue Hefenfelth, or the Heavenly Field,[1] which name it undoubtedly re-

---

[1] For another instance of a name with an inner meaning, cf. II, 15. The site of the battle is probably seven or eight miles north of Hexham (*v.* next note), Oswald having taken up his position on the northern side of the Roman wall between the Tyne and the Solway (*i.e.*, the wall attributed to Hadrian, cf. I, 12, p. 25, note). According to tradition the battle was finally won at a place called Halydene (Hallington?), two miles to the east.

ceived of old as a presage of what was afterwards to
happen, denoting, that the heavenly trophy was to be
erected, the heavenly victory begun, and heavenly
miracles shown forth to this day. The place is near the
wall in the north which the Romans formerly drew
across the whole of Britain from sea to sea, to restrain
the onslaught of the barbarous nations, as has been
said before. Hither also the brothers of the church of
Hagustald,[1] which is not far distant, long ago made it
their custom to resort every year, on the day before that
on which King Oswald was afterwards slain, to keep
vigils there for the health of his soul, and having sung
many psalms of praise, to offer for him in the morning
the sacrifice of the Holy Oblation. And since that good
custom has spread, they have lately built a church there,
which has attached additional sanctity and honour in the
eyes of all men to that place;[2] and this with good
reason; for it appears that there was no symbol of the
Christian faith, no church, no altar erected throughout
all the nation of the Bernicians, before that new leader
in war, prompted by the zeal of his faith, set up this
standard of the Cross as he was going to give battle to
his barbarous enemy.

Nor is it foreign to our purpose to relate one of the
many miracles that have been wrought at this cross.
One of the brothers of the same church of Hagulstald,
whose name is Bothelm, and who is still living, a few
years ago, walking carelessly on the ice at night,
suddenly fell and broke his arm; he was soon tormented
with a most grievous pain in the broken part, so that he
could not lift his arm to his mouth for the anguish. Hearing one morning that one of the brothers designed to go
up to the place of the holy cross, he desired him, on his

---

[1] **Hexham.** Wilfrid built a magnificent church there between
the years 672-678 on land given by Ethelthryth, wife of Egfrid,
king of Northumbria. It became the see of a bishop in 678 when
the great northern diocese was subdivided by Theodore (v. IV,
12). Bede's own monastery of Wearmouth and Jarrow was in the
diocese of Hexham. The bishopric became extinct in 821.

[2] The place is still called St. Oswald's, and a little chapel probably marks the spot.

return, to bring him a piece of that sacred wood, saying, he believed that with the mercy of God he might thereby be healed. The brother did as he was desired; and returning in the evening, when the brothers were sitting at table, gave him some of the old moss which grew on the surface of the wood. As he sat at table, having no place to bestow the gift which was brought him, he put it into his bosom; and forgetting, when he went to bed, to put it away, left it in his bosom. Awaking in the middle of the night, he felt something cold lying by his side, and putting his hand upon it to feel what it was, he found his arm and hand as sound as if he had never felt any such pain.

CHAP. III. *How the same king Oswald, asking a bishop of the Scottish nation, had Aidan sent him, and granted him an episcopal see in the Isle of Lindisfarne.* [635 A.D.]

THE same Oswald, as soon as he ascended the throne, being desirous that all the nation under his rule should be endued with the grace of the Christian faith, whereof he had found happy experience in vanquishing the barbarians, sent to the elders of the Scots,[1] among whom himself and his followers, when in banishment, had received the sacrament of Baptism, desiring that they would send him a bishop, by whose instruction and ministry the English nation, which he governed, might learn the privileges and receive the Sacraments of the faith of our Lord. Nor were they slow in granting his request; for they sent him Bishop Aidan, a man of singular gentleness, piety, and moderation; having a zeal of God, but not fully according to knowledge: for he was wont to keep Easter Sunday according to the custom of his country, which we have before so often mentioned,[2] from the fourteenth to the twentieth of the moon; the northern province of the Scots, and all the nation of the Picts, at

[1] *I.e.*, Irish.
[2] Cf. II, 2, note on Paschal Controversy.

that time still celebrating Easter after that manner, and believing that in this observance they followed the writings of the holy and praiseworthy Father Anatolius.[1] Whether this be true, every instructed person can easily judge. But the Scots which dwelt in the South of Ireland had long since, by the admonition of the Bishop of the Apostolic see, learned to observe Easter according to the canonical custom.[2]

On the arrival of the bishop, the king appointed him his episcopal see in the island of Lindisfarne,[3] as he desired. Which place, as the tide ebbs and flows, is twice a day enclosed by the waves of the sea like an island; and again, twice, when the beach is left dry, becomes contiguous with the land. The king also humbly and willingly in all things giving ear to his admonitions, industriously applied himself to build up and extend the Church of Christ in his kingdom; wherein, when the bishop, who was not perfectly skilled in the English tongue, preached the Gospel, it was a fair sight to see the king himself interpreting the Word of God to his ealdormen and thegns, for he had thoroughly learned the language of the Scots during his long banishment. From that time many came daily into Britain from the country of the Scots, and with great devotion preached the Word to those provinces of the English, over which King Oswald reigned, and those among them that had re-

[1] Bishop of Laodicea, *circ.* 284 A.D. According to Eusebius, he was the first to arrange the cycle of nineteen years. The Canon quoted by the Celts in support of their observance of Easter is proved to be a forgery, probably of the seventh century and of British origin.

[2] Probably they adopted Catholic customs about 633, after the return of their delegates sent to consult the Roman Church on this question in 631.

[3] Cf. Preface, p. 4, note 3. The Celtic missionaries were generally attracted to remote sites, and this, the first mission station of the Celtic Church in Northumbria, was doubtless chosen for the resemblance of its physical features to Iona. The constitution was also modelled on that of Iona, with this difference, that it was an episcopal see as well as a monastery. It was included in the "province" of the Abbot of Iona. The Bishop and all the clergy were monks, and Aidan himself was Abbot as well as Bishop.

ceived priest's orders,[1] administered the grace of Baptism
to the believers. Churches were built in divers places;
the people joyfully flocked together to hear the Word;
lands and other property were given of the king's bounty
to found monasteries; English children, as well as their
elders, were instructed by their Scottish teachers in study
and the observance of monastic discipline. For most of
those who came to preach were monks. Bishop Aidan
was himself a monk, having been sent out from the
island called Hii,[2] whereof the monastery was for a long
time the chief of almost all those of the northern Scots,[3]
and all those of the Picts, and had the direction of their
people. That island belongs to Britain, being divided
from it by a small arm of the sea, but had been long
since given by the Picts, who inhabit those parts of
Britain, to the Scottish monks, because they had received
the faith of Christ through their preaching.

CHAP. IV. *When the nation of the Picts received the
faith of Christ.* [565 A.D.]

IN the year of our Lord 565, when Justin, the younger,
the successor of Justinian, obtained the government of
the Roman empire, there came into Britain from Ireland
a famous priest and abbot, marked as a monk by habit
and manner of life, whose name was Columba,[4] to

---

[1] "Sacerdotali," perhaps (but not necessarily here)="episcopal," as often. There may have been a number of the Irish
non-diocesan bishops in the mission.
[2] Iona, a name supposed to have arisen from a mistaken reading
of *Ioua*, an adjectival form used by Adamnan (*v. infra* note 4),
feminine, agreeing with *insula*, formed from the Irish name, I, Ii,
Hii, etc. (the forms vary greatly). Then "Iona" was fancifully
regarded as the Hebrew equivalent for *Columba* (=a dove), and
this helped to preserve the name.   [3] *I.e.*, Irish.
[4] For St. Columba, *v.* Dr. Reeves's edition of the life by Adamnan, Abbot of Iona, 679-704 (cf. V, 15, note). Authorities are
divided with regard to the date of his coming to Britain. Dr.
Reeves and Mr. Skene, following the Annals of Tighernach,
decide in favour of 563. For his name, "Columcille," cf. V, 9,
note. He was of Irish birth, connected with the Dalriadic Scots.

preach the word of God to the provinces of the northern Picts, who are separated from the southern parts belonging to that nation by steep and rugged mountains. For the southern Picts, who dwell on this side of those mountains, had, it is said, long before forsaken the errors of idolatry, and received the true faith by the preaching of Bishop Ninias,[1] a most reverend and holy man of the British nation, who had been regularly instructed at Rome in the faith and mysteries of the truth; whose episcopal see, named after St. Martin the bishop, and famous for a church dedicated to him (wherein Ninias himself and many other saints rest in the body), is now in the possession of the English nation. The place belongs to the province of the Bernicians, and is commonly called the White House,[2] because he there

and of royal descent on both sides of his house. He was ordained priest at Clonard, but was never a bishop. Many ecclesiastical and monastic foundations throughout Ireland and Scotland are attributed to him. He travelled much in both countries, visited Bruide (*v. infra*) at Inverness, and founded churches all over the north of Scotland. He also worked indefatigably in his own monastery of Iona. In his earlier years his excitable, impatient temperament seems to have involved him in various wars. He is said to have stirred up his kinsmen against the Irish king, Diarmaid; and it has been supposed that his mission to the Picts was undertaken in expiation of the bloodshed for which he was responsible.

[1] There is much that is legendary in the account of St. Ninias, and Bede only professes to give the tradition. He was a Briton, probably a native of Strathclyde. He studied at Rome and received episcopal consecration there; came under the influence of St. Martin of Tours, to whom he afterwards dedicated his church in Galloway, and returned as a missionary to Britain. His preaching led to the conversion of the Picts of Galloway and those to whom Bede alludes here as situated to the south of the Grampians. Irish tradition, difficult to reconcile with Bede's statement that he was buried at Whitern, tells that he spent the last years of his life in Ireland and founded a church at Leinster. He was commemorated there on September 16th, under the name of Moinenn. The traditional date of his death, September 16th, 432, has no authority.

[2] Whitern, on Wigton Bay, so called from the white appearance of the stone church, as compared with the usual wooden buildings. The dedication must have been subsequent to St. Martin's death, *circ.* 397. The see was revived as an Anglian one in Bede's own time (*v.* V. 23, p. 381). For the form of the name, " Ad Candidam Casam," cf. II, 14, p. 119, note 5.

built a church of stone, which was not usual among the Britons.

Columba came into Britain in the ninth year of the reign of Bridius, who was the son of Meilochon,[1] and the powerful king of the Pictish nation, and he converted that nation to the faith of Christ, by his preaching and example. Wherefore he also received of them the gift of the aforesaid island whereon to found a monastery. It is not a large island, but contains about five families, according to the English computation; his successors hold it to this day; he was also buried therein, having died at the age of seventy-seven, about thirty-two years after he came into Britain to preach.[2] Before he crossed over into Britain, he had built a famous monastery in Ireland, which, from the great number of oaks, is in the Scottish tongue called Dearmach—The Field of Oaks.[3] From both these monasteries, many others had their beginning through his disciples, both in Britain and Ireland; but the island monastery where his body lies, has the pre-eminence among them all.

That island has for its ruler an abbot, who is a priest, to whose jurisdiction all the province, and even the bishops, contrary to the usual method, are bound to be subject, according to the example of their first teacher, who was not a bishop, but a priest and monk;[4] of whose

[1] Bruide Mac Maelchon had defeated the Dalriadic Scots in 560 A.D. and driven them back to Cantyre. Northwards his dominion extended as far as the Orkneys and it is probable that it included the eastern lowlands north of the Forth (cf. Rhŷs, "Celtic Britain"). Another tradition (Irish) represents Conall, King of the Dalriadic Scots, as the donor of Iona, but the earliest Irish authority (ninth or tenth century) agrees with Bede.

[2] The year in which he died, as well as the ultimate resting-place of his relics, is uncertain. Dr. Reeves places his death in 597, the year of St. Augustine's landing.

[3] I.e., in Irish. The place is Durrow in Leinster.

[4] There was no diocesan episcopate in the early Irish Church; it was organized on a monastic system. Bishops performed all episcopal functions (ordination, etc.), but they lived in the monastery, subject to the supreme authority of the abbot, who was aided in the government by a council of senior monks. Bishops were also sent out as missionaries. The functions of abbot and bishop might

life and discourses some records are said to be preserved by his disciples. But whatsoever he was himself, this we know for certain concerning him, that he left successors renowned for their continence, their love of God, and observance of monastic rules. It is true they employed doubtful cycles in fixing the time of the great festival, as having none to bring them the synodal decrees for the observance of Easter, by reason of their being so far away from the rest of the world; but they earnestly practised such works of piety and chastity as they could learn from the Prophets, the Gospels and the Apostolic writings. This manner of keeping Easter continued among them no little time, to wit, for the space of 150 years, till the year of our Lord 715.

But then the most reverend and holy father and priest, Egbert,[1] of the English nation, who had long lived in banishment in Ireland for the sake of Christ, and was most learned in the Scriptures, and renowned for long perfection of life, came among them, corrected their error, and led them to observe the true and canonical day of Easter; which, nevertheless, they did not always keep on the fourteenth of the moon with the Jews, as some imagined, but on Sunday, although not in the proper week.[2] For, as Christians, they knew that the Resurrection of our Lord, which happened on the first day of the week, was always to be celebrated on the first day of the week; but being rude and barbarous, they had not learned when that same first day after the Sabbath, which is now called the Lord's day, should come. But because they had not failed in the grace of fervent charity, they were accounted worthy to receive the full

be combined in one man, but the abbot, as such, could discharge no episcopal duties. A great monastery was head of a "provincia" ("diocesis," "parochia"), and had many monasteries and churches dependent on it.

[1] Cf. c. 27, IV, 3, 26; V, 9, 10, 22, 23, 24. Perhaps "sacerdos" should be translated "bishop" here (v. supra c. 3, note; infra c. 27, note). Early writers allude to him as a bishop, e.g., Alcuin, Ethelwulf. In the life of St. Adalbert, one of Wilbrord's companions (cf. V. 10), he is called "Northumbrorum episcopus."

[2] I.e., they were not "Quartodecimans" (cf. II, 2, p. 84, note 3).

knowledge of this matter also, according to the promise
of the Apostle, "And if in any thing ye be otherwise
minded, God shall reveal even this unto you."[1] Of which
we shall speak more fully hereafter in its proper place.

CHAP. V. *Of the life of Bishop Aidan.* [635 A.D.]

FROM this island, then, and the fraternity of these monks,
Aidan was sent to instruct the English nation in Christ,
having received the dignity of a bishop. At that time
Segeni,[2] abbot and priest, presided over that monastery.
Among other lessons in holy living, Aidan left the
clergy a most salutary example of abstinence and continence; it was the highest commendation of his doctrine
with all men, that he taught nothing that he did not
practise in his life among his brethren; for he neither
sought nor loved anything of this world, but delighted
in distributing immediately among the poor whom he
met whatsoever was given him by the kings or rich men
of the world. He was wont to traverse both town and
country on foot, never on horseback, unless compelled
by some urgent necessity; to the end that, as he went,
he might turn aside to any whomsoever he saw, whether
rich or poor, and call upon them, if infidels, to receive
the mystery of the faith, or, if they were believers,
strengthen them in the faith, and stir them up by words
and actions to giving of alms and the performance of
good works.

His course of life was so different from the slothfulness
of our times, that all those who bore him company,
whether they were tonsured or laymen, had to study
either reading the Scriptures, or learning psalms. This
was the daily employment of himself and all that were
with him, wheresoever they went; and if it happened,
which was but seldom, that he was invited to the king's

---

[1] Phil., iii, 15.
[2] Cf. II, 19. He is probably to be identified with the Segenus
mentioned there as one of the priests to whom Pope John's letter
was addressed. He was Abbot of Iona, 623-652.

table, he went with one or two clerks, and having taken
a little food, made haste to be gone, either to read with
his brethren or to pray. At that time, many religious
men and women, led by his example, adopted the custom
of prolonging their fast on Wednesdays and Fridays, till
the ninth hour, throughout the year, except during the
fifty days after Easter. Never, through fear or respect
of persons, did he keep silence with regard to the sins of
the rich; but was wont to correct them with a severe
rebuke. He never gave money to the powerful men of
the world, but only food, if he happened to entertain
them; and, on the contrary, whatsoever gifts of money
he received from the rich, he either distributed, as has
been said, for the use of the poor, or bestowed in ran-
soming such as had been wrongfully sold for slaves.
Moreover, he afterwards made many of those he had
ransomed his disciples, and after having taught and
instructed them, advanced them to priest's orders.

It is said, that when King Oswald had asked a bishop
of the Scots to administer the Word of faith to him and
his nation, there was first sent to him another man of
more harsh disposition,[1] who, after preaching for some
time to the English and meeting with no success, not
being gladly heard by the people, returned home, and in
an assembly of the elders reported, that he had not been
able to do any good by his teaching to the nation to
whom he had been sent, because they were intractable
men, and of a stubborn and barbarous disposition. They
then, it is said, held a council and seriously debated
what was to be done, being desirous that the nation
should obtain the salvation it demanded, but grieving
that they had not received the preacher sent to them.
Then said Aidan, who was also present in the council,
to the priest in question, "Methinks, brother, that you
were more severe to your unlearned hearers than you
ought to have been, and did not at first, conformably to
the Apostolic rule, give them the milk of more easy
doctrine, till, being by degrees nourished with the Word

---

[1] Hector Boethius gives his name as Corman.

L

of God, they should be capable of receiving that which is more perfect and of performing the higher precepts of God." Having heard these words, all present turned their attention to him and began diligently to weigh what he had said, and they decided that he was worthy to be made a bishop, and that he was the man who ought to be sent to instruct the unbelieving and unlearned; since he was found to be endued preeminently with the grace of discretion, which is the mother of the virtues. So they ordained him and sent him forth to preach; and, as time went on, his other virtues became apparent, as well as that temperate discretion which had marked him at first.

CHAP. VI. *Of King Oswald's wonderful piety and religion.* [635-642 A.D.]

KING OSWALD, with the English nation which he governed, being instructed by the teaching of this bishop, not only learned to hope for a heavenly kingdom unknown to his fathers, but also obtained of the one God, Who made heaven and earth, a greater earthly kingdom than any of his ancestors. In brief, he brought under his dominion all the nations and provinces of Britain, which are divided into four languages, to wit, those of the Britons, the Picts, the Scots, and the English.[1] Though raised to that height of regal power, wonderful to relate, he was always humble, kind, and generous to the poor and to strangers.

To give one instance, it is told, that when he was once sitting at dinner, on the holy day of Easter, with the aforesaid bishop, and a silver dish full of royal dainties was set before him, and they were just about to put forth their hands to bless the bread, the servant, whom he had appointed to relieve the needy, came in on a sudden, and told the king, that a great multitude of poor folk from all parts was sitting in the streets begging alms of

[1] Cf. I, 1, p. 6. note 2.

the king; he immediately ordered the meat set before him to be carried to the poor, and the dish to be broken in pieces and divided among them. At which sight, the bishop who sat by him, greatly rejoicing at such an act of piety, clasped his right hand and said, "May this hand never decay." This fell out according to his prayer; for his hands with the arms being cut off from his body, when he was slain in battle, remain uncorrupted to this day, and are kept in a silver shrine, as revered relics, in St. Peter's church in the royal city,[1] which has taken its name from Bebba, one of its former queens. Through this king's exertions the provinces of the Deiri and the Bernicians, which till then had been at variance, were peacefully united and moulded into one people. He was nephew to King Edwin through his sister Acha; and it was fit that so great a predecessor should have in his own family such an one to succeed him in his religion and sovereignty.

CHAP. VII. *How the West Saxons received the Word of God by the preaching of Birinus; and of his successors, Agilbert and Leutherius.* [635-670 A.D.]

AT that time, the West Saxons, formerly called Gewissae,[2] in the reign of Cynegils,[3] received the faith of Christ, through the preaching of Bishop Birinus,[4] who came into Britain by the counsel of Pope Honorius;[5] having promised in his presence that he would sow the

[1] Bamborough (Bebbanburh, Bebburgh, Babbanburch, etc. There are many forms of the name). It is uncertain who the queen was. Nennius says she was the wife of Ethelfrid. His wife, Oswald's mother, was Acha (*v. infra*), but he may have been married twice. It was Ida, the first king of Bernicia, who founded Bamborough (Sax. Chron.).

[2] Cf. II, 5 *ad fin.*, note.

[3] Cf. note on Cuichelm, II, 9. Cynegils began to reign in 611 and reigned about thirty-one years.

[4] This account tells us substantially all that is known of him. Additional details are either legendary or conjectural. He was made a missionary ("regionary") bishop, *i.e.*, had no fixed see assigned to him.   [5] II, 17, 18, 19, 20.

seed of the holy faith in the farthest inland regions of
the English, where no other teacher had been before
him. Hereupon at the bidding of the Pope he received
episcopal consecration from Asterius, bishop of Genoa;[1]
but on his arrival in Britain, he first came to the nation
of the Gewissae, and finding all in that place confirmed
pagans, he thought it better to preach the Word there,
than to proceed further to seek for other hearers of his
preaching.

Now, as he was spreading the Gospel in the aforesaid
province, it happened that when the king himself, having
received instruction as a catechumen, was being baptized together with his people, Oswald, the most holy
and victorious king of the Northumbrians, being present,
received him as he came forth from baptism, and by an
honourable alliance most acceptable to God, first adopted
as his son, thus born again and dedicated to God, the
man whose daughter[2] he was about to receive in
marriage. The two kings gave to the bishop the city
called Dorcic,[3] there to establish his episcopal see;
where having built and consecrated churches, and by his
pious labours called many to the Lord, he departed to
the Lord, and was buried in the same city; but many
years after, when Haedde was bishop,[4] he was translated

[1] He was Archbishop of Milan, residing at Genoa. "Asterius
. . . like his predecessors from 568, avoided contact with the
dominant Arian Lombards by residing within the imperial territory
at Genoa" (Bright).

[2] Called Cyneburga by Reginald of Durham (Life of St. Oswald).

[3] Dorchester, about nine miles from Oxford, near the junction of
the Thame and the Thames. The Abbey Church of SS. Peter and
Paul stands on the traditional site of Cynegil's baptism. The see
became extinct on the retirement of Agilbert (*v. infra*), but there
are some grounds for believing that it was revived for a short time
as a Mercian see in 679 (*v.* p. 272, note), after which it again disappeared till, in the ninth century, the Bishop of Leicester moved
his see to Dorchester.

[4] IV, 12; V, 18. Haedde became bishop in 676 (Sax. Chron.).
His see was at Winchester. He removed the bones of Birinus,
because Dorchester had ceased to be an episcopal see. Winchester continued to be the only West Saxon see till the diocese
was again divided (*v.* V, 18), when Daniel was established at Winchester, and Aldhelm at Sherborne.

thence to the city of Venta,[1] and laid in the church of the blessed Apostles, Peter and Paul.

When the king died, his son Coinwalch[2] succeeded him on the throne, but refused to receive the faith and the mysteries of the heavenly kingdom; and not long after he lost also the dominion of his earthly kingdom; for he put away the sister of Penda, king of the Mercians, whom he had married, and took another wife; whereupon a war ensuing, he was by him deprived of his kingdom, and withdrew to Anna, king of the East Angles, where he lived three years in banishment, and learned and received the true faith; for the king, with whom he lived in his banishment, was a good man, and happy in a good and saintly offspring, as we shall show hereafter.[3]

But when Coinwalch was restored to his kingdom, there came into that province out of Ireland, a certain bishop called Agilbert,[4] a native of Gaul, but who had then lived a long time in Ireland, for the purpose of reading the Scriptures. He attached himself to the king, and voluntarily undertook the ministry of preaching. The king, observing his learning and industry, desired him to accept an episcopal see there and remain as the bishop of his people. Agilbert complied with the request, and

---

[1] Winchester; *Gwent* (Celtic)=a plain. This, the "old Church," as distinguished from the present Cathedral, was built by Coinwalch on his restoration to his kingdom. There are legends of early British churches on the site, the first founded by "King Lucius" (I, 4), the second dedicated to "St. Amphibalus" (I, 7, p. 15, note).

[2] Cuichelm (*v.* II, 9, and note) had died before his father, Cynegils.

[3] Bede reverts more than once to the subject of Anna's pious offspring, *v. infra* cc. 8, 18; IV, 19, 20. He had four daughters: Sexburg (c. 8, IV, 19, 22), Ethelberg (c. 8), Ethelthryth (IV, 19, 20; cf. IV, 3, 22), and Witberg (not mentioned by Bede); two granddaughters, Earcongota (c. 8) and Ermingild, the wife of Wulfhere of Mercia; all of whom entered convents, as did also his step-daughter, Saethryth (c. 8).

[4] Cc. 25, 26, 28; IV, 1; V, 19. The name is a Frankish form of the English "Aethelbert." He was apparently consecrated in Gaul, but not appointed to any diocese.

presided over that nation as their bishop for many years. At length the king, who understood only the language of the Saxons, weary of his barbarous tongue, privately brought into the province another bishop, speaking his own language, by name Wini,[1] who had also been ordained in Gaul; and dividing his province into two dioceses, appointed this last his episcopal see in the city of Venta, by the Saxons called Wintancaestir.[2] Agilbert, being highly offended, that the king should do this without consulting him, returned into Gaul, and being made bishop of the city of Paris, died there, being old and full of days. Not many years after his departure out of Britain, Wini was also expelled from his bishopric by the same king, and took refuge with Wulfhere, king of the Mercians, of whom he purchased for money the see of the city of London,[3] and remained bishop thereof till his death. Thus the province of the West Saxons continued no small time without a bishop.

During which time, the aforesaid king of that nation, sustaining repeatedly very great losses in his kingdom from his enemies, at length bethought himself, that as he had been before expelled from the throne for his unbelief, he had been restored when he acknowledged the faith of Christ; and he perceived that his kingdom, being deprived of a bishop, was justly deprived also of the Divine protection. He, therefore, sent messengers into Gaul to Agilbert, with humble apologies entreating him to return to the bishopric of his nation. But he excused himself, and protested that he could not go, because he was bound to the bishopric of his own city and diocese; notwithstanding, in order to give him some help in answer to his earnest request, he sent thither in his stead the priest

[1] Cf. c. 28. It is not known why he was expelled (v. infra). There is a tradition that he spent the last three years of his life at Winchester as a penitent, doubtless for the act of simony related below, but this is inconsistent with Bede's statement that he remained Bishop of London till his death.

[2] Winchester; v.s. pp. 148-9, notes.

[3] London was an East Saxon bishopric, but Wulfhere (v. c. 24, ad fin.) had acquired the supremacy over the East Saxons (v. c. 30).

Leutherius,[1] his nephew, to be ordained as his bishop, if he thought fit, saying that he thought him worthy of a bishopric. The king and the people received him honourably, and asked Theodore, then Archbishop of Canterbury, to consecrate him as their bishop. He was accordingly consecrated in the same city, and many years diligently governed the whole bishopric of the West Saxons by synodical authority.

CHAP. VIII. *How Earconbert, King of Kent, ordered the idols to be destroyed; and of his daughter Earcongota, and his kinswoman Ethelberg, virgins consecrated to God.* [640 A.D.]

IN the year of our Lord 640, Eadbald,[2] king of Kent, departed this life, and left his kingdom to his son Earconbert, who governed it most nobly twenty-four years and some months. He was the first of the English kings that of his supreme authority commanded the idols throughout his whole kingdom to be forsaken and destroyed, and the fast of forty days to be observed; and that the same might not be lightly neglected, he appointed fitting and condign punishments for the offenders. His daughter Earcongota, as became the offspring of such a parent, was a most virtuous virgin, serving God in a monastery in the country of the Franks, built by a most noble abbess, named Fara, at a place called In Brige;[3] for at that time but few monasteries had been built in the country of the Angles, and many were wont, for the sake of monastic life, to repair to the monasteries of the Franks or Gauls; and they also sent

[1] Hlothere, consecrated 670. Apparently he was appointed by a West Saxon Synod ("ex synodica sanctione"). Dr. Bright thinks the term is used loosely for a Witenagemot.

[2] II, 5-9, 20; V, 24.

[3] Faremoûtier-en-Brie (Farae Monasterium in Brige), founded *circ.* 617 by Fara, or Burgundofara, a Burgundian lady of noble birth, said to have been dedicated by St. Columba in her infancy. The monastery was a double one, *i.e.*, consisted of monks and nuns (cf. *infra*, "many of the brethren").

their daughters there to be instructed, and united to
their Heavenly Bridegroom, especially in the monasteries
of Brige, of Cale,[1] and Andilegum.[2] Among whom was
also Saethryth,[3] daughter of the wife of Anna, king of the
East Angles, above mentioned; and Ethelberg,[4] the
king's own daughter; both of whom, though strangers,
were for their virtue made abbesses of the monastery of
Brige. Sexburg,[5] that king's elder daughter, wife to
Earconbert, king of Kent, had a daughter called Earcongota,[6] of whom we are about to speak.

Many wonderful works and miracles of this virgin,
dedicated to God, are to this day related by the inhabitants of that place; but for us it shall suffice to say
something briefly of her departure out of this world to
the heavenly kingdom. The day of her summoning
drawing near, she began to visit in the monastery the
cells of the infirm handmaidens of Christ, and particularly those that were of a great age, or most noted for
their virtuous life, and humbly commending herself
to their prayers, she let them know that her death was
at hand, as she had learnt by revelation, which she
said she had received in this manner. She had seen a
band of men, clothed in white, come into the monastery,
and being asked by her what they wanted, and what
they did there, they answered, "They had been sent
thither to carry away with them the gold coin that had
been brought thither from Kent." Towards the close of
that same night, as morning began to dawn, leaving the
darkness of this world, she departed to the light of
heaven. Many of the brethren of that monastery who
were in other houses, declared they had then plainly
heard choirs of singing angels, and, as it were, the
sound of a multitude entering the monastery. Whereupon going out immediately to see what it might be,
they beheld a great light coming down from heaven,

---

[1] Chelles, near Paris, founded by Clothilde, wife of Clovis I,
restored and enlarged by Bathild, wife of Clovis II (v. V, 19, note).
[2] Andeley-sur-Seine, also founded by Clothilde, wife of Clovis I.
[3] Cf. *supra* c. 7, note on Anna.
[4] *Ibid.*   [5] *Ibid.*   [6] *Ibid.*

which bore that holy soul, set loose from the bonds of
the flesh, to the eternal joys of the celestial country.
They also tell of other miracles that were wrought that
night in the same monastery by the power of God; but
as we must proceed to other matters, we leave them to
be related by those whose concern they are. The body
of this venerable virgin and bride of Christ was buried in
the church of the blessed protomartyr, Stephen. It was
thought fit, three days after, to take up the stone that
covered the tomb, and to raise it higher in the same
place, and whilst they were doing this, so sweet a
fragrance rose from below, that it seemed to all the
brethren and sisters there present, as if a store of balsam
had been opened.

Her aunt also, Ethelberg, of whom we have spoken,
preserved the glory, acceptable to God, of perpetual
virginity, in a life of great self-denial, but the extent
of her virtue became more conspicuous after her death.
Whilst she was abbess, she began to build in her
monastery a church, in honour of all the Apostles,
wherein she desired that her body should be buried;
but when that work was advanced half way, she was
prevented by death from finishing it, and was buried in
the place in the church which she had chosen. After her
death, the brothers occupied themselves with other
things, and this structure was left untouched for seven
years, at the expiration whereof they resolved, by reason
of the greatness of the work, wholly to abandon the
building of the church, and to remove the abbess's bones
thence to some other church that was finished and consecrated. On opening her tomb, they found the body as
untouched by decay as it had been free from the corruption of carnal concupiscence, and having washed it again
and clothed it in other garments, they removed it to the
church of the blessed Stephen, the Martyr. And her
festival is wont to be celebrated there with much honour
on the 7th of July.

CHAP. IX. *How miracles of healing have been frequently wrought in the place where King Oswald was killed; and how, first, a traveller's horse was restored and afterwards a young girl cured of the palsy.* [642 A.D.]

OSWALD, the most Christian king of the Northumbrians, reigned nine years, including that year which was held accursed for the barbarous cruelty of the king of the Britons and the reckless apostacy of the English kings; for, as was said above,[1] it is agreed by the unanimous consent of all, that the names and memory of the apostates should be erased from the catalogue of the Christian kings, and no year assigned to their reign. After which period, Oswald was killed in a great battle, by the same pagan nation and pagan king of the Mercians, who had slain his predecessor Edwin, at a place called in the English tongue Maserfelth,[2] in the thirty-eighth year of his age, on the fifth day of the month of August.[3]

How great his faith was towards God, and how remarkable his devotion, has been made evident by miracles even after his death; for, in the place where he was killed by the pagans, fighting for his country, sick men and cattle are frequently healed to this day. Whence it came to pass that many took up the very dust of the place where his body fell, and putting it into water, brought much relief with it to their friends who were sick. This custom came so much into use, that the earth being carried away by degrees, a hole was made as deep as the height of a man. Nor is it surprising that the sick should be healed in the place where he died; for, whilst he lived, he never ceased to provide for the poor and the sick, and to bestow alms on them, and assist them.

[1] Cf. c. 1.
[2] The place is commonly supposed to be near Oswestry in Shropshire (*i.e.*, Oswald's Tree). There is a legend (related by Reginald) which tells of a tree near the spot, to which a large bird carried the king's right arm from the stake (cf. c. 12 *ad fin.*). The Welsh name of the place, "Croes Oswallt" (Cross-Oswald), points to the explanation that the "tree" was a wooden cross set up to mark the site. [3] 642, *i.e.*, nine years after the death of Edwin.

Many miracles are said to have been wrought in that place, or with the dust carried from it; but we have thought it sufficient to mention two, which we have heard from our elders.

It happened, not long after his death, that a man was travelling on horseback near that place, when his horse on a sudden fell sick, stood still, hung his head, and foamed at the mouth, and, at length, as his pain increased, he fell to the ground; the rider dismounted, and taking off his saddle,[1] waited to see whether the beast would recover or die. At length, after writhing for a long time in extreme anguish, the horse happened in his struggles to come to the very place where the great king died. Immediately the pain abated, the beast ceased from his frantic kicking, and, after the manner of horses, as if resting from his weariness, he rolled from side to side, and then starting up, perfectly recovered, began to graze hungrily on the green herbage. The rider observing this, and being an intelligent man, concluded that there must be some wonderful sanctity in the place where the horse had been healed, and he marked the spot. After which he again mounted his horse, and went on to the inn where he intended to stop. On his arrival he found a girl, niece to the landlord, who had long been sick of the palsy; and when the members of the household, in his presence, lamented the girl's grievous calamity, he gave them an account of the place where his horse had been cured. In brief, she was put into a wagon and carried to the place and laid down there. At first she slept awhile, and when she awoke, found herself healed of her infirmity. Upon which she called for water, washed her face, arranged her hair, put a kerchief on her head, and returned home on foot, in good health, with those who had brought her.

---

[1] Reading *stramine subtracto*, on the authority of the oldest MSS., in which case we must assume (with Plummer) that *stramen* is used incorrectly for *stragulus* in the sense of "saddle," or "horse-cloth," from the classical use, *sternere equum* = to saddle. Cf. "stratus regaliter," c. 14. Later MSS. read *stramine substrato* (= "spreading straw under him ").

CHAP. X. *How the dust of that place prevailed against fire.* [After 642 A.D.]

ABOUT the same time, another traveller, a Briton, as is reported, happened to pass by the same place, where the aforesaid battle was fought. Observing one particular spot of ground greener and more beautiful than any other part of the field, he had the wisdom to infer that the cause of the unusual greenness in that place must be that some person of greater holiness than any other in the army had been killed there. He therefore took along with him some of the dust of that piece of ground, tying it up in a linen cloth, supposing, as was indeed the case, that it would be of use for curing sick people, and proceeding on his journey, came in the evening to a certain village, and entered a house where the villagers were feasting at supper. Being received by the owners of the house, he sat down with them at the entertainment, hanging the cloth, with the dust which he had carried in it, on a post in the wall. They sat long at supper and drank deep. Now there was a great fire in the middle of the room, and it happened that the sparks flew up and caught the roof of the house, which being made of wattles and thatch, was suddenly wrapped in flames; the guests ran out in panic and confusion, but they were not able to save the burning house, which was rapidly being destroyed. Wherefore the house was burnt down, and only that post on which the dust hung in the linen cloth remained safe and untouched by the fire. When they beheld this miracle, they were all amazed, and inquiring into it diligently, learned that the dust had been taken from the place where the blood of King Oswald had been shed. These wonderful works being made known and reported abroad, many began daily to resort to that place, and received the blessing of health for themselves and their friends.

CHAP. XI. *How a light from Heaven stood all night over his relics, and how those possessed with devils were healed by them.* [679-697 A.D.]

AMONG the rest, I think we ought not to pass over in silence the miracles and signs from Heaven that were shown when King Oswald's bones were found, and translated into the church where they are now preserved. This was done by the zealous care of Osthryth, queen of the Mercians,[1] the daughter of his brother Oswy, who reigned after him, as shall be said hereafter.

There is a famous monastery in the province of Lindsey, called Beardaneu,[2] which that queen and her husband Ethelred greatly loved and venerated, conferring upon it many honours. It was here that she was desirous to lay the revered bones of her uncle. When the wagon in which those bones were carried arrived towards evening at the aforesaid monastery, they that were in it were unwilling to admit them, because, though they knew him to be a holy man, yet, as he was a native of another province, and had obtained the sovereignty over them, they retained their ancient aversion to him even after his death. Thus it came to pass that the relics were left in the open air all that night, with only a large tent spread over the wagon which contained them. But it was revealed by a sign from Heaven with how much reverence they ought to be received by all the faithful; for all that night, a pillar of light, reaching from the wagon up to heaven, was visible in almost every part of the province of Lindsey. Hereupon, in the morning, the brethren of that monastery who had refused it the day before, began themselves earnestly to pray that those holy relics, beloved of God, might be laid among them. Accordingly, the bones, being washed, were put into a shrine which they had made for that purpose, and placed

---

[1] Wife of Ethelred of Mercia (cf. IV, 21), murdered by her own people in 697 (V, 24).
[2] Bardney, in Lincolnshire. Ethelred became first a monk, afterwards abbot of the monastery.

in the church, with due honour; and that there might be a perpetual memorial of the royal character of this holy man, they hung up over the monument his banner of gold and purple. Then they poured out the water in which they had washed the bones, in a corner of the cemetery.[1] From that time, the very earth which received that holy water, had the power of saving grace in casting out devils from the bodies of persons possessed.

Lastly, when the aforesaid queen afterwards abode some time in that monastery, there came to visit her a certain venerable abbess, who is still living, called Ethelhild, the sister of the holy men, Ethelwin[2] and Aldwin, the first of whom was bishop in the province of Lindsey, the other abbot of the monastery of Peartaneu;[3] not far from which was the monastery of Ethelhild. When this lady was come, in a conversation between her and the queen, the discourse, among other things, turning upon Oswald, she said, that she also had that night seen the light over his relics reaching up to heaven. The queen thereupon added, that the very dust of the pavement on which the water that washed the bones had been poured out, had already healed many sick persons. The abbess thereupon desired that some of that health-bringing dust might be given her, and, receiving it, she tied it up in a cloth, and, putting it into a casket, returned home. Some time after, when she was in her monastery, there came to it a guest, who was wont often in the night to be on a sudden grievously tormented with an unclean spirit; he being hospitably entertained, when he had gone to bed after supper, was suddenly seized by the Devil, and began to cry out, to gnash his teeth, to foam at the mouth, and to writhe and distort his limbs. None being able to hold or bind him, the servant ran, and knocking at the door, told

---

[1] "Sacrarium." Probably here=the cemetery. But we find it elsewhere in Bede for the sacristy, and it is also used of the sanctuary.

[2] Cf. c. 27; IV, 12.

[3] Partney: cf. II, 16, and note. This is the only mention of its abbot, Aldwin.

the abbess. She, opening the monastery door, went out
herself with one of the nuns to the men's apartment, and
calling a priest, desired that he would go with her to the
sufferer. Being come thither, and seeing many present,
who had not been able, by their efforts, to hold the tormented person and restrain his convulsive movements,
the priest used exorcisms, and did all that he could to
assuage the madness of the unfortunate man, but, though
he took much pains, he could not prevail. When no
hope appeared of easing him in his ravings, the abbess
bethought herself of the dust, and immediately bade
her handmaiden go and fetch her the casket in which
it was. As soon as she came with it, as she had been
bidden, and was entering the hall of the house, in the
inner part whereof the possessed person was writhing in
torment, he suddenly became silent, and laid down his
head, as if he had been falling asleep, stretching out all
his limbs to rest. " Silence fell upon all and intent they
gazed," [1] anxiously waiting to see the end of the matter.
And after about the space of an hour the man that had
been tormented sat up, and fetching a deep sigh, said,
" Now I am whole, for I am restored to my senses."
They earnestly inquired how that came to pass, and he
answered, " As soon as that maiden drew near the hall
of this house, with the casket she brought, all the evil
spirits that vexed me departed and left me, and were
no more to be seen." Then the abbess gave him a little
of that dust, and the priest having prayed, he passed
that night in great peace; nor was he, from that time
forward, alarmed by night, or in any way troubled by his
old enemy.

CHAP. XII.   *How a little boy was cured of a fever at his
tomb.*

SOME time after, there was a certain little boy in the said
monastery, who had been long grievously troubled with

---

[1] Aen. II, 1. Quotations from Vergil are frequent in Bede.
Cf. II, 13, *ad fin.* ; v. 12, p. 327.

a fever; he was one day anxiously expecting the hour
when his fit was to come on, when one of the brothers,
coming in to him, said, "Shall I tell you, my son, how
you may be cured of this sickness? Rise, enter the
church, and go close to Oswald's tomb; sit down and
stay there quiet and do not leave it; do not come away,
or stir from the place, till the time is past, when the fever
leaves you: then I will go in and fetch you away." The
boy did as he was advised, and the disease durst not
assail him as he sat by the saint's tomb; but fled in such
fear that it did not dare to touch him, either the second
or third day, or ever after. The brother that came from
thence, and told me this, added, that at the time when
he was talking with me, the young man was then still
living in the monastery, on whom, when a boy, that
miracle of healing had been wrought. Nor need we
wonder that the prayers of that king who is now reigning with our Lord, should be very efficacious with Him,
since he, whilst yet governing his temporal kingdom,
was always wont to pray and labour more for that which
is eternal. Nay, it is said, that he often continued in
prayer from the hour of morning thanksgiving[1] till it
was day; and that by reason of his constant custom of
praying or giving thanks to God, he was wont always,
wherever he sat, to hold his hands on his knees with the
palms turned upwards. It is also commonly affirmed
and has passed into a proverb, that he ended his life in
prayer; for when he was beset with the weapons of his
enemies, and perceived that death was at hand, he
prayed for the souls of his army. Whence it is proverbially said, "'Lord have mercy on their souls,' said
Oswald, as he fell to the ground."

Now his bones were translated to the monastery which
we have mentioned, and buried therein: but the king
who slew him commanded his head, and hands, with the
arms, to be cut off from the body, and set upon stakes.
But his successor in the throne, Oswy, coming thither
the next year with his army, took them down, and buried

---

[1] *I.e.*, matins (between midnight and 3 A.M.).

his head in the cemetery of the church of Lindisfarne,[1] and the hands and arms in his royal city.[2]

CHAP. XIII. *How a certain person in Ireland was restored, when at the point of death, by his relics.*

NOR was the fame of the renowned Oswald confined to Britain, but, spreading rays of healing light even beyond the sea, reached also to Germany and Ireland. For the most reverend prelate, Acca,[3] is wont to relate, that when, in his journey to Rome,[4] he and his bishop Wilfrid stayed some time with Wilbrord,[5] the holy archbishop of the Frisians, he often heard him tell of the wonders which had been wrought in that province at the relics of that most worshipful king. And he used to say that in Ireland, when, being yet only a priest, he led the life of a stranger and pilgrim for love of the eternal country, the fame of that king's sanctity was already spread far and near in that island also. One of the miracles, among the rest, which he related, we have thought fit to insert in this our history.

[1] It was removed in 875, during the Danish invasions, in the coffin of St. Cuthbert, and finally interred in the same tomb with the body of Cuthbert at Durham, where it was found in 1827. Hence St. Cuthbert is often represented holding St. Oswald's head in his hands.

[2] Bamborough: cf. c. 6, note.

[3] Bishop of Hexham, 709-731: *v.* V, 20 (cf. also IV, 14; V, 19). He was a much loved friend of Bede, many of whose works were undertaken at his instigation. He was devotedly attached to Wilfrid, whom he succeeded at Hexham. The "Continuation" says that he was expelled from his see in 731, and he probably never regained it.

[4] Cf. V. 19, p. 353. This was probably Wilfrid's third journey to Rome, undertaken in 703-704, for, at the time of his earlier journey (in 678), when he spent the winter in Frisland, Wilbrord was not yet there.

[5] The great missionary archbishop of the Frisians. He was trained as a boy in Wilfrid's abbey at Ripon, studied some time in Ireland, and with eleven companions undertook in 690 the mission to Frisland planned by Egbert: *v.* V, 10, 11. (For Egbert, *v.* c. 4, p. 143, and note.)

M

"At the time," said he, " of the plague which made such widespread havoc in Britain and Ireland, among others, a certain scholar of the Scottish race was smitten with the disease, a man learned in the study of letters, but in no way careful or studious of his eternal salvation; who, seeing his death near at hand, began to fear and tremble lest, as soon as he was dead, he should be hurried away to the prison-house of Hell for his sins. He called me, for I was near, and trembling and sighing in his weakness, with a lamentable voice made his complaint to me, after this manner: ' You see that my bodily distress increases, and that I am now reduced to the point of death. Nor do I question but that after the death of my body, I shall be immediately snatched away to the everlasting death of my soul, and cast into the torments of hell, since for a long time, amidst all my reading of divine books, I have suffered myself to be ensnared by sin, instead of keeping the commandments of God. But it is my resolve, if the Divine Mercy shall grant me a new term of life, to correct my sinful habits, and wholly to devote anew my mind and life to obedience to the Divine will. But I know that I have no merits of my own whereby to obtain a prolongation of life, nor can I hope to have it, unless it shall please God to forgive me, wretched and unworthy of pardon as I am, through the help of those who have faithfully served him. We have heard, and the report is widespread, that there was in your nation a king, of wonderful sanctity, called Oswald, the excellency of whose faith and virtue has been made famous even after his death by the working of many miracles. I beseech you, if you have any relics of his in your keeping, that you will bring them to me; if haply the Lord shall be pleased, through his merits, to have mercy on me.' I answered, ' I have indeed a part of the stake on which his head was set up by the pagans, when he was killed, and if you believe with steadfast heart, the Divine mercy may, through the merits of so great a man, both grant you a longer term of life here, and render you worthy to be admitted into eternal life.' He answered immediately that he had entire faith therein. Then I blessed some water, and put into it a splinter of the aforesaid oak, and gave it to the sick man to drink. He presently found ease, and, recovering of his sickness, lived a long time after; and, being entirely converted to God in heart and deed, wherever he went, he spoke of the goodness of his merciful Creator, and the honour of His faithful servant."

CHAP. XIV. *How on the death of Paulinus, Ithamar was made bishop of Rochester in his stead; and of the wonderful humility of King Oswin, who was cruelly slain by Oswy.* [644-651 A.D.]

OSWALD being translated to the heavenly kingdom, his brother Oswy,[1] a young man of about thirty years of age, succeeded him on the throne of his earthly kingdom, and held it twenty-eight years with much trouble, being attacked by the pagan nation of the Mercians, that had slain his brother, as also by his son Alchfrid,[2] and by his nephew Oidilwald,[3] the son of his brother who reigned before him. In his second year, that is, in the year of our Lord 644, the most reverend Father Paulinus, formerly Bishop of York, but at that time Bishop of the city of Rochester, departed to the Lord, on the 10th day of October, having held the office of a bishop nineteen years, two months, and twenty-one days; and was buried in the sacristy of the blessed Apostle Andrew,[4] which King Ethelbert had built from the foundation, in the same city of Rochester. In his place, Archbishop Honorius

---

[1] The third of Ethelfrid's seven sons (*v.* Sax. Chron.) to succeed to the sovereignty. With his brothers he had spent his youth in banishment among the Picts and Scots (*v.s.* c. 1).

[2] Cc. 21, 24, 25, 28. The pupil and friend of Wilfrid. He was made sub-king of Deira in place of Ethelwald (*v.* next note). The date and circumstances of his rebellion are not known. A cross at Bewcastle in Cumberland, erected in 670 or 671, commemorates him and asks prayers for his soul.

[3] Ethelwald, *v.* cc. 23, 24.

[4] Cf. II, 3.

ordained Ithamar,[1] of the Kentish nation, but not inferior
to his predecessors in learning and conduct of life.

Oswy, during the first part of his reign, had a partner
in the royal dignity called Oswin, of the race of King
Edwin, and son to Osric[2] of whom we have spoken
above, a man of wonderful piety and devotion, who
governed the province of the Deiri seven years in very
great prosperity, and was himself beloved by all men.
But Oswy, who governed all the other northern part of
the nation beyond the Humber, that is, the province of
the Bernicians, could not live at peace with him; and at
last, when the causes of their disagreement increased,
he murdered him most cruelly. For when each had
raised an army against the other, Oswin perceived that
he could not maintain a war against his enemy who had
more auxiliaries than himself, and he thought it better at
that time to lay aside all thoughts of engaging, and to
reserve himself for better times. He therefore disbanded
the army which he had assembled, and ordered all his
men to return to their own homes, from the place that
is called Wilfaraesdun,[3] that is, Wilfar's Hill, which is
about ten miles distant from the village called Cataract,
towards the north-west. He himself, with only one
trusty thegn, whose name was Tondhere, withdrew and
lay concealed in the house of Hunwald, a noble,[4] whom
he imagined to be his most assured friend. But, alas!
it was far otherwise; for Hunwald betrayed him, and
Oswy, by the hands of his reeve, Ethilwin, foully slew
him and the thegn aforesaid. This happened on the 20th
of August, in the ninth year of his reign, at a place
called Ingetlingum, where afterwards, to atone for this

---

[1] The first bishop of English birth. For Honorius, v. II, 15,
note.

[2] The apostate king of Deira, Osric, son of Aelfric, was first
cousin to Edwin (cf. c. 1). Oswald united the two Northumbrian
kingdoms, but at his death, Oswin, son of Osric, succeeded to
Deira. He was canonised, and his tragic death led him to be
regarded as a martyr.

[3] Not identified. The village ("a vico Cataractone") is probably
the one called Cataracta in II, 14 (v. note, ad loc.).

[4] Comes, A.S. gesith.

crime, a monastery was built,[1] wherein prayers should
be daily offered up to God for the redemption of the
souls of both kings, to wit, of him that was murdered,
and of him that commanded the murder.

King Oswin was of a goodly countenance, and tall of
stature, pleasant in discourse, and courteous in behaviour; and bountiful to all, gentle and simple alike;
so that he was beloved by all men for the royal dignity
of his mind and appearance and actions, and men of the
highest rank came from almost all provinces to serve
him. Among all the graces of virtue and moderation by
which he was distinguished and, if I may say so, blessed
in a special manner, humility is said to have been the
greatest, which it will suffice to prove by one instance.

He had given a beautiful horse to Bishop Aidan, to use
either in crossing rivers, or in performing a journey upon
any urgent necessity, though the Bishop was wont to
travel ordinarily on foot. Some short time after, a poor
man meeting the Bishop, and asking alms, he immediately
dismounted, and ordered the horse, with all his royal
trappings, to be given to the beggar; for he was very
compassionate, a great friend to the poor, and, in a
manner, the father of the wretched. This being told to
the king, when they were going in to dinner, he said to
the Bishop, "What did you mean, my lord Bishop, by
giving the poor man that royal horse, which it was fitting
that you should have for your own use? Had not we
many other horses of less value, or things of other sorts,
which would have been good enough to give to the poor,
instead of giving that horse, which I had chosen and
set apart for your own use?" Thereupon the Bishop
answered, "What do you say, O king? Is that son of a
mare more dear to you than that son of God?" Upon
this they went in to dinner, and the Bishop sat in his
place; but the king, who had come in from hunting,
stood warming himself, with his attendants, at the fire.
Then, on a sudden, whilst he was warming himself, calling

---

[1] At Queen Eanfled's request (*v.* c. 24, p. 191). The place is
generally identified with Gilling in the North Riding of Yorkshire.
For the form of the name, *v.* II, 14, p. 119, note 5.

to mind what the bishop had said to him, he ungirt his sword, and gave it to a servant, and hastened to the Bishop and fell down at his feet, beseeching him to forgive him; "For from this time forward," said he, "I will never speak any more of this, nor will I judge of what or how much of our money you shall give to the sons of God." The bishop was much moved at this sight, and starting up, raised him, saying that he was entirely reconciled to him, if he would but sit down to his meat, and lay aside all sorrow. The king, at the bishop's command and request, was comforted, but the bishop, on the other hand, grew sad and was moved even to tears. His priest then asking him, in the language of his country, which the king and his servants did not understand, why he wept, "I know," said he, "that the king will not live long; for I never before saw a humble king; whence I perceive that he will soon be snatched out of this life, because this nation is not worthy of such a ruler." Not long after, the bishop's gloomy foreboding was fulfilled by the king's sad death, as has been said above. But Bishop Aidan himself was also taken out of this world, not more than twelve days after the death of the king he loved, on the 31st of August,[1] to receive the eternal reward of his labours from the Lord.

CHAP. XV. *How Bishop Aidan foretold to certain seamen that a storm would arise, and gave them some holy oil to calm it.* [Between 642 and 645 A.D.]

How great the merits of Aidan were, was made manifest by the Judge of the heart, with the testimony of miracles, whereof it will suffice to mention three, that they may not be forgotten. A certain priest, whose name was Utta,[2] a man of great weight and sincerity, and on that account honoured by all men, even the princes of the world, was sent to Kent, to bring thence, as wife for

---

[1] In 651 A.D. Cf. v. 24.   [2] Cf. c. 21.

King Oswy, Eanfled,[1] the daughter of King Edwin, who had been carried thither when her father was killed. Intending to go thither by land, but to return with the maiden by sea, he went to Bishop Aidan, and entreated him to offer up his prayers to the Lord for him and his company, who were then to set out on so long a journey. He, blessing them, and commending them to the Lord, at the same time gave them some holy oil, saying, "I know that when you go on board ship, you will meet with a storm and contrary wind; but be mindful to cast this oil I give you into the sea, and the wind will cease immediately; you will have pleasant calm weather to attend you and send you home by the way that you desire."

All these things fell out in order, even as the bishop had foretold. For first, the waves of the sea raged, and the sailors endeavoured to ride it out at anchor, but all to no purpose; for the sea sweeping over the ship on all sides and beginning to fill it with water, they all perceived that death was at hand and about to overtake them. The priest at last, remembering the bishop's words, laid hold of the phial and cast some of the oil into the sea, which at once, as had been foretold, ceased from its uproar. Thus it came to pass that the man of God, by the spirit of prophecy, foretold the storm that was to come to pass, and by virtue of the same spirit, though absent in the body, calmed it when it had arisen. The story of this miracle was not told me by a person of little credit, but by Cynimund, a most faithful priest of our church,[2] who declared that it was related to him by Utta, the priest, in whose case and through whom the same was wrought.

[1] II, 9, 20; III, 24, 25, 29; V, 19.
[2] The monastery of Wearmouth and Jarrow. Cf. IV, 18; V, 21 ad init., 24.

CHAP. XVI. *How the same Aidan, by his prayers, saved
the royal city when it was fired by the enemy.* [Before
651 A.D.]

ANOTHER notable miracle of the same father is related by
many such as were likely to have knowledge thereof;
for during the time that he was bishop, the hostile army
of the Mercians, under the command of Penda, cruelly
ravaged the country of the Northumbrians far and near,
even to the royal city,[1] which has its name from Bebba,
formerly its queen. Not being able to take it by storm
or by siege, he endeavoured to burn it down; and having
pulled down all the villages in the neighbourhood of the
city, he brought thither an immense quantity of beams,
rafters, partitions, wattles and thatch, wherewith he encompassed the place to a great height on the land side,
and when he found the wind favourable, he set fire to it
and attempted to burn the town.

At that time, the most reverend Bishop Aidan was
dwelling in the Isle of Farne,[2] which is about two miles
from the city; for thither he was wont often to retire to
pray in solitude and silence; and, indeed, this lonely
dwelling of his is to this day shown in that island.
When he saw the flames of fire and the smoke carried
by the wind rising above the city walls, he is said to have
lifted up his eyes and hands to heaven, and cried with
tears, "Behold, Lord, how great evil is wrought by
Penda!" These words were hardly uttered, when the
wind immediately veering from the city, drove back the
flames upon those who had kindled them, so that some
being hurt, and all afraid, they forebore any further
attempts against the city, which they perceived to be
protected by the hand of God.

[1] Bamborough, *v.* cc. 6, 12.
[2] The scene of St. Cuthbert's hermit life: *v.* IV, 27, 28, 29; V, 1.
It is called the "House Island," and is the largest of the Farne
group of seventeen islands off the coast of Northumberland,
opposite Bamborough, famous in modern times for the rescue of a
shipwrecked crew by Grace Darling.

CHAP. XVII. *How a prop of the church on which Bishop Aidan was leaning when he died, could not be consumed when the rest of the Church was on fire; and concerning his inward life.* [651 A.D.]

AIDAN was in the king's township, not far from the city of which we have spoken above, at the time when death caused him to quit the body, after he had been bishop sixteen [1] years; for having a church and a chamber in that place, he was wont often to go and stay there, and to make excursions from it to preach in the country round about, which he likewise did at other of the king's townships, having nothing of his own besides his church and a few fields about it. When he was sick they set up a tent for him against the wall at the west end of the church, and so it happened that he breathed his last, leaning against a buttress that was on the outside of the church to strengthen the wall. He died in the seventeenth year of his episcopate, on the 31st of August.[2] His body was thence presently translated to the isle of Lindisfarne, and buried in the cemetery of the brethren. Some time after, when a larger church was built there and dedicated in honour of the blessed prince of the Apostles, his bones were translated thither, and laid on the right side of the altar, with the respect due to so great a prelate.

Finan,[3] who had likewise been sent thither from Hii, the island monastery of the Scots, succeeded him, and continued no small time in the bishopric. It happened some years after, that Penda, king of the Mercians, coming into these parts with a hostile army, destroyed all he could with fire and sword, and the village where the bishop died, along with the church above

[1] *v.l.* seventeen. The MS. authority is about equal; but cf. *infra*, the statement that he died in the seventeenth year of his episcopate, which seems to be correct.
[2] 651 A.D.; *v.s.* c. 14 *ad fin.*
[3] Cc. 21, 22, 25, 26, 27. For his character, *v.* c. 25 (though some suppose the reference to be to Ronan). For Hii, *v.* c. 3, note.

mentioned, was burnt down; but it fell out in a wonderful manner that the buttress against which he had been leaning when he died, could not be consumed by the fire which devoured all about it. This miracle being noised abroad, the church was soon rebuilt in the same place, and that same buttress was set up on the outside, as it had been before, to strengthen the wall. It happened again, some time after, that the village and likewise the church were carelessly burned down the second time. Then again, the fire could not touch the buttress; and, miraculously, though the fire broke through the very holes of the nails wherewith it was fixed to the building, yet it could do no hurt to the buttress itself. When therefore the church was built there the third time, they did not, as before, place that buttress on the outside as a support of the building, but within the church, as a memorial of the miracle; where the people coming in might kneel, and implore the Divine mercy. And it is well known that since then many have found grace and been healed in that same place, as also that by means of splinters cut off from the buttress, and put into water, many more have obtained a remedy for their own infirmities and those of their friends.[1]

I have written thus much concerning the character and works of the aforesaid Aidan, in no way commending or approving his lack of wisdom with regard to the observance of Easter; nay, heartily detesting it, as I have most manifestly proved in the book I have written, " De Temporibus "; [2] but, like an impartial historian, unreservedly relating what was done by or through him, and commending such things as are praiseworthy in his actions, and preserving the memory thereof for the benefit of the readers; to wit, his love of peace and charity; of continence and humility; his mind superior to anger and avarice, and despising pride and

[1] The church and the buttress were evidently both of wood.
[2] He probably refers to the " De Temporum Ratione," the longer of his two chronological works. It treats the Paschal question at length. But in the " De Temporibus " he also briefly discusses it.

vainglory; his industry in keeping and teaching the Divine commandments, his power of study and keeping vigil; his priestly authority in reproving the haughty and powerful, and at the same time his tenderness in comforting the afflicted, and relieving or defending the poor. To be brief, so far as I have learnt from those that knew him, he took care to neglect none of those things which he found in the Gospels and the writings of Apostles and prophets, but to the utmost of his power endeavoured to fulfil them all in his deeds.

These things I greatly admire and love in the aforesaid bishop, because I do not doubt that they were pleasing to God; but I do not approve or praise his observance of Easter at the wrong time, either through ignorance of the canonical time appointed, or, if he knew it, being prevailed on by the authority of his nation not to adopt it.[1] Yet this I approve in him, that in the celebration of his Easter, the object which he had at heart and reverenced and preached was the same as ours, to wit, the redemption of mankind, through the Passion, Resurrection and Ascension into Heaven of the Man Christ Jesus, who is the mediator between God and man. And therefore he always celebrated Easter, not as some falsely imagine, on the fourteenth of the moon, like the Jews, on any day of the week, but on the Lord's day, from the fourteenth to the twentieth of the moon; and this he did from his belief that the Resurrection of our Lord happened on the first day of the week, and for the hope of our resurrection, which also he, with the holy Church, believed would truly happen on that same first day of the week, now called the Lord's day.

CHAP. XVIII. *Of the life and death of the religious King Sigbert.* [*Circ.* 631 A.D.]

AT this time, the kingdom of the East Angles, after the death of Earpwald, the successor of Redwald, was

---

[1] Cf. c. 3.

governed by his brother Sigbert,[1] a good and religious man, who some time before had been baptized in Gaul, whilst he lived in banishment, a fugitive from the enmity of Redwald. When he returned home, as soon as he ascended the throne, being desirous to imitate the good institutions which he had seen in Gaul, he founded a school wherein boys should be taught letters, and was assisted therein by Bishop Felix, who came to him from Kent, and who furnished them with masters and teachers after the manner of the people of Kent.[2]

This king became so great a lover of the heavenly kingdom, that at last, quitting the affairs of his kingdom, and committing them to his kinsman Ecgric, who before had a share in that kingdom, he entered a monastery, which he had built for himself, and having received the tonsure, applied himself rather to do battle for a heavenly throne. A long time after this, it happened that the nation of the Mercians, under King Penda, made war on the East Angles; who finding themselves no match for their enemy, entreated Sigbert to go with them to battle, to encourage the soldiers. He was unwilling and refused, upon which they drew him against his will out of the monastery, and carried him to the army, hoping that the soldiers would be less afraid and less disposed to flee in the presence of one who had formerly been an active and distinguished commander. But he, still mindful of his profession, surrounded, as he was, by a royal army, would carry nothing in his hand but a wand, and was killed with King Ecgric; and the pagans pressing on, all their army was either slaughtered or dispersed.

They were succeeded in the kingdom by Anna,[3] the son of Eni, of the blood royal, a good man, and the

---

[1] II, 15, and note.

[2] Cf. *ib.* The school was probably in the episcopal city of Dunwich, though it has been maintained that it was the origin of Cambridge University. For this there seems to be no authority except a seventeenth century addition to this passage in a twelfth or thirteenth century MS: "Grantebrig schola a Sigberto Rege."

[3] Cf. c. 7, p. 149, and note.

father of good children, of whom, in the proper place, we shall speak hereafter. He also was afterwards slain like his predecessors by the same pagan chief of the Mercians.

CHAP. XIX. *How Fursa built a monastery among the East Angles, and of his visions and sanctity, to which, his flesh remaining uncorrupted after death bore testimony. [Circ. 633 A.D.]*

WHILST Sigbert still governed the kingdom, there came out of Ireland a holy man called Fursa,[1] renowned both for his words and actions, and remarkable for singular virtues, being desirous to live as a stranger and pilgrim for the Lord's sake, wherever an opportunity should offer. On coming into the province of the East Angles, he was honourably received by the aforesaid king, and performing his wonted task of preaching the Gospel, by the example of his virtue and the influence of his words, converted many unbelievers to Christ, and confirmed in the faith and love of Christ those that already believed.

Here he fell into some infirmity of body, and was thought worthy to see a vision of angels; in which he was admonished diligently to persevere in the ministry of the Word which he had undertaken, and indefatigably to apply himself to his usual watching and prayers; inasmuch as his end was certain, but the hour thereof uncertain, according to the saying of our Lord, "Watch therefore, for ye know neither the day nor the hour."[2] Being confirmed by this vision, he set himself with all speed to build a monastery on the ground which had been given him by King Sigbert, and to establish a rule

---

[1] For a full account of St. Fursa and his brothers, and other companions mentioned in this chapter, *v.* Miss Margaret Stokes's "Three months in the Forests of France, a pilgrimage in search of vestiges of the Irish Saints in France." Bede's narrative is taken from an extant ancient Latin life of St. Fursa (or Fursey), the "libellus de vita ejus conscriptus" to which he refers several times (*v. infra*).

[2] St. Matt., xxv, 13.

of life therein. This monastery was pleasantly situated in the woods, near the sea; it was built within the area of a fort, which in the English language is called Cnobheresburg, that is, Cnobhere's Town;[1] afterwards, Anna, king of that province, and certain of the nobles, embellished it with more stately buildings and with gifts.

This man was of noble Scottish[2] blood, but much more noble in mind than in birth. From his boyish years, he had earnestly applied himself to reading sacred books and observing monastic discipline, and, as is most fitting for holy men, he carefully practised all that he learned to be right.

Now, in course of time he himself built a monastery,[3] wherein he might with more freedom devote himself to his heavenly studies. There, falling sick, as the book concerning his life clearly informs us, he fell into a trance, and quitting his body from the evening till cockcrow, he was accounted worthy to behold the sight of the choirs of angels, and to hear their glad songs of praise. He was wont to declare, that among other things he distinctly heard this refrain: "The saints shall go from strength to strength."[4] And again, "The God of gods shall be seen in Sion."[5] Being restored to his body, and again taken from it three days after, he not only saw the greater joys of the blessed, but also fierce conflicts of evil spirits, who by frequent accusations wickedly endeavoured to obstruct his journey to heaven; but the angels protected him, and all their endeavours were in vain. Concerning all these matters, if any one desires to be more fully informed, to wit, with what subtlety of deceit the devils recounted both his actions and idle words, and even his thoughts, as if they had been written down in a book;

[1] Burgh Castle in Suffolk, where there was a Roman fortress, Garianonum.

[2] *I.e.*, Irish.

[3] His monastery on Lough Corrib. It is obvious from the sequel that this vision was prior to his journey to Britain, and is distinct from the vision mentioned above.

[4] Ps. lxxxiv, 7; (lxxxiii, 8, in the Vulgate). The reading is that of the Vulgate and the Gallican Psalter: "Ibunt de virtute in virtutem: videbitur Deus deorum in Sion."   [5] *Ibid.*

and what joyous or grievous tidings he learned from the holy angels and just men who appeared to him among the angels; let him read the little book of his life which I have mentioned, and I doubt not that he will thereby reap much spiritual profit.

But there is one thing among the rest, which we have thought it may be beneficial to many to insert in this history. When he had been taken up on high, he was bidden by the angels that conducted him to look back upon the world. Upon which, casting his eyes downward, he saw, as it were, a dark valley in the depths underneath him. He also saw four fires in the air, not far distant from each other. Then asking the angels, what fires those were, he was told, they were the fires which would kindle and consume the world. One of them was of falsehood, when we do not fulfil that which we promised in Baptism, to renounce the Devil and all his works. The next was of covetousness, when we prefer the riches of the world to the love of heavenly things. The third was of discord, when we do not fear to offend our neighbour even in needless things. The fourth was of ruthlessness when we think it a light thing to rob and to defraud the weak. These fires, increasing by degrees, extended so as to meet one another, and united in one immense flame. When it drew near, fearing for himself, he said to the angel, "Lord, behold the fire draws near to me." The angel answered, "That which you did not kindle will not burn you; for though this appears to be a terrible and great pyre, yet it tries every man according to the merits of his works; for every man's concupiscence shall burn in this fire; for as a man burns in the body through unlawful pleasure, so, when set free from the body, he shall burn by the punishment which he has deserved."

Then he saw one of the three angels, who had been his guides throughout both visions, go before and divide the flaming fires, whilst the other two, flying about on both sides, defended him from the danger of the fire. He also saw devils flying through the fire, raising the flames of war against the just. Then followed

accusations of the envious spirits against himself, the
defence of the good spirits, and a fuller vision of the
heavenly hosts; as also of holy men of his own nation,
who, as he had learnt, had worthily held the office of
priesthood in old times, and who were known to fame;
from whom he heard many things very salutary to himself, and to all others that would listen to them. When
they had ended their discourse, and returned to Heaven
with the angelic spirits, there remained with the blessed
Fursa, the three angels of whom we have spoken
before, and who were to bring him back to the body.
And when they approached the aforesaid great fire, the
angel divided the flame, as he had done before; but
when the man of God came to the passage so opened
amidst the flames, the unclean spirits, laying hold of
one of those whom they were burning in the fire, cast
him against him, and, touching his shoulder and jaw,
scorched them. He knew the man, and called to mind
that he had received his garment when he died. The
holy angel, immediately laying hold of the man, threw
him back into the fire, and the malignant enemy said,
" Do not reject him whom you before received; for as you
received the goods of the sinner, so you ought to share
in his punishment." But the angel withstood him, saying, " He did not receive them through avarice, but in
order to save his soul." The fire ceased, and the angel,
turning to him, said, " That which you kindled burned
you; for if you had not received the money of this man
that died in his sins, his punishment would not burn
you." And he went on to speak with wholesome counsel
of what ought to be done for the salvation of such as
repented in the hour of death.

Being afterwards restored to the body, throughout
the whole course of his life he bore the mark of the fire
which he had felt in the spirit, visible to all men on his
shoulder and jaw; and the flesh openly showed, in a
wonderful manner, what the spirit had suffered in secret.
He always took care, as he had done before, to teach
all men the practice of virtue, as well by his example,
as by preaching. But as for the story of his visions, he

would only relate them to those who, from desire of repentance, questioned him about them. An aged brother of our monastery is still living, who is wont to relate that a very truthful and religious man told him, that he had seen Fursa himself in the province of the East Angles, and heard those visions from his lips; adding, that though it was in severe winter weather and a hard frost, and the man was sitting in a thin garment when he told the story, yet he sweated as if it had been in the heat of mid-summer, by reason of the great terror or joy of which he spoke.

To return to what we were saying before, when, after preaching the Word of God many years in Scotland,[1] he could not well endure the disturbance of the crowds that resorted to him, leaving all that he looked upon as his own, he departed from his native island, and came with a few brothers through the Britons into the province of the English, and preaching the Word there, as has been said, built a famous monastery.[2] When this was duly carried out, he became desirous to rid himself of all business of this world, and even of the monastery itself, and forthwith left the care of it and of its souls, to his brother Fullan, and the priests Gobban and Dicull,[3] and being himself free from all worldly affairs, resolved to end his life as a hermit. He had another brother called Ultan, who, after a long monastic probation, had also adopted the life of an anchorite. So, seeking him out alone, he lived a whole year with him in self-denial and prayer, and laboured daily with his hands.

Afterwards seeing the province thrown into confusion by the irruptions of the pagans,[4] and foreseeing that the

---

[1] *I.e.*, Ireland.　　　　[2] The monastery at Burgh Castle.

[3] Fullan, or Foillan, was apparently a bishop (the others are called " presbyteri "). He and Ultan after Fursa's death (*circ.* 650) went to South Brabant. Ultan founded a monastery at Fosse in the diocese of Liège (then of Maestricht), and Fullan laboured in conjunction with St. Gertrude in the double monastery of Nivelles. Ultan became abbot, first of Fosse and later of Péronne. The name Gobban occurs frequently in Irish Church History, Dicull occasionally. There is a Dicull mentioned in IV, 13.

[4] *I.e.*, the Mercians; *v.s.* c. 18.

N

monasteries would also be in danger, he left all things in order, and sailed over into Gaul, and being there honourably entertained by Clovis, king of the Franks,[1] or by the patrician Ercinwald, he built a monastery in the place called Latineacum,[2] and falling sick not long after, departed this life. The same Ercinwald, the patrician, took his body, and kept it in the porch of a church he was building in his town of Perrona,[3] till the church itself should be dedicated. This happened twenty-seven days after, and the body being taken from the porch, to be re-buried near the altar, was found as whole as if he had died that very hour. And again, four years after, when a more beautiful shrine had been built to receive his body to the east of the altar, it was still found without taint of corruption, and was translated thither with due honour; where it is well known that his merits, through the divine operation, have been declared by many miracles. We have briefly touched upon these matters as well as the incorruption of his body, that the lofty nature of the man may be better known to our readers. All which, as also concerning the comrades of his warfare, whosoever will read it, will find more fully described in the book of his life.

CHAP. XX. *How, when Honorius died, Deusdedit became Archbishop of Canterbury; and of those who were at that time bishops of the East Angles, and of the church of Rochester.* [653 A.D.]

IN the meantime, Felix, bishop of the East Angles, dying, when he had held that see seventeen years,[4]

---

[1] Clovis II, King of Neustria, 638-656. Ercinwald was his Mayor of the Palace.

[2] Lagny on the Marne, near Paris.

[3] Péronne on the Somme. The monastery founded there after his death was called "Perrona Scotorum" from the number of Irish who resorted to it.

[4] *Circ.* 647. The rapid increase in the number of native bishops may be seen from this chapter. The only one before Thomas was Ithamar (cf. c. 14, p. 164).

Honorius ordained Thomas his deacon, of the province of the Gyrwas,[1] in his place; and he being taken from this life when he had been bishop five years, Bertgils, surnamed Boniface,[2] of the province of Kent, was appointed in his stead. Honorius[3] himself also, having run his course, departed this life in the year of our Lord 653, on the 30th of September; and when the see had been vacant a year and six months, Deusdedit[4] of the nation of the West Saxons, was chosen the sixth Archbishop of Canterbury. To ordain him, Ithamar,[5] bishop of Rochester, came thither. His ordination was on the 26th of March, and he ruled the church nine years, four months, and two days; and when Ithamar died, he consecrated in his place Damian,[6] who was of the race of the South Saxons.

CHAP. XXI. *How the province of the Midland Angles became Christian under King Peada.* [653 A.D.]

AT this time, the Middle Angles, that is, the Angles of the Midland country,[7] under their Prince Peada, the son of King Penda, received the faith and mysteries of the truth.

[1] The Fen country. The province included part of the counties of Lincoln, Northampton, Huntingdon, and Cambridge.
[2] Such changes of name were frequent: cf. Benedict for Biscop (IV, 18), Boniface for Winfrid (*v.* " Continuation "), Clement for Wilbrord (V, 11), and cf. *infra*, " Deusdedit."
[3] II, 15, note.
[4] The first archbishop of English birth. He died in 664 (*v.* IV, 1). His original name is said to have been Frithonas; Deusdedit is the Latin form of Theodore. There was a Pope of the same name, 615-618 (*v.* II, 7). Similar names were common in the African Church, *e.g.*, " Adeodatus," " Habetdeus," " Quodvultdeus," " Deogratias." [5] Cf. c. 14, and note.
[6] Cf. IV, 2. It has been supposed that he died of the plague of 664. After his death the see was vacant for several years. It is remarkable that he came of a race which had not yet become Christian. The South Saxons continued to be pagan till Wilfrid evangelized them, 681-686 (IV, 13).
[7] For their origin, *v.* I, 15. Their country, which was subject to Mercia, was the present Leicestershire. They are probably to be identified with the Southern Mercians; *v.* c. 24, where we find Peada confirmed by Oswy in the government of that people.

Being an excellent youth, and most worthy of the name
and office of a king, he was by his father elevated to the
throne of that nation, and came to Oswy, king of the
Northumbrians, requesting to have his daughter Alch-
fled [1] given him to wife; but he could not obtain his desire
unless he would receive the faith of Christ, and be baptized, with the nation which he governed. When he
heard the preaching of the truth, the promise of the
heavenly kingdom, and the hope of resurrection and
future immortality, he declared that he would willingly
become a Christian, even though he should not obtain
the maiden; being chiefly prevailed on to receive the
faith by King Oswy's son Alchfrid,[2] who was his brother-
in-law and friend, for he had married his sister Cyne-
burg,[3] the daughter of King Penda.

Accordingly he was baptized by Bishop Finan, with
all his his nobles and thegns,[4] and their servants, that
came along with him, at a noted township, belonging to
the king, called At the Wall.[5] And having received four
priests, who by reason of their learning and good life
were deemed proper to instruct and baptize his nation,
he returned home with much joy. These priests were
Cedd and Adda, and Betti and Diuma;[6] the last of whom
was by nation a Scot, the others English. Adda was
brother to Utta, whom we have mentioned before,[7] a
renowned priest, and abbot of the monastery which is
called At the Goat's Head.[8] The aforesaid priests,

[1] She caused his death by treachery: v. c. 24 *ad fin.*
[2] C. 14, *ad init.*, and note.
[3] After Alchfrid's death, she took the veil and ruled the monastery of Caistor (? Cyneburgacaster) in Northamptonshire. She
was one of the five children of the heathen Penda, who were
canonized as saints.
[4] *Comitibus ac militibus.* A.S. "geferum" (companions) and
"king's thegns."
[5] Cf. c. 22. Variously identified with Walton and Walbottle,
both near Newcastle. For the preposition, v. II, 14, p. 119, note 5.
[6] For Cedd, v. Preface, and *infra* cc. 22, 23, 25, 26. The names
of Adda and Betti do not occur again. For Diuma: v. *infra* and
c. 24. [7] III, 15.
[8] Gateshead on the Tyne, opposite Newcastle. For the prepos
tion, cf. II, 14, p. 119, note 5.

arriving in the province with the prince, preached the Word, and were heard willingly; and many, as well of the nobility as the common sort, renouncing the abominations of idolatry, were daily washed in the fountain of the faith.

Nor did King Penda forbid the preaching of the Word even among his people, the Mercians, if any were willing to hear it; but, on the contrary, he hated and despised those whom he perceived to be without the works of faith, when they had once received the faith of Christ, saying, that they were contemptible and wretched who scorned to obey their God, in whom they believed. These things were set on foot two years before the death of King Penda.

But when he was slain, and the most Christian king, Oswy, succeeded him in the throne, as we shall hereafter relate, Diuma,[1] one of the aforesaid four priests, was made bishop of the Midland Angles, as also of the Mercians, being ordained by Bishop Finan; for the scarcity of priests made it necessary that one prelate should be set over two nations. Having in a short time gained many people to the Lord, he died among the Midland Angles, in the country called Infeppingum;[2] and Ceollach, also of the Scottish nation, succeeded him in the bishopric. But he, not long after, left his bishopric, and returned to the island of Hii,[3] which, among the Scots, was the chief and head of many monasteries. His successor in the bishopric was Trumhere,[4] a godly man, and trained in the monastic life, an Englishman, but ordained bishop by the Scots. This happened in the days of King Wulfhere, of whom we shall speak hereafter.

[1] Penda was killed in 655. Diuma was probably consecrated in 656.
[2] Not identified. Perhaps Repton (Reppington) in Derbyshire, where it is supposed that Diuma had fixed his see. For the form of the name, cf. II, 14, p. 119, note 5.
[3] He probably returned at the time of the rebellion of Mercia in 658; v. c. 24, ad fin. For Hii, v.s. c. 3, ad fin.
[4] Abbot of Gilling. He was a kinsman of Oswin: v. c. 24, p. 191.

CHAP. XXII. *How under King Sigbert, through the preaching of Cedd, the East Saxons again received the faith, which they had before cast off.* [653 A.D.]

AT that time, also, the East Saxons, at the instance of King Oswy, again received the faith, which they had formerly cast off when they expelled Mellitus, their bishop.[1] For Sigbert,[2] who reigned next to Sigbert surnamed The Little, was then king of that nation, and a friend to King Oswy, who, when Sigbert came to the province of the Northumbrians to visit him, as he often did, used to endeavour to convince him that those could not be gods that had been made by the hands of men; that a stock or a stone could not be proper matter to form a god, the residue whereof was either burned in the fire, or framed into any vessels for the use of men, or else was cast out as refuse, trampled on and turned into dust. That God is rather to be understood as incomprehensible in majesty and invisible to human eyes, almighty, eternal, the Creator of heaven and earth and of mankind; Who governs and will judge the world in righteousness, Whose eternal abode must be believed to be in Heaven, and not in base and perishable metal; and that it ought in reason to be concluded, that all those who learn and do the will of Him by Whom they were created, will receive from Him eternal rewards. King Oswy having often, with friendly counsel, like a brother, said this and much more to the like effect to King Sigbert, at length, aided by the consent of his friends, he believed, and after he had consulted with those about him, and exhorted them, when they all agreed and assented to the faith, he was baptized with them by Bishop Finan, in the king's township above spoken of, which is called At the Wall,[3] because it is close by the

---

[1] Cf. II, 5. Since then, the East Saxons had remained pagan.
[2] Sometimes surnamed the "Good." (He must not be confused with Sigbert, King of the East Angles, II, 15, and III, 18, 19.) Sigbert the Little was the successor of the three young kings who expelled Mellitus (II, 5).　　　　　　[3] C. 21 and note.

wall which the Romans formerly drew across the island of Britain, at the distance of twelve miles from the eastern sea.

King Sigbert, having now become a citizen of the eternal kingdom, returned to the seat of his temporal kingdom, requesting of King Oswy that he would give him some teachers, to convert his nation to the faith of Christ, and cleanse them in the fountain of salvation. Wherefore Oswy, sending into the province of the Midland Angles, summoned the man of God, Cedd,[1] and, giving him another priest for his companion, sent them to preach the Word to the East Saxons. When these two, travelling to all parts of that country, had gathered a numerous Church to the Lord, it happened once that Cedd returned home, and came to the church of Lindisfarne to confer with Bishop Finan; who, finding that the work of the Gospel had prospered in his hands, made him bishop of the nation of the East Saxons, calling to him two other bishops[2] to assist at the ordination. Cedd, having received the episcopal dignity, returned to his province, and pursuing the work he had begun with more ample authority, built churches in divers places, and ordained priests and deacons to assist him in the Word of faith, and the ministry of Baptism,[3] especially in the city which, in the language of the Saxons, is called Ythancaestir,[4] as also in that which is named Tilaburg.[5] The first of these places is on the bank of the Pant, the other on the bank of the Thames. In these, gathering a flock of Christ's servants, he taught them to observe the discipline of a rule of life, as far as those rude people were then capable of receiving it.

[1] C. 21 and note.
[2] They must have been Celtic bishops, probably of the Irish Church and subject to the authority of Iona. Cedd seems to have had no fixed see. He is not called Bishop of London, like Mellitus.
[3] Dr. Bright regards this organization as a foreshadowing of the parochial system, which, however, was not thoroughly established till long after.
[4] Identified with the Roman military station, Othona, on the Blackwater, formerly called the Pant, in Essex. The town is now submerged.   [5] Tilbury.

Whilst the teaching of the everlasting life was thus, for no small time, making daily increase in that province to the joy of the king and of all the people, it happened that the king, at the instigation of the enemy of all good men, was murdered by his own kindred. They were two brothers who did this wicked deed; and being asked what had moved them to it, they had nothing else to answer, but that they had been incensed against the king, and hated him, because he was too apt to spare his enemies, and calmly forgave the wrongs they had done him, upon their entreaty. Such was the crime for which the king was killed, because he observed the precepts of the Gospel with a devout heart; but in this innocent death his real offence was also punished, according to the prediction of the man of God. For one of those nobles[1] that murdered him was unlawfully married, and when the bishop was not able to prevent or correct the sin, he excommunicated him, and commanded all that would give ear to him not to enter this man's house, nor to eat of his meat. But the king made light of this command, and being invited by the noble, went to a banquet at his house. As he was going thence, the bishop met him. The king, beholding him, immediately dismounted from his horse, trembling, and fell down at his feet, begging pardon for his offence; for the bishop, who was likewise on horse-back, had also alighted. Being much incensed, he touched the prostrate king with the rod he held in his hand, and spoke thus with the authority of his office: "I tell thee, forasmuch as thou wouldest not refrain from the house of that sinful and condemned man, thou shalt die in that very house." Yet it is to be believed, that such a death of a religious man not only blotted out his offence, but even added to his merit; because it happened on account of his piety and his observance of the commands of Christ.

Sigbert was succeeded in the kingdom by Suidhelm,[2] the son of Sexbald, who was baptized by the same

[1] *Comes.* A.S. "gesith."
[2] He was his brother probably. But the relationships of these East Saxon kings are very difficult to determine.

Cedd, in the province of the East Angles, in the royal township, called Rendlaesham,[1] that is, Rendil's Dwelling; and Ethelwald,[2] king of the East Angles, brother to Anna, king of the same people, received him as he came forth from the holy font.

CHAP. XXIII. *How Bishop Cedd, having a place for building a monastery given him by King Ethelwald, consecrated it to the Lord with prayer and fasting; and concerning his death.* [659-664 A.D.]

THE same man of God, whilst he was bishop among the East Saxons, was also wont oftentimes to visit his own province, Northumbria, for the purpose of exhortation. Oidilwald,[3] the son of King Oswald, who reigned among the Deiri, finding him a holy, wise, and good man, desired him to accept some land whereon to build a monastery, to which the king himself might frequently resort, to pray to the Lord and hear the Word, and where he might be buried when he died; for he believed faithfully that he should receive much benefit from the daily prayers of those who were to serve the Lord in that place. The king had before with him a brother of the same bishop, called Caelin, a man no less devoted to God, who, being a priest, was wont to administer to him and his house the Word and the Sacraments of the faith; by whose means he chiefly came to know and love the bishop. So then, complying with the king's desires, the Bishop chose himself a place whereon to build a monastery among steep and distant mountains, which looked more like lurking-places for robbers and dens of wild beasts, than dwellings of men; to the end that, according

[1] Rendlesham in Suffolk.
[2] Distinguish from Ethelwald, or Oidilwald, sub-King of Deira (*v.s.* c. 14, and *infra* cc. 23, 24). Ethelwald, King of the East Angles, succeeded his brother, Ethelhere, who was the successor of Anna (cf. *supra* cc. 7, 18, 19), and was killed in the battle of the Winwaed (*v. infra* c. 24).
[3] Cf. *supra* c. 14; *infra* c. 24. Apparently he succeeded Oswin as sub-King of Deira.

to the prophecy of Isaiah, "In the habitation of dragons, where each lay, might be grass with reeds and rushes;"[1] that is, that the fruits of good works should spring up, where before beasts were wont to dwell, or men to live after the manner of beasts.

But the man of God, desiring first to cleanse the place which he had received for the monastery from stain of former crimes, by prayer and fasting, and so to lay the foundations there, requested of the king that he would give him opportunity and leave to abide there for prayer all the time of Lent, which was at hand. All which days, except Sundays, he prolonged his fast till the evening, according to custom, and then took no other sustenance than a small piece of bread, one hen's egg, and a little milk and water. This, he said, was the custom of those of whom he had learned the rule of regular discipline, first to consecrate to the Lord, by prayer and fasting, the places which they had newly received for building a monastery or a church. When there were ten days of Lent still remaining, there came a messenger to call him to the king; and he, that the holy work might not be intermitted, on account of the king's affairs, entreated his priest, Cynibill, who was also his own brother, to complete his pious undertaking. Cynibill readily consented, and when the duty of fasting and prayer was over, he there built the monastery, which is now called Laestingaeu,[2] and established therein religious customs according to the use of Lindisfarne, where he had been trained.

When Cedd had for many years held the office of bishop in the aforesaid province, and also taken charge of this monastery, over which he placed provosts,[3] it happened that he came thither at a time when there was plague, and fell sick and died. He was first buried

[1] Isaiah, xxxv, 7.
[2] Lastingham (v. Preface). Cedd was its first abbot, though it was not in his own diocese.
[3] Doubtless only one at a time. The "Provost" is the prior of later times. The charge of the monastery would devolve upon him while Cedd was absent in his diocese.

without the walls; but in the process of time a church was built of stone in the monastery, in honour of the Blessed Mother of God, and his body was laid in it, on the right side of the altar.

The bishop left the monastery to be governed after him by his brother Ceadda,[1] who was afterwards made bishop, as shall be told hereafter. For, as it rarely happens, the four brothers we have mentioned, Cedd and Cynibill, and Caelin and Ceadda, were all celebrated priests of the Lord, and two of them also came to be bishops. When the brethren who were in his monastery, in the province of the East Saxons,[2] heard that the bishop was dead and buried in the province of the Northumbrians, about thirty men of that monastery came thither, being desirous either to live near the body of their father, if it should please God, or to die and be buried there. Being gladly received by their brethren and fellow soldiers in Christ, all of them died there struck down by the aforesaid pestilence, except one little boy, who is known to have been saved from death by the prayers of his spiritual father. For being alive long after, and giving himself to the reading of Scripture, he was told that he had not been regenerated by the water of Baptism, and being then cleansed in the laver of salvation, he was afterwards promoted to the order of priesthood, and was of service to many in the church. I do not doubt that he was delivered at the point of death, as I have said, by the intercession of his father, to whose body he had come for love of him, that so he might himself avoid eternal death, and by teaching, offer the ministry of life and salvation to others of the brethren.

[1] Or, as he is commonly called, St. Chad, the greatest of this remarkable group of brothers; *v.* Preface and *infra passim.*
[2] Ythancaestir, or Tilbury (*v.* c. 22).

CHAP. XXIV. *How when King Penda was slain, the province of the Mercians received the faith of Christ, and Oswy gave possessions and territories to God, for building monasteries, as a thank offering for the victory obtained.* [655 A.D.]

AT this time, King Oswy was exposed to the cruel and intolerable invasions of Penda, king of the Mercians, whom we have so often mentioned, and who had slain his brother;[1] at length, compelled by his necessity, he promised to give him countless gifts and royal marks of honour greater than can be believed, to purchase peace; provided that he would return home, and cease to waste and utterly destroy the provinces of his kingdom. The pagan king refused to grant his request, for he had resolved to blot out and extirpate all his nation, from the highest to the lowest; whereupon King Oswy had recourse to the protection of the Divine pity for deliverance from his barbarous and pitiless foe, and binding himself by a vow, said, "If the pagan will not accept our gifts, let us offer them to Him that will, the Lord our God." He then vowed, that if he should win the victory, he would dedicate his daughter to the Lord in holy virginity, and give twelve pieces of land whereon to build monasteries. After this he gave battle with a very small army: indeed, it is reported that the pagans had thirty times the number of men; for they had thirty legions, drawn up under most noted commanders.[2] King Oswy and his son Alchfrid met them with a very small army, as has been said, but trusting in Christ as their Leader; his other son, Egfrid,[3] was then kept as a hostage at the court of Queen Cynwise,[4]

---

[1] Oswald; *v.s.* c. 9.

[2] "Ealdormen," Green, "Making of England," p. 301. But they probably included many British chiefs (*v.* Nennius, and cf. *infra* "duces regii ").

[3] Oswy's younger son. He succeeded his father in 670 or 671 (*v.* IV, 5, and for the events of his reign, IV, V, *passim*).

[4] The wife of Penda.

in the province of the Mercians. King Oswald's son
Oidilwald,[1] who ought to have supported them, was on
the enemy's side, and led them on to fight against his
country and his uncle; though, during the battle, he withdrew, and awaited the event in a place of safety. The
engagement began, the pagans were put to flight or
killed, the thirty royal commanders, who had come to
Penda's assistance, were almost all of them slain; among
whom was Ethelhere,[2] brother and successor to Anna,
king of the East Angles. He had been the occasion of
the war, and was now killed, having lost his army
and auxiliaries. The battle was fought near the river
Winwaed,[3] which then, owing to the great rains, was in
flood, and had overflowed its banks, so that many more
were drowned in the flight than destroyed in battle by
the sword.

Then King Oswy, according to the vow he had made to
the Lord, returned thanks to God for the victory granted
him, and gave his daughter Elfled,[4] who was scarce a
year old, to be consecrated to Him in perpetual virginity;
bestowing also twelve small estates of land, wherein the

[1] Cc. 14 and 23. The reason for his conduct is not explained.
Probably he had hoped to establish his claims on Northumbria
through Penda's assistance, but shrank from actually fighting
against his country.

[2] Cf. c. 22, *ad fin.*, note. How he gave occasion for the war is
not known.

[3] The river has not been identified, and there is great uncertainty
even with regard to the district. Below, Bede says that Oswy
concluded the war in the district of "Loidis," by which he must
mean Leeds, as in II, 14, and most commentators adopt this view.
In this case, the river may be the Aire, or more probably the
Went, a tributary of the Don. Others believe the district to be the
Lothians, following the account in Nennius, who describes Oswy
as taking refuge before the battle in a city called Iudeu, supposed to be either Edinburgh or Carriden (cf. I, 12, note), and
the river has been supposed to be the Avon in Linlithgow.

[4] She is mentioned as joint-abbess with her mother, Eanfled, of
the monastery of Whitby (IV, 26). Eddius calls her " sapientissima
virgo," " semper totius provinciae consolatrix optimaque consilia-
trix." Her influence helped to restore Wilfrid to the bishopric.
She was the friend of St. Cuthbert, who is said to have wrought a
miraculous cure on her behalf. It was to her that he prophesied
the death of her brother Egfrid (IV, 26, p. 285, note).

expelling the ealdormen of the foreign king, they bravely
recovered at once their liberty and their lands; and being
thus free, together with their king, they rejoiced to serve
Christ the true King, for the sake of an everlasting
kingdom in heaven. This king governed the Mercians
seventeen years, and had for his first bishop Trumhere,[1]
above spoken of; the second was Jaruman;[2] the third
Ceadda;[3] the fourth Wynfrid.[4] All these, succeeding
each other in order under King Wulfhere, discharged
episcopal duties to the Mercian nation.

CHAP. XXV. *How the question arose about the due time
of keeping Easter, with those that came out of Scotland.*[5]
[664 A.D.]

IN the meantime, Bishop Aidan being taken away from
this life, Finan, who was ordained and sent by the
Scots, succeeded him in the bishopric, and built a church
in the Isle of Lindisfarne, fit for the episcopal see;
nevertheless, after the manner of the Scots, he made it,
not of stone, but entirely of hewn oak, and covered it
with reeds; and it was afterwards dedicated in honour
of the blessed Peter the Apostle, by the most reverend
Archbishop Theodore. Eadbert,[6] also bishop of that
place, took off the thatch, and caused it to be covered
entirely, both roof and walls, with plates of lead.

his power to the north of the Humber ended in 675 in his disastrous
defeat by Egfrid, King of Northumbria (IV, 12) and his death
followed immediately after. He was the first Christian king of all
Mercia, and he was zealous in putting down idolatry (Florence of
Worcester).
    [1] Cf. *supra* and c. 21.
    [2] He succeeded in 662. Cf. c. 30.
    [3] C. 23, p. 187, and note.
    [4] IV, 3, 5, 6. He was deposed by Theodore for some act of
disobedience not known (IV, 6), and went to the Continent, where,
travelling in Neustria, he was mistaken for Wilfrid and cruelly ill-
treated by the emissaries of Ebroin (*v.* V, 19, note), " errore bono
unius syllabae seducti," as Eddius, the biographer of Wilfrid,
remarks.   [5] *I.e.*, Ireland.
    [6] He succeeded Cuthbert as Bishop of Lindisfarne; *v.* IV, 29, 30.

At this time, a great and frequently debated question arose about the observance of Easter;[1] those that came from Kent or Gaul affirming, that the Scots celebrated Easter Sunday contrary to the custom of the universal Church. Among them was a most zealous defender of the true Easter, whose name was Ronan,[2] a Scot by nation, but instructed in the rule of ecclesiastical truth in Gaul or Italy. Disputing with Finan, he convinced many, or at least induced them to make a more strict inquiry after the truth; yet he could not prevail upon Finan, but, on the contrary, embittered him the more by reproof, and made him a professed opponent of the truth, for he was of a violent temper. James,[3] formerly the deacon of the venerable Archbishop Paulinus, as has been said above, observed the true and Catholic Easter, with all those that he could instruct in the better way. Queen Eanfled and her followers also observed it as she had seen it practised in Kent, having with her a Kentish priest who followed the Catholic observance, whose name was Romanus. Thus it is said to have sometimes happened in those times that Easter was twice celebrated in one year; and that when the king, having ended his fast, was keeping Easter, the queen and her followers were still fasting, and celebrating Palm Sunday. Whilst Aidan lived, this difference about the observance of Easter was patiently tolerated by all men, for they well knew, that though he could not keep Easter contrary to the custom of those who had sent him, yet he industriously laboured to practise the works of faith, piety, and love, according to the custom of all holy men; for which reason he was deservedly beloved by all, even by those who differed in opinion concerning Easter, and was held in veneration, not only by less important persons, but even by the bishops, Honorius of Canterbury, and Felix of the East Angles.

But after the death of Finan, who succeeded him,

---

[1] Cf. II, 2, p. 84, note 3.
[2] Nothing certain is known of him.
[3] II, 16, 20; IV, 2.

O

when Colman, who was also sent from Scotland,[1] came to be bishop, a greater controversy arose about the observance of Easter, and other rules of ecclesiastical life. Whereupon this question began naturally to influence the thoughts and hearts of many who feared, lest haply, having received the name of Christians, they might run, or have run, in vain. This reached the ears of the rulers, King Oswy and his son Alchfrid. Now Oswy, having been instructed and baptized by the Scots, and being very perfectly skilled in their language, thought nothing better than what they taught; but Alchfrid, having for his teacher in Christianity the learned Wilfrid,[2] who had formerly gone to Rome to study ecclesiastical doctrine, and spent much time at Lyons with Dalfinus,[3] archbishop of Gaul, from whom also he had received the crown of ecclesiastical tonsure, rightly thought that this man's doctrine ought to be preferred before all the traditions of the Scots. For this reason he had also given him a monastery of forty families, at a place called Inhrypum;[4] which place, not long before, he had given for a monastery to those that were followers of the Scots; but forasmuch as they afterwards, being left to their choice, preferred to quit the place rather than alter their custom, he gave it to him, whose life and doctrine were worthy of it.

Agilbert, bishop of the West Saxons,[5] above-men-

---

[1] *I.e.*, Iona: cf. IV, 4, *ad init.* Colman succeeded in 661.

[2] For his life: *v.* V, 19.

[3] Really Annemundus. He was Archbishop of Lyons. Cf. V, 8, note on Godwin. He is confused with his brother Dalfinus, Count of Lyons: *v.* V, 19, p. 348, note.

[4] Ripon. For the preposition, cf. II, 14, p. 119, note 5. The monastery was first given to Eata (*v.* c. 26), to be organized by him, and among the monks he brought with him from Melrose was Cuthbert (cf. IV, 27). They were forced to retire in 661, but after the Synod of Whitby they conformed to the Catholic rules.

[5] Cf. c. 7, where Bede's summary account obscures the sequence of events. Here he is still called Bishop of the West Saxons. It is probable that he had retired from Wessex by this time, but had not yet gone to Gaul. He did not become Bishop of Paris before 666, for in that year we find his predecessor, Importunus, witnessing a "privilegium" for a nunnery at Soissons.

tioned, a friend of King Alchfrid and of Abbot Wilfrid, had at that time come into the province of the Northumbrians, and was staying some time among them; at the request of Alchfrid, he made Wilfrid a priest in his aforesaid monastery. He had in his company a priest, whose name was Agatho.[1] The question being raised there .concerning Easter and the tonsure and other ecclesiastical matters, it was arranged, (that a synod should be held in the monastery of Streanaeshalch,[2] which signifies the Bay of the Lighthouse, where the Abbess Hilda,[3] a woman devoted to the service of God, then ruled; and that there this question should be decided.) The kings, both father and son, came thither, and the bishops, Colman with his Scottish clerks, and Agilbert with the priests Agatho and Wilfrid. James and Romanus were on their side; but the Abbess Hilda and her followers were for the Scots, as was also the venerable Bishop Cedd,[4] long before ordained by the Scots, as has been said above, and he acted in that council as a most careful interpreter for both parties.

King Oswy first made an opening speech, in which he said that it behoved those who served one God to observe one rule of life; and as they all expected the same kingdom in heaven, so they ought not to differ in the celebration of the heavenly mysteries; but rather to inquire which was the truer tradition, that it might be followed by all in common; he then commanded his bishop, Colman, first to declare what the custom was which he observed, and whence it derived its origin. Then Colman said, "The Easter which I keep, I received from my elders, who sent me hither as bishop; all our forefathers, men beloved of God, are known to have celebrated it after the same manner; and that it may not seem to any contemptible and worthy to be

[1] We hear nothing more of this priest.
[2] C. 24. The etymology is generally considered impossible. But cf. Bright, "Early English Church History," p. 213.
[3] C. 24. After the Synod it appears that she conformed to the Catholic usages. But she continued to be an opponent of Wilfrid till the end of her life.   [4] Cc. 21, 22, 23.

rejected, it is the same which the blessed John the Evangelist, the disciple specially beloved of our Lord, with all the churches over which he presided, is recorded to have celebrated."[1] When he had said thus much, and more to the like effect, the king commanded Agilbert to make known the manner of his observance and to show whence it was derived, and on what authority he followed it. Agilbert answered, "I beseech you, let my disciple, the priest Wilfrid, speak in my stead; because we both concur with the other followers of the ecclesiastical tradition that are here present, and he can better and more clearly explain our opinion in the English language, than I can by an interpreter."

Then Wilfrid, being ordered by the king to speak, began thus:—"The Easter which we keep, we saw celebrated by all at Rome, where the blessed Apostles, Peter and Paul, lived, taught, suffered, and were buried; we saw the same done by all in Italy and in Gaul, when we travelled through those countries for the purpose of study and prayer. We found it observed in Africa, Asia, Egypt, Greece, and all the world, wherever the Church of Christ is spread abroad, among divers nations and tongues, at one and the same time; save only among these and their accomplices in obstinacy, I mean the Picts and the Britons, who foolishly, in these two remote islands of the ocean, and only in part even of them, strive to oppose all the rest of the world." When he had so said, Colman answered, "It is strange that you choose to call our efforts foolish, wherein we follow the example of so great an Apostle, who was thought worthy to lean on our Lord's bosom, when all the world knows him to have lived most wisely." Wilfrid replied, "Far be it from us to charge John with folly, for he literally observed the precepts of the Mosaic Law, whilst the

[1] The practice of the churches of Asia, traditionally derived from St. John, was to disregard the day of the week and observe as Easter Day the 14th of the month Nisan. Therefore the claim to the authority of St. John, advanced by the Celts, was inaccurate and gives some colour to the charge, often brought against them, of being "Quartodecimans."

Church was still Jewish in many points, and the Apostles, lest they should give cause of offence to the Jews who were among the Gentiles, were not able at once to cast off all the observances of the Law which had been instituted by God, in the same way as it is necessary that all who come to the faith should forsake the idols which were invented by devils. For this reason it was, that Paul circumcised Timothy,[1] that he offered sacrifice in the temple,[2] that he shaved his head with Aquila and Priscilla at Corinth;[3] for no other advantage than to avoid giving offence to the Jews. Hence it was, that James said to the same Paul, "Thou seest, brother, how many thousands of Jews there are which believe; and they are all zealous of the Law."[4] And yet, at this time, when the light of the Gospel is spreading throughout the world, it is needless, nay, it is not lawful, for the faithful either to be circumcised, or to offer up to God sacrifices of flesh. So John, according to the custom of the Law, began the celebration of the feast of Easter, on the fourteenth day of the first month, in the evening, not regarding whether the same happened on a Saturday, or any other week-day. But when Peter preached at Rome, being mindful that our Lord arose from the dead, and gave to the world the hope of resurrection, on the first day of the week, he perceived that Easter ought to be kept after this manner: he always awaited the rising of the moon on the fourteenth day of the first month in the evening, according to the custom and precepts of the Law, even as John did. And when that came, if the Lord's day, then called the first day of the week, was the next day, he began that very evening to celebrate Easter, as we all do at the present time. But if the Lord's day did not fall the next morning after the fourteenth moon, but on the sixteenth, or the seventeenth, or any other moon till the twenty-first, he waited for that, and on the Saturday before, in the evening, began to observe the holy solemnity of Easter. Thus it came

[1] Acts, xvi, 3.
[3] *Ibid.*, xviii, 18.
[2] *Ibid.*, xxi, 26.
[4] *Ibid.*, xxi, 20.

to pass, that Easter Sunday was only kept from the fifteenth moon to the twenty-first. Nor does this evangelical and apostolic tradition abolish the Law, but rather fulfil it; the command being to keep the passover from the fourteenth moon of the first month in the evening to the twenty-first moon of the same month in the evening; which observance all the successors of the blessed John in Asia, since his death, and all the Church throughout the world, have since followed; and that this is the true Easter, and the only one to be celebrated by the faithful, was not newly decreed by the council of Nicaea, but only confirmed afresh; as the history of the Church informs us.[1]

'Thus it is plain, that you, Colman, neither follow the example of John, as you imagine, nor that of Peter, whose tradition you oppose with full knowledge, and that you neither agree with the Law nor the Gospel in the keeping of your Easter. For John, keeping the Paschal time according to the decree of the Mosaic Law, had no regard to the first day of the week, which you do not practise, seeing that you celebrate Easter only on the first day after the Sabbath. Peter celebrated Easter Sunday between the fifteenth and the twenty-first moon, which you do not practise, seeing that you observe Easter Sunday from the fourteenth to the twentieth moon; so that you often begin Easter on the thirteenth moon in the evening, whereof neither the Law made any mention, nor did our Lord, the Author and Giver of the Gospel, on that day either eat the old passover in the evening, or deliver the Sacraments of the New Testament, to be celebrated by the Church, in memory of His Passion, but on the fourteenth. Besides, in your celebration of Easter, you utterly exclude the twenty-first moon, which the Law ordered to be specially observed. Thus, as I have said before, you agree neither with John nor Peter, nor with the Law, nor the Gospel, in the celebration of the greatest festival."

To this Colman rejoined: "Did the holy Anatolius,[2]

---

[1] Cf. II, 19, note.   [2] Cf. c. 3, note.

much commended in the history of the Church, judge contrary to the Law and the Gospel, when he wrote, that Easter was to be celebrated from the fourteenth to the twentieth moon? Is it to be believed that our most reverend Father Columba and his successors, men beloved by God, who kept Easter after the same manner, judged or acted contrary to the Divine writings? Whereas there were many among them, whose sanctity was attested by heavenly signs and miracles which they wrought; whom I, for my part, doubt not to be saints, and whose life, customs, and discipline I never cease to follow."

" It is evident," said Wilfrid, " that Anatolius was a most holy, learned, and commendable man; but what have you to do with him, since you do not observe his decrees? For he undoubtedly, following the rule of truth in his Easter, appointed a cycle of nineteen years, which either you are ignorant of, or if you know it, though it is kept by the whole Church of Christ, yet you despise it as a thing of naught. He so computed the fourteenth moon in our Lord's Paschal Feast, that according to the custom of the Egyptians, he acknowledged it to be the fifteenth moon on that same day in the evening; so in like manner he assigned the twentieth to Easter-Sunday, as believing that to be the twenty-first moon, when the sun had set. That you are ignorant of the rule of this distinction is proved by this, that you sometimes manifestly keep Easter before the full moon, that is, on the thirteenth day. Concerning your Father Columba and his followers, whose sanctity you say you imitate, and whose rule and precepts confirmed by signs from Heaven you say that you follow, I might answer, then when many, in the day of judgement, shall say to our Lord, that in His name they have prophesied, and have cast out devils, and done many wonderful works, our Lord will reply, that He never knew them. But far be it from me to speak thus of your fathers, for it is much more just to believe good than evil of those whom we know not. Wherefore I do not deny those also to have been God's servants, and beloved of God, who with rude simplicity, but pious intentions, have themselves loved Him. Nor do I think that such observance of Easter did them much harm, as long as none came to show them a more perfect rule to follow; for assuredly I believe that, if any teacher, reckoning after the Catholic manner, had come among them, they would have as readily followed his admonitions, as they are known to have kept those commandments of God, which they had learned and knew.

"But as for you and your companions, you certainly sin, if, having heard the decrees of the Apostolic see, nay, of the universal Church, confirmed, as they are, by Holy Scripture, you scorn to follow them; for, though your fathers were holy, do you think that those few men, in a corner of the remotest island, are to be preferred before the universal Church of Christ throughout the world? And if that Columba of yours, (and, I may say, ours also, if he was Christ's servant,) was a holy man and powerful in miracles, yet could he be preferred before the most blessed chief of the Apostles, to whom our Lord said, ' Thou art Peter, and upon this rock I will build my Church, and the gates of hell shall not prevail against it, and I will give unto thee the keys of the kingdom of Heaven?' "[1]

When Wilfrid had ended thus, the king said, " Is it true, Colman, that these words were spoken to Peter by our Lord?" He answered, "It is true, O king!" Then said he, "Can you show any such power given to your Columba?" Colman answered, "None." Then again the king asked, "Do you both agree in this, without any controversy, that these words were said above all to Peter, and that the keys of the kingdom of Heaven were given to him by our Lord?" They both answered, "Yes." Then the king concluded, "And I also say unto you, that he is the door-keeper, and I will not gainsay him, but I desire, as far as I know and am able, in all things to obey his laws, lest haply when I come to the gates of the kingdom of Heaven, there should be

---

[1] St. Matt., xvi, 18-19.

none to open them, he being my adversary who is proved to have the keys." The king having said this, all who were seated there or standing by, both great and small, gave their assent, and renouncing the less perfect custom, hastened to conform to that which they had found to be better.

CHAP. XXVI. *How Colman, being worsted, returned home; and Tuda succeeded him in the bishopric; and of the state of the church under those teachers.* [664 A.D.]

THE disputation being ended, and the assembly broken up, Agilbert returned home. Colman, perceiving that his doctrine was rejected, and his party despised, took with him those who wished to follow him, to wit, such as would not accept the Catholic Easter and the tonsure in the form of a crown,[1] (for there was no small dispute about that also,) and went back into Scotland,[2] to consult with his people what was to be done in this case. Cedd, forsaking the practices of the Scots, returned to his bishopric, having submitted to the Catholic observance of Easter. This debate took place in the year of our Lord 664, which was the twenty-second year of the reign of King Oswy, and the thirtieth of the episcopate of the Scots among the English; for Aidan was bishop seventeen years, Finan ten, and Colman three.

When Colman had gone back into his own country, Tuda, the servant of Christ, was made bishop of the Northumbrians[3] in his place, having been instructed and ordained bishop among the Southern Scots, having also the crown of the ecclesiastical tonsure, according to the custom of that province, and observing the Catholic rule with regard to the time of Easter.[4] He was a good and religious man, but he governed the church a very short time; he had come from Scotland[5] whilst Colman was

---

[1] Cf. II, 2, p. 85, note 1.   [2] To Iona; *v.* IV, 4, *ad init.*
[3] Fourth Bishop of Lindisfarne and the last of the Irish bishops in that see. He died of the plague in 664: *v.* c. 27.
[4] Cf. c. 3, p. 139, and note.   [5] *I.e.*, Ireland.

yet bishop, and, both by word and deed, diligently taught all men those things that appertain to the faith and truth. But Eata,[1] who was abbot of the monastery called Mailros,[2] a man most reverend and gentle, was appointed abbot over the brethren that chose to remain in the church of Lindisfarne, when the Scots went away. It is said that Colman, upon his departure, requested and obtained this of King Oswy, because Eata was one of Aidan's twelve boys of the English nation,[3] whom he received in the early years of his episcopate, to be instructed in Christ; for the king greatly loved Bishop Colman on account of his innate discretion. This is that Eata, who, not long after, was made bishop of the same church of Lindisfarne. Colman carried home with him part of the bones of the most reverend Father Aidan, and left part of them in the church where he had presided, ordering them to be interred in the sacristy.

The place which they governed shows how frugal and temperate he and his predecessors were, for there were very few houses besides the church found at their departure; indeed, no more than were barely sufficient to make civilized life possible; they had also no money, but only cattle; for if they received any money from rich persons, they immediately gave it to the poor; there being no need to gather money, or provide houses for the entertainment of the great men of the world; for such never resorted to the church, except to pray and hear the Word of God. The king himself, when occasion required, came only with five or six servants, and having performed his devotions in the church, departed. But if they happened to take a repast there, they were satisfied with the plain, daily food of the brethren, and

[1] IV, 12, 27, 28; V, 2.
[2] Old Melrose, "Quod Tuidi fluminis circumflexu maxima ex parte' clauditur," V, 12. The more famous monastery is of later date and is to the west of the older site.
[3] Cf. c. 3, *ad fin.* (where, however, there is only a general allusion to the instruction of English children). It has been suggested that they may have been redeemed from slavery. Cf. c. 5, p. 145.

required no more. For the whole care of those teachers
was to serve God, not the world—to feed the soul, and
not the belly.

For this reason the religious habit was at that time
held in great veneration; so that wheresoever any clerk
or monk went, he was joyfully received by all men, as
God's servant; and even if they chanced to meet him
upon the way, they ran to him, and with bowed head,
were glad to be signed with the cross by his hand, or
blessed by his lips. Great attention was also paid to
their exhortations; and on Sundays they flocked eagerly
to the church, or the monasteries, not to feed their
bodies, but to hear the Word of God; and if any priest
happened to come into a village, the inhabitants came
together and asked of him the Word of life; for the
priests and clerks went to the villages for no other reason
than to preach, baptize, visit the sick, and, in a word,
to take care of souls; and they were so purified from all
taint of avarice, that none of them received lands and
possessions for building monasteries, unless they were
compelled to do so by the temporal authorities; which
custom was for some time after universally observed in
the churches of the Northumbrians. But enough has
now been said on this subject.

CHAP. XXVII. *How Egbert, a holy man of the English
nation, led a monastic life in Ireland.* [664 A.D.]

IN the same year of our Lord 664, there happened an
eclipse of the sun, on the third day of May,[1] about the
tenth hour of the day. In the same year, a sudden
pestilence[2] depopulated first the southern parts of

[1] Really on the 1st.
[2] Called the "Yellow Pest" from the colour of its victims. It
was a bubonic plague; it probably came from the East and was
the same as that which raged in Europe in Justinian's reign.
There were several outbreaks in England in the seventh century,
but this was the most virulent. For subsequent visitations, cf. IV,
7, 14, 19.

Britain, and afterwards attacking the province of the
Northumbrians, ravaged the country far and near, and
destroyed a great multitude of men. By this plague the
aforesaid priest of the Lord, Tuda,[1] was carried off, and
was honourably buried in the monastery called Paegnalaech.[2] Moreover, this plague prevailed no less dis-
astrously in the island of Ireland. Many of the nobility,
and of the lower ranks of the English nation, were
there at that time, who, in the days of the Bishops
Finan and Colman, forsaking their native island, retired
thither, either for the sake of sacred studies, or of a
more ascetic life; and some of them presently devoted
themselves faithfully to a monastic life, others chose
rather to apply themselves to study, going about from
one master's cell to another. The Scots willingly received them all, and took care to supply them with daily
food without cost, as also to furnish them with books
for their studies, and teaching free of charge.

Among these were Ethelhun and Egbert,[3] two youths
of great capacity, of the English nobility. The former
of whom was brother to Ethelwin,[4] a man no less beloved by God, who also at a later time went over into
Ireland to study, and having been well instructed, returned into his own country, and being made bishop in the
province of Lindsey, long and nobly governed the Church.
These two being in the monastery which in the language
of the Scots is called Rathmelsigi,[5] and having lost all
their companions, who were either cut off by the plague,
or dispersed into other places, were both seized by the
same sickness, and grievously afflicted. Of these, Egbert, (as I was informed by a priest venerable for his

---

[1] Cf. c. 26, p. 201.
[2] The Saxon Chronicle has "on Wagele," which is supposed to
be Whalley, on the borders of Lancashire, Cheshire, and Yorkshire, but the name varies greatly in different chroniclers. Smith
considers that Bede's form "Paegnalaech" or "Paegnalech"
points to Finchale (Wincanheale, in Simeon of Durham, or Pin-
cahala), near Durham.
[3] Cf. c. 4.   [4] Cf. c. 11; IV, 12.
[5] Said, on doubtful authority, to be Melfont, or Mellifont, in
County Louth.

age, and of great veracity, who declared he had heard
the story from his own lips,) concluding that he was
at the point of death, went out of the chamber, where
the sick lay, in the morning, and sitting alone in a fitting
place, began seriously to reflect upon his past actions,
and, being full of compunction at the remembrance of
his sins, bedewed his face with tears, and prayed fer-
vently to God that he might not die yet, before he could
forthwith more fully make amends for the careless
offences which he had committed in his boyhood and
infancy, or might further exercise himself in good works.
He also made a vow that he would spend all his life abroad
and never return into the island of Britain, where he was
born; that besides singing the psalms at the canonical
hours, he would, unless prevented by bodily infirmity,
repeat the whole Psalter daily to the praise of God; and
that he would every week fast one whole day and night.
Returning home, after his tears and prayers and vows,
he found his companion asleep; and going to bed himself, he began to compose himself to rest. When he
had lain quiet awhile, his comrade awaking, looked
on him, and said, "Alas! Brother Egbert, what have
you done? I was in hopes that we should have entered
together into life everlasting; but know that your prayer
is granted." For he had learned in a vision what the
other had requested, and that he had obtained his
request.

In brief, Ethelhun died the next night; but Egbert,
throwing off his sickness, recovered and lived a long
time after to grace the episcopal office, which he received, by deeds worthy of it; [1] and blessed with many
virtues, according to his desire, lately, in the year of
our Lord 729, being ninety years of age, he departed to
the heavenly kingdom. He passed his life in great perfection of humility, gentleness, continence, simplicity,
and justice. Thus he was a great benefactor, both to
his own people, and to those nations of the Scots and
Picts among whom he lived in exile, by the example of

---

[1] "Acceptum sacerdotii gradum," A.S. "biscophade onfeng" =
he received the episcopate. Cf. c. 4, note.

his life, his earnestness in teaching, his authority in reproving, and his piety in giving away of those things which he received from the rich. He also added this to the vows which we have mentioned: during Lent, he would eat but one meal a day, allowing himself nothing but bread and thin milk, and even that by measure. The milk, new the day before, he kept in a vessel, and skimming off the cream in the morning, drank the rest, as has been said, with a little bread. Which sort of abstinence he likewise always observed forty days before the Nativity of our Lord, and as many after the solemnity of Pentecost, that is, of the fifty days' festival.

CHAP. XXVIII. *How, when Tuda was dead, Wilfrid was ordained, in Gaul, and Ceadda, among the West Saxons, to be bishops for the province of the Northumbrians.* [664 A.D.]

IN the meantime, King Alchfrid sent the priest, Wilfrid, to the king of Gaul,[1] in order that he should cause him to be consecrated bishop for himself and his people. That prince sent him to be ordained by Agilbert,[2] of whom we have before spoken, and who, having left Britain, was made bishop of the city of Paris;[3] and by him Wilfrid was honourably consecrated, several bishops meeting together for that purpose in a village belonging to the king, called In Compendio.[4] He stayed some

[1] In 664. This was the young "Fainéant" king of Neustria, Clotaire III. Wilfrid was probably sent abroad at his own request. Doubtless he desired to have the canonical number of three bishops at his consecration, and Boniface of Dunwich (c. 20; IV, 5) was the only prelate in England whose orders he would have regarded as entirely satisfactory, for Wini might be considered a usurper, and Cedd and Jaruman had been consecrated by schismatics. Archbishop Deusdedit was dead (III, 20, note) and so probably was Damian of Rochester.

[2] He was Wilfrid's friend: *v.s.* c. 25, pp. 194-5.

[3] Cf. *ibid.*, note.

[4] Compiègne, a royal "villa." For the preposition, *v.* II, 14, note. The ceremony was a specially magnificent one, Wilfrid being carried in a golden chair by twelve bishops in choral procession, according to an ancient custom of the Gallican Church.

time in the parts beyond the sea for his ordination, and King Oswy, following the example of his son's zeal, sent into Kent a holy man, of modest character, well read in the Scripture, and diligently practising those things which he had learned therein, to be ordained bishop of the church of York. This was a priest called Ceadda,[1] brother to the most reverend prelate Cedd, of whom mention has been often made, and abbot of the monastery of Laestingaeu. With him the king also sent his priest Eadhaed,[2] who was afterwards, in the reign of Egfrid,[3] made bishop of the church of Ripon. Now when they arrived in Kent, they found that Archbishop Deusdedit had departed this life, and no other bishop was as yet appointed in his place; whereupon they betook themselves to the province of the West Saxons, where Wini was bishop, and by him Ceadda was consecrated; two bishops of the British nation, who kept Easter Sunday, as has been often said, contrary to the canonical manner, from the fourteenth to the twentieth moon, being called in to assist at the ordination; for at that time there was no other bishop in all Britain canonically ordained, except Wini.[4]

So Ceadda, being consecrated bishop, began immediately to labour for ecclesiastical truth and purity of

---

[1] Preface, III, 23, *et saep.* Why Oswy, who had consented to Wilfrid's consecration (*v.* V, 19) acted in this manner is not clear. Probably it implies that the Celtic party, during Wilfrid's prolonged absence, had to some extent recovered their ascendency; and, if it was at this time that Alchfrid (who is not heard of again) rebelled against his father (*v.s.* c. 14, *ad init.*) and was deprived of his kingdom, Wilfrid would have lost his warmest supporter.

[2] He retired to Ripon from Lindsey, of which he was the first separate bishop, when Ethelred recovered that province for Mercia in 679. But cf. IV, 12, *ad fin.*, note, for the statement that he was "Bishop" of Ripon.

[3] King of Northumbria, *v.s.* c. 24, p. 188, note 3.

[4] It does not appear why Boniface (Bertgils) of Dunwich, Bishop of the East Angles, 652-669 (c. 20, IV, 5), is ignored. Ceadda's consecration was afterwards regarded as of doubtful validity and was completed by Theodore (*v.* IV, 12). The British (probably Cornish) bishops were schismatical, and Wini's position was irregular. Moreover, the see to which Ceadda was consecrated was not vacant.

doctrine; to apply himself to humility, self-denial, and study; to travel about, not on horseback, but after the manner of the Apostles, on foot, to preach the Gospel in towns, the open country, cottages, villages, and castles; for he was one of the disciples of Aidan, and endeavoured to instruct his people by the same manner of life and character, after his and his own brother Cedd's example. Wilfrid also having been now made a bishop, came into Britain, and in like manner by his teaching brought into the English Church many rules of Catholic observance. Whence it followed, that the Catholic principles daily gained strength, and all the Scots that dwelt in England either conformed to these, or returned into their own country.

CHAP. XXIX. *How the priest Wighard was sent from Britain to Rome, to be ordained archbishop; of his death there, and of the letters of the Apostolic Pope giving an account thereof.* [667 A.D.]

AT this time the most noble kings of the English, Oswy, of the province of the Northumbrians, and Egbert of Kent, consulted together to determine what ought to be done about the state of the English Church, for Oswy, though educated by the Scots, had rightly perceived that the Roman was the Catholic and Apostolic Church. They selected, with the consent and by the choice of the holy Church of the English nation, a priest named Wighard,[1] one of Bishop Deusdedit's clergy, a good man and fitted for the episcopate, and sent him to Rome to be ordained bishop, to the end that, having been raised to the rank of an archbishop, he might ordain Catholic prelates for the Churches of the English nation throughout all Britain. But Wighard, arriving at Rome, was cut off by death, before he could be consecrated bishop, and the following letter was sent back into Britain to King Oswy:—

" *To the most excellent lord, our son, Oswy, king of the*

[1] IV, 1.

Saxons, Vitalian,[1] *bishop, servant of the servants of God.*
We have received to our comfort your Excellency's letters;
by reading whereof we are acquainted with your most
pious devotion and fervent love of the blessed life; and
know that by the protecting hand of God you have been
converted to the true and Apostolic faith, in hope that even
as you reign in your own nation, so you may hereafter
reign with Christ. Blessed be the nation, therefore, that
has been found worthy to have as its king one so wise
and a worshipper of God; forasmuch as he is not himself alone a worshipper of God, but also studies day and
night the conversion of all his subjects to the Catholic
and Apostolic faith, to the redemption of his own soul.
Who would not rejoice at hearing such glad tidings?
Who would not exult and be joyful at these good works?
For your nation has believed in Christ the Almighty
God, according to the words of the Divine prophets, as
it is written in Isaiah, 'In that day there shall be a root
of Jesse, which shall stand for an ensign of the people;
to it shall the Gentiles seek.'[2] And again, 'Listen, O
isles, unto me, and hearken ye people from far.'[3] And a
little after, 'It is a light thing that thou shouldst be my
servant to raise up the tribes of Jacob, and to restore the
outcast of Israel. I have given thee for a light to the
Gentiles, that thou mayst be my salvation unto the end
of the earth.'[4] And again, 'Kings shall see, princes
also shall arise and worship.'[5] And immediately after,
'I have given thee for a covenant of the people, to
establish the earth, and possess the scattered heritages;
that thou mayest say to the prisoners, Go forth; to
them that are in darkness, Show yourselves.'[6] And
again, 'I the Lord have called thee in righteousness,
and have held thine hand, and have kept thee, and have
given thee for a covenant of the people, for a light of
the Gentiles; to open the blind eyes, to bring out the
prisoner from the prison, and them that sit in darkness
from the prison-house.'[7]

---

[1] Consecrated in 657—died in 672.   [2] Isaiah, xi, 10.
[3] *Ibid.*, xlix, 1.   [4] *Ibid.*, 6.   [5] *Ibid.*, 7.   [6] *Ibid.*, 8-9.
[7] *Ibid.*, xlii, 6-7. The readings are from the Vulgate.

P

"Behold, most excellent son, how it is plain as day that it was prophesied not only of you, but also of all the nations, that they should believe in Christ, the Creator of all things. Wherefore it behoves your Highness, as being a member of Christ, in all things continually to follow the pious rule of the chief of the Apostles, in celebrating Easter, and in all things delivered by the holy Apostles, Peter and Paul, whose doctrine daily enlightens the hearts of believers, even as the two lights of heaven illumine the world."

And after some lines, wherein he speaks of celebrating the true Easter uniformly throughout all the world,—

"Finally," he adds, "we have not been able now, on account of the length of the journey, to find a man, apt to teach, and qualified in all respects to be a bishop, according to the tenor of your letters.[1] But, assuredly, as soon as such a fit person shall be found, we will send him well instructed to your country, that he may, by word of mouth, and through the Divine oracles, with the blessing of God, root out all the enemy's tares throughout your island. We have received the presents sent by your Highness to the blessed chief of the Apostles, for an eternal memorial of him, and return you thanks, and always pray for your safety with the clergy of Christ. But he that brought these presents has been removed out of this world, and is buried at the threshold of the Apostles, for whom we have been much grieved, because he died here. Nevertheless, we have caused the blessed gifts of the saints, that is, the relics of the blessed Apostles, Peter and Paul, and of the holy martyrs, Laurentius, John, and Paul, and Gregory, and Pancratius,[2] to be given to your servants, the bearers of

[1] It has not been stated that Oswy and Egbert asked the Pope to provide an archbishop, failing Wighard. But this seems to be implied in IV, 1: "episcopum, quem petierant." Or, as is generally supposed, Vitalian may have arbitrarily assumed this to be the intention of their letter.

[2] There were several martyrs of the name of Laurentius, but the best known is the Roman deacon, St. Laurence, who suffered at Rome in 258 A.D. He was buried in the Via Tiburtina, where a church dedicated to him is said to have been founded by Con-

these our letters, to be by them delivered to your Excellency. And to your consort[1] also, our spiritual daughter, we have by the aforesaid bearers sent a cross, with a gold key to it, made out of the most holy chains of the blessed Apostles, Peter and Paul; for, hearing of her pious zeal, all the Apostolic see rejoices with us, even as her pious works smell sweet and blossom before God.

"We therefore desire that your Highness should hasten, according to our wish, to dedicate all your island to Christ our God; for assuredly you have for your Protector, the Redeemer of mankind, our Lord Jesus Christ, Who will prosper you in all things, that you may gather together a new people of Christ, establishing there the Catholic and Apostolic faith. For it is written, 'Seek ye first the kingdom of God and His righteousness, and all these things shall be added unto you.'[2] Truly your Highness seeks, and shall obtain, and all your islands shall be made subject to you, even as we desire. Saluting your Excellency with fatherly affection, we never cease to pray to the Divine Goodness, to vouchsafe to assist you and yours in all good works, that you may reign with Christ in the world to come. May the Heavenly Grace preserve your Excellency in safety!"

In the next book we shall have a more suitable occasion to show who was selected and consecrated in Wighard's place.

stantine the Great. On the site stands the present Church of S. Lorenzo fuori le Mura, the older part of which dates from the sixth century at least. One of Aldhelm's foundations (V, 18) was a little church dedicated to St. Laurence at Bradford-on-Avon in 705, probably the small Saxon church which still stands there. There were many martyrs named John and Paul, and more than one Gregory. St. Pancras was a boy-martyr, a Phrygian by birth, who suffered at Rome in 304 A.D., when he was only fourteen years of age. His martyrdom was widely celebrated, and miraculous powers were attributed to his tomb outside the walls of Rome. An old British church at Canterbury, which had been desecrated by the heathen invaders, was restored for Christian use and dedicated to St. Pancras by Augustine.

[1] Eanfled, v.s. c. 15 and note.   [2] St. Matt., vi, 33.

CHAP. XXX. *How the East Saxons, during a pestilence, returned to idolatry, but were soon brought back from their error by the zeal of Bishop Jaruman.* [665 A.D.]

AT the same time, the Kings Sighere and Sebbi,[1] though themselves subject to Wulfhere, king of the Mercians, governed the province of the East Saxons after Suidhelm, of whom we have spoken above.[2] When that province was suffering from the aforesaid disastrous plague, Sighere, with his part of the people, forsook the mysteries of the Christian faith, and turned apostate. For the king himself, and many of the commons and nobles, loving this life, and not seeking after another, or even not believing in any other, began to restore the temples that had been abandoned, and to adore idols, as if they might by those means be protected against the plague. But Sebbi, his companion and co-heir in the kingdom, with all his people, very devoutly preserved the faith which he had received, and, as we shall show hereafter, ended his faithful life in great felicity.

King Wulfhere, hearing that the faith of the province was in part profaned, sent Bishop Jaruman,[3] who was successor to Trumhere, to correct their error, and recall the province to the true faith. He acted with much discretion, as I was informed by a priest who bore him company in that journey, and had been his fellow labourer in the Word, for he was a religious and good man, and travelling through all the country, far and near, brought back both the people and the aforesaid king to the way of righteousness, so that, either forsaking or destroying the temples and altars which they had erected, they opened the churches, and gladly confessed the Name of Christ, which they had opposed, choosing rather to die in the faith of resurrection in Him, than to live in the abominations of unbelief among their idols. Having thus accomplished their works, the priests and teachers returned home with joy.

[1] Cf. IV, 6. Sighere was the son, Sebbi the brother, of Sigbert the Little (*v.s.* c. 22, *ad init.*).

[2] C. 22, *ad fin.*

[3] C. 24, *ad fin.*; IV, 3.

BOOK IV

CHAP. I. *How when Deusdedit died, Wighard was sent to Rome to receive the episcopate; but he dying there, Theodore was ordained archbishop, and sent into Britain with the Abbot Hadrian.* [664-669 A.D.]

IN the above-mentioned year of the aforesaid eclipse [1] and of the pestilence which followed it immediately, in which also Bishop Colman, being overcome by the united effort of the Catholics, returned home,[2] Deusdedit,[3] the sixth bishop of the church of Canterbury, died on the 14th of July. Earconbert,[4] also, king of Kent, departed this life the same month and day; leaving his kingdom to his son Egbert, who held it for nine years. The see then became vacant for no small time, until, the priest Wighard,[5] a man of great learning in the teaching of the Church, of the English race, was sent to Rome by King Egbert and Oswy, king of the Northumbrians, as was briefly mentioned in the foregoing book,[6] with a request that he might be ordained Archbishop of the Church of England; and at the same time presents were sent to the Apostolic pope, and many vessels of gold and silver. Arriving at Rome, where Vitalian[7] presided at that time over the Apostolic see, and having made known to the aforesaid Apostolic pope the occasion of his journey, he was not long after carried off, with almost all his companions who had come with him, by a pestilence which fell upon them.

But the Apostolic pope having consulted about that matter, made diligent inquiry for some one to send to be

[1] 664 A.D.: cf. III, 27, *ad init.*
[2] Cf. III, 26, *ad init.*   [3] Cf. III, 20 and note.
[4] Cf. III, 8; V, 19, p. 348.
[5] Cf. III, 29. From Bede's "History of the Abbots" we learn that he was a pupil of Pope Gregory's Roman disciples in Kent.
[6] III, 29.   [7] *Ibid.*, and note.

archbishop of the English Churches. There was then in
the monastery of Niridanum, which is not far from
Naples in Campania, an abbot called Hadrian,[1] by nation
an African, well versed in Holy Scripture, trained in monastic and ecclesiastical teaching, and excellently skilled
both in the Greek and Latin tongues. The pope, sending
for him, commanded him to accept the bishopric and go
to Britain. He answered, that he was unworthy of so
great a dignity, but said that he could name another,
whose learning and age were fitter for the episcopal
office. He proposed to the pope a certain monk named
Andrew, belonging to a neighbouring nunnery[2] and he
was by all that knew him judged worthy of a bishopric;
but the weight of bodily infirmity prevented him from
becoming a bishop. Then again Hadrian was urged to
accept the episcopate; but he desired a respite, to see
whether in time he could find another to be ordained
bishop.

There was at that time in Rome, a monk, called
Theodore,[3] known to Hadrian, born at Tarsus in Cilicia,
a man instructed in secular and Divine writings, as also
in Greek and Latin; of high character and venerable
age, being sixty-six years old. Hadrian proposed him to
the pope to be ordained bishop, and prevailed; but upon
the condition that he should himself conduct him into
Britain, because he had already travelled through Gaul
twice upon different occasions, and was, therefore, better
acquainted with the way, and was, moreover, sufficiently
provided with men of his own; as also, to the end that,
being his fellow labourer in teaching, he might take special
care that Theodore should not, according to the custom of
the Greeks, introduce any thing contrary to the truth of
the faith into the Church where he presided.[4] Theodore,
being ordained subdeacon, waited four months for his
hair to grow, that it might be shorn into the shape of a

[1] Cf. Preface, p. 2, note 3.
[2] He was probably chaplain of the nunnery.
[3] Cf. Preface, p. 2, note 2.
[4] Cf. Bright, cc. 252, 253. He sees here an allusion to the
Monothelite controversy.

crown; for he had before the tonsure of St. Paul,[1] the Apostle, after the manner of the eastern people. He was ordained by Pope Vitalian, in the year of our Lord 668, on Sunday, the 26th of March, and on the 27th of May was sent with Hadrian to Britain.[2]

They proceeded together by sea to Marseilles, and thence by land to Arles, and having there delivered to John, archbishop of that city,[3] Pope Vitalian's letters of recommendation, were by him detained till Ebroin,[4] the king's mayor of the palace, gave them leave to go where they pleased. Having received the same, Theodore went to Agilbert, bishop of Paris,[5] of whom we have spoken above, and was by him kindly received, and long entertained. But Hadrian went first to Emme, Bishop of the Senones,[6] and then to Faro,[7] bishop of the Meldi, and lived in comfort with them a considerable time; for the approach of winter had obliged them to rest wherever they could. King Egbert, being informed by sure messengers that the bishop they had asked of the Roman prelate was in the kingdom of the Franks, sent thither his reeve,[8] Raedfrid, to conduct him. He, having arrived there, with Ebroin's leave took Theodore and conveyed him to the port called Quentavic;[9] where, falling sick,

[1] *I.e.*, the Eastern, which consisted in shaving the whole head. This method was supposed to have the authority of St. Paul (an idea derived from Acts, xviii, 18), and of St. James "the Less." Cf. II, 2, p. 85, note.

[2] They were accompanied by Benedict Biscop (*v.* c. 18) whom Vitalian had asked to act as their guide and interpreter ("Hist. Abb.," § 3).

[3] Archbishop of Arles, 658-675.

[4] From this it has been inferred that Arles belonged to Neustria. The king was Clothaire III, king of Neustria. Ebroin had succeeded Ercinwald (*v.* III, 19, *ad fin.*) as Mayor of the Palace. He was murdered in 681.

[5] III, 7, 25, 26, 28.

[6] Called also Emmo, or Haymo; Bishop of Sens, 658-675.

[7] Or Burgundofarus, Bishop of Meaux, 626-672. He was brother of Fara, mentioned III, 8.

[8] "Praefectus."

[9] Etaples in Picardy; "Quentae (or "ad Quantiam") vicus" = the village at the mouth of the Canche. It was an important commercial town and port.

he stayed some time, and as soon as he began to recover, sailed over into Britain. But Ebroin detained
Hadrian, suspecting that he went on some mission from
the Emperor to the kings of Britain, to the prejudice of
the kingdom of which he at that time had the chief
charge; however, when he found that in truth he had
never had any such commission, he discharged him, and
permitted him to follow Theodore. As soon as he came
to him, Theodore gave him the monastery of the blessed
Peter the Apostle,[1] where the archbishops of Canterbury
are wont to be buried, as I have said before; for at his
departure, the Apostolic lord had enjoined upon Theodore
that he should provide for him in his province, and give
him a suitable place to live in with his followers.

CHAP. II. *How Theodore visited all places; how the
Churches of the English began to be instructed in the
study of Holy Scripture, and in the Catholic truth; and
how Putta was made bishop of the Church of Rochester
in the room of Damianus.* [669 A.D.]

THEODORE came to his Church in the second year after
his consecration, on Sunday, the 27th of May, and spent
in it twenty-one years, three months, and twenty-six
days. Soon after, he visited all the island, wherever the
tribes of the English dwelt, for he was gladly received
and heard by all persons; and everywhere attended and
assisted by Hadrian, he taught the right rule of life, and
the canonical custom of celebrating Easter. This was
the first archbishop whom all the English Church consented to obey. And forasmuch as both of them were, as
has been said before, fully instructed both in sacred and
in secular letters, they gathered a crowd of disciples,
and rivers of wholesome knowledge daily flowed from
them to water the hearts of their hearers; and, together
with the books of Holy Scripture, they also taught them

---

[1] SS. Peter and Paul (St. Augustine's): cf. I, 33. Theodore had
placed Benedict Biscop over it while Hadrian was still abroad.

the metrical art, astronomy, and ecclesiastical arithmetic. A testimony whereof is, that there are still living at this day some of their scholars, who are as well versed in the Greek and Latin tongues as in their own, in which they were born. Nor were there ever happier times since the English came into Britain; for having brave Christian kings, they were a terror to all barbarous nations, and the minds of all men were bent upon the joys of the heavenly kingdom of which they had but lately heard; and all who desired to be instructed in sacred studies had masters at hand to teach them.

From that time also they began in all the churches of the English to learn Church music, which till then had been only known in Kent. And, excepting James, of whom we have spoken above,[1] the first teacher of singing in the churches of the Northumbrians was Eddi, surnamed Stephen,[2] invited from Kent by the most reverend Wilfrid, who was the first of the bishops of the English nation that learned to deliver to the churches of the English the Catholic manner of life.[3]

Theodore, journeying through all parts, ordained bishops in fitting places, and with their assistance corrected such things as he found faulty. Among the rest, when he charged Bishop Ceadda with not having been duly consecrated,[4] he, with great humility, answered, " If you know that I have not duly received episcopal ordination, I willingly resign the office, for I never thought myself worthy of it; but, though unworthy, for obedience sake I submitted, when bidden to undertake it." Theodore, hearing his humble answer, said that he should not resign the bishopric, and he himself completed his ordination after the Catholic manner. Now at the time when Deusdedit died, and a bishop for the

---

[1] II, 16, 20.

[2] Eddius, the biographer of Wilfrid. He mentions himself (" Life of Wilfrid," Chapter XIV) as a " cantor."

[3] Bede can scarcely mean to impeach the orthodoxy of the bishops of native birth prior to Wilfrid. Probably the reference is mainly to the prominent part he took in bringing about the decision at Whitby.   [4] Cf. III, 28, note.

church of Canterbury was by request ordained and sent, Wilfrid was also sent from Britain into Gaul to be ordained; and because he returned before Theodore, he ordained priests and deacons in Kent till the archbishop should come to his see. But when Theodore came to the city of Rochester, where the bishopric had been long vacant by the death of Damian,[1] he ordained a man named Putta,[2] trained rather in the teaching of the Church and more addicted to simplicity of life than active in worldly affairs, but specially skilful in Church music, after the Roman use, which he had learned from the disciples of the blessed Pope Gregory.[3]

CHAP. III. *How the above-mentioned Ceadda was made Bishop of the province of Mercians. Of his life, death, and burial.* [669 A.D.]

AT that time, the province of the Mercians was governed by King Wulfhere, who, on the death of Jaruman,[4] desired of Theodore that a bishop should be given to him and his people; but Theodore would not ordain a new one for them, but requested of King Oswy that Ceadda might be their bishop. He then lived in retirement at his monastery, which is at Laestingaeu,[5] while Wilfrid administered the bishopric of York, and of all

---

[1] Cf. III, 20, and note.

[2] Cc. 5, 12. Florence of Worcester mentions a Putta, Bishop of Hereford, who died in 688, but it is very doubtful whether he can be identified with the above. Bede's words in Chapter 12 do not imply that Putta, Bishop of Rochester, became Bishop of Hereford. Hereford was not one of the five sees into which Florence tells us that Theodore divided the great Mercian bishopric, but it appears soon after as a separate see for Hecana (Herefordshire). Possibly Putta, who is traditionally reckoned as its first bishop, may have acted as Sexwulf's deputy there.

[3] Cf. II, 20 *ad fin.*, note.

[4] III, 24, 30. He had probably died two years before Chad's appointment, *i.e.*, in 667, and the see had been vacant in the interval, for Wilfrid, then in retirement at Ripon, is said (by Eddius) to have discharged episcopal functions for the Mercians.

[5] Lastingham. Cf. Preface, p. 3; III, 23, 28.

the Northumbrians, and likewise of the Picts, as far as King Oswy was able to extend his dominions. And, seeing that it was the custom of that most reverend prelate to go about the work of the Gospel everywhere on foot rather than on horseback, Theodore commanded him to ride whenever he had a long journey to undertake; and finding him very unwilling, in his zeal and love for his pious labour, he himself, with his own hands, lifted him on horseback; for he knew him to be a holy man, and therefore obliged him to ride wherever he had need to go. Ceadda having received the bishopric of the Mercians and of Lindsey,[1] took care to administer it with great perfection of life, according to the example of the ancient fathers. King Wulfhere also gave him land of the extent of fifty families, to build a monastery, at the place called Ad Barvae,[2] or "At the Wood," in the province of Lindsey, wherein traces of the monastic life instituted by him continue to this day.

He had his episcopal see in the place called Lyccidfelth,[3] in which he also died, and was buried, and where the see of the succeeding bishops of that province continues to this day. He had built himself a retired habitation not far from the church, wherein he was wont to pray and read in private, with a few, it might be seven or eight of the brethren, as often as he had any spare

---

[1] Lindsey at this time belonged to Mercia. Cf. c. 12, p. 243, note 5.

[2] Smith believed this place to be Barton-on-Humber. It is now generally identified with Barrow in Lincolnshire. For the preposition, cf. II, 14, p. 119, note 5.

[3] It had not previously been an episcopal see, though Wulfhere had wished to establish Wilfrid there during the vacancy in the Mercian bishopric (p. 218, note 4). When the bishopric of Mercia and Lindsey was subdivided by Theodore in 679, Lichfield remained the see of the bishopric of Mercia proper. In 787, under Offa, King of Mercia, with the consent of Pope Hadrian, it was raised into a separate archbishopric for Mercia and East Anglia, but in 802 Canterbury was re-established as the sole archbishopric for the Southern Province. The popular derivation of the name, Lichfield ("Field of the Dead") is from *lic*=a corpse, and the place is traditionally connected with the martyrdom of a great number of British Christians. Another derivation, however (from *leccian*=to irrigate), points to the meaning "the watered field."

time from the labour and ministry of the Word. When he had most gloriously governed the church in that province for two years and a half, the Divine Providence so ordaining, there came round a season like that of which Ecclesiastes says, "That there is a time to cast away stones, and a time to gather stones together;"[1] for a plague fell upon them, sent from Heaven, which, by means of the death of the flesh, translated the living stones of the Church from their earthly places to the heavenly building. And when, after many of the Church of that most reverend prelate had been taken away out of the flesh, his hour also drew near wherein he was to pass out of this world to the Lord, it happened one day that he was in the aforesaid habitation with only one brother, called Owini,[2] his other companions having upon some due occasion returned to the church. Now Owini was a monk of great merit, having forsaken the world with the sole desire of the heavenly reward; worthy in all respects to have the secrets of the Lord revealed to him in special wise, and worthy to have credit given by his hearers to what he said. For he had come with Queen Ethelthryth[3] from the province of the East Angles, and was the chief of her thegns, and governor of her house. As the fervour of his faith increased, resolving to renounce the secular life, he did not go about it slothfully, but so entirely forsook the things of this world, that, quitting all that he had, clad in a plain garment, and carrying an axe and hatchet in his hand, he came to the monastery of the same most reverend father, which is called Laestingaeu. He said that he was not entering the monastery in order to live in idleness, as some do, but to labour; which he also confirmed by practice; for as he was less capable of studying the Scriptures, the more earnestly he applied himself to

[1] Eccl., iii. 5.
[2] A stone which is believed to have formed part of Owini's tomb was found at the end of the eighteenth century at Haddenham, near Ely, and is now in Ely Cathedral. It bears the inscription, "Lucem tuam Ovino da Deus et requiem. Amen" (Mayor and Lumley).　　　　　　　　　　　　[3] Cf. c. 19.

the labour of his hands. So then, forasmuch as he was reverent and devout, he was kept by the bishop in the aforesaid habitation with the brethren, and whilst they were engaged within in reading, he was without, doing such things as were necessary.

One day, when he was thus employed abroad, his companions having gone to the church, as I began to tell, and the bishop was alone reading or praying in the oratory of that place, on a sudden, as he afterwards said, he heard a sweet sound of singing and rejoicing descend from heaven to earth. This sound he said he first heard coming from the sky in the south-east, above the winter sunrise, and that afterwards it drew near him gradually, till it came to the roof of the oratory where the bishop was, and entering therein, filled all the place and encompassed it about. He listened attentively to what he heard, and after about half an hour, perceived the same song of joy to ascend from the roof of the said oratory, and to return to heaven in the same way as it came, with unspeakable sweetness. When he had stood some time amazed, and earnestly considering in his mind what this might be, the bishop opened the window of the oratory, and making a sound with his hand, as he was often wont to do, bade anyone who might be without to come in to him. He went hastily in, and the bishop said to him, " Make haste to the church, and cause those seven brothers to come hither, and do you come with them." When they were come, he first admonished them to preserve the virtue of love and peace among themselves, and towards all the faithful; and with unwearied earnestness to follow the rules of monastic discipline, which they had either been taught by him, and had seen him observe, or had found in the words and actions of the former fathers. Then he added that the day of his death was at hand; for, said he, " that gracious guest, who was wont to visit our brethren, has vouchsafed also to come to me this day, and to call me out of this world. Return, therefore, to the church, and speak to the brethren, that in their prayers they commend my departure to the Lord, and that they be

mindful to prepare for their own, the hour whereof is
uncertain, by watching, and prayer, and good works."

When he had spoken thus much and more to the same
end, and they, having received his blessing, had gone
away in great sorrow, he who had heard the heavenly
song returned alone, and prostrating himself on the
ground, said, "I beseech you, father, may I be permitted to ask a question?"—"Ask what you will,"
answered the bishop. Then he said, "I beseech you to
tell me what was that song which I heard as of a joyful
company coming from heaven upon this oratory, and
after some time returning to heaven?" The bishop
answered: "If you heard the singing, and know of the
coming of the heavenly company, I command you, in
the Name of the Lord, that you tell it not to any before
my death. But in truth they were angelic spirits, who
came to call me to my heavenly reward, which I have
always loved and longed after, and they promised that
they would return seven days hence, and take me away
with them." Which was indeed fulfilled, as had been
said to him; for being presently seized with bodily infirmity, and the same daily increasing, on the seventh
day, as had been promised to him, when he had prepared for death by receiving the Body and Blood of our
Lord, his saintly soul being delivered from the prison of
the body, led, as may justly be believed, by the attendant
angels, he departed to the joys of Heaven.

It is no wonder that he joyfully beheld the day of his
death, or rather the day of the Lord, the coming whereof
he had always been mindful to await with earnest ex-
pectation. For with all his merits of continence, humility,
teaching, prayer, voluntary poverty, and other virtues,
he was so filled with the fear of the Lord, so mindful of
his latter end in all his actions, that, as I was wont to
hear from one of the brothers who instructed me in the
Scriptures, and who had been bred in his monastery,
and under his direction, whose name was Trumbert, if
it happened that there blew a sudden strong gust of
wind, when he was reading or doing any other thing, he
forthwith called upon the Lord for mercy, and begged

that it might be granted to all mankind. If the wind grew stronger, he closed his book, and fell on his face, praying still more earnestly. But, if a violent storm of wind or rain came on, or if the earth and air were filled with the terror of thunder and lightning, he would go to the church, and anxiously devote himself with all his heart to prayers and psalms till the weather became calm. Being asked by his brethren why he did so, he answered, " Have not you read—' The Lord also thundered in the heavens, and the Highest gave his voice. Yea, he sent out his arrows and scattered them; and he shot out lightnings, and discomfited them.' [1] For the Lord moves the air, raises the winds, hurls lightning, and thunders from heaven, to rouse the inhabitants of the earth to fear him; to put them in mind of judgement to come; to dispel their pride, and confound their boldness, by recalling to their thoughts that dread time, when the heavens and the earth being on fire, He will come in the clouds, with great power and majesty, to judge the quick and the dead. Wherefore," said he, "it behoves us to respond to His heavenly admonition with due fear and love; that, as often as the air is moved and He puts forth His hand threatening to strike, but does not yet let it fall, we may immediately implore His mercy; and searching the recesses of our hearts, and casting out the dregs of our sins, we may carefully so act that we may never deserve to be struck down."

With this revelation and narrative of the aforesaid brother, concerning the death of this prelate, agrees the account of the most reverend Father Egbert, above spoken of,[2] who long and zealously led a monastic life with the same Ceadda, when both were youths, in Ireland, in prayer and self-denial and meditation on the Holy Scriptures. But whereas Ceadda afterwards returned into his own country, Egbert continued to live abroad for the Lord's sake till the end of his life. A long time after, Hygbald, a man of great holiness and con-

[1] Ps. xviii, 13, 14.
[2] III, 4, 27.

tinence, who was an abbot in the province of Lindsey,[1] came from Britain to visit him, and whilst, as became holy men, they were discoursing of the life of the former fathers, and rejoicing to imitate the same, mention was made of the most reverend prelate, Ceadda; whereupon Egbert said, "I know a man in this island, still in the flesh, who, when Ceadda passed away from this world, saw the soul of his brother Cedd, with a company of angels, descending from heaven, who, having taken Ceadda's soul along with them, returned again to the heavenly kingdom." Whether he said this of himself, or some other, we do not certainly know; but because it was said by so great a man, there can be no doubt of the truth thereof.

Ceadda died on the 2nd of March,[2] and was first buried by St. Mary's Church, but afterwards, when the church of the most blessed chief of the Apostles, Peter, was built in the same place, his bones were translated into it. In both which places, as a testimony of his virtue, frequent miracles of healing are wont to be wrought. And of late, a certain man that had a frenzy, wandering about everywhere, arrived there in the evening, unperceived or disregarded by the keepers of the place, and having rested there the whole of the night, came forth in his right mind the next morning, to the surprise and joy of all, and told what a cure had been wrought on him through the goodness of God. The place of the sepulchre is a wooden monument, made like a little house, covered, having a hole in the wall, through which those that go thither for devotion are wont to put in their hand and take out some of the dust. This they put into water and give to sick cattle or men to drink, whereupon they are presently eased of their infirmity, and restored to their desired health.

In his place, Theodore ordained Wynfrid,[3] a man of

---

[1] He is said to have been Abbot of Bardney.
[2] In 672. The original Church of St. Mary at Lichfield, said to have been built by Oswy in 656-657, was replaced about 1140 by the new Cathedral, and Ceadda's relics were soon after removed to it.   [3] Cf. III, 24, *ad fin.*, note.

good and sober life, to preside, like his predecessors, over the bishoprics of the Mercians, the Midland Angles, and Lindsey, of all which, Wulfhere, who was still living, was king. Wynfrid was one of the clergy of the prelate he succeeded, and had for no small time filled the office of deacon under him.

CHAP. IV. *How Bishop Colman, having left Britain, built two monasteries in the country of the Scots; the one for the Scots, the other for the English whom he had taken along with him.* [667 A.D.]

IN the meantime, Colman, the Scottish bishop, departing from Britain,[1] took along with him all the Scots whom he had gathered about him in the isle of Lindisfarne, and also about thirty of the English nation, for both these companies had been trained in duties of the monastic life; and leaving some brothers in his church, he went first to the isle of Hii,[2] whence he had been sent to preach the Word of God to the English nation. Afterwards he retired to a small island, which is to the west of Ireland, and at some distance from it, called in the language of the Scots, Inisboufinde,[3] the Island of the White Heifer. Arriving there, he built a monastery, and placed in it the monks he had brought of both nations. But they could not agree among themselves, by reason that the Scots, in the summer season, when the harvest was to be brought in, leaving the monastery, wandered about through places known to them; but returned again the next winter, and desired to use in common what the English had provided. Colman sought to put an end to this dissension, and travelling about far and near, he found a place in the island of Ireland fitted to be the site of a monastery, which, in the language of the

[1] Cf. III, 26, *ad init.*
[2] Iona. Cf. III, 3, *ad fin.*, note.
[3] Innisboffin, off the coast of Mayo. The annals of Ulster give 667 as the date of his retirement to it.

Q

Scots, is called Mageo.[1] He bought a small part of it of
the chief to whom it belonged, to build his monastery
thereon; upon condition, that the monks dwelling there
should pray to the Lord for him who let them have the
place. Then at once building a monastery, with the
assistance of the chief and all the neighbouring people, he
placed the English there, leaving the Scots in the aforesaid island. This monastery is to this day occupied by
English inhabitants; being the same that, grown from a
small beginning to be very large, is commonly called
Muigeo; and as all have long since been brought to
adopt better customs, it contains a notable society of
monks, who are gathered there from the province of the
English, and live by the labour of their own hands, after
the example of the venerable fathers, under a rule and
a canonical abbot, in much continence and singleness of
life.

CHAP. V. *Of the death of the kings Oswy and Egbert,
and of the synod held at the place Herutford,[2] in which
Archbishop Theodore presided.* [670-673 A.D.]

IN the year of our Lord 670,[3] being the second year after
Theodore arrived in England, Oswy, king of the Northumbrians, fell sick, and died, in the fifty-eighth year of
his age.[4] He at that time bore so great affection to the
Roman Apostolic usages, that he had designed, if he
recovered from his sickness, to go to Rome, and there

[1] Mayo, called from this settlement, "Mayo of the Saxons." It
continued to be an English monastery (*v. infra*), and after awhile
adopted those usages, to avoid which Colman had left England.
It became an episcopal see, which in 1559 was annexed to the
archbishopric of Tuam.   [2] Hertford.
[3] It seems probable that we ought to read 671; cf. Plummer *ad
loc.*
[4] Oswy is the last king in Bede's list of those who held an
"imperium" (*v.* II, 5). With the rise of Mercia under Wulfhere
(III, 24), the supremacy of Northumbria had virtually passed away.
After Oswy's death, the position of Northumbria was an isolated
one, and it was by conquests over Britons, not Englishmen, that
Egfrid enlarged the bounds of his kingdom.

to end his days at the holy places, having asked Bishop Wilfrid, with a promise of no small gift of money, to conduct him on his journey. He died on the 15th of February, leaving his son Egfrid[1] his successor in the kingdom. In the third year of his reign, Theodore assembled a council of bishops, along with many other teachers of the church, who loved and were acquainted with the canonical statutes of the fathers. When they were met together, he began, in the spirit which became a bishop, to enjoin the observance of such things as were in accordance with the unity and the peace of the Church. The purport of the proceedings of this synod is as follows:—[2]

" In the name of our Lord God and Saviour Jesus Christ, Who reigns for ever and governs His Church, it was thought meet that we should assemble, according to the custom prescribed in the venerable canons, to treat about the necessary affairs of the Church. We met on the 24th day of September, the first indiction,[3] at the place which is called Herutford: I, Theodore, albeit unworthy, appointed by the Apostolic see bishop of the church of Canterbury; our fellow priest and brother, the most reverend Bisi, bishop of the East Angles; and with

---

[1] In his youth he had been a hostage at the court of Queen Cynwise, wife of Penda (III, 24, p. 188).

[2] This is of supreme importance as the first English provincial Council and the first national assembly of the English. The rule laid down at Nicaea and confirmed by later councils was that provincial synods should meet twice a year to settle all ecclesiastical matters which affected the province as a unity.

[3] 24th September, 673, falls in the first indiction, whether the Pontifical or the " Caesarean " system is meant (v. Haddan and Stubbs, III, 121). Bede himself used the Caesarean indiction, of which we get the first notice in his " De Temporum Ratione." It began on 24th September. It does not, however, follow that Theodore also used it. The oldest scheme, viz., the Constantinopolitan, began on 1st September; the Roman or Pontifical, on New Year's Day as received at the time, i.e., 25th December, 1st January, or 21st March. For Indictions, v. " Dictionary of Christian Antiquities." They were cycles of fifteen years, a mode of reckoning dates which appeared in the fourth century, based upon the Imperial fiscal system, but which came to be used irrespective of taxation. " 1st indiction " stands for " 1st year of the indiction."

us also our brother and fellow priest, Wilfrid, bishop of
the nation of the Northumbrians, represented by his
proxies. There were present also our brothers and fellow
priests, Putta, bishop of the Kentish castle, called Rochester; Leutherius, bishop of the West Saxons, and
Wynfrid, bishop of the province of the Mercians.[1] When
we were all met together, and had sat down in order, I
said, ' I beseech you, most dear brothers, for the fear
and love of our Redeemer, that we may all treat in
common on behalf of our faith; to the end that whatsoever has been decreed and defined by holy and approved
fathers, may be inviolably observed by all of us.' This
and much more I spoke tending to charity and the preservation of the unity of the Church; and when I had
ended my preface, I asked every one of them in order,
whether they consented to observe the things that had
been of old canonically decreed by the fathers? To which
all our fellow priests answered, ' Most assuredly we are
all resolved to observe willingly and heartily whatsoever
is laid down in the canons of the holy fathers.' Then
forthwith I produced the said book of canons,[2] and in
the presence of them all showed ten articles in the same,
which I had marked in several places, because I knew
them to be of the most importance to us, and entreated
that these might be most particularly received by them all.

"Article I. That we all in common keep the holy day
of Easter on the Sunday after the fourteenth moon of the
first month.

"II. That no bishop intrude into the diocese of

---

[1] Of the six suffragans only four were present. Wilfrid was at
this time (669-678) in possession of his see; why he did not appear
in person is not explained. Possibly his action foreshadows the
future troubles between him and Theodore. Wini, Bishop of
London, was still alive (v. III, 7, and note). If the story of his
retirement to Winchester is true, this would account for his
absence. For Bisi, v. infra. His see was at Dunwich (cf. II, 15).
For Putta, v.s. c. 2 and note; for Leutherius, v. III, 7; for Wynfrid, III, 24; IV, 3, ad fin.
[2] The collection of Canons approved by the Council of Chalcedon, translated into Latin by Dionysius Exiguus (early in the sixth
century, cf. V, 21, p. 369, note) and adopted by the Western Church.

another, but be satisfied with the government of the people committed to him.

" III. That it shall not be lawful for any bishop to disturb in any matter monasteries dedicated to God, nor to take away forcibly any part of their property.

" IV. That the monks themselves do not move from one place to another, that is, from monastery to monastery, unless with the consent of their own abbot; but that they continue in the obedience which they promised at the time of their conversion.

" V. That no clerk, forsaking his own bishop, shall wander about, or be anywhere received without commendatory letters from his diocesan. But if he shall be once received, and will not return when summoned, both the receiver, and he that is received shall be under excommunication.

" VI. That bishops and clergy, when travelling, shall be content with the hospitality that is afforded them; and that it be not lawful for any one of them to exercise any priestly function without leave of the bishop in whose diocese he is known to be.

" VII. That a synod be assembled twice a year; but on account of divers hindrances, it was approved by all, that we should meet once a year, on the 1st of August, at the place called Clofeshoch.[1]

" VIII. That no bishop, through ambition, shall set himself above another; but that they shall all observe the time and order of their consecration.

" IX. The ninth Article was discussed in common, to the effect that more bishops should be made, as the number of the faithful increased; but this matter for the present was passed over.[2]

[1] This place used to be identified with Cliff-at-Hoe near Rochester, but the theory rests mainly on the similarity of name. As in the recorded Councils of Clovesho the supremacy of Mercia is clearly indicated, it is generally assumed that the place must have been either in Mercia or a kingdom subject to it, as Kent was at the time. Except one Council in 716, we find none mentioned as having taken place at Clovesho till seventy years after this time (747), but councils were held at other places.

[2] The subdivision of the great bishoprics was an important part

" X. Of marriages; that nothing be allowed but lawful wedlock; that none commit incest; no man leave his own wife, except it be, as the holy Gospel teaches, for fornication. And if any man shall put away his own wife, lawfully joined to him in matrimony, that he take no other, if he wishes to be a true Christian, but continue as he is, or else be reconciled to his own wife.

"These articles being thus discussed and defined in common, to the end, that for the future, no stumbling-block of contention might arise from any one of us, or that things be falsely set forth, it was thought fit that every one of us should, by the subscription of his own hand, confirm all the particulars so defined. Which judgement, as defined by us, I dictated to be written by Titillus our notary. Given in the month and indiction aforesaid. Whosoever, therefore, shall attempt in any way to oppose or infringe this decision, confirmed by our consent, and by the subscription of our hands, according to the decree of the canons, must know, that he is excluded from all sacerdotal functions, and from our fellowship. May the Grace of God keep us in safety, living in the unity of His Holy Church."

This synod was held in the year of our Lord 673. In which year Egbert, king of Kent,[1] died in the month of July; his brother Hlothere[2] succeeded him on the throne, which he held eleven years and seven months. Bisi, the bishop of the East Angles, who is said to have been in the aforesaid synod, a man of great saintliness and piety, was successor to Boniface,[3] before spoken of; for when Boniface died, after having been bishop seventeen years, he was ordained by Theodore and made bishop in his place. Whilst he was still alive, but hindered by grievous infirmity from administering his episcopal functions, two

---

of Theodore's policy, and though at this Council he failed to carry his point, possibly through the opposition of Wilfrid's representatives, in the succeeding years he effected a great change in the organization of the episcopate, creating dioceses co-extensive with tribal territories.

[1] III, 29; IV, 1.
[2] Cc. 22, 26.
[3] His original name was Bertgils, v. III, 20.

bishops, Aecci and Badwin, were elected and consecrated in his place; from which time to the present, that province has had two bishops.[1]

CHAP. VI. *How Wynfrid being deposed, Sexwulf received his bishopric, and Earconwald was made bishop of the East Saxons.* [675 A.D.]

NOT long after these events, Theodore, the archbishop, taking offence at some act of disobedience of Wynfrid, bishop of the Mercians,[2] deposed him from his bishopric when he had held it but a few years, and in his place ordained Sexwulf bishop,[3] who was founder and abbot of the monastery which is called Medeshamstead,[4] in the country of the Gyrwas.[5] Wynfrid, thus deposed, returned to his monastery which is called Ad Barvae,[6] and there ended his life in holy conversation.

Theodore then also appointed Earconwald,[7] bishop of

[1] Theodore availed himself of this opportunity for subdivision. Aecci was appointed to Dunwich and Badwin to the new see of Elmham. Suffolk and Norfolk thus each received a separate bishopric. The Danish invasions broke up this arrangement; Dunwich disappeared as an episcopal see, and the succession to Elmham was interrupted for a time. In 1075 the see of the single East Anglian bishopric was removed to Thetford, and in 1094 to Norwich.

[2] It has been conjectured that he resisted the subdivision of his diocese. For his subsequent adventures, *v.* III, 24, p. 192, note 4.

[3] This was probably in 675 (Flor. of Wor.). Sexwulf (*v. infra* c. 12) had been a rich thegn who became a monk and was made first abbot of Medeshamstead.

[4] Peterborough, as the town which grew up around the monastery came to be called in the tenth century, the monastery being dedicated to St. Peter. Peada is said to have planned the foundation (*v.* Peterborough additions to the Saxon Chronicle), but the accounts are late and untrustworthy.

[5] III, 20, note.   [6] C. 3, p. 219, note 2.

[7] He succeeded Wini (III, 7) in 675 and died about 693. He was canonized. It was in his house that the reconciliation between Theodore and Wilfrid took place. It is said that as a boy he had heard Mellitus preach in London. He was present at the West Saxon Witenagemot which enacted the "Dooms of Ine" (c. 15 and V, 7), and is spoken of as one of Ine's bishops, Essex being probably subject to Wessex at that time.

the East Saxons, in the city of London, over whom at that time reigned Sebbi and Sighere, of whom mention has been made above.[1] This Earconwald's life and conversation, as well when he was bishop as before that time, is said to have been most holy, as is even now testified by heavenly miracles; for to this day, his horse-litter, in which he was wont to be carried when sick, is kept by his disciples, and continues to cure many of fevers and other ailments; and not only sick persons who are laid under that litter, or close by it, are cured; but the very splinters cut from it, when carried to the sick, are wont immediately to bring healing to them.

This man, before he was made bishop, had built two famous monasteries, the one for himself, and the other for his sister Ethelburg,[2] and established them both in regular discipline of the best kind. That for himself was in the district of Sudergeona, by the river Thames, at a place called Cerotaesei,[3] that is, the Island of Cerot; that for his sister in the province of the East Saxons, at a place called In Berecingum,[4] wherein she might be a mother and nurse of women devoted to God. Being put into the government of that monastery, she showed herself in all respects worthy of her brother the bishop, by her own holy life and by her regular and pious care of those under her rule, as was also manifested by heavenly miracles.

CHAP. VII. *How it was indicated by a light from heaven where the bodies of the nuns should be buried in the monastery of Berecingum.* [675 A.D.?]

In this monastery many miracles were wrought, accounts of which have been committed to writing by those who

[1] In III, 30.
[2] Cc. 7-10. She is not to be confused with Ethelberg, daughter of Anna (III, 8), Abbess of Faremoûtier-en-Brie.
[3] Chertsey in Surrey. William of Malmesbury tells us that it was a flourishing monastery till it was destroyed by the Danes.
[4] Barking in Essex, *v. infra* cc. 7-10. For the preposition, *v.* II, 14, p. 119, note 5.

were acquainted with them, that their memory might be
preserved, and succeeding generations edified, and these
are in the possession of many persons; some of them we
also have taken pains to include in our History of the
Church. At the time of the pestilence, already often
mentioned,[1] which ravaged all the country far and wide,
it had also seized on that part of this monastery where
the men abode, and they were daily hurried away to the
Lord. The careful mother of the community began often
to inquire of the sisters, when they were gathered together, in what part of the monastery they desired to be
buried and a cemetery to be made, when the same affliction should fall upon that part of the monastery in which
the handmaids of the Lord dwelt together apart from the
men, and they should be snatched away out of this world
by the same destruction as the rest. Receiving no certain answer from the sisters, though she often questioned
them, she and all of them received a most certain answer
from the Divine Providence. For one night, after matins
had been sung, and those handmaids of Christ had gone
out of their chapel to the tombs of the brothers who had
departed this life before them, and were singing the
customary songs of praise to the Lord, on a sudden a
light from heaven, like a great sheet, came down upon
them all, and struck them with such amazement, that, in
consternation, they even left off singing their hymn.
But that resplendent light, in comparison wherewith the
sun at noon-day might seem dark, soon after, rising from
that place, removed to the south side of the monastery,
that is, to the westward of the chapel, and having continued there some time, and rested upon those parts, in
the sight of them all withdrew itself again to heaven,
leaving no doubt in the minds of all, but that the same
light, which was to lead or to receive the souls of those
handmaids of Christ into Heaven, also showed the place
in which their bodies were to rest and await the day of
the resurrection. The radiance of this light was so great,

[1] The plague of 664 has been mentioned in III, 27; IV, 1, 3; but
this may have been a later visitation. Barking is generally supposed to have been founded in 666.

that one of the older brethren, who at the same time was
in their chapel with another younger than himself, related in the morning, that the rays of light which came
in at the crannies of the doors and windows, seemed to
exceed the utmost brightness of daylight.

CHAP. VIII. *How a little boy, dying in the same monastery, called upon a virgin that was to follow him; and
how another nun, at the point of leaving her body, saw
some small part of the future glory.* [675 A.D.?]

THERE was, in the same monastery, a boy, not above
three years old, called Aesica; who, by reason of his
tender age, was being brought up among the virgins
dedicated to God, there to learn his lessons. This child
being seized by the aforesaid pestilence, when his last
hour was come, called three times upon one of the
virgins consecrated to Christ, speaking to her by her
own name, as if she had been present, Eadgyth! Eadgyth! Eadgyth! and thus ending his temporal life,
entered into that which is eternal. The virgin, to whom
he called, as he was dying, was immediately seized,
where she was, with the same sickness, and departing
this life the same day on which she had been summoned,
followed him that called her into the heavenly kingdom.

Likewise, one of the same handmaids of God, being
smitten with the same disease, and reduced to the last
extremity, began on a sudden, about midnight, to cry
out to them that ministered to her, desiring they would
put out the lamp that was lighted there. And, when she
had done this many times, and yet no one did her will,
at last she said, "I know that you think I am raving,
when I say this, but be assured that it is not so; for I
tell you truly, that I see this house filled with so great a
light, that that lamp of yours seems to me to be altogether
dark." And when still no one replied to what she said,
or did her bidding, she added, "Burn your lamp, then,
as long as you will; but know, that it is not my light,
for my light will come to me at the dawn of day." Then

she began to tell, that a certain man of God, who had died that same year, had appeared to her, telling her that at the break of day she should depart to the eternal light. The truth of which vision was speedily proved by the maiden's death as soon as the day appeared.

CHAP. IX. *Of the signs which were shown from Heaven when the mother of that community departed this life.* [675 A.D.?]

Now when Ethelburg herself, the pious mother of that community devoted to God, was about to be taken out of this world, a wonderful vision appeared to one of the sisters, called Tortgyth; who, having lived many years in that monastery, always endeavoured, in all humility and sincerity, to serve God herself, and to help the mother to maintain regular discipline, by instructing and re- proving the younger ones. Now, in order that her virtue might, according to the Apostle, be made perfect in weakness, she was suddenly seized with a most grievous bodily disease, under which, through the merciful pro- vidence of our Redeemer, she was sorely tried for the space of nine years; to the end, that whatever stain of evil remained amidst her virtues, either through ignor- ance or neglect, might all be purified in the furnace of long tribulation. This woman, going out of the chamber where she abode one night, at dusk, plainly saw as it were a human body, which was brighter than the sun, wrapped in fine linen, and lifted up on high, being taken out of the house in which the sisters used to sleep. Then looking earnestly to see what it was that drew up that appearance of the glorious body which she beheld, she perceived that it was raised on high as it were by cords brighter than gold, until, entering into the open heavens, it could no longer be seen by her. Reflecting on this vision, she made no doubt that some one of the com- munity would soon die, and her soul be lifted up to heaven by the good works which she had wrought, as it were by golden cords. And so in truth it befell; for a

few days after, the beloved of God, Ethelburg, mother of
that community, was delivered out of the prison of the
flesh; and her life is proved to have been such that no
one who knew her ought to doubt that an entrance into
the heavenly country was open to her, when she departed
from this life.

There was also, in the same monastery, a certain nun,
of noble origin in this world, and still nobler in the love
of the world to come; who had, for many years, been so
disabled in all her body, that she could not move a single
limb. When she heard that the body of the venerable
abbess had been carried into the church, till it should be
buried, she desired to be carried thither, and to be placed
bending towards it, after the manner of one praying;
which being done, she spoke to her as if she had been
living, and entreated her that she would obtain of the
mercy of our pitiful Creator, that she might be delivered
from such great and long-continued pains; nor was it
long before her prayer was heard: for being delivered
from the flesh twelve days after, she exchanged her
temporal afflictions for an eternal reward.

For three years after the death of her Superior, the
aforesaid handmaid of Christ, Tortgyth, was detained in
this life and was so far spent with the sickness before
mentioned, that her bones scarce held together. At
last, when the time of her release was at hand, she
not only lost the use of her other limbs, but also of her
tongue; in which state having continued three days
and as many nights, she was, on a sudden, restored by
a spiritual vision, and opened her lips and eyes, and
looking up to heaven, began thus to speak to the vision
which she saw: "Very acceptable to me is thy coming,
and thou art welcome!" Having so said, she was silent
awhile, as it were, waiting for the answer of him whom
she saw and to whom she spoke; then, as if somewhat
displeased, she said, "I can in no wise gladly suffer
this;" then pausing awhile, she said again, "If it can
by no means be to-day, I beg that the delay may not be
long;" and again holding her peace a short while, she
concluded thus; "If it is certainly so determined, and

the decree cannot be altered, I beg that it may be no longer deferred than this next night." Having so said, and being asked by those about her with whom she talked, she said, "With my most dear mother, Ethelburg;" by which they understood, that she was come to acquaint her that the time of her departure was at hand; for, as she had desired, after one day and night, she was delivered alike from the bonds of the flesh and of her infirmity and entered into the joys of eternal salvation.

CHAP. X. *How a blind woman, praying in the burial-place of that monastery, was restored to her sight.* [675 A.D.?]

HILDILID, a devout handmaid of God, succeeded Ethelburg in the office of abbess and presided over that monastery with great vigour many years, till she was of an extreme old age,[1] in the observance of regular discipline, and carefully providing all things for the common use. The narrowness of the space where the monastery is built, led her to determine that the bones of the servants and handmaidens of Christ, who had been there buried, should be taken up, and should all be translated into the church of the Blessed Mother of God, and interred in one place. How often a brightness of heavenly light was seen there, when this was done, and a fragrancy of wonderful sweetness arose, and what other signs were revealed, whosoever reads will find in the book from which we have taken these tales.[2]

But in truth, I think it by no means fit to pass over

---

[1] Two different dates are given for her succession, 664 and 675. If the former is right, the plague (c. 7) must have been that of 664. and Ethelburg probably died of it. It appears from a letter of St. Boniface that Hildilid was alive in 709. She was one of Aldhelm's numerous women-scholars. He dedicated the prose version of his work in praise of virginity (v. V, 18) to her and others of the sisterhood, and speaks highly of their scholarly attainments.

[2] Apparently a life of St. Ethelburg not known to exist now.

the miracle of healing, which the same book informs us
was wrought in the cemetery of that community dedicated to God.   There lived in that neighbourhood a certain thegn, whose wife was seized with a sudden dimness
in her eyes, and as the malady increased daily, it became
so burdensome to her, that she could not see the least
glimpse of light.   Having continued some time wrapped
in the night of this blindness, on a sudden she bethought
herself that she might recover her lost sight, if she were
carried to the monastery of the nuns, and there prayed
at the relics of the saints.   Nor did she lose any time in
fulfilling that which she had conceived in her mind: for
being conducted by her maids to the monastery, which
was very near, and professing that she had perfect faith
that she should be there healed, she was led into the
cemetery, and having long prayed there on her knees,
she did not fail to be heard, for as she rose from prayer,
before she went out of the place, she received the gift of
sight which she had desired; and whereas she had been
led thither by the hands of her maids, she now returned
home joyfully without help: as if she had lost the light
of this world to no other end than that she might show
by her recovery how great a light is vouchsafed to the
saints of Christ in Heaven, and how great a grace of
healing power.

CHAP. XI.   *How Sebbi, king of the same province, ended
his life in a monastery.*   [694 A.D.]

AT that time, as the same little book informs us, Sebbi,[1]
a very devout man, of whom mention has been made
above, governed the kingdom of the East Saxons.   His
mind was set on religious acts, frequent prayer and pious
fruits of almsgiving; he esteemed a private and monastic
life better than all the wealth and honours of his kingdom, and he would have long before left his kingdom
and adopted that life, had not his wife firmly refused to

[1] Cf. III, 30; IV, 6.

be divorced from him; for which reason many were of
opinion and often said that a man of such a disposition
ought rather to have been made a bishop than a king.
When he had spent thirty years as a king and a soldier
of the heavenly kingdom, he fell into great bodily infirmity, of which he afterwards died, and he admonished
his wife, that they should then at least together devote
themselves to the service of God, since they could no
longer together enjoy, or rather serve, the world.
Having with much difficulty obtained this of her, he
went to Waldhere, bishop of London, who had succeeded Earconwald,[1] and with his blessing received the
religious habit, which he had long desired. He also
carried to him a considerable sum of money, to be given
to the poor, reserving nothing to himself, but rather
coveting to remain poor in spirit for the sake of the
kingdom of Heaven.

When the aforesaid sickness increased, and he perceived the day of his death to be drawing near, being a
man of a royal disposition, he began to apprehend lest,
when in great pain, at the approach of death, he might
commit anything unworthy of his character, either by
word or gesture. Wherefore, calling to him the aforesaid
bishop of London, in which city he then was, he entreated him that none might be present at his death,
besides the bishop himself, and two of his own attendants. The bishop having promised that he would most
willingly grant his request, not long after the man of
God composed himself to sleep, and saw a consoling
vision, which took from him all anxiety concerning the
aforesaid uneasiness; and, moreover, showed him on
what day he was to end his life. For, as he afterwards
related, he saw three men in shining garments come to
him; one of whom sat down by his bed, whilst his companions who had come with him stood and inquired

[1] For Earconwald, v.s. c. 6. Waldhere is the first of a long list
of undistinguished bishops of London given by William of Malmesbury. A letter of his to Archbishop Bertwald survives, and there is
a charter in which Swefred (v. next note) grants lands at Twick-
enham to him in 704.

about the state of the sick man they had come to visit, and he said that the king's soul should quit his body without any pain, and with a great splendour of light; and told him that he should die the third day after. Both these things came to pass, as he had learnt from the vision; for on the third day after, at the ninth hour, he suddenly fell, as it were, into a light slumber, and without any sense of pain he gave up the ghost.

A stone coffin had been prepared for his burial, but when they came to lay him in it, they found his body a span longer than the coffin. Hereupon they chipped away as much of the stone as they could, and made the coffin about two inches longer; but not even so would it contain the body. Wherefore because of this difficulty of entombing him, they had thoughts either to get another coffin, or else to shorten the body, by bending it at the knees, if they could, so that the coffin might contain it. But Heaven interposed and a miracle prevented the execution of either of those designs; for on a sudden, in the presence of the bishop and Sighard, who was the son of that same king and monk, and who reigned after him jointly with his brother Suefred,[1] and of no small number of men, that coffin was found to fit the length of the body, insomuch that a pillow might even be put in at the head; and at the feet the coffin was four inches longer than the body. He was buried in the church of the blessed teacher of the Gentiles,[2] by whose doctrine he had learned to hope for heavenly things.

[1] Cf. V, 8, note on Suaebhard.
[2] St. Paul's, London. Sebbi's tomb is believed to have survived till the fire of 1666.

CHAP. XII. *How Haedde succeeded Leutherius in the bishopric of the West Saxons; how Cuichelm succeeded Putta in the bishopric of the church of Rochester, and was himself succeeded by Gebmund; and who were then bishops of the Northumbrians.* [673-681 A.D.]

LEUTHERIUS was the fourth bishop of the West Saxons; for Birinus was the first, Agilbert the second, and Wini the third.[1] When Coinwalch,[2] in whose reign the said Leutherius was made bishop, died, the sub-kings took upon them the government of the nation, and dividing it among themselves, held it for about ten years; and during their rule he died, and Haedde[3] succeeded him in the bishopric, having been consecrated by Theodore, in the city of London. During his episcopate, Caedwalla,[4] having subdued and removed the sub-kings, took upon himself the supreme authority. When he had held it for two years, and whilst the same bishop still governed the church, at length impelled by love of the heavenly kingdom, he quitted it and, going away to Rome, ended his days there, as shall be said more fully hereafter.

In the year of our Lord 676, when Ethelred, king of the Mercians,[5] ravaged Kent with a hostile army, and

---

[1] For these bishops, cf. III, 7.

[2] *Ibid.* He died in 672 (Sax. Chron.). Of the sub-kings the most prominent were Aescwine and Centwine, a brother of Coinwalch. The Saxon Chronicle gives a different account. According to it, Coinwalch's widow, Sexburg, reigned for one year after him and was succeeded by Aescwine, who was succeeded by Centwine.

[3] Cf. III, 7, and for his character, V, 18. The Saxon Chronicle says he succeeded in 676 and died in 703. Bede places his death in 705 (V, 18).

[4] Cc. 15, 16, and V, 7. He was of Ceaulin's line (II, 5) and so belonged to a younger branch of the West Saxon royal house. Welsh writers confuse him with the British king, Caedwalla (II, 20), and with his son, Cadwalader.

[5] A son of Penda. He succeeded his brother Wulfhere in 675. In 704 he became a monk (V, 24) and afterwards Abbot of Bardney Monastery (cf. III, 11), which he is said to have founded. His invasion of Kent was probably provoked by an attempt on the part of

profaned churches and monasteries, without regard to pity, or the fear of God, in the general destruction he laid waste the city of Rochester; Putta,[1] who was bishop, was absent at that time, but when he understood that his church was ravaged, and everything taken away from it, he went to Sexwulf, bishop of the Mercians,[2] and having received of him a certain church, and a small piece of land, ended his days there in peace; in no way endeavouring to restore his bishopric, for, as has been said above, he was more industrious in ecclesiastical than in worldly affairs; serving God only in that church, and going wherever he was desired, to teach Church music. Theodore consecrated Cuichelm bishop of Rochester in his stead; but he, not long after, departing from his bishopric for want of necessaries, and withdrawing to other parts, Gebmund was put in his place by Theodore.[3]

In the year of our Lord 678, which is the eighth of the reign of Egfrid, in the month of August, appeared a star, called a comet, which continued for three months, rising in the morning, and sending forth, as it were, a tall pillar of radiant flame. The same year a dissension broke out between King Egfrid and the most reverend prelate, Wilfrid, who was driven from his see,[4] and two bishops substituted for him, to preside over the nation

that kingdom, at Wulfhere's death, to resume a position of independence towards Mercia. In spite of his conduct on this raid, Theodore, Florence of Worcester, and others, speak of the saintliness of his character. [1] Cc. 2 (and note), 5.
[2] C. 6, and note, and *infra*, p. 244.
[3] The dates of these changes in the episcopate are uncertain. Probably Gebmund was consecrated in 678. For his death, *v.* V, 8 *ad fin.*, and note.
[4] This was Wilfrid's first expulsion (*v.* V, 19). Bede's reticence on the subject is noteworthy. Egfrid's hostility to his former friend, Wilfrid, was doubtless caused by Wilfrid's encouragement of Queen Ethelthryth (cc. 19, 20) in her desire to take the veil. It was probably increased by Egfrid's second wife, Eormenburg, who is said to have resented Wilfrid's power and magnificence. Theodore, carrying out his policy of subdivision, availed himself of the opportunity afforded by this dissension. He consulted some of his suffragans (we do not know who they were; it was apparently

of the Northumbrians,[1] namely, Bosa,[2] to govern the
province of the Deiri; and Eata[3] that of the Bernicians;
the former having his episcopal see in the city of York,
the latter either in the church of Hagustald, or of Lindisfarne; both of them promoted to the episcopal dignity
from a community of monks. With them also Eadhaed[4]
was ordained bishop for the province of Lindsey, which
King Egfrid had but newly acquired, having defeated
Wulfhere and put him to flight;[5] and this was the first
bishop of its own which that province had; the second
was Ethelwin;[6] the third Edgar;[7] the fourth Cyni-

at a mixed council of ecclesiastics and laymen), but did not communicate with Wilfrid, being, no doubt, conscious of the useless-
ness of trying to get his consent. Wilfrid, after demanding an
explanation from the archbishop and the king in a Northumbrian
" gemot," and receiving no satisfaction, appealed to Rome (cf.
V, 19, p. 351). For the importance of this step, v. Bright, " Early
English Church History," pp. 323-326.

[1] Probably the intention was that Wilfrid should keep the larger
part of Deira, with his see at York, and that three new dioceses
should be formed. But, on his departure to appeal to Rome, it was
assumed that he had resigned his bishopric, and Bosa was consecrated Bishop of Deira with his see at York, Eata, Bishop of
the Bernicians, with the option of fixing his see either at Lindisfarne or Hagustald (Hexham). These two were " substituted for
him." Lindsey, which at this time belonged to Northumbria, became for the first time a separate diocese. When it passed again
to Mercia in 679 it was included in the subdivision of the Mercian
bishopric, and Ethelwin (v. infra note 6) became its bishop with
his see at Sidnacaestir (generally identified with Stow, but the
locality is unknown).

[2] He was one of the bishops educated in Hilda's monastery (v.
c. 23). Bede speaks highly of him (V, 3, 20), and Alcuin calls him
" vir sine fraude bonus." He retired from York when Wilfrid was
restored, but appears to have been reinstated on Wilfrid's second
expulsion.

[3] Abbot of Melrose, afterwards of Lindisfarne (III, 26, and
note; IV, 27; V, 9).

[4] III, 28, and this Chapter, ad fin., and note.

[5] In 675. Lindsey which had been Northumbrian under Edwin
and Oswald, had passed through many vicissitudes. Penda conquered it, Oswy recovered it (in 655), Wulfhere conquered it
again, Egfrid recovered it (675). It passed finally to Mercia under
Ethelred in 679 (v. infra this Chapter, ad fin.).   [6] III, 11, 27.

[7] He was still Bishop of Lindsey in 706, when he signed a charter
of Ethelward, " subregulus " of the Hwiccas.

bert,[1] who is there at present. Before Eadhaed, Sexwulf[2] was bishop as well of that province as of the Mercians and Midland Angles; so that, when expelled from Lindsey, he continued in the government of those provinces. Eadhaed, Bosa, and Eata, were ordained at York by archbishop Theodore;[3] who also, three years after the departure of Wilfrid, added two bishops to their number: Tunbert,[4] appointed to the church of Hagustald, Eata still continuing in that of Lindisfarne; and Trumwine[5] to the province of the Picts, which at that time was subject to English rule. Eadhaed returning from Lindsey, because Ethelred had recovered that province,[6] was placed by Theodore over the church of Ripon.[7]

[1] Preface, p. 4, and V, 23. Simeon of Durham says that he died in 732.
[2] Lindsey was at that time subject to Mercia. Sexwulf was expelled when Egfrid conquered it in 675. When the Mercian diocese was subdivided, he retained his see at Lichfield (v.s. c. 3, p. 219, note) as Bishop of the Mercians proper.
[3] By Theodore alone. The suffragans did not take part in the consecration.
[4] In 681 a fresh subdivision took place. The Bernician diocese was divided, Eata retaining Lindisfarne and giving up Hexham to Tunbert. Afterwards Eata retired from Lindisfarne in favour of Cuthbert and took Hexham (v. infra c. 28). Tunbert had been Abbot of Gilling (In Getlingum, III, 14, 24). He was deposed by Theodore from Hexham three years after his consecration (v. infra c. 28), like Wynfrid, "pro culpa cujusdam inobedientiae" (Vita Eatae in "Miscellanea Biographica," Surtees Society).
[5] His see was not at Whitern among the Picts of Galloway, as has been supposed (Florence of Worcester, Richard of Hexham, and others), but at the monastery of Abercorn on the Forth (I, 12; IV, 26), the Picts north of the Forth being at this time subject to Northumbria. After Egfrid's disastrous expedition in 685, they freed themselves from Northumbrian rule, the see was abandoned, and Trumwine retired to Whitby (c. 26). We hear of him as one of the deputation to Cuthbert in 684 (c. 28).
[6] In 679; v.s., p. 243, note 5.
Whether Ripon became for a time an episcopal see seems doubtful. In III, 28, Bede says distinctly that Eadhaed became "praesul" of the church there, and it does not seem consistent with his use to understand it as = abbot. Probably there was an attempt to subdivide the diocese of Deira (Eddius mentions it as one of Wilfrid's grievances), but the scheme was abandoned when Wilfrid was restored in 705. Ripon did not finally become an episcopal see till 1836.

CHAP. XIII. *How Bishop Wilfrid converted the province of the South Saxons to Christ.* [681 A.D.]

BUT Wilfrid was expelled from his bishopric, and having long travelled in many lands, went to Rome,[1] and afterwards returned to Britain. Though he could not, by reason of the enmity of the aforesaid king, be received into his own country or diocese, yet he could not be restrained from the ministry of the Gospel; for, taking his way into the province of the South Saxons,[2] which extends from Kent to the south and west, as far as the West Saxons, containing land of 7,000 families, and was at that time still in bondage to pagan rites, he administered to them the Word of faith, and the Baptism of salvation. Ethelwalch,[3] king of that nation, had been, not long before, baptized in the province of the Mercians, at the instance of King Wulfhere,[4] who was present, and received him as his godson when he came forth from the font, and in token of this adoption gave him two provinces, to wit, the Isle of Wight, and the province of the Meanware, in the country of the West Saxons.[5] The bishop, therefore, with the king's consent, or rather to his great joy, cleansed in the sacred font the foremost ealdormen and thegns of that country; and the priests, Eappa,[6] and Padda, and Burghelm, and Oiddi, either then, or

[1] For a fuller account, *v.* V, 19, and notes.
[2] For the early importance of this kingdom under Aelli, *v.* II, 5. It had become a small insignificant nation, cut off from its neighbours by forests (the " Andredsweald ") and marshes, and though we read (III, 20) that Damian, bishop of Rochester, was of the South Saxon race, it was almost untouched by Christian influences.
[3] Cf. *infra* c. 15.
[4] He also brought about the reconversion of the East Saxons by sending Bishop Jaruman to them. Cf. III, 30.
[5] Wulfhere had invaded Wessex, probably in 661 (Sax. Chron.), and conquered the Isle of Wight and the district of the Meanware, *i.e.*, the district from Southampton Water to the South Downs. The inhabitants were Jutes. The name survives in the hundreds, Meonstoke, and East and West Meon. For the termination " ware "=dwellers, cf. Lindisfari, Cantuarii, Boructuari, etc.
[6] Cf. c. 14.

afterwards, baptized the rest of the people. The queen, whose name was Eabae, had been baptized in her own country, the province of the Hwiccas.[1] She was the daughter of Eanfrid, the brother of Aenhere,[2] who were both Christians, as were their people; but all the province of the South Saxons was ignorant of the Name of God and the faith. But there was among them a certain monk of the Scottish nation, whose name was Dicul,[3] who had a very small monastery, at the place called Bosanhamm,[4] encompassed by woods and seas, and in it there were five or six brothers, who served the Lord in humility and poverty; but none of the natives cared either to follow their course of life, or hear their preaching.

But Bishop Wilfrid, while preaching the Gospel to the people, not only delivered them from the misery of eternal damnation, but also from a terrible calamity of temporal death. For no rain had fallen in that district for three years before his arrival in the province, whereupon a grievous famine fell upon the people and pitilessly destroyed them; insomuch that it is said that often forty or fifty men, wasted with hunger, would go together to some precipice, or to the sea-shore, and there, hand in hand, in piteous wise cast them themselves down either to perish by the fall, or be swallowed up by the waves. But on the very day on which the nation received the Baptism of the faith, there fell a soft but plentiful rain; the earth revived, the fields grew green again, and the season was pleasant and fruitful. Thus the old superstition was cast away, and idolatry renounced, the heart and flesh of all rejoiced in the living God, for they perceived that He Who is the true God had enriched them by His heavenly grace with both inward and outward

---

[1] Cf. II, 2, p. 84, note 2.

[2] They were probably joint kings of the Hwiccas.

[3] "Scottish," as usual, means Irish. There is another Dicul mentioned in III, 19. Stevenson suggests the identification of this Dicul with the Irish monk who wrote a geographical work, the "De Mensura Orbis Terrae," but he lived in the ninth century.

[4] Bosham, near Chichester. It was the favourite South Saxon abode of Harold and Godwine (Freeman, "Norman Conquest").

blessings. For the bishop, when he came into the province, and found so great misery from famine there, taught them to get their food by fishing; for their sea and rivers abounded in fish, but the people had no skill to take any of them, except eels alone. The bishop's men having gathered eel-nets everywhere, cast them into the sea, and by the blessing of God took three hundred fishes of divers sorts, which being divided into three parts, they gave a hundred to the poor, a hundred to those of whom they had the nets, and kept a hundred for their own use. By this benefit the bishop gained the affections of them all, and they began more readily at his preaching to hope for heavenly blessings, seeing that by his help they had received those which are temporal.

At this time, King Ethelwalch gave to the most reverend prelate, Wilfrid, land to the extent of eighty-seven families, to maintain his company who were wandering in exile. The place is called Selaeseu,[1] that is, the Island of the Sea-Calf; it is encompassed by the sea on all sides, except the west, where is an entrance about the cast of a sling in width; which sort of place is by the Latins called a peninsula, by the Greeks, a cherronesos. Bishop Wilfrid, having this place given him, founded therein a monastery, chiefly of the brethren he had brought with him, and established a rule of life; and his successors are known to be there to this day. He himself, both in word and deed performed the duties of a bishop in those parts during the space of five years, until the death of King Egfrid,[2] and was justly honoured by all. And forasmuch as the king, together with the said place, gave him all the goods that were therein, with the lands and men, he instructed all the people in

[1] Selsey, the island of the seal ("sea-calf"), south of Chichester. It was a royal "vill." It became the episcopal see for the South Saxons at some time about 709 (cf. V, 18, *ad fin.* and note), transferred to Chichester in 1075.
[2] Egfrid fell at the battle of Nechtansmere in 685 (*v.* c. 26), and Wilfrid was restored to his bishopric "in the second year of Aldfrid," Egfrid's successor (V, 19, p. 353). He was in Wessex with Caedwalla for part of the year 686 (cf. c. 16).

the faith of Christ, and cleansed them in the water of Baptism. Among whom were two hundred and fifty bondsmen and bondswomen, all of whom he saved by Baptism from slavery to the Devil, and in like manner, by giving them their liberty, set them free from slavery to man.

CHAP. XIV. *How a pestilence ceased through the intercession of King Oswald.* [681-686 A.D.]

IN this monastery, at that time, certain special manifestations of the heavenly grace are said to have been shown forth; in as much as the tyranny of the Devil had been recently cast out and Christ had begun to reign there. Of these I have thought it proper to perpetuate the memory of one which the most reverend Bishop Acca [1] was wont often to relate to me, affirming that it had been told him by most creditable brothers of the same monastery. About the same time that this province had received the faith of Christ, a grievous pestilence fell upon many provinces of Britain; which, also, by the Divine dispensation, reached to the aforesaid monastery, then governed by the most religious priest of Christ, Eappa; [2] and many, as well of those that had come thither with the bishop, as of those of the same province of the South Saxons who had been lately called to the faith, were snatched away out of this world. The brethren, therefore, thought fit to keep a fast of three days, and humbly to implore the Divine goodness to vouchsafe to have mercy on them, either by delivering from instant death those that were in danger by reason of the disease, or by saving those who were hurried out of this life from the eternal damnation of their souls.

There was at that time in the monastery, a little boy, of the Saxon nation, lately called to the faith, who had been attacked by the same infirmity, and had long kept his bed. On the second day of the aforesaid fasting and

[1] III, 13, note.   [2] C. 13.

prayer, it happened about the second hour of the day, that this boy was left alone in the place where he lay sick, when on a sudden, through the Divine disposition, the most blessed chiefs of the Apostles vouchsafed to appear to him; for he was a boy of a very simple and gentle disposition, and with sincere devotion observed the mysteries of the faith which he had received. The Apostles therefore, greeting him with loving words, said, "My son, fear not death, concerning which thou art troubled; for this day we will bring thee to the kingdom of Heaven; but first thou must needs wait till the Masses are celebrated, that having received thy voyage provision,[1] the Body and Blood of our Lord, and so being set free from sickness and death, thou mayest be taken up to the everlasting joys in Heaven.

"Call therefore to thee the priest, Eappa, and tell him, that the Lord has heard your prayers, and has favourably looked upon your devotion and your fast, and not one more shall die of this plague, either in the monastery or the lands adjacent to it; but all your people who any where labour under this sickness, shall be raised up from their weakness, and restored to their former health, saving thee alone, who art this day to be delivered from death, and to be carried into Heaven, to behold our Lord Christ, whom thou hast faithfully served. This favour the Divine mercy has vouchsafed to grant you, through the intercession of the godly King Oswald, beloved of God, who formerly nobly ruled over the nation of the Northumbrians, with the authority of a temporal kingdom and the devotion of Christian piety which leads to the eternal kingdom. For this very day that king was killed in body by the infidels in war, and straightway taken up to Heaven to the everlasting joys of souls, and brought into fellowship with the number of the elect. Let them look in their records,[2] wherein the

[1] This English equivalent for "viaticum" is used by Stapleton in his translation (1565).
[2] Calendars to show the proper days for commemorative Masses, cf. *infra* " chronicle " (" annale "). The burial was generally on the day of death, hence " depositio " of the festival of a saint.

burial of the dead is set down, and they will find that he
was, this day, as we have said, taken out of this world.
Let them, therefore, celebrate Masses in all the oratories
of this monastery, either in thanksgiving because their
prayers are heard, or else in memory of the aforesaid
King Oswald, who once governed their nation,[1] and
therefore humbly prayed to the Lord for them, as for
converts of his nation; and let all the brethren assemble
in the church, and all communicate in the heavenly
Sacrifices, and so let them cease to fast, and refresh the
body also with the food that belongs to it."

The boy called the priest, and repeated all these
words to him; and the priest carefully inquired after the
habit and form of the men that had appeared to him.
He answered, "Their habit was altogether noble, and
their countenances most pleasant and beautiful, such as
I had never seen before, nor did I think there could be
any men so fair and comely. One of them indeed was
shorn like a clerk, the other had a long beard; and they
said that one of them was called Peter, the other Paul;
and they were the servants of our Lord and Saviour
Jesus Christ, sent by Him from Heaven to protect our
monastery." The priest believed what the boy said, and
going thence immediately, looked in his chronicle, and
found that King Oswald had been killed on that very
day. He then called the brethren, ordered dinner to be
provided, Masses to be said, and all of them to communicate as usual; causing also a part of the same
Sacrifice of the Lord's Oblation to be carried to the
sick boy.

Soon after this, the boy died, on that same day; and
by his death proved that the words which he had heard
from the Apostles of Christ were true. And this moreover bore witness to the truth of his words, that none
besides himself, belonging to the same monastery, was
taken away at that time. And without doubt, by this
vision, many that heard of it were wonderfully excited

[1] It must be remembered that this was a monastery of Northumbrians. But Oswald is said to have held an "imperium" over
all England except Kent (II, 5).

to implore the Divine mercy in adversity, and to submit to the wholesome remedy of fasting. From that time, the day of commemoration of that king and soldier of Christ began to be yearly honoured with the celebration of Masses, not only in that monastery, but in many other places.

CHAP. XV. *How King Caedwalla, king of the Gewissae, having slain Ethelwalch, wasted that Province with cruel slaughter and devastation.* [685 A.D.]

IN the meantime, Caedwalla,[1] a young man of great vigour, of the royal race of the Gewissae,[2] an exile from his country, came with an army, slew Ethelwalch,[3] and wasted that province with cruel slaughter and devastation; but he was soon expelled by Berthun and Andhun, the king's ealdormen, who held in succession the government of the province. The first of them was afterwards killed by the same Caedwalla, when he was king of the Gewissae, and the province was reduced to more grievous slavery: Ini,[4] likewise, who reigned after Caedwalla, oppressed that country with the like servitude for many years; for which reason, during all that time, they could have no bishop of their own; but their first bishop, Wilfrid, having been recalled home, they were subject to the bishop of the Gewissae, that is, the West Saxons, who were in the city of Venta.[5]

[1] C. 12, note.
[2] The West Saxons, v. II, 5 and note. Cf. III, 7.
[3] C. 13.
[4] v. V, 7 *ad fin.* Like Caedwalla, a descendant of Ceaulin, "A king who deserves the name of great" (Bright), great both as a conqueror and a legislator. He was probably the first king to introduce written law into Wessex, viz., his famous "Dooms," enacted by a West Saxon witenagemot in the early years of his reign.
[5] Winchester. At this time Haedde was bishop there (c. 12). For the creation of a South Saxon bishopric v. V, 18 *ad fin.*

CHAP. XVII. *Of the Synod held in the plain of Haeth-felth, Archbishop Theodore being president.* [680 A.D.]

ABOUT this time, Theodore being informed that the faith of the Church at Constantinople was much perplexed by the heresy of Eutyches,[1] and desiring that the Churches of the English, over which he presided, should remain free from all such taint, convened an assembly of venerable bishops and many learned men, and diligently inquired into the faith of each. He found them all of one mind in the Catholic faith, and this he caused to be committed to writing by the authority of the synod as a memorial, and for the instruction of succeeding generations; the beginning of which document is as follows:

"In the name of our Lord and Saviour Jesus Christ, under the rule of our most pious lords, Egfrid, king of of the Northumbrians, in the tenth year of his reign, the seventeenth of September, the eighth indiction; Ethelred, king of the Mercians, in the sixth year of his reign; Aldwulf king of the East Angles, in the seventeenth year of his reign; and Hlothere, king of Kent, in the seventh year of his reign;[2] Theodore, by the grace of God, archbishop of the island of Britain, and of the city of Canter-

[1] Eutyches was Archimandrite of a monastery near Constantinople. He was condemned by the synod of Constantinople in 448, and by the council of Chalcedon in 451. He was the originator of the Monophysite heresy which denied the existence of the two natures, the Divine and human, in the Incarnate Son. Monothelitism, which was the subject of the controversy alluded to here, arose out of an attempt to reconcile the Monophysites by the assertion of one will and operation (activity, ἐνέργεια) in our Lord. It was condemned in the General Council of Constantinople, 680-681. In anticipation of this council various provincial synods were held, as well as the synod at Rome assembled by Pope Agatho, at which Wilfrid represented the English church (*v.* V. 19).

[2] The year was 680 (cf. V, 24), but it falls in the eighth year of Hlothere of Kent, who succeeded in July, 673. For Egfrid, *v. s.* c. 5, *ad init.* Probably he succeeded in 671. Ethelred of Mercia succeeded in 675 (V, 24), so that Sept., 680, might easily fall in his sixth year; Aldwulf, of East Anglia, in 663 or 664 (*v.* II, 15; IV, 23). The eighth indiction, whether Cæsarean or Pontifical (*v.s.* c. 5, note), includes Sept. 17, 680.

bury, being president, and the other venerable bishops of the island of Britain sitting with him, the holy Gospels being laid before them, at the place which, in the Saxon tongue, is called Haethfelth,[1] we conferred together, and set forth the right and orthodox faith, as our Lord Jesus Christ in the flesh delivered the same to His disciples, who beheld His Presence and heard His words, and as it is delivered by the creed of the holy fathers, and by all holy and universal synods in general, and by the consent of all approved doctors of the Catholic Church. We, therefore, following them, in piety and orthodoxy, and professing accordance with their divinely inspired doctrine, do believe agreeably to it, and with the holy fathers confess the Father, and Son, and Holy Ghost, to be properly and truly a Trinity consubstantial in Unity, and Unity in Trinity, that is, one God in three Subsistences or consubstantial persons, of equal glory and honour."

And after much more of the same sort, appertaining to the confession of the right faith, this holy synod added to its document, "We acknowledge the five holy and general councils[2] of the blessed fathers acceptable to God; that is, of the 318 assembled at Nicaea, against the most impious Arius and his tenets; and at Constantino-

[1] Generally identified with Hatfield in Hertfordshire, but T. Kerslake ("Vestiges of the supremacy of Mercia") supposes it to be Clovesho (Cliff-at-Hoe); *v.s.* c. 5, and note.

[2] The five Oecumenical Councils which had been held before this time, viz., Nicaea, in 325; Constantinople, in 381-382; Ephesus, in 431; Chalcedon, in 451; Constantinople, in 553. For the Arian heresy, *v.* I, 8 (and note), where "madness" ("vesania") is, as here, the word used to describe it. Macedonius was a "semi-Arian," Eudoxius an Arian; both were bishops of Constantinople. Nestorius was consecrated Bishop of Constantinople in 428. He popularized the heresy which originated with Theodore, Bishop of Mopsuestia, 392-428. It consisted in emphasizing the human element in our Lord's Nature to the practical exclusion of the Divine, as a reaction against Apollinarianism which explained away His real Humanity. "The Christ of Nestorius was, after all, simply a deified man, not God incarnate" (Gore, "Bampton Lectures"). Theodoret, Bishop of Cyrus in Syria (died 457) and Ibas, Bishop of Edessa, 435-457, were disciples of Theodore, Bishop of Mopsuestia, and opponents of Cyril of Alexandria, who is accused of Apollinarianism in the letter of Ibas.

ple, of 150, against the madness of Macedonius and Eudoxius, and their tenets; and at Ephesus, for the first
time, of 200, against the most wicked Nestorius, and his
tenets; and at Chalcedon, of 630, against Eutyches and
Nestorius, and their tenets; and again, at Constantinople,
in a fifth council, in the time of Justinian the younger,[1]
against Theodorus, and the epistles of Theodoret and
Ibas, and their tenets in opposition to Cyril." And again
a little lower, "the synod held in the city of Rome, in the
time of the blessed Pope Martin,[2] in the eighth indiction,
and in the ninth year of the most pious Emperor Constantine,[3] we also acknowledge. And we glorify our Lord Jesus
Christ, as they glorified Him, neither adding aught nor
taking away; anathematizing with hearts and lips those
whom they anathematized, and receiving those whom
they received; glorifying God the Father, Who is without
beginning, and His only-begotten Son, begotten of the
Father before the worlds, and the Holy Ghost proceeding
ineffably from the Father and the Son,[4] even as those
holy Apostles, prophets, and doctors, whom we have
above-mentioned, did declare. And all we, who, with
Archbishop Theodore, have thus set forth the Catholic
faith, thereto subscribe."

[1] Justinian I, 527-565.
[2] The first Lateran Council, in 649, against the Monothelites.
Martin I, Pope 649-655, died in the Crimea, exiled and imprisoned
by the Emperor Constans II in consequence of his resistance to
the heresy.
[3] Constantine IV, more generally known as Constans II, 641-688.
[4] We have here, under the auspices of an Eastern Archbishop, a
clear enunciation of the doctrine which afterwards divided the
east and west: the Double Procession of the Holy Spirit. The
"filioque" clause, which formed no part of the Nicene Creed, nor of
its Constantinopolitan recension, had been formally adopted at the
Third Council of Toledo in 589 and at subsequent Spanish councils.
The English prelates at Hatfield were probably influenced by this
precedent.

CHAP. XVIII. *Of John, the precentor of the Apostolic see, who came into Britain to teach.* [680 A.D.]

AMONG those who were present at this synod, and confirmed the decrees of the Catholic faith, was the venerable John,[1] archchanter of the church of the holy Apostle Peter,[2] and abbot of the monastery of the blessed Martin, who had come lately from Rome, by order of Pope Agatho, together with the most reverend Abbot Biscop, surnamed Benedict,[3] of whom mention has been made above. For the said Benedict, having built a monastery in Britain, in honour of the most blessed chief of the Apostles, at the mouth of the river Wear, went to Rome with Ceolfrid,[4] his companion and fellow-labourer in that work, who was after him abbot of the same monastery; he had been several times before at Rome, and was now honourably received by Pope Agatho of blessed memory; from whom he also asked and obtained, in order to

[1] Cf. Bede's "History of the Abbots," § 6.
[2] *I.e.*, St. Peter's at Rome. The Monastery of St. Martin was on the Esquiline. It was founded by Pope Symmachus in honour of SS. Sylvester and Martin.
[3] Cf. c. 1, notes. (For his life, *v.* Bede's "History of the Abbots," and the Anon. "History of the Abbots.") He has not been mentioned before in this history. His ecclesiastical surname was Benedict, "Baducing" was probably his patronymic. He was of noble birth and a thegn of King Oswy, born in 628. He was the companion of Wilfrid on his first journey to Rome (V, 19). In his native province of Northumbria he founded the monasteries of Wearmouth (in 674) and Jarrow (*circ.* 681), where Bede's life was passed, and enriched them with furniture, vestments, relics, pictures, and a library of valuable books which he brought from the Continent. The rule which he framed for his monasteries was Benedictine, compiled from seventeen different monasteries which he had visited. He died Jan. 12, 689.
[4] Cf. V, 21. Bede's "History of the Abbots," and Anon. "History of the Abbots." He added to Benedict's library. He had been a monk at Ripon under Wilfrid, became Abbot of Jarrow in 681, and of Wearmouth in addition to Jarrow in 688. In 716 he resigned and set out for Rome, but died at Langres in the same year. Bede was trained under him (V, 24) and was probably the little boy left alone with him to recite the offices when the pestilence of 686 swept away the monks. Anon. Hist. Abb. § 14.)

S

secure the immunities of the monastery which he had founded, a letter of privilege confirmed by apostolic authority, according to what he knew to be the will and grant of King Egfrid, by whose consent and gift of land he had built that monastery.

He was also allowed to take the aforesaid Abbot John with him into Britain, that he might teach in his monastery the system of singing throughout the year, as it was practised at St. Peter's at Rome.[1] The Abbot John did as he had been commanded by the Pope, teaching the singers of the said monastery the order and manner of singing and reading aloud, and committing to writing all that was requisite throughout the whole course of the year for the celebration of festivals; and these writings are still preserved in that monastery, and have been copied by many others elsewhere. The said John not only taught the brothers of that monastery, but such as had skill in singing resorted from almost all the monasteries of the same province to hear him, and many invited him to teach in other places.

Besides his task of singing and reading, he had also received a commission from the Apostolic Pope, carefully to inform himself concerning the faith of the English Church, and to give an account thereof on his return to Rome. For he also brought with him the decision of the synod of the blessed Pope Martin, held not long before at Rome,[2] with the consent of one hundred and five bishops, chiefly to refute those who taught that there is but one operation and will in Christ, and he gave it to be transcribed in the aforesaid monastery of the most religious Abbot Benedict. The men who followed such opinion greatly perplexed the faith of the Church of Constantinople at that time; but by the help of God they were then discovered and overcome.[3] Wherefore, Pope Agatho, being desirous to be informed concerning the state of the Church in Britain, as well as in other provinces, and to

[1] Cf. II, 20, *ad fin.*, note.
[2] Cf. c. 17, and note.
[3] In the Council of Constantinople, 680-681 (*v.s.* c. 17 *ad init.* note.

what extent it was clear from the contagion of heretics, gave this matter in charge to the most reverend Abbot John, then appointed to go to Britain. The synod we have spoken of having been called for this purpose in Britain, the Catholic faith was found untainted in all, and a report of the proceedings of the same was given him to carry to Rome.

But in his return to his own country, soon after crossing the sea, he fell sick and died; and his body, for the sake of St. Martin, in whose monastery he presided, was by his friends carried to Tours,[1] and honourably buried; for he had been kindly entertained by the Church there on his way to Britain, and earnestly entreated by the brethren, that in his return to Rome he would take that road, and visit their Church, and moreover he was there supplied with men to conduct him on his way, and assist him in the work enjoined upon him. Though he died by the way, yet the testimony of the Catholic faith of the English nation was carried to Rome, and received with great joy by the Apostolic Pope, and all those that heard or read it.

CHAP. XIX. *How Queen Ethelthryth always preserved her virginity, and her body suffered no corruption in the grave.* [660-696 A.D.]

KING EGFRID took to wife Ethelthryth, the daughter of Anna,[2] king of the East Angles, of whom mention has been often made; a man of true religion, and altogether noble in mind and deed. She had before been given in marriage to another, to wit, Tondbert, ealdorman[3] of the Southern Gyrwas; but he died soon after he had married her, and she was given to the aforesaid king. Though she lived with him twelve years, yet she preserved the glory of perfect virginity, as I was informed by Bishop

---

[1] To St. Martin's own church at Tours, where, as Abbot of St. Martin's monastery at Rome, it was specially fitting that he should find burial.   [2] Cf. III, 7, note.
[3] "Princeps," A.S. Ealdorman. The county of the Southern Gyrwas was South Cambridgeshire. Cf. III, 20, note.

Wilfrid, of blessed memory, of whom I inquired, because some questioned the truth thereof; and he told me that he was an undoubted witness to her virginity, forasmuch as Egfrid promised to give him many lands and much money if he could persuade the queen to consent to fulfil her marriage duty, for he knew the queen loved no man more than himself. And it is not to be doubted that this might take place in our age, which true histories tell us happened sometimes in former ages, by the help of the same Lord who promises to abide with us always, even unto the end of the world. For the divine miracle whereby her flesh, being buried, could not suffer corruption, is a token that she had not been defiled by man.

She had long asked of the king that he would permit her to lay aside worldly cares, and to serve only Christ, the true King, in a monastery; and having at length with difficulty prevailed, she entered the monastery of the Abbess Aebba,[1] who was aunt to King Egfrid, at the place called the city of Coludi,[2] having received the veil of the religious habit from the hands of the aforesaid Bishop Wilfrid; but a year after she was herself made abbess in the district called Elge,[3] where, having built a monastery, she began, by the example of a heavenly life and by her teaching, to be the virgin mother of many virgins dedicated to God. It is told of her that from the time of her entering the monastery, she would never wear any linen but only woollen garments, and would

[1] Cf. c. 25. Bede tells us in the "Life of Cuthbert," that she was a half sister of Oswy's on the mother's side. Her name survives in Ebchester on the Derwent, where she founded a nunnery; in St. Abb's Head, near which she afterwards founded the double monastery of Coldingham; and in St. Ebbe's, Oxford. She was the friend of Cuthbert, and it was to her exhortations to Egfrid that Wilfrid owed his release from prison.

[2] Coldingham in Berwickshire. It was a mixed monastery. Cf. c. 25.

[3] Ely. The Isle of Ely was her jointure from her first husband. She received the help and support of Aldwulf, king of East Anglia (II, 15; IV, 17, 23), her cousin (he was the son of Ethelhere and nephew of Anna). The monastery was founded in 673. It was exempted from the jurisdiction of the East Anglian bishop, and subject to Wilfrid.

seldom wash in a hot bath, unless just before the greater festivals, as Easter, Whitsuntide, and the Epiphany, and then she did it last of all, when the other handmaids of Christ who were there had been washed, served by her and her attendants. She seldom ate more than once a day, excepting on the greater festivals, or some urgent occasion. Always, except when grievous sickness prevented her, from the time of matins till day-break, she continued in the church at prayer. Some also say, that by the spirit of prophecy she not only foretold the pestilence of which she was to die, but also, in the presence of all, revealed the number of those that should be then snatched away from this world out of her monastery. She was taken to the Lord, in the midst of her flock, seven years after she had been made abbess; and, as she had ordered, was buried among them in a wooden coffin in her turn, according to the order in which she had passed away.

She was succeeded in the office of abbess by her sister Sexburg,[1] who had been wife to Earconbert, king of Kent. This abbess, when her sister had been buried sixteen years, thought fit to take up her bones, and, putting them into a new coffin, to translate them into the church. Accordingly she ordered some of the brothers to find a stone whereof to make a coffin for this purpose. They went on board ship, for the district of Ely is on every side encompassed with water and marshes, and has no large stones, and came to a small deserted city, not far from thence, which, in the language of the English, is called Grantacaestir,[2] and presently, near the city walls, they found a white marble coffin,[3] most beautifully

---

[1] III, 8, cf. III, 7, note. After her husband's death she acted as regent for a time, then founded a monastery in the Isle of Sheppey, and became abbess of it. Thence she retired to Ely, where, after being a simple nun, she succeeded Ethelthryth as abbess. She was herself succeeded first at Sheppey, and afterwards at Ely, by her daughter Ermingild, widow of Wulfhere of Mercia.

[2] Grantchester, near Cambridge.

[3] A Roman sarcophagus. A number of fragments of very ancient stone coffins have been found there, built into the wall of the church (Mayor and Lumby).

wrought, and fitly covered with a lid of the same sort of stone. Perceiving, therefore, that the Lord had prospered their journey, they returned thanks to Him and carried it to the monastery.

When the grave was opened and the body of the holy virgin and bride of Christ was brought into the light of day, it was found as free from corruption as if she had died and been buried on that very day; as the aforesaid Bishop Wilfrid, and many others that know it, testify. But the physician, Cynifrid, who was present at her death, and when she was taken up out of the grave, had more certain knowledge. He was wont to relate that in her sickness she had a very great tumour under her jaw. "And I was ordered," said he, "to lay open that tumour to let out the noxious matter in it, which I did, and she seemed to be somewhat more easy for two days, so that many thought she might recover from her infirmity; but on the third day she was attacked by the former pains, and being soon snatched out of the world, she exchanged all pain and death for everlasting life and health. And when, so many years after, her bones were to be taken out of the grave, a pavilion being spread over it, and all the congregation, the brothers on the one side, and the sisters on the other, standing about it singing, while the abbess, with a few others, had gone within to take up and wash the bones, on a sudden we heard the abbess within cry out with a loud voice, 'Glory be to the name of the Lord.' Not long after they called me in, opening the door of the pavilion, and I found the body of the holy virgin taken out of the grave and laid on a bed, like one asleep; then taking off the veil from the face, they also showed me that the incision which I had made was healed up; so that, in marvellous wise, instead of the open gaping wound with which she had been buried, there then appeared only the slightest trace of a scar. Besides, all the linen clothes in which the body had been wrapped, appeared entire and as fresh as if they had been that very day put about her chaste limbs."

It is said that when she was sore troubled with the aforesaid tumour and pain in her jaw and neck, she took great pleasure in that sort of sickness, and was wont to say, "I know of a surety that I deservedly bear the weight of my trouble on my neck, for I remember that, when I was a young maiden, I bore on it the needless weight of necklaces;[1] and therefore I believe the Divine goodness would have me endure the pain in my neck, that so I may be absolved from the guilt of my needless levity, having now, instead of gold and pearls, the fiery heat of a tumour rising on my neck." It happened also that by the touch of those same linen clothes devils were expelled from bodies possessed, and other diseases were at divers times healed; and the coffin wherein she was first buried is said to have cured some of infirmities of the eyes, who, praying with their heads resting upon that coffin, were presently relieved of the pain or dimness in their eyes. So they washed the virgin's body, and having clothed it in new garments, brought it into the church, and laid it in the sarcophagus that had been brought, where it is held in great veneration to this day. The sarcophagus was found in a wonderful manner to fit the virgin's body as if it had been made purposely for her, and the place for the head, which was fashioned separately, appeared exactly shaped to the measurement of her head.

Elge is in the province of the East Angles, a district of about six hundred families, of the nature of an island, encompassed, as has been said, with marshes or waters, and therefore it has its name from the great plenty of eels taken in those marshes; there the aforesaid handmaid of Christ desired to have a monastery, because, as we have before mentioned, she came, according to the flesh, of that same province of the East Angles.

---

[1] "Audrey" is the popular form of the name Ethelthryth. A "tawdry lace" (*i.e.* St. Audrey lace) is a necklace; cf. "Winter's Tale," iv. 3. Hence our word "tawdry," which possibly only derives its meaning from the cheap necklaces, etc., sold at St. Audrey's fair at Ely on the saint's day, October 17 (the day of her translation), but may also be a reminiscence of this anecdote.

CHAP. XX. *A Hymn concerning her.*

IT seems fitting to insert in this history a hymn concerning virginity, which we composed in elegiac verse many years ago, in praise and honour of the same queen and bride of Christ, and therefore truly a queen, because the bride of Christ; and to imitate the method of Holy Scripture, wherein many songs are inserted in the history, and these, as is well known, are composed in metre and verse.

"Trinity,[1] Gracious, Divine, Who rulest all the ages; favour my task, Trinity, Gracious, Divine.

"Let Maro sound the trumpet of war, let us sing the gifts of peace; the gifts of Christ we sing, let Maro sound the trumpet of war.

"Chaste is my song, no rape of guilty Helen; light tales shall be told by the wanton, chaste is my song.

"I will tell of gifts from Heaven, not wars of hapless Troy; I will tell of gifts from Heaven, wherein the earth is glad.

"Lo! the high God comes to the womb of a holy virgin, to be the Saviour of men, lo! the high God comes.

"A hallowed maid gives birth to Him Who gave the world its being; Mary, the gate of God, a maiden gives Him birth.

"The company of her fellows rejoices over the Virgin Mother of Him Who wields the thunder; a shining virgin band, the company of her fellows rejoices.

"Her honour has made many a blossom to spring

---

[1] The poem is (1) alphabetical; *i.e.*, the first letters of the hexameter lines form the alphabet, and there are four additional couplets at the end, in which the first letters form the word "Amen"; (2) "serpentine," reciprocal or echoing; *i.e.*, the last half of the pentameter repeats the first two and a half feet of the hexameter. Such verses are common in mediaeval Latin, and are doubtless a development from the occasional instances of echoing lines which occur in the classical poets (*e.g.*, Martial VIII, xxi, 1-2; IX, 97; Ovid, Fasti IV, 365-366), as the extreme form of that impulse to give emphasis by iteration which is a marked feature of Latin poetry, particularly of the Ovidian elegiac.

from that pure shoot, virgin blossoms her honour has made to spring.

"Scorched by the fierce flames, the maiden Agatha [1] yielded not; in like manner Eulalia endures, scorched by the fierce flames.

"The lofty soul of chaste Tecla overcomes the wild beasts; chaste Euphemia overcomes the accursed wild beasts.

"Agnes joyously laughs at the sword, herself stronger than steel, Cecilia joyously laughs at the foemen's sword.

"Many a triumph is mighty throughout the world in temperate hearts; throughout the world love of the temperate life is mighty.

"Yea, and our day likewise a peerless maiden has blessed; peerless our Ethelthryth shines.

"Child of a noble sire, and glorious by royal birth, more noble in her Lord's sight, the child of a noble sire.

"Thence she receives queenly honour and a sceptre in this world; thence she receives honour, awaiting higher honour above.

"What need, gracious lady, to seek an earthly lord, even now given to the Heavenly Bridegroom?

[1] Agatha suffered 5th February, 251 A.D., in the Decian persecution, according to her "Acta" (the Diocletian, according to the Martyrology and Aldhelm). Eulalia was burnt to death at the age of twelve in the Diocletian persecution, having denounced herself. The legend tells that a white dove hovered over her ashes till snow fell and covered them. Tecla, the disciple of St. Paul, is said to have been the first virgin martyr. She was miraculously saved from her martyrdom and died in peace long after. Euphemia was torn by wild beasts at Chalcedon in 307 A.D. in the Diocletian persecution. Asterius, Bishop of Amasea, 400 A.D., says that he saw a tablet in the church at Chalcedon depicting her sufferings. We have thus very early evidence for her history. Agnes is said to have been beheaded in 304 A.D., in the Diocletian persecution, at the age of twelve or thirteen. The date of St. Cecilia is very uncertain; Fortunatus, Bishop of Poitiers, says that she died *circ.* 176-180 A.D., but another account places her martyrdom as late as the time of Diocletian. Her connection with music does not appear in the legends, and is probably due to the fact that Pope Paschal endowed the monastery which he built in connection with her church at Rome to provide for musical services at her tomb day and night.

"Christ is at hand, the Bridegroom (why seek an earthly lord?) that thou mayst follow even now, methinks, in the steps of the Mother of Heaven's King, that thou too mayst be a mother in God.

"Twelve years [1] she had reigned, a bride dedicated to God, then in the cloister dwelt, a bride dedicated to God.

"To Heaven all consecrated she lived, abounding in lofty deeds, then to Heaven all consecrated she gave up her soul.

"Twice eight Novembers [2] the maid's fair flesh lay in the tomb, nor did the maid's fair flesh see corruption in the tomb.

"This was Thy work, O Christ, that her very garments were bright and undefiled even in the grave; O Christ, this was Thy work.

"The dark serpent [3] flies before the honour due to the holy raiment; disease is driven away, and the dark serpent flies.

"Rage fills the foe who of old conquered Eve; exultant the maiden triumphs and rage fills the foe.

"Behold, O bride of God, thy glory upon earth; the glory that awaits thee in the Heavens behold, O bride of God.

"In gladness thou receivest gifts, bright amidst the festal torches; behold! the Bridegroom comes, in gladness thou receivest gifts.

"And a new song thou singest to the tuneful harp; a new-made bride, thou exultest in the tuneful hymn.

"None can part her from them which follow the Lamb

[1] She had not been a queen twelve years. The dates are probably these: she was born about 630 at Ermynge (Ixning) in Suffolk, and married to Tondbert in 652. Tondbert died in 655, and she was married to Egfrid (who must then have been only fifteen) in 660. Egfrid succeeded to the throne in 670 or 671, and it must have been in 672 that she retired to Coldingham. She was, therefore, queen for not more than two years, though perhaps we may accept the statement of the Liber Eliensis that Egfrid was sub-king of Deira for some years before his accession.

[2] *I.e.*, she had been buried sixteen years; *v.s.* c. 19.

[3] Literally the water snake, ὕδρος, used generally for any serpent, and so=the Devil; *Chelydrus* is similarly used (*v.* Ducange).

enthroned on high, whom none had severed from the Love enthroned on high."

CHAP. XXI. *How Bishop Theodore made peace between the kings Egfrid and Ethelred.* [679 A.D.]

IN the ninth year of the reign of King Egfrid, a great battle[1] was fought between him and Ethelred, king of the Mercians, near the river Trent, and Aelfwine,[2] brother to King Egfrid, was slain, a youth about eighteen years of age, and much beloved by both provinces; for King Ethelred had married his sister Osthryth.[3] There was now reason to expect a more bloody war, and more lasting enmity between those kings and their fierce nations; but Theodore, the bishop, beloved of God, relying on the Divine aid, by his wholesome admonitions wholly extinguished the dangerous fire that was breaking out; so that the kings and their people on both sides were appeased, and no man was put to death, but only the due mulct[4] paid to the king who was the avenger for the death of his brother; and this peace continued long after between those kings and between their kingdoms.

CHAP. XXII. *How a certain captive's chains fell off when Masses were sung for him.* [679 A.D.]

IN the aforesaid battle, wherein King Aelfwine was killed, a memorable incident is known to have happened,

[1] The Battle of the Trent in 679 (cf. V, 24). It was on the anniversary of Wilfrid's expulsion; he is said to have foretold a calamity. The place may, perhaps, be identified with Elford-on-Trent, in Staffordshire; it is supposed that the name may be a reminiscence of Aelfwine. By this battle Mercia regained Lindsey, which never again became Northumbrian (cf. c. 12, *ad fin.*).

[2] Cf. c. 22, where he is called "King Aelfwine," as also twice in Eddius. He may have been sub-king of Deira.

[3] III, 11; V, 24. When Wilfrid took refuge in Mercia in 681, she and her husband expelled him "pro adulatione Egfridi regis" (Eddius).

[4] The "Wergild," *i.e.,* pecuniary value set upon every man's life according to his status (*v.* Stubbs, "Constitutional History").

which I think ought by no means to be passed over in
silence; for the story will be profitable to the salvation
of many. In that battle a youth called Imma, one of
the king's thegns, was struck down, and having lain as
if dead all that day and the next night among the bodies
of the slain, at length he came to himself and revived,
and sitting up, bound his own wounds as best as he
could. Then having rested awhile, he stood up, and
went away to see if he could find any friends to take
care of him; but in so doing he was discovered and
taken by some of the enemy's army, and carried before
their lord, who was one of King Ethelred's nobles.[1]
Being asked by him who he was, and fearing to own
himself a thegn, he answered that he was a peasant, a
poor man and married, and he declared that he had
come to the war with others like himself to bring provisions to the army." The noble entertained him, and
ordered his wounds to be dressed, and when he began
to recover, to prevent his escaping, he ordered him to be
bound at night. But he could not be bound, for as soon
as they that bound him were gone, his bonds were loosed.

Now he had a brother called Tunna, who was a priest
and abbot of a monastery in the city which is still called
Tunnacaestir after him.[2] This man, hearing that his
brother had been killed in the battle, went to see if haply
he could find his body; and finding another very like
him in all respects, he believed it to be his. So he carried
it to his monastery, and buried it honourably, and took
care often to say Masses for the absolution of his soul;
the celebration whereof occasioned what I have said,
that none could bind him but he was presently loosed
again. In the meantime, the noble that had kept him
was amazed, and began to inquire why he could not be

---

[1] " Comes," A.S. " gesith." Above, Imma is described as " de
militia ejus juvenis," *i.e.,* a young " king's thegn" (the term
applied to him in the A.S. version).
[2] Towcester (" Tovecester," in Domesday Book) in Northamptonshire, Doncaster, and Littleborough have all been suggested,
but the place has not been identified. The name indicates that it
had been a Roman station.

bound; whether perchance he had any spells about him, such as are spoken of in stories. He answered that he knew nothing of those arts; " but I have," said he, " a brother who is a priest in my country, and I know that he, supposing me to be killed, is saying frequent Masses for me; and if I were now in the other life, my soul there, through his intercession, would be delivered from penalty."

When he had been a prisoner with the noble some time, those who attentively observed him, by his countenance, habit, and discourse, took notice, that he was not of the meaner sort, as he had said, but of some quality. The noble then privately sending for him, straitly questioned him, whence he came, promising to do him no harm on that account if he would frankly confess who he was. This he did, declaring that he had been a thegn of the king's, and the noble answered, " I perceived by all your answers that you were no peasant. And now you deserve to die, because all my brothers and relations were killed in that fight; yet I will not put you to death, that I may not break my promise."

As soon, therefore, as he was recovered, he sold him to a certain Frisian at London, but he could not in any wise be bound either by him, or as he was being led thither. But when his enemies had put all manner of bonds on him, and the buyer perceived that he could in no way be bound, he gave him leave to ransom himself if he could. Now it was at the third hour, when the Masses were wont to be said, that his bonds were most frequently loosed. He, having taken an oath that he would either return, or send his owner the money for the ransom, went into Kent to King Hlothere, who was son to the sister of Queen Ethelthryth,[1] above spoken of, for he had once been that queen's thegn. From him he asked and obtained the price of his freedom, and as he had promised, sent it to his master for his ransom.

Returning afterwards into his own country, and coming to his brother, he gave him an exact account of all his

---

[1] Sexburg. Cf. III, 8; IV, 19, p. 261, and note.

misfortunes, and the consolation afforded to him in
them; and from what his brother told him he understood, that his bonds had been generally loosed at those
times when Masses had been celebrated for him; and he
perceived that other advantages and blessings which
had fallen to his lot in his time of danger, had been conferred on him from Heaven, through the intercession of
his brother, and the Oblation of the saving Sacrifice.
Many, on hearing this account from the aforesaid man,
were stirred up in faith and pious devotion to prayer, or
to alms-giving, or to make an offering to God of the
Sacrifice of the holy Oblation, for the deliverance of their
friends who had departed this world; for they knew that
such saving Sacrifice availed for the eternal redemption
both of body and soul. This story was also told me by
some of those who had heard it related by the man himself to whom it happened; therefore, since I had a clear
understanding of it, I have not hesitated to insert it in
my Ecclesiastical History.

CHAP. XXIII. *Of the life and death of the Abbess Hilda.*
[614-680 A.D.]

IN the year after this, that is the year of our Lord 680,
the most religious handmaid of Christ, Hilda,[1] abbess of
the monastery that is called Streanaeshalch,[2] as we mentioned above, after having done many heavenly deeds on
earth, passed thence to receive the rewards of the
heavenly life, on the 17th of November, at the age of
sixty-six years. Her life falls into two equal parts, for
the first thirty-three years of it she spent living most
nobly in the secular habit; and still more nobly dedicated
the remaining half to the Lord in the monastic life. For
she was nobly born, being the daughter of Hereric,[3]
nephew to King Edwin, and with that king she also re-

---

[1] Cf. III, 24, 25; IV, 24; V, 24.   [2] *Ibid.*
[3] Cf. *infra*, this Chapter. He was the son of Edwin's elder
brother, who died in exile after the invasion of Deira by Ethelric,
king of Bernicia, in 589.

ceived the faith and mysteries of Christ, at the preaching of Paulinus, of blessed memory,[1] the first bishop of the Northumbrians, and preserved the same undefiled till she attained to the vision of our Lord in Heaven.

When she had resolved to quit the secular habit, and to serve Him alone, she withdrew into the province of the East Angles, for she was allied to the king there;[2] being desirous to cross over thence into Gaul, forsaking her native country and all that she had, and so to live a stranger for our Lord's sake in the monastery of Cale,[3] that she might the better attain to the eternal country in heaven. For her sister Heresuid, mother to Aldwulf,[4] king of the East Angles, was at that time living in the same monastery, under regular discipline, waiting for an everlasting crown; and led by her example, she continued a whole year in the aforesaid province, with the design of going abroad; but afterwards, Bishop Aidan recalled her to her home, and she received land to the extent of one family on the north side of the river Wear;[5] where likewise for a year she led a monastic life, with very few companions.

After this she was made abbess in the monastery called Heruteu,[6] which monastery had been founded, not long before, by the pious handmaid of Christ, Heiu,[7] who is said to have been the first woman in the province of the Northumbrians who took upon her the vows and habit of a nun, being consecrated by Bishop Aidan; but she, soon after she had founded that monastery, retired to the city of Calcaria,[8] which is called Kaelcacaestir

[1] II, 9, foll.
[2] Her sister, Heresuid, had married Ethelhere, brother of Anna, of East Anglia, whom he succeeded. In 647, when Hilda took the veil, Anna was still king.   [3] III, 8, note.
[4] Cf. II, 15; IV, 17.   [5] A small cell, not otherwise known.
[6] Hartlepool, v. III, 24, p. 190, note.
[7] Bede is the sole authority for her life. A fifteenth century gloss on one of the MSS. has led to her being wrongly identified with the Irish Bega, the supposed foundress of St. Bees.
[8] A Roman station on the Wharfe, now Tadcaster. Probably the nunnery was at Healaugh (Heiu's *laeg*=territory), three miles north of Calcaria. A gravestone bearing Heiu's name has been found there.

by the English, and there fixed her dwelling. Hilda, the handmaid of Christ, being set over that monastery, began immediately to order it in all things under a rule of life, according as she had been instructed by learned men; for Bishop Aidan, and others of the religious that knew her, frequently visited her and loved her heartily, and diligently instructed her, because of her innate wisdom and love of the service of God.

When she had for some years governed this monastery, wholly intent upon establishing a rule of life, it happened that she also undertook either to build or to set in order a monastery in the place called Streanaeshalch, and this work which was laid upon her she industriously performed; for she put this monastery under the same rule of monastic life as the former; and taught there the strict observance of justice, piety, chastity, and other virtues, and particularly of peace and charity; so that, after the example of the primitive Church, no one there was rich, and none poor, for they had all things common, and none had any private property. Her prudence was so great, that not only meaner men in their need, but sometimes even kings and princes, sought and received her counsel; she obliged those who were under her direction to give so much time to reading of the Holy Scriptures, and to exercise themselves so much in works of justice, that many might readily be found there fit for the priesthood and the service of the altar.

Indeed we have seen five from that monastery who afterwards became bishops, and all of them men of singular merit and sanctity, whose names were Bosa,[1] Aetla,[2]

[1] Cf. c. 12.
[2] His name does not appear in any of the lists of bishops. There is no evidence that a see of Dorchester (cf. III, 7, and note) existed at this time, except from this passage and the statement of Florence of Worcester to the effect that a fivefold division of the Mercian diocese took place in 679, that Dorchester was included in Mercia, and that Aetla was appointed as its bishop. Probably this latter statement is derived from Bede. It has been proposed to identify Aetla with Haedde, Bishop of the West Saxons (III, 7; IV, 12; V, 18), but it seems unlikely that Bede should not have mentioned their identity. The most probable explanation seems to be that a see was established about 679 at Dorchester (which may

Oftfor,[1] John,[2] and Wilfrid.[3] Of the first we have said above that he was consecrated bishop of York; of the second, it may be briefly stated that he was appointed bishop of Dorchester. Of the last two we shall tell hereafter, that the former was ordained bishop of Hagustald, the other of the church of York; of the third, we may here mention that, having applied himself to the reading and observance of the Scriptures in both the monasteries of the Abbess Hilda,[4] at length being desirous to attain to greater perfection, he went into Kent, to Archbishop Theodore, of blessed memory; where having spent some time in sacred studies, he resolved to go to Rome also, which, in those days, was esteemed a very salutary undertaking. Returning thence into Britain, he took his way into the province of the Hwiccas,[5] where King Osric then ruled,[6] and continued there a long time, preaching the Word of faith, and showing an example of good life to all that saw and heard him. At that time, Bosel, the bishop of that province,[7] laboured under

have been under Mercia at the time) and that Aetla was its bishop, but that it had only a very short existence.

[1] Cf. *infra*, notes.

[2] John of Beverley, "Inderauuda" (*v.* V, 2). He and Berthun (*ibid.*) are said to have founded Beverley. He was consecrated Bishop of Hexham, probably in 687, transferred to York 705, when Wilfrid was restored to Hexham, and died in 721, soon after his retirement to Beverley (V, 6, *ad fin.*). As Bishop of Hexham he ordained Bede both deacon and priest (V. 24). He had been a pupil of Archbishop Theodore (cf. V. 3).

[3] Wilfrid II, Bishop of York. He succeeded John (V, 6) in 718, and was still Bishop of York in 731 when Bede finished the History (cf. V, 23). In 732 he resigned and was succeeded by Egbert (to whom Bede addressed the Ep. ad Egb., and who in 735 received the pallium as Archbishop of York). Wilfrid died in 745 (*v.* Continuation, 732, 735, and 745). His character is highly praised by Alcuin (De Sanct. Ebor.).

[4] Hartlepool and Whitby, both apparently double monasteries.

[5] Cf. II, 2, p. 84.

[6] Dr. Stubbs suggests that this sub-king of the Hwiccas may possibly be the same as Osric of Northumbria, *v.* V, 23, and note.

[7] The see was at Worcester. The foundation of the bishopric is assigned by Florence of Worcester to the year 679, the date of the alleged fivefold division of the Mercian diocese (*v.s.* p. 272, note 2), Bosel being appointed bishop.

such weakness of body, that he could not himself perform episcopal functions; for which reason, Oftfor was, by universal consent, chosen bishop in his stead, and by order of King Ethelred,[1] consecrated by Bishop Wilfrid,[2] of blessed memory, who was then Bishop of the Midland Angles, because Archbishop Theodore was dead, and no other bishop ordained in his place. A little while before, that is, before the election of the aforesaid man of God, Bosel, Tatfrid,[3] a man of great industry and learning, and of excellent ability, had been chosen bishop for that province, from the monastery of the same abbess, but had been snatched away by an untimely death, before he could be ordained.

Thus this handmaid of Christ, the Abbess Hilda, whom all that knew her called Mother, for her singular piety and grace, was not only an example of good life, to those that lived in her monastery, but afforded occasion of amendment and salvation to many who lived at a distance, to whom the blessed fame was brought of her industry and virtue. For it was meet that the dream of her mother, Bregusuid, during her infancy, should be fulfilled. Now Bregusuid, at the time that her husband, Hereric, lived in banishment, under Cerdic,[4] king of the Britons, where he was also poisoned, fancied, in a dream, that he was suddenly taken away from her and she was seeking for him most carefully, but could find no sign of him anywhere. After an anxious search for him, all at once she found a most precious necklace under her garment, and whilst she was looking on it very attentively, it seemed to shine forth with such a blaze of light that it filled all Britain with the glory of its brilliance. This dream was doubtless fulfilled in her daughter that

[1] Cf. c. 12 and note.
[2] The consecration of Oftfor is generally placed in 691. It was after Wilfrid's second expulsion, when he was acting as Bishop of Leicester. Theodore had died in 690, and Bertwald was not consecrated till 693 (v. V, 8).
[3] So Florence of Worcester.
[4] He was king of the Britons of Loidis and Elmet. It was probably to avenge the death of his nephew, Hereric, that Edwin conquered Loidis and drove out Cerdic.

we speak of, whose life was an example of the works of light, not only blessed to herself, but to many who desired to live aright.

When she had governed this monastery many years, it pleased Him Who has made such merciful provision for our salvation, to give her holy soul the trial of a long infirmity of the flesh, to the end that, according to the Apostle's example, her virtue might be made perfect in weakness. Struck down with a fever, she suffered from a burning heat, and was afflicted with the same trouble for six years continually; during all which time she never failed either to return thanks to her Maker, or publicly and privately to instruct the flock committed to her charge; for taught by her own experience she admonished all men to serve the Lord dutifully, when health of body is granted to them, and always to return thanks faithfully to Him in adversity, or bodily infirmity. In the seventh year of her sickness, when the disease turned inwards, her last day came, and about cockcrow, having received the voyage provision[1] of Holy Housel, and called together the handmaids of Christ that were within the same monastery, she admonished them to preserve the peace of the Gospel among themselves, and with all others; and even as she spoke her words of exhortation, she joyfully saw death come, or, in the words of our Lord, passed from death unto life.

That same night it pleased Almighty God, by a manifest vision, to make known her death in another monastery, at a distance from hers, which she had built that same year, and which is called Hacanos.[2] There was in that monastery, a certain nun called Begu,[3] who, having dedicated her virginity to the Lord, had served Him upwards of thirty years in the monastic life. This nun was resting

---

[1] Cf. c. 14, note.

[2] Hackness, thirteen miles from Whitby and three to the west of Scarborough. It was a cell belonging to Whitby. At the dissolution under Henry VIII, it contained only four monks, of the Benedictine order (Dugdale, "Monasticon").

[3] She has been confused with Heiu and with Bega, v.s. p. 271, note 7.

in the dormitory of the sisters, when on a sudden she heard in the air the well-known sound of the bell, which used to awake and call them to prayers, when any one of them was taken out of this world, and opening her eyes, as she thought, she saw the roof of the house open, and a light shed from above filling all the place. Looking earnestly upon that light, she saw the soul of the aforesaid handmaid of God in that same light, being carried to heaven attended and guided by angels. Then awaking, and seeing the other sisters lying round about her, she perceived that what she had seen had been revealed to her either in a dream or a vision; and rising immediately in great fear, she ran to the virgin who then presided in the monastery in the place of the abbess,[1] and whose name was Frigyth, and, with many tears and lamentations, and heaving deep sighs, told her that the Abbess Hilda, mother of them all, had departed this life, and had in her sight ascended to the gates of eternal light, and to the company of the citizens of heaven, with a great light, and with angels for her guides. Frigyth having heard it, awoke all the sisters, and calling them to the church, admonished them to give themselves to prayer and singing of psalms, for the soul of their mother; which they did earnestly during the remainder of the night; and at break of day, the brothers came with news of her death, from the place where she had died. They answered that they knew it before, and then related in order how and when they had learnt it, by which it appeared that her death had been revealed to them in a vision that same hour in which the brothers said that she had died. Thus by a fair harmony of events Heaven ordained, that when some saw her departure out of this world, the others should have knowledge of her entrance into the eternal life of souls. These monasteries are about thirteen miles distant from each other.

It is also told, that her death was, in a vision, made known the same night to one of the virgins dedicated to

[1] *I.e.*, the Prioress.

ved her with a great love, in the same
\ere the said handmaid of God died. This
\oul ascend to heaven in the company of
\:s she openly declared, in the very same
\.\.\.\.t happened, to those handmaids of Christ
\.\.\.\.o were with her; and aroused them to pray for her
soul, even before the rest of the community had heard of
her death. The truth of which was known to the whole
community in the morning. This same nun was at that
time with some other handmaids of Christ, in the remotest part of the monastery, where the women who
had lately entered the monastic life were wont to pass
their time of probation, till they were instructed according to rule, and admitted into the fellowship of the
community.

CHAP. XXIV. *That there was in her monastery a brother, on whom the gift of song was bestowed by Heaven.*[1]
[680 A.D.]

THERE was in the monastery of this abbess a certain
brother, marked in a special manner by the grace of God,
for he was wont to make songs of piety and religion, so
that whatever was expounded to him out of Scripture,
he turned ere long into verse expressive of much sweetness and penitence, in English, which was his native
language. By his songs the minds of many were often
fired with contempt of the world, and desire of the
heavenly life. Others of the English nation after him

---

[1] Obviously ballads, probably of a warlike character, existed
before Caedmon, but he is regarded as the father of English
sacred poetry. It is a question how far the new impulse arose in-
dependently among the Anglo-Saxons, or is to be connected with
Old Saxon religious poetry of which the "Heliand" is the only
extant specimen (cf. Plummer, *ad loc.*). Of the mass of poetry
attributed to Caedmon, much must be regarded as not his actual
work. The fragment translated here by Bede has been accepted
as genuine by most critics. It exists in the Northumbrian dialect
at the end of the Moore MS. of Bede, and in a West Saxon form
in other MSS., as well as in the Anglo-Saxon translation of Bede's
History, the Northumbrian version being the oldest.

attempted to compose religious poems, but none could equal him, for he did not learn the art of poetry from men, neither was he taught by man, but by God's grace he received the free gift of song, for which reason he never could compose any trivial or vain poem, but only those which concern religion it behoved his religious tongue to utter./; For having lived in the secular habit till he was well advanced in years, he had never learned anything of versifying; and for this reason sometimes at a banquet, when it was agreed to make merry by singing in turn, if he saw the harp come towards him, he would rise up from table and go out and return home.

Once having done so and gone out of the house where the banquet was, to the stable, where he had to take care of the cattle that night, he there composed himself to rest at the proper time. Thereupon one stood by him in his sleep, and saluting him, and calling him by his name, said, "Cædmon, sing me something." But he answered, "I cannot sing, and for this cause I left the banquet and retired hither, because I could not sing." Then he who talked to him replied, "Nevertheless thou must needs sing to me." "What must I sing?" he asked. "Sing the beginning of creation," said the other. Having received this answer he straightway began to sing verses to the praise of God the Creator, which he had never heard, the purport whereof was after this manner: "Now must we praise the Maker of the heavenly kingdom, the power of the Creator and His counsel, the deeds of the Father of glory, How He, being the eternal God, became the Author of all wondrous works, Who being the Almighty Guardian of the human race, first created heaven for the sons of men to be the covering of their dwelling place, and next the earth." This is the sense but not the order of the words as he sang them in his sleep; for verses, though never so well composed, cannot be literally translated out of one language into another without loss of their beauty and loftiness. Awaking from his sleep, he remembered all that he had sung in his dream, and soon added more after the same manner, in words which worthily expressed the praise of God.

In the morning he came to the reeve [1] who was over him, and having told him of the gift he had received, was conducted to the abbess, and bidden, in the presence of many learned men, to tell his dream, and repeat the verses, that they might all examine and give their judgement upon the nature and origin of the gift whereof he spoke. And they all judged that heavenly grace had been granted to him by the Lord. They expounded to him a passage of sacred history or doctrine, enjoining upon him, if he could, to put it into verse. Having undertaken this task, he went away, and returning the next morning, gave them the passage he had been bidden to translate, rendered in most excellent verse. Whereupon the abbess, joyfully recognizing the grace of God in the man, instructed him to quit the secular habit, and take upon him monastic vows; and having received him into the monastery, she and all her people admitted him to the company of the brethren, and ordered that he should be taught the whole course of sacred history. So he, giving ear to all that he could learn, and bearing it in mind, and as it were ruminating, like a clean animal, [2] turned it into most harmonious verse; and sweetly singing it, made his masters in their turn his hearers. He sang the creation of the world, the origin of man, and all the history of Genesis, the departure of the children of Israel out of Egypt, their entrance into the promised land, and many other histories from Holy Scripture; the Incarnation, Passion, Resurrection of our Lord, and His Ascension into heaven; the coming of the Holy Ghost, and the teaching of the Apostles; likewise he made many songs concerning the terror of future judgement, the horror of the pains of hell, and the joys of heaven; besides many more about the blessings and the judgements of God, by all of which he endeavoured to draw men away from the love of sin, and to excite in them devotion to well-doing and perseverance therein. For he was

[1] "Villicus," A.S. "tun-gerefa" = town-reeve, *i.e.*, headman of the township. Cædmon was apparently a herdsman on a farm belonging to the monastery.
[2] Cf. Levit., xi, 3, and Deut., xiv, 6.

a very religious man, humbly submissive to the discipline of monastic rule, but inflamed with fervent zeal against those who chose to do otherwise; for which reason he made a fair ending of his life.

For when the hour of his departure drew near, it was preceded by a bodily infirmity under which he laboured for the space of fourteen days, yet it was of so mild a nature that he could talk and go about the whole time. In his neighbourhood was the house to which those that were sick, and like to die, were wont to be carried. He desired the person that ministered to him, as the evening came on of the night in which he was to depart this life, to make ready a place there for him to take his rest. The man, wondering why he should desire it, because there was as yet no sign of his approaching death, nevertheless did his bidding. When they had lain down there, and had been conversing happily and pleasantly for some time with those that were in the house before, and it was now past midnight, he asked them, whether they had the Eucharist within?[1] They answered, "What need of the Eucharist? for you are not yet appointed to die, since you talk so merrily with us, as if you were in good health." "Nevertheless," said he, "bring me the Eucharist." Having received It into his hand, he asked, whether they were all in charity with him, and had no complaint against him, nor any quarrel or grudge. They answered, that they were all in perfect charity with him, and free from all anger; and in their turn they asked him to be of the same mind towards them. He answered at once, "I am in charity, my children, with all the servants of God." Then strengthening himself with the heavenly Viaticum, he prepared for the entrance into another life, and asked how near the time was when the brothers should be awakened to sing the nightly praises of the Lord?[2] They answered, "It is not far off." Then he said, "It is well, let us await that hour;" and signing

---

[1] Apparently reserved and kept in the Infirmary for the Communion of the dying.

[2] Matins were sung soon after midnight.

himself with the sign of the Holy Cross, he laid his head on the pillow, and falling into a slumber for a little while, so ended his life in silence.

Thus it came to pass, that as he had served the Lord with a simple and pure mind, and quiet devotion, so he now departed to behold His Presence, leaving the world by a quiet death; and that tongue, which had uttered so many wholesome words in praise of the Creator, spake its last words also in His praise, while he signed himself with the Cross, and commended his spirit into His hands; and by what has been here said, he seems to have had foreknowledge of his death.

CHAP. XXV. *Of the vision that appeared to a certain man of God before the monastery of the city Coludi was burned down.*

AT this time, the monastery of virgins, called the city of Coludi,[1] above-mentioned, was burned down, through carelessness; and yet all that knew it might have been aware that it happened by reason of the wickedness of those who dwelt in it, and chiefly of those who seemed to be the greatest. But there wanted not a warning of the approaching punishment from the Divine mercy whereby they might have been led to amend their ways, and by fasting and tears and prayers, like the Ninevites, have averted the anger of the just Judge.

For there was in that monastery a man of the Scottish race, called Adamnan,[2] leading a life entirely devoted to God in continence and prayer, insomuch that he never took any food or drink, except only on Sundays and Thursdays; and often spent whole nights in watching and prayer. This strictness in austerity of life he had first adopted from the necessity of correcting the evil that

---

[1] Coldingham, *v.s.* c. 19 and note.
[2] Not the Abbot of Iona who wrote the the life of St. Columba (V, 15, 21). This Adamnan is found in the Martyrology of Wilson, in Colgan's "Lives of the Irish Saints," and in Bollandus, "Acta Sanctorum."

was in him; but in process of time the necessity became
a custom.

For in his youth he had been guilty of some sin for
which, when he came to himself, he conceived a great
horror, and dreaded lest he should be punished for the
same by the righteous Judge. Betaking himself, therefore, to a priest, who, he hoped, might show him the
way of salvation, he confessed his guilt, and desired to be
advised how he might escape the wrath to come. The
priest having heard his offence, said, " A great wound
requires greater care in the healing thereof; wherefore
give yourself as far as you are able to fasting and psalms,
and prayer, to the end that thus coming before the presence of the Lord in confession,[1] you may find Him merciful. But he, being oppressed with great grief by reason
of his guilty conscience, and desiring to be the sooner
loosed from the inward fetters of sin, which lay heavy
upon him, answered, "I am still young in years and
strong of body, and shall, therefore, easily bear all whatsoever you shall enjoin me to do, if so be that I may be
saved in the day of the Lord, even though you should bid
me spend the whole night standing in prayer, and pass
the whole week in abstinence." The priest replied, "It
is much for you to continue for a whole week without
bodily sustenance; it is enough to observe a fast for two
or three days; do this till I come again to you in a short
time, when I will more fully show you what you ought to
do, and how long to persevere in your penance." Having
so said, and prescribed the measure of his penance, the
priest went away, and upon some sudden occasion passed
over into Ireland, which was his native country, and returned no more to him, as he had appointed. But the
man remembering this injunction and his own promise,
gave himself up entirely to tears of penitence, holy vigils
and continence; so that he only took food on Thursdays
and Sundays, as has been said; and continued fasting
all the other days of the week. When he heard that his
priest had gone to Ireland, and had died there, he ever

---

[1] From the Vulgate, Ps. xciv, 2. (xcv in our Psalter.)

after observed this manner of abstinence, which had been
appointed for him as we have said; and as he had begun
that course through the fear of God, in penitence for his
guilt, so he still continued the same unremittingly for the
love of God, and through delight in its rewards.

Having practised this carefully for a long time, it happened that he had gone on a certain day to a distance
from the monastery, accompanied by one the brothers;
and as they were returning from this journey, when they
drew near to the monastery, and beheld its lofty buildings, the man of God burst into tears, and his countenance discovered the trouble of his heart. His companion, perceiving it, asked what was the reason, to
which he answered: "The time is at hand when a de-
vouring fire shall reduce to ashes all the buildings which
you here behold, both public and private." The other,
hearing these words, when they presently came into the
monastery, told them to Aebba,[1] the mother of the community. She with good cause being much troubled at
that prediction, called the man to her, and straitly questioned him concerning the matter and how he came to
know it. He answered, "Being engaged one night lately
in watching and singing psalms, on a sudden I saw one
standing by me whose countenance I did not know, and I
was startled at his presence, but he bade me not to fear,
and speaking to me like a friend he said, 'You do well
in that you have chosen rather at this time of rest not
to give yourself up to sleep, but to continue in watching
and prayer.' I answered, 'I know I have great need to
continue in wholesome watching and earnest prayer to
the Lord to pardon my transgressions.' He replied,
'You speak truly, for you and many more have need to
redeem their sins by good works, and when they cease
from temporal labours, then to labour the more eagerly
for desire of eternal blessings; but this very few do; for
I, having now gone through all this monastery in order,
have looked into the huts[2] and beds of all, and found

---

[1] C. 19 and note.
[2] The detached dwellings built round the principal buildings of
the community. Irish monasteries were built after this fashion.

none of them except yourself busy about the health of
his soul; but all of them, both men and women, are
either sunk in slothful sleep, or are awake in order to
commit sin; for even the cells that were built for prayer
or reading, are now converted into places of feasting,
drinking, talking, and other delights; the very virgins
dedicated to God, laying aside the respect due to their profession, whensoever they are at leisure, apply themselves
to weaving fine garments, wherewith to adorn themselves
like brides, to the danger of their state, or to gain the
friendship of strange men; for which reason, as is meet,
a heavy judgement from Heaven with raging fire is
ready to fall on this place and those that dwell therein.'"
The abbess said, "Why did you not sooner reveal to
me what you knew?" He answered, "I was afraid to
do it, out of respect to you, lest you should be too much
afflicted; yet you may have this comfort, that the blow
will not fall in your days." This vision being made
known, the inhabitants of that place were for a few days
in some little fear, and leaving off their sins, began to
do penance; but after the death of the abbess they returned to their former defilement, nay, they committed
worse sins; and when they said "Peace and safety,"
the doom of the aforesaid judgement came suddenly
upon them.

That all this fell out after this manner, was told me
by my most reverend fellow-priest, Aedgils, who then
lived in that monastery. Afterwards, when many of the
inhabitants had departed thence, on account of the destruction, he lived a long time in our monastery,[1] and died
there. We have thought fit to insert this in our History,
to admonish the reader of the works of the Lord, how
terrible He is in His doing toward the children of men,
lest haply we should at some time or other yield to the
snares of the flesh, and dreading too little the judgement
of God, fall under His sudden wrath, and either in His
righteous anger be brought low with temporal losses, or
else be more strictly tried and snatched away to eternal
perdition.

[1] Wearmouth and Jarrow.

CHAP. XXVI. *Of the death of the Kings Egfrid and Hlothere.* [684-685 A.D.]

IN the year of our Lord 684, Egfrid, king of the Northumbrians, sending his general, Berct,[1] with an army into Ireland, miserably laid waste that unoffending nation, which had always been most friendly to the English; insomuch that the invading force spared not even the churches or monasteries. But the islanders, while to the utmost of their power they repelled force with force, implored the assistance of the Divine mercy, and with constant imprecations invoked the vengeance of Heaven; and though such as curse cannot inherit the kingdom of God, yet it was believed, that those who were justly cursed on account of their impiety, soon suffered the penalty of their guilt at the avenging hand of God. For the very next year, when that same king had rashly led his army to ravage the province of the Picts,[2] greatly against the advice of his friends, and particularly of Cuthbert,[3] of blessed memory, who had been lately ordained bishop, the enemy made a feigned retreat, and the king was drawn into a narrow pass among remote mountains,[4] and slain, with the greater part of the forces he had led thither, on the 20th of May, in the fortieth year of his age, and the fifteenth of his reign.[5] His friends,

---

[1] For Berct, cf. V, 24 (*sub* 698), note. The circumstances which led to the invasion are not known.

[2] The Picts north of the Forth, cf. c. 12, *ad fin.* Their king at this time was Bruide mac Bili, who was Egfrid's distant kinsman. In 672 Egfrid had crushed a rising of Picts under the same king.

[3] Cf. cc. 27-32. He had a mysterious intimation of the disaster at the hour of the king's defeat and death, and warned the queen (Eormenburg), who was with him at Carlisle (*v.* Bede's Life of Cuthbert, and the Anonymous Life). He is also said to have prophesied the king's death a year before to Elfled, Egfrid's sister (*v.* III, 24).

[4] At Nechtansmere or Dunnechtan, identified with Dunnichen, near Forfar. Egfrid was buried in Iona, where Adamnan, the friend of his successor, was Abbot.

[5] Cf. c. 5 *ad init.*, note. If he succeeded in February, 670, this would be his sixteenth year.

as has been said, advised him not to engage in this war; but since he had the year before refused to listen to the most reverend father, Egbert,[1] advising him not to attack the Scots, who were doing him no harm, it was laid upon him as a punishment for his sin, that he should now not listen to those who would have prevented his death.

From that time the hopes and strength of the Anglian kingdom "began to ebb and fall away;[2] for the Picts recovered their own lands, which had been held by the English, and so did also the Scots that were in Britain; and some of the Britons[3] regained their liberty, which they have now enjoyed for about forty-six years. Among the many English that then either fell by the sword, or were made slaves, or escaped by flight out of the country of the Picts, the most reverend man of God, Trumwine,[4] who had been made bishop over them, withdrew with his people that were in the monastery of Aebbercurnig,[5] in the country of the English, but close by the arm of the sea which is the boundary between the lands of the English and the Picts. Having commended his followers, wheresoever he could, to his friends in the monasteries, he chose his own place of abode in the monastery, which we have so often mentioned, of servants and handmaids of God, at Streanaeshalch;[6] and there for many years, with a few of his own brethren, he led a life in all monastic austerity, not only to his own benefit, but to the benefit of many others, and dying there, he was buried in the church of the blessed Peter the Apostle,[7] with the honour due to his life and rank. The royal virgin, Elfled,[8] with her mother, Eanfled, whom we have mentioned before, then presided over that monastery; but when the

---

[1] III, 4, 27; IV, 3; V, 9, 10, 22, 24. His English birth and long residence in Ireland fitted him to be a mediator.

[2] Vergil, Aen. II, 169.

[3] The Dalriadic Scots (Cf. I, 1, note; I, 34) and the Britons of Strathclyde.   [4] Cf. c. 12.

[5] Abercorn on the Forth, cf. I, 12; IV, 12, and note.

[6] III, 24, 25; IV, 23; V, 24.   [7] Cf. III, 24, p. 190.

[8] III, 24, and note. Elfled succeeded Hilda as abbess, and apparently ruled jointly with her mother.

bishop came thither, that devout teacher found in him the greatest help in governing, and comfort in her private life. Aldfrid[1] succeeded Egfrid in the throne, being a man most learned in the Scriptures, said to be brother to Egfrid, and son to King Oswy; he nobly retrieved the ruined state of the kingdom, though within narrower bounds.

The same year, being the 685th from the Incarnation of our Lord, Hlothere,[2] king of Kent, died on the 6th of February, when he had reigned twelve years after his brother Egbert,[3] who had reigned nine years: he was wounded in battle with the South Saxons, whom Edric,[4] the son of Egbert, had raised against him, and died whilst his wound was being dressed. After him, this same Edric reigned a year and a half. On his death, kings of doubtful title, or of foreign origin,[5] for some time wasted the kingdom, till the lawful king, Wictred,[6] the son of Egbert, being settled in the throne, by his piety and zeal delivered his nation from foreign invasion.

[1] Cf. V, *passim*, and Bede's two lives of Cuthbert. His mother's name is said by the Irish authorities to have been Fina. He had lived among the Irish islands ("in insulis Scottorum," and "in regionibus Scottorum") for the sake of study, according to Bede, but William of Malmesbury implies that Egfrid may have been responsible for his exile. He was a man of great learning and of scholarly tastes. In Bede's "History of the Abbots," we are told that he gave eight hides of land for a MS. which Benedict Biscop had brought from Rome.

[2] Cc. 5, 17, 22.

[3] Cc. 1, 5.

[4] Apparently at one time joint-king with Hlothere. Certain dooms are ascribed to them both. According to Thomas of Elmham, he was killed in war against Caedwalla, king of Wessex, and his brother, Mul, who were at this time encroaching on Kent.

[5] Mul seems to have usurped the throne for a time.

[6] In 692 we find him reigning as joint-king with Swaebhard (V, 8 *ad fin.*). He must have succeeded in 690, if Bede's dates are correct; cf. V, 23, where it is said that he died on April 23, 725, after a reign of thirty-four and a half years.

CHAP. XXVII. *How Cuthbert, a man of God, was made bishop; and how he lived and taught whilst still in the monastic life.* [685 A.D.]

IN the same year in which King Egfrid departed this life,[1] he, as has been said, caused the holy and venerable Cuthbert[2] to be ordained bishop of the church of Lindisfarne. He had for many years led a solitary life, in great continence of body and mind, in a very small island, called Farne,[3] in the ocean about nine miles distant from that same church. From his earliest childhood[4] he had always been inflamed with the desire of a religious life; and he adopted the name and habit of a monk when he was quite a young man: he first entered the monastery of Mailros,[5] which is on the bank of the river Tweed, and was then governed by the Abbot Eata,[6] a man of great gentleness and simplicity, who was afterward made bishop of the church of Hagustald or Lindisfarne,[7] as has been said above. The provost of the monastery at that time was Boisil,[8] a priest of great virtue and of a prophetic spirit. Cuthbert, humbly submitting himself

---

[1] *I.e.*, 685. [2] C. 26 and note.
[3] Cf. III, 16 and note.
[4] As a boy he had been remarkable for his high spirits and love of athletic exercises. The rebuke of a little boy of three is said to have turned his thoughts to a more serious life, and a vision which he saw as he watched his sheep on the Lammermuir Hills on the night of Aidan's death, led him to form the resolve of entering a monastery. (Bede's Life of Cuthbert.)
[5] Melrose; cf. III, 26 and note.
[6] *Ibid.* and V, 9.
[7] C. 12, p. 243, note 1.
[8] C. 28; V. 9. Probably here "sacerdos"=priest, A.S. version: "masse-preost." But Aelfric calls him bishop. The town of St. Boswells on the Tweed is called after him. For an instance of his prophetic spirit, *v. infra,* c. 28. It was his fame which drew Cuthbert to Melrose. When he saw the youth on his arrival, he exclaimed, "Behold a servant of the Lord!" He is generally supposed to have been carried off by the plague of 664. For an account of his last days spent in reading the Gospel of St. John with Cuthbert, *v.* Bede's Prose Life of Cuthbert. The "codex" which they used was extant in Durham in Simeon of Durham's time.

to this man's direction, from him received both a knowledge of the Scriptures, and an example of good works.

After he had departed to the Lord, Cuthbert became provost of that monastery, where he instructed many in the rule of monastic life, both by the authority of a master, and the example of his own behaviour. Nor did he bestow his teaching and his example in the monastic life on his monastery alone, but laboured far and wide to convert the people dwelling round about from the life of foolish custom, to the love of heavenly joys; for many profaned the faith which they held by their wicked actions; and some also, in the time of a pestilence, neglecting the mysteries of the faith which they had received, had recourse to the false remedies of idolatry, as if they could have put a stop to the plague sent from God, by incantations, amulets, or any other secrets of the Devil's art. In order to correct the error of both sorts, he often went forth from the monastery, sometimes on horseback, but oftener on foot, and went to the neighbouring townships, where he preached the way of truth to such as had gone astray; which Boisil also in his time had been wont to do. It was then the custom of the English people, that when a clerk or priest came to a township, they all, at his summons, flocked together to hear the Word; willingly heard what was said, and still more willingly practised those things that they could hear and understand. And such was Cuthbert's skill in speaking, so keen his desire to persuade men of what he taught, such a light shone in his angelic face, that no man present dared to conceal from him the secrets of his heart, but all openly revealed in confession what they had done, thinking doubtless that their guilt could in nowise be hidden from him; and having confessed their sins, they wiped them out by fruits worthy of repentance, as he bade them. He was wont chiefly to resort to those places and preach in those villages which were situated afar off amid steep and wild mountains, so that others dreaded to go thither, and whereof the poverty and barbarity rendered them inaccessible to other teachers. But he, devoting himself entirely to that pious labour, so industriously ministered

U

to them with his wise teaching, that when he went forth
from the monastery, he would often stay a whole week,
sometimes two or three, or even sometimes a full month,
before he returned home, continuing among the hill folk to
call that simple people by his preaching and good works
to the things of Heaven.

This venerable servant of the Lord, having thus spent
many years in the monastery of Mailros, and there become conspicuous by great tokens of virtue, his most
reverend abbot, Eata, removed him to the isle of Lindisfarne, that he might there also, by his authority as provost and by the example of his own practice, instruct
the brethren in the observance of regular discipline; for
the same reverend father then governed that place also
as abbot. From ancient times, the bishop was wont
to reside there with his clergy, and the abbot with his
monks, who were likewise under the paternal care of the
bishop; because Aidan, who was the first bishop of the
place, being himself a monk, brought monks thither,
and settled the monastic institution there;[1] as the blessed
Father Augustine is known to have done before in Kent,
when the most reverend Pope Gregory wrote to him, as
has been said above, to this effect: " But in that you, my
brother, having been instructed in monastic rules, must
not live apart from your clergy in the Church of the English, which has been lately, by the will of God, converted to the faith, you must establish the manner of
conversation of our fathers in the primitive Church,
among whom, none said that aught of the things which
they possessed was his own; but they had all things
common."[2]

[1] Cf. III, 3, p. 139, note 3.
[2] Cf. I, 27 *ad init.*

CHAP. XXVIII. *How the same St. Cuthbert, living the life of an Anchorite, by his prayers obtained a spring in a dry soil, and had a crop from seed sown by the labour of his hands out of season.* [676 A.D.]

AFTER this, Cuthbert, as he grew in goodness and intensity of devotion, attained also to a hermit's life of contemplation in silence and solitude, as we have mentioned. But forasmuch as many years ago we wrote enough concerning his life and virtues, both in heroic verse and prose,[1] it may suffice at present only to mention this, that when he was about to go to the island, he declared to the brothers, "If by the grace of God it shall be granted to me, that I may live in that place by the labour of my hands, I will willingly abide there; but if not, God willing, I will very soon return to you." The place was quite destitute of water, corn, and trees; and being infested by evil spirits, was very ill suited for human habitation; but it became in all respects habitable, at the desire of the man of God; for at his coming the wicked spirits departed. When, after expelling the enemy, he had, with the help of the brethren, built himself a narrow dwelling, with a mound about it, and the necessary cells in it, to wit, an oratory and a common living room, he ordered the brothers to dig a pit in the floor of the room, although the ground was hard and stony, and no hopes appeared of any spring. When they had done this relying upon the faith and prayers of the servant of God, the next day it was found to be full of water, and to this day affords abundance of its heavenly bounty to all that resort thither. He also desired that instruments for husbandry might be brought him, and some wheat; but having prepared the ground and sown the wheat at the proper season, no sign of a blade, not to speak of ears, had sprouted from it by the summer. Hereupon, when the brethren visited him according to custom, he ordered barley to be brought him, if haply it

---

[1] Much of the account given here is from the prose life.

were either the nature of the soil, or the will of God, the
Giver of all things, that such grain rather should grow
there. He sowed it in the same field, when it was brought
him, after the proper time of sowing, and therefore without any likelihood of its bearing fruit; but a plentiful crop
immediately sprang up, and afforded the man of God
the means which he had desired of supporting himself
by his own labour.

When he had here served God in solitude many years,
the mound which encompassed his dwelling being so
high, that he could see nothing from it but heaven,
which he thirsted to enter, it happened that a great synod
was assembled in the presence of King Egfrid, near the
river Alne, at a place called Adtuifyrdi,[1] which signifies
"at the two fords," in which Archbishop Theodore, of
blessed memory, presided, and there Cuthbert was, with
one mind and consent of all, chosen bishop of the church
of Lindisfarne. They could not, however, draw him from
his hermitage, though many messengers and letters were
sent to him. At last the aforesaid king himself, with the
most holy Bishop Trumwine,[2] and other religious and
powerful men, sailed to the island; many also of the
brothers from the isle of Lindisfarne itself, assembled
together for the same purpose: they all knelt, and con-
jured him by the Lord, with tears and entreaties, till
they drew him, also in tears, from his beloved retreat,
and forced him to go to the synod. When he arrived
there, he was very reluctantly overcome by the unanimous
resolution of all present, and compelled to take upon himself the duties of the episcopate; being chiefly prevailed
upon by the words of Boisil, the servant of God, who,
when he had prophetically[3] foretold all things that were
to befall him, had also predicted that he should be a
bishop. Nevertheless, the consecration was not appointed

---

[1] The synod of Twyford, a mixed assembly of clergy and laity,
met in the autumn of 684. The place is "perhaps where the Aln
is crossed by two fords near Whittingham" (in Northumberland)
(Bright). This is another instance of the preposition prefixed to
the name, cf. II, 14, p. 119, note 5.

[2] Cc. 12, 26.   [3] Cf. c. 27, p. 288.

immediately; but when the winter, which was then at hand, was over, it was carried out at Easter,[1] in the city of York, and in the presence of the aforesaid King Egfrid; seven bishops coming together for his consecration, among whom, Theodore, of blessed memory, was Primate. He was first elected bishop of the church of Hagustald, in the place of Tunbert,[2] who had been deposed from the episcopate; but because he chose rather to be placed over the church of Lindisfarne, in which he had lived, it was thought fit that Eata should return to the see of the church of Hagustald, to which he had been first ordained, and that Cuthbert should take upon him the government of the church of Lindisfarne.[3]

Following the example of the blessed Apostles, he adorned the episcopal dignity by his virtuous deeds; for he both protected the people committed to his charge by constant prayer, and roused them, by wholesome admonitions, to thoughts of Heaven. He first showed in his own life what he taught others to do, a practice which greatly strengthens all teaching; for he was above all things inflamed with the fire of Divine charity, of sober mind and patient, most diligently intent on devout prayers, and kindly to all that came to him for comfort. He thought it stood in the stead of prayer to afford the weak brethren the help of his exhortation, knowing that he who said " Thou shalt love the Lord thy God," said likewise, " Thou shalt love thy neighbour." He was noted for penitential abstinence, and was always through the grace of compunction, intent upon heavenly things. And when he offered up to God the Sacrifice of the saving Victim, he commended his prayer to the Lord, not with uplifted voice, but with tears drawn from the bottom of his heart.

---

[1] In 685.   [2] Cf. c. 12 and note.   [3] *Ibid.*

CHAP. XXIX. *How this bishop foretold that his own death was at hand to the anchorite Herebert.* [687 A.D.]

HAVING spent two years in his bishopric, he returned to his island and hermitage,[1] being warned of God that the day of his death, or rather of his entrance into that life which alone can be called life, was drawing near; as he, at that time, with his wonted candour, signified to certain persons, though in words which were somewhat obscure, but which were nevertheless afterwards plainly understood; while to others he declared the same openly.

There was a certain priest, called Herebert, a man of holy life, who had long been united with the man of God, Cuthbert, in the bonds of spiritual friendship. This man leading a solitary life in the island of that great lake from which the river Derwent flows at its beginning,[2] was wont to visit him every year, and to receive from him the teaching of everlasting salvation. Hearing that Bishop Cuthbert was come to the city of Lugubalia,[3] he went thither to him, according to his custom, seeking to be more and more inflamed in heavenly desires through his wholesome admonitions. Whilst they alternately entertained one another with draughts of the celestial life, the bishop, among other things, said, "Brother Herebert, remember at this time to ask me and speak to me concerning all whereof you have need to ask and speak; for, when we part, we shall never again see one another with bodily eyesight in this world. For I know of a surety that the time of my departure is at hand, and that shortly I must put off this my tabernacle." Hearing these words, Herebert fell down at his feet, with tears and lamentations, and said, "I beseech you, by the Lord, not to forsake me; but to remember your most

[1] Soon after Christmas, 686. In February, 687, his last illness began.
[2] St. Herbert's Island in Derwentwater. Strictly speaking, the Derwent flows through Derwentwater: it rises in Borrowdale. An indulgence of forty days was granted by Thomas Appleby, Bishop of Carlisle, in 1374 to pilgrims who visited the island.
[3] Carlisle, called also Luel by Simeon of Durham.

faithful companion, and entreat the mercy óf God that, as we have served Him together upon earth, so we may depart together to behold His grace in Heaven. For you know that I have always endeavoured to live according to the words of your lips, and likewise whatsoever faults I have committed, either through ignorance or frailty, I have instantly sought to amend according to the judgement of your will." The bishop applied himself to prayer, and having presently had intimation in the spirit that he had obtained what he asked of the Lord, he said, "Rise, brother, and do not weep, but rejoice greatly because the mercy of Heaven has granted what we desired."

The event established the truth of this promise and prophecy, for after their parting, they never again saw one another in the flesh; but their spirits quitting their bodies on one and the same day, to wit, the 20th of March,[1] were immediately united in fellowship in the blessed vision, and together translated to the heavenly kingdom by the ministry of angels. But Herebert was first wasted by a long-continued infirmity, through the dispensation of the Lord's mercy, as may be believed, to the end that if he was in any wise inferior in merit to the blessed Cuthbert, that which was lacking might be supplied by the chastening pain of a long sickness, that being thus made equal in grace to his intercessor, as he departed out of the body at one and the same time with him, so he might be accounted worthy to be received into the like abode of eternal bliss.

The most reverend father died in the isle of Farne, earnestly entreating the brothers that he might also be buried there, where he had served no small time under the Lord's banner. But at length yielding to their entreaties, he consented to be carried back to the isle of Lindisfarne, and there buried in the church.[2] This being

[1] In 687.
[2] In St. Peter's Church. In 875, when the monks fled from Lindisfarne before the Danes, his relics were removed, first to Chester-le-Street, then to Ripon, and eventually to Durham. Simeon of Durham says the body was found to be uncorrupted, when it was placed in the new Cathedral there in 1104.

done, the venerable Bishop Wilfrid held the episcopal see of that church one year,[1] till such time as a bishop should be chosen to be ordained in the room of Cuthbert. Afterwards Eadbert[2] was ordained, a man renowned for his knowledge of the Holy Scriptures, as also for his observance of the heavenly precepts, and chiefly for almsgiving, so that, according to the law, he gave every year the tenth part, not only of four-footed beasts, but also of all corn and fruit, as also of his garments, to the poor.

CHAP. XXX. *How his body was found altogether uncorrupted after it had been buried eleven years; and how his successor in the bishopric departed this world not long after.* [698 A.D.]

IN order to show forth the great glory of the life after death of the man of God, Cuthbert, whereas the loftiness of his life before his death had been revealed by the testimony of many miracles, when he had been buried eleven years, Divine Providence put it into the minds of the brethren to take up his bones. They thought to find them dry and all the rest of the body consumed and turned to dust, after the manner of the dead, and they desired to put them into a new coffin, and to lay them in the same place, but above the pavement, for the honour due to him. They made known their resolve to Bishop Eadbert, and he consented to it, and bade them to be mindful to do it on the anniversary of his burial. They did so, and opening the grave, found all the body whole, as if he were still alive, and the joints of the limbs pliable, like one asleep rather than dead; besides, all the vestments in which he was clothed were not only un-

[1] The year in which he administered the bishopric falls between his restoration to York, Hexham, and the monastery of Ripon, and his second expulsion.
[2] Cf. III, 25, *ad init.*, and *infra* c. 30. In the life of Cuthbert he is described as a man "magnarum virtutum" (miraculous powers?). Alcuin tells that he calmed the winds by his prayers.

defiled, but marvellous to behold, being fresh and bright
as at the first. The brothers seeing this, were struck
with a great dread, and hastened to tell the bishop what
they had found; he being then alone in a place remote
from the church, and encompassed on all sides by the
shifting waves of the sea. There he always used to
spend the time of Lent, and was wont to pass the forty
days before the Nativity of our Lord, in great devotion
with abstinence and prayer and tears. There also his
venerable predecessor, Cuthbert, had for some time
served as the soldier of the Lord in solitude before he
went to the isle of Farne.

They brought him also some part of the garments
that had covered the holy body; which presents he
thankfully accepted, and gladly heard of the miracles,
and he kissed the garments even, with great affection,
as if they had been still upon his father's body, and
said, " Let new garments be put upon the body, in place
of these you have brought, and so lay it in the coffin
which you have prepared; for I know of a surety that
the place will not long remain empty, which has been
hallowed with so great grace of heavenly miracles; and
how happy is he to whom the Lord, the Author and
Giver of all bliss, shall vouchsafe to grant the privilege
of resting therein." When the bishop had made an end
of saying this and more in like manner, with many tears
and great compunction and with faltering tongue, the
brothers did as he had commanded them, and when they
had wrapped the body in new garments, and laid it in a
new coffin, they placed it above the pavement of the
sanctuary. Soon after, Bishop Eadbert, beloved of God,
fell grievously sick, and his fever daily increasing in
severity, ere long, that is, on the 6th of May,[1] he also
departed to the Lord, and they laid his body in the grave
of the blessed father Cuthbert, placing over it the coffin,
with the uncorrupted remains of that father. The
miracles of healing, sometimes wrought in that place
testify to the merits of them both; of some of these we

----

[1] 698 A.D.

have before preserved the memory in the book of his life. But in this History we have thought fit to add some others which have lately come to our knowledge.

CHAP. XXXI. *Of one that was cured of a palsy at his tomb.*

THERE was in that same monastery a brother whose name was Badudegn, who had for no small time ministered to the guests of the house, and is still living, having the testimony of all the brothers and strangers resorting thither, of being a man of much piety and religion, and serving the office put upon him only for the sake of the heavenly reward. This man, having one day washed in the sea the coverings or blankets which he used in the guest chamber, was returning home, when on the way, he was seized with a sudden infirmity, insomuch that he fell to the ground, and lay there a long time and could scarce at last rise again. When he got up, he felt one half of his body, from the head to the foot, struck with palsy, and with great trouble made his way home by the help of a staff. The disease increased by degrees, and as night approached, became still worse, so that when day returned, he could scarcely rise or walk alone. Suffering from this trouble, he conceived the wise resolve to go to the church, as best he could, and approach the tomb of the reverend father Cuthbert, and there, on his knees, humbly beseech the mercy of God that he might either be delivered from that disease, if it were well for him, or if by the grace of God it was ordained for him to be chastened longer by this affliction, that he might bear the pain which was laid upon him with patience and a quiet mind.

He did accordingly as he had determined, and supporting his weak limbs with a staff, entered the church. There prostrating himself before the body of the man of God, he prayed with pious earnestness, that, through his intercession, the Lord might be propitious to him. As he prayed, he seemed to fall into a deep sleep, and, as he was afterwards wont to relate, felt a large and broad hand touch his head, where the pain lay, and likewise pass over all that part of his body which had been benumbed by the disease, down to his feet. Gradually the pain departed and health returned. Then he awoke, and rose up in perfect health, and returning thanks to the Lord for his recovery, told the brothers what had been done for him; and to the joy of them all, returned the more zealously, as if chastened by the trial of his affliction, to the service which he was wont before to perform with care.

Moreover, the very garments which had been on Cuthbert's body, dedicated to God, either while he was alive, or after his death, were not without the virtue of healing, as may be seen in the book of his life and miracles, by such as shall read it.

CHAP. XXXII. *Of one who was lately cured of a disease in his eye at the relics of St. Cuthbert.*

NOR is that cure to be passed over in silence, which was performed by his relics three years ago, and was told me lately by the brother himself, on whom it was wrought. It happened in the monastery, which, being built near the river Dacore,[1] has taken its name from the same, over which, at that time, the religious Suidbert[2] presided as abbot. In that monastery was a youth whose eyelid was disfigured by an unsightly tumour, which growing daily greater, threatened the loss of the eye. The physicians endeavoured to mitigate it by applying ointments, but in vain. Some said it ought to be cut off; others opposed this course, for fear of greater danger. The brother having long laboured under this malady, when no human means availed to save his eye, but rather, it grew daily worse, on a sudden, through the grace of the

---

[1] The Dacre, a small stream near Penrith. There are the ruins of a castle, and Smith says there is a tradition of a monastery on its banks.

[2] Not the missionary in V, 11.

mercy of God, it came to pass that he was cured by the relics of the holy father, Cuthbert. For when the brethren found his body uncorrupted, after having been many years buried, they took some part of the hair, to give, as relics, to friends who asked for them, or to show, in testimony of the miracle.

One of the priests of the monastery, named Thruidred, who is now abbot there, had a small part of these relics by him at that time. One day he went into the church and opened the box of relics, to give some part of them to a friend who asked for it, and it happened that the youth who had the diseased eye was then in the church. The priest, having given his friend as much as he thought fit, gave the rest to the youth to put back into its place. But he having received the hairs of the holy head, prompted by some salutary impulse, applied them to the diseased eyelid, and endeavoured for some time, by the application of them, to abate and mitigate the tumour. Having done this, he again laid the relics in the box, as he had been bidden, believing that his eye would soon be cured by the hairs of the man of God, which had touched it; nor did his faith disappoint him. It was then, as he is wont to relate, about the second hour of the day; but while he was occupied with other thoughts and business of the day, on a sudden, about the sixth hour of the same, touching his eye, he found it and the eyelid as sound as if there never had been any disfigurement or tumour on it.

BOOK V

CHAP. I. *How Ethelwald, successor to Cuthbert, leading a hermit's life, calmed a tempest by his prayers when the brethren were in danger at sea.* [687-699 A.D.]

THE venerable Ethelwald[1] succeeded the man of God, Cuthbert, in the exercise of a solitary life, which he spent in the isle of Farne[2] before he became a bishop. After he had received the priesthood, he consecrated his office by deeds worthy of that degree for many years in the monastery which is called Inhrypum.[3] To the end that his merit and manner of life may be the more certainly made known, I will relate one miracle of his, which was told me by one of the brothers for and on whom the same was wrought; to wit, Guthfrid, the venerable servant and priest of Christ, who also, afterwards, as abbot, presided over the brethren of the same church of Lindisfarne, in which he was educated.

"I came," says he, "to the island of Farne, with two others of the brethren, desiring to speak with the most reverend father, Ethelwald. Having been refreshed with his discourse, and asked for his blessing, as we were returning home, behold on a sudden, when we were in the midst of the sea, the fair weather in which we were sailing, was broken, and there arose so great and terrible a tempest, that neither sails nor oars were of any use to us, nor had we anything to expect but death. After long struggling with the wind and waves to no effect, at last we looked back to see whether it was possible by any means at least to return to the island whence we came, but we found that we were on all sides alike cut off by the storm, and that there was no hope of escape by our own

---

[1] "Innumera miracula" are ascribed to him by Florence of Worcester.

[2] III, 16, and note; IV, 27-30.

[3] Ripon, v. III, 25, p. 194; V, 19.

efforts. But looking further, we perceived, on the island of Farne, our father Ethelwald, beloved of God, come out of his retreat to watch our course; for, hearing the noise of the tempest and raging sea, he had come forth to see what would become of us. When he beheld us in distress and despair, he bowed his knees to the Father of our Lord Jesus Christ, in prayer for our life and safety; and as he finished his prayer, he calmed the swelling water, in such sort that the fierceness of the storm ceased on all sides, and fair winds attended us over a smooth sea to the very shore. When we had landed, and had pulled up our small vessel from the waves, the storm, which had ceased a short time for our sake, presently returned, and raged furiously during the whole day; so that it plainly appeared that the brief interval of calm had been granted by Heaven in answer to the prayers of the man of God, to the end that we might escape."

The man of God remained in the isle of Farne twelve years, and died there; but was buried in the church of the blessed Apostle Peter, in the isle of Lindisfarne, beside the bodies of the aforesaid bishops.[1] These things happened in the days of King Aldfrid,[2] who, after his brother Egfrid, ruled the nation of the Northumbrians for nineteen years.

CHAP. II.   *How Bishop John cured a dumb man by his blessing.* [687 A.D.]

In the beginning of Aldfrid's reign, Bishop Eata[3] died, and was succeeded in the bishopric of the church of Hagustald by the holy man John,[4] of whom those that knew him well are wont to tell many miracles, and more particularly Berthun,[5] a man worthy of all reverence and

---

[1] Cuthbert and Eadbert (IV, 29, 30). His relics were removed with Cuthbert's and finally interred at Durham.

[2] IV, 26, and V, 18. He reigned from 685 to 705.

[3] III, 26; IV, 12, 27, 28. He died in 686.

[4] John of Beverley, *v.* IV, 23, p. 273, and note. Wilfrid administered the bishopric during the vacancy between Eata's death and John's consecration in 687.   [5] Cf. *ibid.*

of undoubted truthfulness, and once his deacon, now abbot of the monastery called Inderauuda,[1] that is, " In the wood of the Deiri ": some of which miracles we have thought fit to hand on to posterity. There is a certain remote dwelling[2] enclosed by a mound, among scattered trees, not far from the church of Hagustald, being about a mile and a half distant and separated from it by the river Tyne, having an oratory[3] dedicated to St. Michael the Archangel, where the man of God used frequently, as occasion offered, and specially in Lent, to abide with a few companions and in quiet give himself to prayer and study. Having come hither once at the beginning of Lent to stay, he bade his followers find out some poor man labouring under any grievous infirmity, or want, whom they might keep with them during those days, to receive alms, for so he was always used to do.

There was in a township not far off, a certain youth who was dumb, known to the bishop, for he often used to come into his presence to receive alms. He had never been able to speak one word; besides, he had so much scurf and scab on his head, that no hair could ever grow on the top of it, but only some rough hairs stood on end round about it. The bishop caused this young man to be brought, and a little hut to be made for him within the enclosure of the dwelling, in which he might abide, and receive alms from him every day. When one week of Lent was over, the next Sunday he bade the poor

[1] Beverley. The present name is said to be derived from a colony of beavers in the Hull river. In 866 the minster was destroyed by the Danes, but it was repaired three years later. In 925 Athelstan restored it and made it collegiate, giving it lands and various privileges. (For the preposition, v. II, 14, p. 119, note 5.)

[2] Supposed to have been at St. John's Lee, near Hexham. The old name is Erneshow or Herneshaw. (Richard of Hexham, Folcard.)

[3] The reading of the best MSS., "Clymeterium" (v. ll. clymiterium, climiterium, clymitorium) seems inexplicable. Smith reads "coemeterium," probably on the authority of a gloss ("id est cimeterium ") on some of the later MSS., and it has generally been translated "cemetery." The AS. version has "gebæd hus 7 ciricean"=oratory and church.

man come to him, and when he had come, he bade him put his tongue out of his mouth and show it him; then taking him by the chin, he made the sign of the Holy Cross on his tongue, directing him to draw it back so signed into his mouth and to speak. "Pronounce some word," said he; "say 'gae,'" which, in the language of the English, is the word of affirming and consenting, that is, yes. The youth's tongue was immediately loosed, and he spoke as he was bidden. The bishop then added the names of the letters: "Say A." He said A. "Say B;" he said B also. When he had repeated all the letters after the bishop, the latter proceeded to put syllables and words to him, and when he had repeated them all rightly he bade him utter whole sentences, and he did it. Nor did he cease all that day and the next night, as long as he could keep awake, as those who were present relate, to say something, and to express his private thoughts and wishes to others, which he could never do before; after the manner of the man long lame, who, when he was healed by the Apostles Peter and John,[1] leaping up, stood and walked, and entered with them into the temple, walking, and leaping, and praising the Lord, rejoicing to have the use of his feet, which he had so long lacked. The bishop, rejoicing with him at his cure, caused the physician to take in hand the healing of the sores of his head. He did as he was bidden, and with the help of the bishop's blessing and prayers, a goodly head of hair grew as the skin was healed. Thus the youth became fair of countenance, ready of speech, with hair curling in comely fashion, whereas before he had been ill-favoured, miserable, and dumb. Thus filled with joy at his recovered health, notwithstanding that the bishop offered to keep him in his own household, he chose rather to return home.

[1] Acts, iii, 2-8.

CHAP. III. *How he healed a sick maiden by his prayers.*
[705 A.D.]

THE same Berthun told another miracle concerning the
said bishop. When the most reverend Wilfrid, after a
long banishment, was admitted to the bishopric of the
church of Hagustald,[1] and the aforesaid John, upon the
death of Bosa,[2] a man of great sanctity and humility,
was, in his place, appointed bishop of York, he himself
came, once upon a time, to the monastery of nuns, at
the place called Wetadun,[3] where the Abbess Heriburg
then presided. "When we were come thither," said he,
"and had been received with great and universal joy,
the abbess told us, that one of the nuns, who was her
own daughter after the flesh, laboured under a grievous
sickness, for she had been lately let blood in the arm,
and whilst she was under treatment,[4] was seized with an
attack of sudden pain, which speedily increased, while the
wounded arm became worse, and so much swollen, that
it could scarce be compassed with both hands; and she
lay in bed like to die through excess of pain. Wherefore
the abbess entreated the bishop that he would vouchsafe
to go in and give her his blessing; for she believed that
she would soon be better if he blessed her or laid his
hands upon her. He asked when the maiden had been
let blood, and being told that it was on the fourth day
of the moon, said, 'You did very indiscreetly and un-
skilfully to let blood on the fourth day of the moon; for I

---

[1] This was Wilfrid's second restoration. He recovered Hexham
and the monastery of Ripon at the Synod on the Nidd in 705.
[2] Bosa (IV, 12, 23) died *circ.* 705.
[3] Watton in the East Riding of Yorkshire. ("Hodie Watton,
i.e., humida villa ex aquis et paludibus quibus septa est." Smith.)
It is called Betendune by Folcard, the biographer of Bishop John.
[4] For "studium"=medical treatment, *v.* Plummer, *ad loc.*
Under the verb, *studere*, Ducange gives instances of this meaning:
"Iussitque rex, ut studeretur a medicis"; Greg. Turon., vi, 32.
"Episcopus, adhibito mulomedico, jussit ei (equo) studium im-
pendere, quo scilicet sanari potuisset"; St. Audoënus, lib. 2; Vit.
St. Eligii, 44.

X

remember that Archbishop Theodore,[1] of blessed memory, said, that blood-letting at that time was very dangerous, when the light of the moon is waxing and the tide of the ocean is rising. And what can I do for the maiden if she is like to die?'

"But the abbess still earnestly entreated for her daughter, whom she dearly loved, and designed to make abbess in her stead,[2] and at last prevailed with him to go in and visit the sick maiden. Wherefore he went in, taking me with him to the maid, who lay, as I said, in sore anguish, and her arm swelling so greatly that it could not be bent at all at the elbow; and he stood and said a prayer over her, and having given his blessing, went out. Afterwards, as we were sitting at table, at the usual hour, some one came in and called me out, saying, 'Quoenburg' (that was the maid's name) 'desires that you should immediately go back to her.' This I did, and entering the chamber, I found her of more cheerful countenance, and like one in good health. And while I was sitting beside her, she said, "Shall we call for something to drink?'—'Yes,' said I, 'and right glad am I, if you can.' When the cup was brought, and we had both drunk, she said, 'As soon as the bishop had said the prayer for me and given me his blessing and had gone out, I immediately began to mend; and though I have not yet recovered my former strength, yet all the pain is quite gone both from my arm, where it was most burning, and from all my body, as if the bishop had carried it away with him; notwithstanding the swelling of the arm still seems to remain.' But when we departed thence, the cure of the pain in her limbs was followed by the assuaging of the grievous swelling; and the maiden

---

[1] Bishop John had studied under Theodore. Cf. IV, 23, note.

[2] Note the tendency to hereditary succession in monasteries (v. Haddan and Stubbs, III, 337-338). Instances are, however, rare in England, though common in Ireland, where the clan system affected ecclesiastical preferments. Eanfled and Elfled at Whitby are not a case in point, as Eanfled did not precede her daughter, but was only associated with her in some way in the government of the monastery.

being thus delivered from pains and death, returned praise to our Lord and Saviour, in company with His other servants who were there."

CHAP. IV. *How he healed a thegn's wife that was sick, with holy water.*

THE same abbot related another miracle, not unlike the former, of the aforesaid bishop. " Not very far from our monastery," he said, "to wit, about two miles off, was the township[1] of one Puch, a thegn, whose wife had lain sick of a very grievous disease for nearly forty days, insomuch that for three weeks she could not be carried out of the chamber where she lay. It happened that the man of God was, at that time, called thither by the thegn to consecrate a church; and when that was done, the thegn desired him to come into his house and dine. The bishop declined, saying that he must return to the monastery, which was very near. The thegn, entreating him more earnestly, vowed he would also give alms to the poor, if so be that the bishop would vouchsafe to enter his house that day and break his fast. I joined my entreaties to his, promising in like manner to give alms for the relief of the poor,[2] if he would but go and dine at the thegn's house, and give his blessing. Having at length, with much difficulty, prevailed, we went in to refresh ourselves. The bishop had sent to the woman that lay sick some of the holy water, which he had blessed for the consecration of the church, by one of the brothers who had come with me, ordering him to give her some to drink, and wash that part of her where he found that her pain was greatest, with some of the same water. This being done, the woman immediately got up whole and sound, and perceiving that she had not only been delivered from her long sickness, but at the same time had recovered the strength which she had lost for

[1] This "vill" was at South Burton (Folcard), now called Bishop Burton, between two and three miles from Beverley.
[2] To redeem his fast, as the A.S. version explains.

so great a time, she presented the cup to the bishop and to us, and continued serving us with meat and drink as she had begun, till dinner was over; following the example of the blessed Peter's wife's mother, who, having been sick of a fever, arose at the touch of our Lord's hand, and having forthwith received health and strength, ministered to them."[1]

CHAP. V. *How he likewise recalled by his prayers a thegn's servant from death.*

AT another time also, being called to consecrate the church[2] of a thegn named Addi, when he had performed the required duty, he was entreated by the thegn to go in to one of his servants, who lay dangerously ill, insomuch that having lost all use of his limbs, he seemed to be at the point of death; and moreover the coffin had been made ready wherein to bury him after his death. The thegn urged his entreaties with tears, earnestly beseeching him that he would go in and pray for the servant, because his life was of great moment to him; and he believed that if the bishop would lay his hand upon him and give him his blessing, he would soon mend. So the bishop went in, and saw him very near death, and by his side the coffin in which he was to be laid for his burial, whilst all mourned. He said a prayer and blessed him, and going out, spake the wonted words of comfort, "Good health be yours and that speedily." Afterwards, when they were sitting at table, the servant sent to his lord, desiring that he would let him have a cup of wine, because he was thirsty. The thegn, rejoicing greatly that he could drink, sent him a cup of wine, blessed by the bishop; and, as soon as he had drunk it, he immediately got up, and, shaking off the heaviness of his infirmity, dressed himself and went forth, and going in to the bishop, saluted him and the other guests, saying

[1] St. Matt., viii, 14-15; St. Mark, i, 30-31; St. Luke, iv, 38-39.
[2] At North Burton (Dugdale, " Monasticon ").

that he also would gladly eat and drink with them. They bade him sit down with them at table, greatly rejoicing at his recovery. He sat down, ate and drank and made merry, and behaved himself like the rest of the company; and living many years after, continued in the same health which he had gained. The aforesaid abbot says this miracle was not wrought in his presence, but that he had it from those who were present.

CHAP. VI. *How, both by his prayers and blessing, he recalled from death one of his clerks, who had bruised himself by a fall.*

NOR do I think that this miracle, which Herebald,[1] the servant of Christ, says was wrought upon himself by the bishop, is to be passed over in silence. He was then one of that bishop's clergy, but now presides as abbot in the monastery at the mouth of the river Tyne.[2] "Living with him," said he, "and being very well acquainted with his course of life, I found it to be in all points worthy of a bishop, as far as it is lawful for men to judge; but I have known by the experience of others, and more particularly by my own, how great his merit was before Him Who seeth the heart; having been by his prayer and blessing recalled from the threshold of death and brought back to the way of life. For, when in the prime of my youth, I lived among his clergy, applying myself to reading and singing, but not having yet altogether withdrawn my heart from youthful pleasures, it happened one day that, as we were travelling with him, we came into a plain and open road, well fitted for galloping. The young men that were with him, and especially the laymen, began to entreat the bishop to give them leave to gallop, and make trial of their

---

[1] He lived till 745, according to Simeon of Durham.
[2] There were probably two monasteries at Tynemouth, the one mentioned here, and another (*v.* Bede's "Life of Cuthbert"), which had been a house of monks, but afterwards, when Bede wrote, had become a nunnery.

horses one with another. He at first refused, saying
that it was an idle request; but at last, overcome by
the unanimous desire of so many, 'Do so,' said he, 'if
you will, but let Herebald have no part in the trial.'
Then I earnestly prayed that I might have leave to com-
pete with the rest, for I relied on an excellent horse,
which he had himself given me, but I could in no wise
obtain my request.

"When they had several times galloped backwards
and forwards, the bishop and I looking on, my wanton
humour prevailed, and I could no longer refrain, but
though he forbade me, I struck in among them at their
sport, and began to ride with them at full speed; whereat
I heard him call after me with a groan, 'Alas! how
much you grieve me by riding after that manner.'
Though I heard him, I went on against his command;
but immediately the fiery horse taking a great leap over
a hollow place in the way, I fell, and at once lost all
sense and motion, like one dying; for there was in that
place a stone, level with the ground, covered with only
a thin coating of turf, and no other stone was to be
found in all that expanse of plain; and it happened by
chance, or rather by Divine Providence so ordering it, to
punish my disobedience, that my head and my hand,
which in falling I had put under my head, struck upon
that stone, so that my thumb was broken and my skull
fractured, and I became, as I said, like one dead.

"And because I could not move, they stretched a tent
there for me to lie in. It was about the seventh hour of
the day, and having lain still and as it were dead from
that time till the evening, I then revived a little, and was
carried home by my companions, and lay speechless all
the night, vomiting blood, because something was
broken within me by the fall. The bishop was very much
grieved at my fall and my misfortune, for he bore me
extraordinary affection. Nor would he stay that night,
as he was wont, among his clergy; but spent it alone in
watching and prayer, imploring the Divine goodness,
as I suppose, for my preservation. Coming to me early
in the morning, and having said a prayer over me, he

called me by my name, and when I awoke as it were out of a heavy sleep, he asked whether I knew who it was that spoke to me? I opened my eyes and said, 'Yes; you are my beloved bishop.'—'Can you live?' said he. I answered, 'I can, through your prayers, if the Lord will.'

"He then laid his hand on my head, with the words of blessing, and returned to prayer; when he came again to see me, in a short time, he found me sitting and able to talk; and, being moved by Divine inspiration, as it soon appeared, began to ask me, whether I knew for certain that I had been baptized? I answered that I knew beyond all doubt that I had been washed in the font of salvation, for the remission of sins, and I named the priest by whom I knew that I had been baptized. He replied, 'If you were baptized by that priest, your baptism is not perfect; for I know him, and that when he was ordained priest, he could in no wise, by reason of the dulness of his understanding, learn the ministry of catechizing and baptizing; for which reason I enjoined upon him altogether to desist from presuming to exercise that ministry, which he could not duly perform.' This said, he set himself to catechize me that same hour; and it came to pass that when he breathed on my face,[1] straightway I felt better. He called the surgeon and ordered him to set and bind up my skull where it was fractured; and presently having received his blessing, I was so much better that I mounted on horseback the next day, and travelled with him to another place; and being soon after perfectly recovered, I was washed in the water of life."

He continued in his bishopric thirty-three years,[2] and then ascending to the heavenly kingdom, was buried in

[1] Breathing on the face and catechizing were practised in order to exorcise evil spirits from the hearts of catechumens (Bede, Opp., viii, 106).
[2] The Saxon Chronicle is very exact: "Thirty-three years, eight months, and thirteen days." This would date his episcopate from August, 687, to May, 721, for May 7th was observed as the day of his festival at Beverley.

St. Peter's Chapel, in his own monastery, which is called, "In the wood of the Deiri," [1] in the year of our Lord 721. For having, by his great age, become unable to govern his bishopric, he ordained Wilfrid, [2] his priest, bishop of the church of York, and retired to the aforesaid monastery, and there ended his days in godly conversation.

CHAP. VII. *How Caedwalla, king of the West Saxons, went to Rome to be baptized; and his successor Ini, also devoutly journeyed to the same threshold of the holy Apostles.* [688 A.D.]

In the third year of the reign of Aldfrid, [3] Caedwalla, king of the West Saxons, having most vigorously governed his nation for two years, quitted his crown for the sake of the Lord and an everlasting kingdom, and went to Rome, being desirous to obtain the peculiar honour of being cleansed in the baptismal font at the threshold of the blessed Apostles, for he had learned that in Baptism alone the entrance into the heavenly life is opened to mankind; and he hoped at the same time, that being made clean by Baptism, he should soon be freed from the bonds of the flesh and pass to the eternal joys of Heaven; both which things, by the help of the Lord, came to pass according as he had conceived in his mind. For coming to Rome, at the time that Sergius [4] was pope, he was baptized on the Holy Saturday before Easter Day, [5] in the year of our Lord 689, and being still in his white garments, [6] he fell sick, and was set free from the bonds of the flesh on the 20th of April, and obtained an entrance into the kingdom of the blessed in Heaven. At his baptism, the aforesaid pope had given him the name of Peter, to the end, that he might be also united in name to the most blessed chief of the Apostles,

---

[1] Cf. c. 2.   [2] Wilfrid II: *v.* IV, 23, p. 273, and note.
[3] *I.e.*, in 688. For Caedwalla, *v.* IV, 12 (and note), 15, 16.
[4] Sergius I, 687-701.
[5] Cf. II, 9, 14 and notes.   [6] Cf. II, 14 and note.

to whose most holy body his pious love had led him from the utmost bounds of the earth. He was likewise buried in his church, and by the pope's command an epitaph [1] was written on his tomb, wherein the memory of his devotion might be preserved for ever, and the readers or hearers thereof might be stirred up to give themselves to religion by the example of what he had done.

The epitaph was this:—

"High estate, wealth, offspring, a mighty kingdom, triumphs, spoils, chieftains, strongholds, the camp, a home; whatsoever the valour of his sires, whatsoever himself had won, Caedwal, mighty in war, left for the love of God, that, a pilgrim king, he might behold Peter and Peter's seat, receive at his font pure waters of life, and in bright draughts drink of the shining radiance whence a quickening glory streams through all the world. And even as he gained with eager soul the prize of the new life, he laid aside barbaric rage, and, changed in heart, he changed his name with joy. Sergius the Pope bade him be called Peter, himself his father, [2] when he rose born anew from the font, and the grace of Christ, cleansing him, bore him forthwith clothed in white raiment to the heights of Heaven. O wondrous faith of the king, but greatest of all the mercy of Christ, into whose counsels none may enter! For he came in safety from the ends of the earth, even from Britain, through many a nation, over many a sea, by many a path, and saw the city of Romulus and looked upon Peter's sanctuary revered, bearing mystic gifts. He shall walk in white among the sheep of Christ in fellowship with them; for his body is in the tomb, but his soul on high. Thou mightest deem he did but change an earthly for a heavenly sceptre, whom thou seest attain to the kingdom of Christ."

"Here was buried Caedwalla, called also Peter, king of the Saxons, on the twentieth day of April, in the

---

[1] By Benedictus Crispus, Archbishop of Milan. He died in 725.
[2] *I.e.*, Sergius was his godfather (cf. III, 7, where Oswald stands sponsor for Cynegils). The Saxon Chronicle says he also baptized him.

second indiction, aged about thirty years, in the reign of our most pious lord, the Emperor Justinian,[1] in the fourth year of his consulship, in the second year of the pontificate of our Apostolic lord, Pope Sergius."

When Caedwalla went to Rome, Ini[2] succeeded to the kingdom, being of the blood royal; and having reigned thirty-seven years over that nation, he in like manner left his kingdom and committed it to younger men, and went away to the threshold of the blessed Apostles, at the time when Gregory[3] was pope, being desirous to spend some part of his pilgrimage upon earth in the neighbourhood of the holy places, that he might obtain to be more readily received into the fellowship of the saints in heaven. This same thing, about that time, was wont to be done most zealously by many of the English nation, nobles and commons, laity and clergy, men and women.

CHAP. VIII. *How, when Archbishop Theodore died, Bertwald succeeded him as archbishop, and, among many others whom he ordained, he made the learned Tobias bishop of the church of Rochester.* [690 A.D.]

THE year after that in which Caedwalla died at Rome, that is, 690 after the Incarnation of our Lord, Archbishop Theodore, of blessed memory, departed this life, being old and full of days, for he was eighty-eight years of age; which number of years he had been wont long before to foretell to his friends that he should live, the same having been revealed to him in a dream. He held the bishopric twenty-two years,[4] and was buried in St. Peter's church,[5] where all the bodies of the bishops of

[1] Justinian II. He succeeded in 685 and died in 711.
[2] Cf. IV, 15, and note. Thus, according to Bede's reckoning, he reigned from 688 to 725, but the date of his abdication is variously given.
[3] Gregory II, 715-731, *v.* Preface, p. 2.
[4] He was consecrated 26th March, 668, and died, as Bede says here, on 19th September, 690.
[5] The church of SS. Peter and Paul. Cf. II, 3, p. 90.

Canterbury are buried. Of whom, as well as of his fellows of the same degree, it may rightly and truly be said, that their bodies are buried in peace, and their names shall live to all generations. For to say all in few words, the English Churches gained more spiritual increase while he was archbishop, than ever before. His character, life, age, and death, are plainly and manifestly described to all that resort thither, by the epitaph on his tomb, in thirty-four heroic verses.[1] The first whereof are these:

"Here in the tomb rests the body of the holy prelate, called now in the Greek tongue Theodore. Chief pontiff, blest high priest, pure doctrine he set forth to his disciples."

The last are as follow:

"For September had reached its nineteenth day, when his spirit went forth from the prison-bars of the flesh. Mounting in bliss to the gracious fellowship of the new life, he was united to the angelic citizens in the heights of Heaven."

Bertwald[2] succeeded Theodore in the archbishopric, being abbot of the monastery called Racuulfe,[3] which stands at the northern mouth of the river Genlade.[4] He was a man learned in the Scriptures, and perfectly instructed in ecclesiastical and monastic teaching, yet in no wise to be compared to his predecessor. He was chosen bishop in the year of our Lord 692,[5] on the first day of July, when Wictred and Suaebhard were kings

---

[1] They are elegiacs. Cf. I, 10.

[2] Cf. II, 3, and *infra* 19, 23.

[3] The old Roman town Reculver, in Kent. A charter of 679 exists (the oldest original English charter extant) by which King Hlothere of Kent grants land in Thanet to Bertwald and his monastery.

[4] Said to be the Inlade.

[5] The see was, therefore, vacant for two years, possibly owing to the political troubles of the time, cf. IV, 26, *ad fin.* The further delay of a year between Bertwald's election and consecration may have been caused by his desire to obtain greater weight as consecrated by the Primate of a neighbouring Church (Haddan and Stubbs, III, 229).

in Kent;[1] but he was ordained the next year, on Sunday
the 29th of June, by Godwin, metropolitan bishop of
Gaul,[2] and was enthroned on Sunday the 31st of August.
Among the many bishops whom he ordained was Tobias,[3]
a man instructed in the Latin, Greek, and Saxon tongues,
and otherwise of manifold learning, whom he consecrated
in the stead of Gedmund, bishop of the Church of Rochester, who had died.

CHAP. IX. *How the holy man, Egbert, would have gone
into Germany to preach, but could not; and how Wictbert went, but because he availed nothing, returned into
Ireland, whence he came.* [Circ. 688 A.D.]

AT that time the venerable servant of Christ, and priest,
Egbert,[4] who is to be named with all honour, and who,
as was said before, lived as a stranger and pilgrim in
Ireland to obtain hereafter a country in heaven, purposed in his mind to profit many, taking upon him the
work of an apostle, and, by preaching the Gospel, to
bring the Word of God to some of those nations that had
not yet heard it; many of which tribes he knew to be in
Germany, from whom the Angles or Saxons, who now
inhabit Britain, are known to have derived their race
and origin; for which reason they are still corruptly

---

[1] For Wictred, *v.* IV, 26, and note. Thomas of Elmham tries to
identify Suaebhard with Suefred, son of Sebbi, king of the East
Saxons (*v.* IV, 11, *ad fin.*), and says that he made himself king of
Kent by violence, but this seems very improbable.

[2] He was Archbishop of Lyons. The Church of Lyons did not
obtain the primacy over other metropolitan churches till the
eleventh century, but apparently it held a leading position even
before this time.

[3] He was trained under Theodore and Hadrian in the School of
Canterbury; cf. V, 23, *ad init.* The date of Gebmund's death and
the succession of Tobias cannot be earlier than 696, as Gebmund
(*v.* IV, 12) appears to have been present at the Kentish Witenagemot of Bersted in that year. (Haddan and Stubbs, III, 238, 241.)
Tobias died in 726.

[4] III, 4, 27; IV, 3, 26, and *infra* cc. 10, 22, 23, 24.

called "Garmans"[1] by the neighbouring nation of the Britons. Such are the Frisians, the Rugini, the Danes, the Huns, the Old Saxons, and the Boructuari.[2] There are also in the same parts many other peoples still enslaved to pagan rites, to whom the aforesaid soldier of Christ determined to go, sailing round Britain, if haply he could deliver any of them from Satan, and bring them to Christ; or if this might not be, he was minded to go to Rome, to see and adore the thresholds of the holy Apostles and martyrs of Christ.

But a revelation from Heaven and the working of God prevented him from achieving either of these enterprises; for when he had made choice of most courageous companions, fit to preach the Word, inasmuch as they were renowned for their good deeds and their learning, and when all things necessary were provided for the voyage, there came to him on a certain day early in the morning one of the brethren, who had been a disciple of the priest, Boisil,[3] beloved of God, and had ministered to him in Britain, when the said Boisil was provost of the

[1] The name does not occur in any Celtic literature which we possess. All the evidence seems to show that the Celts have always called the English "Saxons." "Ellmyn," for Allemanni, occurs sometimes in Welsh poetry (Rhŷs, "Celtic Britain").

[2] The Frisians at this time occupied the coastland from the Maas to the region beyond the Ems. The Rugini are probably the Rugii (v. Tacitus, Germania, Chapter XLIII). They were on the shores of the Baltic, probably about the mouth of the Oder (the name survives in Rügen and Rügenwalde). They are found with other North German tribes in the army of Attila, and afterwards formed a settlement on the Lower Danube. The Danes were mainly in Jutland, Fünen, and the extreme south of Scandinavia. The Huns, who appeared in Europe towards the end of the fourth century and menaced both the Eastern and Western Empires, were, after Attila's death, driven eastwards, and settled near the Pontus, disappearing among the Bulgarians and other kindred tribes. The Old Saxons, or Saxons of the Continent (cf. I, 15), occupied both sides of the Elbe. The name Saxon does not occur in the oldest accounts of the Germans. Probably it was a new name for a union of nations which comprised the Cherusci, Chauci, Angrivarii (and perhaps other tribes) of Tacitus. The Boructuari are the Bructeri in Westphalia (v. Zeuss, "Die Deutschen und die Nachbarstämme").

[3] Cf. IV, 27 (note) and 28.

monastery of Mailros,[1] under the Abbot Eata, as has
been said above.[2] This brother told him a vision which
he had seen that night. "When after matins," said he,
"I had laid me down in my bed, and was fallen into a
light slumber, Boisil, that was sometime my master and
brought me up in all love, appeared to me, and asked,
whether I knew him? I said, 'Yes, you are Boisil.' He
answered, 'I am come to bring Egbert a message from
our Lord and Saviour, which must nevertheless be delivered to him by you. Tell him, therefore, that he
cannot perform the journey he has undertaken; for it is
the will of God that he should rather go to teach the
monasteries of Columba'"[3] Now Columba was the
first teacher of the Christian faith to the Picts beyond
the mountains northward, and the first founder of the
monastery in the island of Hii, which was for a long time
much honoured by many tribes of the Scots and Picts.
The said Columba is now by some called Columcille, the
name being compounded from "Columba" and "Cella."[4]
Egbert, having heard the words of the vision, charged
the brother that had told it him, not to tell it to any
other, lest haply it should be a lying vision. But when
he considered the matter secretly with himself, he apprehended that it was true, yet would not desist from preparing for his voyage which he purposed to make to
teach those nations.

A few days after the aforesaid brother came again to
him, saying that Boisil had that night again appeared to
him in a vision after matins, and said, "Why did you
tell Egbert so negligently and after so lukewarm a
manner that which I enjoined upon you to say? Yet, go
now and tell him, that whether he will or no, he must go

[1] Melrose; cf. III, 26; IV, 27, and *infra* c. 12.
[2] IV, 27. Cf. III, 26; IV, 12, 28; V, 2.
[3] Cf. III, 3, 4, and notes; *i.e.*, the monasteries which owed their
origin to Columba and were included in the "province" of Iona.
They are distinguished from those which are mentioned in c. 15
as "ab Hiensium dominio liberi."
[4] His baptismal name was Colum (*columba* = a dove). He is said
to have acquired the name of Colum-cille, because in his youth he
was so constantly in the "cell" or oratory.

to Columba's monasteries, because their ploughs are not driven straight; and he must bring them back into the right way." Hearing this, Egbert again charged the brother not to reveal the same to any man. Though now assured of the vision, he nevertheless attempted to set forth upon his intended voyage with the brethren. When they had put aboard all that was requisite for so long a voyage, and had waited some days for fair winds, there arose one night so violent a storm, that part of what was on board was lost, and the ship itself was left lying on its side in the sea. Nevertheless, all that belonged to Egbert and his companions was saved. Then he, saying, in the words of the prophet, "For my sake this great tempest is upon you,"[1] withdrew himself from that undertaking and was content to remain at home.

But one of his companions, called Wictbert,[2] notable for his contempt of the world and for his learning and knowledge, for he had lived many years as a stranger and pilgrim in Ireland, leading a hermit's life in great perfection, took ship, and arriving in Frisland, preached the Word of salvation for the space of two whole years to that nation and to its king, Rathbed;[3] but reaped no fruit of all his great labour among his barbarous hearers. Returning then to the chosen place of his pilgrimage, he gave himself up to the Lord in his wonted life of silence, and since he could not be profitable to strangers by teaching them the faith, he took care to be the more profitable to his own people by the example of his virtue.

---

[1] Jonah, i, 12.

[2] Nothing more is known of him. Alcuin mentions him in his life of Wilbrord. His name is included in a list of the eleven companions of Wilbrord given in a life of St. Suidbert (*v. infra* c. 11), but no value is to be attached to it (*v.* Haddan and Stubbs, III, 225). Bede distinctly says that he retired from missionary efforts after this unsuccessful attempt.

[3] The story is told that at one time Rathbed was about to receive baptism at the hands of St. Wulfram, Archbishop of Sens, but drew back on being told that his ancestors were among the lost, refusing to go to Heaven without them. His perpetual wars with the Franks ended in his defeat and expulsion, and he died in 719.

CHAP. X. *How Wilbrord, preaching in Frisland, converted many to Christ; and how his two companions, the Hewalds, suffered martyrdom.* [690 A.D.]

WHEN the man of God, Egbert, perceived that neither he himself was permitted to go and preach to the nations, being withheld for the sake of some other advantage to the holy Church, whereof he had been forewarned by a revelation; nor that Wictbert, when he went into those parts, had availed to do anything; he nevertheless still attempted to send holy and industrious men to the work of the Word, among whom the most notable was Wilbrord,[1] a man eminent for his merit and rank as priest. They arrived there, twelve in number, and turning aside to Pippin,[2] duke of the Franks, were gladly received by him; and as he had lately subdued the nearer part of Frisland, and expelled King Rathbed,[3] he sent them thither to preach, supporting them at the same time with his sovereign authority, that none might molest them in their preaching, and bestowing many favours on those who consented to receive the faith. Thus it came to pass, that with the help of the Divine grace, in a short time they converted many from idolatry to the faith of Christ.

Following their example, two other priests of the English nation, who had long lived as strangers in Ireland, for the sake of the eternal country, went into the

---

[1] The authority for Wilbrord's life is Alcuin, who wrote it both in prose and verse. Wilbrord was born in 657 or 658 in Northumbria, and was handed over by his mother to the monks at Ripon in his infancy. His father, Wilgils, became a hermit on a promontory at the mouth of the Humber. At the age of twenty he went to Ireland for the sake of study and a stricter life. In 690 he set out for Frisland with eleven others, landed at Katwyk and went to Utrecht, which was afterwards his episcopal see (*v. infra* c. 11).

[2] They turned aside to Pippin on finding Rathbed obdurate. Pippin of Heristal, Mayor of the Palace of the Austrasian kings, had defeated the Neustrians at Testry in 687 and was now the actual ruler of the Franks, though it was his grandson, Pippin the Short, who first assumed royal power.

[3] Cf. c. 9, p. 319, and note.

province of the Old Saxons, if haply they could there win any to Christ by their preaching. They were alike in name as in devotion, Hewald being the name of both, with this distinction, that, on account of the different colour of their hair, the one was called Black Hewald and the other White Hewald.[1] They were both full of religious piety, but Black Hewald was the more learned of the two in Scripture. When they came into the province, these men took up their lodging in the guesthouse of a certain township-reeve, and asked of him that he would conduct them to the ealdorman[2] who was over him, for that they had a message concerning matters of import-ance to communicate to him. For those Old Saxons have no king, but many ealdormen set over their nation; and when any war is on the point of breaking out, they cast lots indifferently, and on whomsoever the lot falls, him they all follow and obey during the time of war; but as soon as the war is ended, all those ealdormen are again equal in power. So the reeve received and entertained them in his house some days, promising to send them to the ealdorman who was over him, as they desired.

But when the barbarians perceived that they were of another religion,—for they continually gave themselves to singing of psalms and prayer, and daily offered up to God the Sacrifice of the saving Victim, having with them sacred vessels and a consecrated table for an altar,— they began to grow suspicious of them, lest if they should come into the presence of their ealdorman, and converse with him, they should turn his heart from their gods, and convert him to the new religion of the Christian

[1] Roger of Wendover places their mission in 695. It must have been later than Wilbrord's in 690.

[2] "Satrap," cf. Stubbs, Constitutional History, i, pp. 41-42. From this passage and similar notices of the Continental Saxons he infers that they had remained free from Roman influences and from any foreign intermixture of blood or institutions. "They had preserved the ancient features of German life in their purest forms. . . . King Alfred, when he translated Bede had no difficulty in recognizing in the satrap the *ealdorman*, in the villicus the *tun-gerefa*, in the vicus the *tunscipe* of his own land."

faith; and thus by degrees all their province should be forced to change its old worship for a new. Wherefore on a sudden they laid hold of them and put them to death; and White Hewald they slew outright with the sword; but they put Black Hewald to lingering torture and tore him limb from limb in horrible fashion, and they threw their bodies into the Rhine. The ealdorman, whom they had desired to see, hearing of it, was very angry that strangers who desired to come to him had not been suffered to come; and therefore he sent and put to death all those villagers and burned their village. The aforesaid priests and servants of Christ suffered on on the 3rd of October.[1]

Miracles from Heaven were not lacking at their martyrdom. For their dead bodies, having been cast into the river by the pagans, as has been said, were carried against the stream for the space of almost forty miles, to the place where their companions were. Moreover, a long ray of light, reaching up to heaven, shone every night above them wheresoever they chanced to be, and that too in the sight of the very pagans that had slain them. Moreover, one of them appeared in a vision by night to one of his companions, whose name was Tilmon, a man of renown and of noble birth in this world, who having been a thegn had become a monk, telling him that he might find their bodies in that place, where he should see rays of light reaching from heaven to the earth. And so it befell; and their bodies being found, were buried with the honour due to martyrs; and the day of their passion or of the finding of their bodies, is celebrated in those parts with fitting veneration. Finally, Pippin, the most glorious duke of the Franks, learning these things, caused the bodies to be brought to him, and buried them with much honour in the church of the city of Cologne, on the Rhine.[2] And it is said that a spring burst forth in the place where they were killed, which to this day affords a plentiful stream in that same place.

[1] The year cannot be fixed.
[2] The Church of St. Cunibert, Cologne (Gallican Martyrology, quoted by Smith).

CHAP. XI. *How the venerable Suidbert in Britain, and Wilbrord at Rome, were ordained bishops for Frisland.* [692 A.D.]

AT their first coming into Frisland, as soon as Wilbrord found that he had leave given him by the prince to preach there, he made haste to go to Rome, where Pope Sergius [1] then presided over the Apostolic see, that he might undertake the desired work of preaching the Gospel to the nations, with his licence and blessing; and hoping to receive of him some relics of the blessed Apostles and martyrs of Christ; to the end, that when he destroyed the idols,[2] and erected churches in the nation to which he preached, he might have the relics of saints at hand to put into them, and having deposited them there, might accordingly dedicate each of those places to the honour of the saint whose relics they were. He desired also there to learn or to receive many other things needful for so great a work. Having obtained his desire in all these matters, he returned to preach.

At which time, the brothers who were in Frisland, attending on the ministry of the Word, chose out of their own number a man of sober life, and meek of heart, called Suidbert,[3] to be ordained bishop for them. He, being sent into Britain, was consecrated, at their request, by the most reverend Bishop Wilfrid, who, having been driven out of his country, chanced then to be living in banishment among the Mercians;[4] for Kent had no bishop at that time, Theodore being dead, and Bertwald, his successor, who had gone beyond the sea to be ordained, having not yet returned to his episcopal see.

[1] Sergius I: *v.s.* c. 7.
[2] Alcuin tells how he killed some of the sacred cattle of the god Fosite, a son of Balder, in Heligoland, and baptized three men in his well.
[3] A life of him by Marcellinus (*v.s.* c. 9, note on Wictbert) is worthless historically. Besides what we learn from Bede, we have the date of his death (713) given by the " Annales Francorum."
[4] This was after Wilfrid's second expulsion (V, 19). Bertwald was elected in July, 692, and returned from the Continent in August, 693 (*v.s.* c. 8).

The said Suidbert, being made bishop, returned from Britain, and not long after departed to the Boructuari; and by his preaching brought many of them into the way of truth; but the Boructuari being not long after subdued by the Old Saxons, those who had received the Word were dispersed abroad; and the bishop himself with certain others went to Pippin, who, at the request of his wife, Blithryda,[1] gave him a place of abode in a certain island on the Rhine, called in their tongue, Inlitore;[2] there he built a monastery, which his successors still possess, and for a time dwelt in it, leading a most continent life, and there ended his days.

When they who had gone thither had spent some years teaching in Frisland, Pippin, with the consent of them all, sent the venerable Wilbrord to Rome, where Sergius was still pope, desiring that he might be consecrated archbishop over the nation of the Frisians; which was accordingly done, as he had made request, in the year of our Lord 696. He was consecrated in the church of the Holy Martyr Cecilia,[3] on her festival; and the said pope gave him the name of Clement, and forthwith sent him back to his bishopric, to wit, fourteen days after his arrival in the city.

Pippin gave him a place for his episcopal see, in his famous fort, which in the ancient language of those people is called Wiltaburg, that is, the town of the Wilts; but, in the Gallic tongue, Trajectum.[4] The most reverend prelate having built a church there,[5] and

[1] The usual form of the name is Plectrude.
[2] Kaiserwerth on the Rhine, where it is believed that his relics still remain in a silver shrine in the thirteenth-century church. (For the preposition, v. II, 14, p. 119, note 5.)
[3] This was Santa Cecilia in Trastevere. The festival is 22nd November. As to the year, Mr. Plummer considers that an entry in an old calendar belonging to Epternach, near Trèves, Wilbrord's own monastery, giving the date 695, is almost certainly by Wilbrord himself.
[4] Utrecht. A distinction has been drawn between the two places, Wiltaburg, or Wiltenburg, being a village near Utrecht, but the names appear to be interchangeable.
[5] The Church of St. Saviour. He also rebuilt a small church which had been destroyed by the pagans, and consecrated it in

preaching the Word of faith far and near, drew many from their errors, and built many churches and not a few monasteries. For not long after he himself constituted other bishops in those parts from the number of the brethren that either came with him or after him to preach there; of whom some are now fallen asleep in the Lord; but Wilbrord himself, surnamed Clement, is still living, venerable for his great age, having been thirty-six years a bishop, and now, after manifold conflicts of the heavenly warfare, he longs with all his heart for the recompense of the reward in Heaven.[1]

CHAP. XII. *How one in the province of the Northumbrians, rose from the dead, and related many things which he had seen, some to be greatly dreaded and some to be desired.* [Circ. 696 A.D.]

AT this time a memorable miracle, and like to those of former days, was wrought in Britain; for, to the end that the living might be roused from the death of the soul, a certain man, who had been some time dead, rose again to the life of the body, and related many memorable things that he had seen; some of which I have thought fit here briefly to describe. There was a certain householder in that district of the Northumbrians which is called Incuneningum,[2] who led a godly life, with all his house. This man fell sick, and his sickness daily increasing, he was brought to extremity, and died in the

honour of St. Martin (Letter of St. Boniface to Pope Stephen). The cathedral stands on the site of this church.

[1] Bede writes in 731. As Alcuin says Wilbrord lived to be eighty-one years of age, he must have died in 738 or 739. Boniface is fairly accurate when he says that he preached for fifty years.

[2] Mr. Skene ("Celtic Scotland," i., p. 219) has shown that the place cannot be Cunningham in Ayrshire, which was not in Northumbria, but in Strathclyde, and not at that time subject to Northumbria. He suggests Tininghame in East Lothian, which Simeon of Durham calls Intiningaham, and places in the diocese of Lindisfarne (C being a scribe's error for T). Chester-le-Street (Saxon: Cunungaceaster) has also been suggested.

beginning of the night; but at dawn he came to life again, and suddenly sat up, whereat all those that sat about the body weeping fled away in great terror, only his wife, who loved him better, though trembling and greatly afraid, remained with him. And he comforting her, said, "Fear not, for I am now in very deed risen from death whereof I was holden, and permitted again to live among men; nevertheless, hereafter I must not live as I was wont, but after a very different manner." Then rising immediately, he went to the oratory of the little town, and continuing in prayer till day, forthwith divided all his substance into three parts; one whereof he gave to his wife, another to his children, and the third, which he kept himself, he straightway distributed among the poor. Not long after, being set free from the cares of this world, he came to the monastery of Mailros,[1] which is almost enclosed by the winding of the river Tweed, and having received the tonsure, went apart into a place of abode which the abbot had provided, and there he continued till the day of his death, in so great contrition of mind and mortifying of the body, that even if his tongue had been silent, his life would have declared that he had seen many things either to be dreaded or coveted, which were hidden from other men.

Thus he related what he had seen.[2] "He that led me had a countenance full of light, and shining raiment, and we went in silence, as it seemed to me, towards the rising of the summer sun. And as we walked we came to a broad and deep valley of infinite length; it lay on our left, and one side of it was exceeding terrible with raging flames, the other no less intolerable for violent hail and cold snows drifting and sweeping through all the place. Both sides were full of the souls of men which seemed to be tossed from one side to the other as it were by a violent storm; for when they could no longer endure the fervent heat, the hapless souls leaped

---

[1] Melrose, v. III, 26; IV, 27; V, 9.
[2] Cf. III, 19. On mediaeval visions, cf. Plummer, *ad loc.*, and Bright, p. 144.

into the midst of the deadly cold; and finding no rest there, they leaped back again to be burnt in the midst of the unquenchable flames. Now whereas an innumerable multitude of misshapen spirits were thus tormented far and near with this interchange of misery, as far as I could see, without any interval of rest, I began to think that peradventure this might be Hell, of whose intolerable torments I had often heard men talk. My guide, who went before me, answered to my thought, saying, 'Think not so, for this is not the Hell you believe it to be.'

"When he had led me farther by degrees, sore dismayed by that dread sight, on a sudden I saw the place before us begin to grow dark and filled with shadows. When we entered into them, the shadows by degrees grew so thick, that I could see nothing else, save only the darkness and the shape and garment of him that led me. As we went on 'through the shades in the lone night,'[1] lo! on a sudden there appeared before us masses of foul flame constantly rising as it were out of a great pit, and falling back again into the same. When I had been led thither, my guide suddenly vanished, and left me alone in the midst of darkness and these fearful sights. As those same masses of fire, without intermission, at one time flew up and at another fell back into the bottom of the abyss, I perceived that the summits of all the flames, as they ascended were full of the spirits of men, which, like sparks flying upwards with the smoke, were sometimes thrown on high, and again, when the vapours of the fire fell, dropped down into the depths below. Moreover, a stench, foul beyond compare, burst forth with the vapours, and filled all those dark places.

"Having stood there a long time in much dread, not knowing what to do, which way to turn, or what end awaited me, on a sudden I heard behind me the sound of a mighty and miserable lamentation, and at the same time noisy laughter, as of a rude multitude insulting captured enemies. When that noise, growing plainer, came up to me, I beheld a crowd of evil spirits dragging

[1] Vergil, Aen. VI, 268.

five souls of men, wailing and shrieking, into the midst
of the darkness, whilst they themselves exulted and
laughed. Among those human souls, as I could discern,
there was one shorn like a clerk, one a layman, and one
a woman. The evil spirits that dragged them went down
into the midst of the burning pit; and it came to pass
that as they went down deeper, I could no longer distinguish between the lamentation of the men and the
laughing of the devils, yet I still had a confused sound
in my ears. In the meantime, some of the dark spirits
ascended from that flaming abyss, and running forward,
beset me on all sides, and with their flaming eyes and
the noisome fire which they breathed forth from their
mouths and nostrils, tried to choke me; and threatened
to lay hold on me with fiery tongs, which they had in
their hands, yet they durst in no wise touch me, though
they assayed to terrify me. Being thus on all sides encompassed with enemies and shades of darkness, and
casting my eyes hither and thither if haply anywhere help
might be found whereby I might be saved, there appeared
behind me, on the way by which I had come, as it were,
the brightness of a star shining amidst the darkness;
which waxing greater by degrees, came rapidly towards
me: and when it drew near, all those evil spirits, that
sought to carry me away with their tongs, dispersed and
fled.

"Now he, whose approach put them to flight, was
the same that led me before; who, then turning towards
the right, began to lead me, as it were, towards the
rising of the winter sun, and having soon brought me
out of the darkness, led me forth into an atmosphere of
clear light. While he thus led me in open light, I saw a
vast wall before us, the length on either side, and the
height whereof, seemed to be altogether boundless. I
began to wonder why we went up to the wall, seeing no
door in it, nor window, nor any way of ascent. But
when we came to the wall, we were presently, I know
not by what means, on the top of it, and lo! there was
a wide and pleasant plain full of such fragrance of
blooming flowers that the marvellous sweetness of the

scents immediately dispelled the foul stench of the dark furnace which had filled my nostrils. So great was the light shed over all this place that it seemed to exceed the brightness of the day, or the rays of the noontide sun. In this field were innumerable companies of men clothed in white, and many seats of rejoicing multitudes. As he led me through the midst of bands of happy inhabitants, I began to think that this perchance might be the kingdom of Heaven, of which I had often heard tell. He answered to my thought, saying, 'Nay, this is not the kingdom of Heaven, as you think.'

"When we had also passed those mansions of blessed spirits, and gone farther on, I saw before me a much more beautiful light than before, and therein heard sweet sounds of singing, and so wonderful a fragrance was shed abroad from the place, that the other which I had perceived before and thought so great, then seemed to me but a small thing; even as that wondrous brightness of the flowery field, compared with this which I now beheld, appeared mean and feeble. When I began to hope that we should enter that delightful place, my guide, on a sudden stood still; and straightway turning, led me back by the way we came.

"In our return, when we came to those joyous mansions of the white-robed spirits, he said to me, 'Do you know what all these things are which you have seen?' I answered, 'No,' and then he said, 'That valley which you beheld terrible with flaming fire and freezing cold, is the place in which the souls of those are tried and punished, who, delaying to confess and amend their crimes, at length have recourse to repentance at the point of death, and so go forth from the body; but nevertheless because they, even at their death, confessed and repented, they shall all be received into the kingdom of Heaven at the day of judgement; but many are succoured before the day of judgement, by the prayers of the living and their alms and fasting, and more especially by the celebration of Masses. Moreover that foul flaming pit which you saw, is the mouth of Hell, into which whosoever falls shall never be delivered to all eternity. This

flowery place, in which you see this fair and youthful
company, all bright and joyous, is that into which the
souls of those are received who, indeed, when they leave
the body have done good works, but who are not so
perfect as to deserve to be immediately admitted into
the kingdom of Heaven; yet they shall all, at the day of
judgement, behold Christ, and enter into the joys of His
kingdom; for such as are perfect in every word and deed
and thought, as soon as they quit the body, forthwith
enter into the kingdom of Heaven; in the neighbourhood
whereof that place is, where you heard the sound of
sweet singing amidst the savour of a sweet fragrance
and brightness of light. As for you, who must now return to the body, and again live among men, if you will
seek diligently to examine your actions, and preserve
your manner of living and your words in righteousness
and simplicity, you shall, after death, have a place of
abode among these joyful troops of blessed souls which
you behold. For when I left you for awhile, it was for
this purpose, that I might learn what should become of
you.' When he had said this to me, I much abhorred returning to the body, being delighted with the sweetness
and beauty of the place which I beheld, and with the
company of those I saw in it. Nevertheless, I durst not
ask my guide anything; but thereupon, on a sudden, I
found myself, I know not how, alive among men."

Now these and other things which this man of God
had seen, he would not relate to slothful men, and such
as lived negligently; but only to those who, being terrified with the dread of torments, or ravished with the
hope of everlasting joys, would draw from his words the
means to advance in piety. In the neighbourhood of his
cell lived one Haemgils, a monk, and eminent in the priesthood, whose good works were worthy of his office: he
is still living, and leading a solitary life in Ireland, supporting his declining age with coarse bread and cold
water. He often went to that man, and by repeated
questioning, heard of him what manner of things he had
seen when out of the body; by whose account those few
particulars which we have briefly set down came also to

our knowledge. And he related his visions to King Ald-frid,[1] a man most learned in all respects, and was by him so willingly and attentively heard, that at his request he was admitted into the monastery above-mentioned, and received the crown of the monastic tonsure; and the said king, whensoever he came into those parts, very often went to hear him. At that time the abbot and priest Ethelwald,[2] a man of godly and sober life, presided over that monastery. He now occupies the episcopal see of the church of Lindisfarne, leading a life worthy of his degree.

He had a place of abode assigned him apart in that monastery, where he might give himself more freely to the service of his Creator in continual prayer. And in-asmuch as that place was on the banks of the river, he was wont often to go into the same for the great desire he had to do penance in his body, and oftentimes to plunge in it, and to continue saying psalms or prayers in the same as long as he could endure it, standing still, while the waves flowed over him, sometimes up to the middle, and sometimes even to the neck in water; and when he went ashore, he never took off his cold, wet garments till they grew warm and dry on his body. And when in the winter the cracking pieces of ice were floating about him, which he had himself sometimes broken, to make room to stand or plunge in the river, and those who beheld it would say, "We marvel, bro-ther Drythelm (for so he was called), that you are able to endure such severe cold;" he answered simply, for he was a simple and sober-spirited man, "I have seen greater cold." And when they said, "We marvel that you choose to observe so hard a rule of continence," he

---

[1] IV, 26; V. 1.
[2] Cf. c. 23. He began life in the service of St. Cuthbert. He became first Prior, or Provost, then Abbot of Melrose, and suc-ceeded Eadfrid, who died in 721, as Bishop of Lindisfarne. He enriched Lindisfarne with two treasures of art: a beautiful stone cross which he erected there, and a cover of gold and jewels for the Lindisfarne Gospels, written by Eadfrid in honour of St. Cuth-bert. The book is now in the British Museum, but the cover is lost.

replied, "I have seen harder things." And so, until the
day of his calling hence, in his unwearied desire of
heavenly bliss, he subdued his aged body with daily
fasting, and forwarded the salvation of many by his
words and life.

CHAP. XIII. *How another contrarywise before his death
saw a book containing his sins, which was shown him by
devils.* [704-709 A.D.]

BUT contrarywise there was a man in the province of the
Mercians, whose visions and words, but not his manner
of life, were of profit to others, though not to himself.
In the reign of Coenred,[1] who succeeded Ethelred, there
was a layman who was a king's thegn, no less acceptable to the king for his outward industry, than displeas-
ing to him for his neglect of his own soul. The king
diligently admonished him to confess and amend, and to
forsake his evil ways, lest he should lose all time for repentance and amendment by a sudden death. But though
frequently warned, he despised the words of salvation, and
promised that he would do penance at some future time.
In the meantime, falling sick he betook himself to his
bed, and was tormented with grievous pains. The king
coming to him (for he loved the man much) exhorted him,
even then, before death, to repent of his offences. But he
answered that he would not then confess his sins, but
would do it when he was recovered of his sickness, lest
his companions should upbraid him with having done that
for fear of death, which he had refused to do in health.
He thought he spoke very bravely, but it afterwards appeared that he had been miserably deceived by the wiles
of the Devil.

The disease increasing, when the king came again to
visit and instruct him, he cried out straightway with a
lamentable voice, "What will you now? What are you

---

[1] 704-709. Cf. *infra,* c. 19, pp. 345, 356, and c. 24. He was the
son of Wulfhere, but being a boy at the time of his father's death,
was passed over in favour of Ethelred, Wulfhere's brother.

come for? for you can no longer do aught for my profit
or salvation." The king answered, "Say not so; take
heed and be of sound mind." "I am not mad," replied
he, "but I now know the worst and have it for certain
before my eyes." "What is that?" said the king. "Not
long since," said he, "there came into this room two fair
youths, and sat down by me, the one at my head, and
the other at my feet. One of them drew forth a book
most beautiful, but very small, and gave it me to read;
looking into it, I there found all the good actions I had
ever done in my life written down, and they were very
few and inconsiderable. They took back the book and
said nothing to me. Then, on a sudden, appeared an army
of evil spirits of hideous countenance, and they beset this
house without, and sitting down filled the greater part of
it within. Then he, who by the blackness of his gloomy
face, and his sitting above the rest, seemed to be the
chief of them, taking out a book terrible to behold, of a
monstrous size, and of almost insupportable weight,
commanded one of his followers to bring it to me to
read. Having read it, I found therein most plainly
written in hideous characters, all the crimes I ever committed, not only in word and deed, but even in the least
thought; and he said to those glorious men in white raiment who sat by me, 'Why sit ye here, since ye know
of a surety that this man is ours?' They answered, 'Ye
speak truly; take him and lead him away to fill up the
measure of your damnation.' This said, they forthwith
vanished, and two wicked spirits arose, having in their
hands ploughshares, and one of them struck me on the
head, and the other on the foot. And these ploughshares
are now with great torment creeping into the inward
parts of my body, and as soon as they meet I shall die,
and the devils being ready to snatch me away, I shall
be dragged into the dungeons of hell."

Thus spoke that wretch in his despair, and soon after
died, and now in vain suffers in eternal torments that
penance which he failed to suffer for a short time with
the fruits of forgiveness. Of whom it is manifest, that
(as the blessed Pope Gregory writes of certain persons)

he did not see these things for his own sake, since they did not avail him, but for the sake of others, who, knowing of his end, should be afraid to put off the time of repentance, whilst they have leisure, lest, being prevented by sudden death, they should perish impenitent. And whereas he saw diverse books laid before him by the good and evil spirits, this was done by Divine dispensation, that we may keep in mind that our deeds and thoughts are not scattered to the winds, but are all kept to be examined by the Supreme Judge, and will in the end be shown us either by friendly angels or by the enemy. And whereas the angels first drew forth a white book, and then the devils a black one; the former a very small one, the latter one very great; it is to be observed, that in his first years he did some good actions, all which he nevertheless obscured by the evil actions of his youth. If, contrarywise, he had taken care in his youth to correct the errors of his boyhood, and by well-doing to put them away from the sight of God, he might have been admitted to the fellowship of those of whom the Psalm says, "Blessed are those whose iniquities are forgiven, and whose sins are covered." [1] This story, as I learned it of the venerable Bishop Pechthelm, [2] I have thought good to set forth plainly, for the salvation of such as shall read or hear it.

CHAP. XIV. *How another in like manner, being at the point of death, saw the place of punishment appointed for him in Hell.*

I MYSELF knew a brother, would to God I had not known him, whose name I could mention if it were of any avail, dwelling in a famous monastery, but himself living infamously. He was oftentimes rebuked by the brethren and elders of the place, and admonished to be converted to a more chastened life; and though he would not give ear to them, they bore with him long and patiently,

---

[1] Ps. xxxi, 1, in the Vulgate (xxxii in our Psalter).
[2] Bishop of Whitern; *v. infra*, cc. 18, 23.

on account of their need of his outward service, for he
was a cunning artificer. But he was much given to
drunkenness, and other pleasures of a careless life, and
more used to stop in his workshop day and night, than
to go to church to sing and pray and hear the Word of
life with the brethren. For which reason it befell him
according to the saying, that he who will not willingly
humble himself and enter the gate of the church must
needs be led against his will into the gate of Hell, being
damned. For he falling sick, and being brought to extremity, called the brethren, and with much lamentation,
like one damned, began to tell them, that he saw Hell
opened, and Satan sunk in the depths thereof; and Caia-
phas, with the others that slew our Lord, hard by him,
delivered up to avenging flames. "In whose neighbourhood," said he, "I see a place of eternal perdition prepared for me, miserable wretch that I am." The brothers,
hearing these words, began diligently to exhort him,
that he should repent even then, whilst he was still in
the flesh. He answered in despair, "There is no time for
me now to change my course of life, when I have myself
seen my judgement passed."

Whilst uttering these words, he died without having
received the saving Viaticum, and his body was buried
in the farthest parts of the monastery, nor did any one
dare either to say Masses or sing psalms, or even to pray
for him.[1] Oh how far asunder hath God put light from
darkness! The blessed Stephen, the first martyr, being
about to suffer death for the truth, saw the heavens
opened, and the glory of God, and Jesus standing on the
right hand of God;[2] and where he was to be after death,
there he fixed the eyes of his mind, that he might die
the more joyfully. But this workman, of darkened mind
and life, when death was at hand, saw Hell opened, and
witnessed the damnation of the Devil and his followers;
he saw also, unhappy wretch! his own prison among
them, to the end that, despairing of salvation, he might
himself die the more miserably, but might by his perdi-

[1] Cf. 1 John, v, 16.   [2] Acts, vii, 56.

tion afford cause of salvation to the living who should hear of it. This befell of late in the province of the Bernicians, and being noised abroad far and near, inclined many to do penance for their sins without delay. Would to God that this also might come to pass through the reading of our words!

CHAP. XV. *How divers churches of the Scots, at the instance of Adamnan, adopted the Catholic Easter; and how the same wrote a book about the holy places.* [703 A.D.]

AT this time a great part of the Scots in Ireland,[1] and some also of the Britons in Britain,[2] by the grace of God, adopted the reasonable and ecclesiastical time of keeping Easter. For when Adamnan,[3] priest and abbot of the monks that were in the island of Hii, was sent by his nation on a mission to Aldfrid, king of the English,[4] he abode some time in that province, and saw the canonical rites of the Church. Moreover, he was earnestly admonished by many of the more learned sort, not to presume to live contrary to the universal custom of the Church, either in regard to the observance of Easter, or any other ordinances whatsoever, with those few followers of his dwelling in the farthest corner of the world.

[1] The northern Irish, and of them only those who were independent of Iona (*v. infra*). The southern Irish had conformed much earlier; cf. III, 3, and note.

[2] It is not clear whether Bede means that any Britons were converted by Adamnan. If so, they must have been Britons of Strathclyde. . The Welsh only conformed 755-777. The reference may be to those of the Cornish Britons, subject to the West Saxons, who were led in 705 by Aldhelm's letter to Geraint to adopt the Catholic Easter (*v. infra*, c. 18).

[3] Ninth Abbot of Iona, 679-704, the author of the Life of St. Columba.

[4] Of Northumbria. Aldfrid, who had studied in Iona during his exile, was his friend. Adamnan visited the king twice, first, *circ.* 686, when he obtained the release of the sixty Irish prisoners taken to England by Berct in 684 (*v.* IV, 26 *ad init.*) and again two years later (cf. *infra* c. 21, p. 372, note 2).

Wherefore he so changed his mind, that he readily preferred those things which he had seen and heard in the
English churches, to the customs which he and and his
people had hitherto followed. For he was a good and
wise man, and excellently instructed in knowledge of the
Scriptures. Returning home, he endeavoured to bring his
own people that were in Hii, or that were subject to that
monastery, into the way of truth, which he had embraced
with all his heart; but he could not prevail. He sailed
over into Ireland,[1] and preaching to those people, and
with sober words of exhortation making known to them
the lawful time of Easter, he brought back many of them,
and almost all that were free from the dominion of those
of Hii, from the error of their fathers to the Catholic
unity, and taught them to keep the lawful time of Easter.

Returning to his island, after having celebrated the
canonical Easter in Ireland, he was instant in preaching
the Catholic observance of the season of Easter in his
monastery, yet without being able to achieve his end;
and it so happened that he departed this life before the
next year came round,[2] the Divine goodness so ordaining
it, that as he was a great lover of peace and unity, he
should be taken away to everlasting life before he should
be obliged, on the return of the season of Easter, to be
at greater variance with those that would not follow him
into the truth.

This same man wrote a book concerning the holy
places, of great profit to many readers; his authority
was the teaching and dictation of Arculf, a bishop of
Gaul,[3] who had gone to Jerusalem for the sake of the

---

[1] The Irish annals mention two voyages to Ireland subsequent
to that in 686 with the prisoners, viz., in 692 and 697, after which
he probably stayed there till after Easter, 704.

[2] On 23rd September, 704. (The dates are those of Tighernach
and the "Annales Cambriae.")

[3] Adamnan's "De.Locis Sanctis," and Bede's account here, are
the only sources of information with regard to this bishop. Adamnan's book is based on the narrative of Arculf compared with
other authorities. Bede, again, in his own work on the the same
subject, made selections from Adamnan, using also other authorities, e.g. Josephus,

Z

holy places; and having wandered over all the Promised
Land, travelled also to Damascus, Constantinople, Alexandria, and many islands in the sea, and returning home
by ship, was cast upon the western coast of Britain by
a great tempest. After many adventures he came to the
aforesaid servant of Christ, Adamnan, and being found
to be learned in the Scriptures, and acquainted with the
holy places, was most gladly received by him and gladly
heard, insomuch that whatsoever he said that he had
seen worthy of remembrance in the holy places, Adamnan straightway set himself to commit to writing. Thus
he composed a work, as I have said, profitable to many,
and chiefly to those who, being far removed from those
places where the patriarchs and Apostles lived, know no
more of them than what they have learnt by reading.
Adamnan presented this book to King Aldfrid, and
through his bounty it came to be read by lesser persons.[1]
The writer thereof was also rewarded by him with many
gifts and sent back into his country. I believe it will be
of advantage to our readers if we collect some passages
from his writings, and insert them in this our History.[2]

CHAP. XVI. *The account given in the aforesaid book of
the place of our Lord's Nativity, Passion, and Resurrection.*

HE wrote concerning the place of the Nativity of our
Lord, after this manner:[3] "Bethlehem, the city of David,
is situated on a narrow ridge, encompassed on all sides
with valleys, being a mile in length from west to east,
and having a low wall without towers, built along the
edge of the level summit. ' In the eastern corner thereof

---

[1] *I.e.*, he had copies made of it.
[2] Nevertheless he quotes his own book rather than Adamnan's.
[3] Cf. Warren and Conder, "Survey of Western Palestine":
"Bethlehem, a well-built stone town, standing on a narrow ridge
which runs east and west . . . towards the east is the open market place, and, beyond this, the convent in which is the fourth
century church of St. Mary, including the Grotto of the Nativity
beneath the main apse."

is a sort of natural half cave, the outward part whereof
is said to have been the place where our Lord was born;
the inner is called the manger of our Lord. This cave
within is all covered with rich marble, and over the particular spot where our Lord is said to have been born,
stands the great church of St. Mary." He likewise wrote
about the place of His Passion and Resurrection in this
manner: "Entering the city of Jerusalem on the north
side, the first place to be visited, according to the disposition of the streets, is the church of Constantine,
called the Martyrium. It was built by the Emperor Constantine, in a royal and magnificent manner, because the
Cross of our Lord was said to have been found there by
his mother Helena. Thence, to the westward, is seen
the church of Golgotha, in which is also to be found the
rock which once bore the Cross to which the Lord's body
was nailed, and now it upholds a large silver cross, having
a great brazen wheel with lamps hanging over it. Under
the place of our Lord's Cross, a crypt is hewn out of the
rock, in which the Sacrifice is offered on an altar for the
dead that are held in honour, their bodies remaining
meanwhile in the street. To the westward of this church
is the round church of the Anastasis or Résurrection of
our Lord, encompassed with three walls, and supported
by twelve columns. Between each of the walls is a broad
passage, which contains three altars at three different
points of the middle wall; to the south, the north, and
the west. It has eight doors or entrances in a straight
line through the three walls; four whereof face the
south-east, and four the east.[1] In the midst of it is the
round tomb of our Lord cut out of the rock, the top of
of which a man standing within can touch with his hand;
on the east is the entrance, against which that great
stone was set. To this day the tomb bears the marks of
the iron tools within, but on the outside it is all covered
with marble to the very top of the roof, which is adorned
with gold, and bears a large golden cross. In the north

---

[1] "Vulturnus" seems to be distinguished from its Greek equivalent, "Eurus."

part of the tomb the sepulchre of our Lord is hewn out of the same rock, seven feet in length, and three hand-breadths above the floor; the entrance being on the south side, where twelve lamps burn day and night, four within the sepulchre, and eight above on the edge of the right side. The stone that was set at the entrance to the tomb is now cleft in two; nevertheless, the lesser part of it stands as an altar of hewn stone before the door of the tomb; the greater part is set up as another altar, four-cornered, at the east end of the same church, and is covered with linen cloths. The colour of the said tomb and sepulchre is white and red mingled together."[1]

CHAP. XVII. *What he likewise wrote of the place of our Lord's Ascension, and the tombs of the patriarchs.*

CONCERNING the place of our Lord's Ascension, the afore-said author writes thus. "The Mount of Olives is equal in height to Mount Sion, but exceeds it in breadth and length; it bears few trees besides vines and olives, and is fruitful in wheat and barley, for the nature of that soil is not such as to yield thickets,[2] but grass and flowers. On the very top of it, where our Lord ascended into heaven, is a large round church,[3] having round about it

[1] The Basilica of the Anastasis was completed by Constantine in 335 A.D., and destroyed in 614 by Chosroes II, King of Persia. Other ancient travellers besides Arculf describe the Holy Places. Eucherius, writing about 427-440, mentions the Martyrium, Golgotha and the Anastasis, and describes their respective sites in similar terms. Theodorus (about 530 A.D.) alludes to the Invention of the Holy Cross by Helena, but the earliest authorities do not connect her with it.

[2] "Brucosa." The adjective is not found in the dictionaries. But Ducange has the following words from which one may, per-haps, infer an adjective of kindred meaning: "*Brua*, idem quod supra *Brossa*, silvula, dumetum," "*Bruarium*, ericetum," and "*Broca*, ager incultus, dumetum."

[3] The Basilica of the Ascension, on the summit of Mount Olivet, is mentioned by the Pilgrim of Bordeaux who was in Jerusalem in 333 A.D. No traces of the church have been found. He also speaks of the Anastasis, which was being built at the time.

three chapels with vaulted roofs. For the inner building could not be vaulted and roofed, by reason of the passage of our Lord's Body; but it has an altar on the east side, sheltered by a narrow roof. In the midst of it are to be seen the last Footprints of our Lord, the place where He ascended being open to the sky; and though the earth is daily carried away by believers, yet still it remains, and retains the same appearance, being marked by the impression of the Feet. Round about these lies a brazen wheel, as high as a man's neck, having an entrance from the west, with a great lamp hanging above it on a pulley and burning night and day. In the western part of the same church are eight windows; and as many lamps, hanging opposite to them by cords, shine through the glass as far as Jerusalem; and the light thereof is said to thrill the hearts of the beholders with a certain zeal and compunction. Every year, on the day of the Ascension of our Lord, when Mass is ended, a strong blast of wind is wont to come down, and to cast to the ground all that are in the church."

Of the situation of Hebron, and the tombs of the fathers,[1] he writes thus. "Hebron, once a habitation and the chief city of David's kingdom, now only showing by its ruins what it then was, has, one furlong to the east of it, a double cave in the valley, where the sepulchres of the patriarchs are encompassed with a wall four-square, their heads lying to the north. Each of the tombs is covered with a single stone, hewn like the stones of a church, and of a white colour, for the three patriarchs. Adam's is of meaner and poorer workmanship, and he lies not far from them at the farthest end of the northern part of that wall. There are also some poorer and

[1] Saewulf (1102 A.D.) writes: "Below is the place called Golgotha, where Adam is said to have been raised to life by the Blood of our Lord which fell upon him, as is said in the Passion, 'And many bodies of the saints which slept arose.' But in the sentences of St. Augustine we read that he was buried in Hebron, where also the three patriarchs were afterwards buried with their wives, Abraham with Sarah, Isaac with Rebecca, and Jacob with Leah, as well as the bones of Joseph which the children of Israel carried with them from Egypt."

smaller monuments of the three women. The hill Mamre
is a mile from these tombs, and is covered with grass and
flowers, having a level plain on the top. In the northern
part of it, the trunk of Abraham's oak, being twice as
high as a man, is enclosed in a church."

Thus much, gathered from the works of the aforesaid
writer, according to the sense of his words, but more
briefly and in fewer words, we have thought fit to insert
in our History for the profit of readers. Whosoever
desires to know more of the contents of that book, may
seek it either in the book itself, or in that abridgement
which we have lately made from it.

CHAP. XVIII. *How the South Saxons received Eadbert
and Eolla, and the West Saxons, Daniel and Aldhelm,
for their bishops; and of the writings of the same Aldhelm.* [705 A.D.]

IN the year of our Lord 705, Aldfrid, king of the Northumbrians, died[1] before the end of the twentieth year of
his reign. His son Osred,[2] a boy about eight years of
age, succeeding him in the throne, reigned eleven years.
In the beginning of his reign, Haedde, bishop of the
West Saxons,[3] departed to the heavenly life; for he was
a good man and a just, and his life and doctrine as a
bishop were guided rather by his innate love of virtue,
than by what he had gained from books. The most

[1] He died at Driffield (supposed to mean the "field of Deira"),
in the East Riding of Yorkshire, on 14th December, 705 (Saxon
Chronicle).

[2] Bede and the Chronicle do not mention the usurper Eadwulf,
who held the sovereignty for eight weeks. With Aldfrid the
greatness of Northumbria, which had begun to decline after
Egfrid's defeat and death, passed away, except for a brief revival
in the time of Eadbert and his brother, Archbishop Egbert. Osred
was a tyrannical and lawless boy, and a period of political and
ecclesiastical trouble set in (cf. Bede, "Epistola ad Egbertum";
Boniface, Ep. 62, etc.).

[3] III, 7; IV, 12.

reverend bishop, Pechthelm, of whom we shall speak
hereafter in the proper place,[1] and who while still
deacon or monk was for a long time with his successor
Aldhelm,[2] was wont to relate that many miracles of healing have been wrought in the place where he died,
through the merit of his sanctity; and that the men of
that province used to carry the dust thence for the sick,
and put it into water, and the drinking thereof, or sprink-
ling with it, brought health to many sick men and beasts;
so that the holy dust being frequently carried away, a
great hole was made there.

Upon his death, the bishopric of that province was
divided into two dioceses.[3] One of them was given to

[1] *Infra* c. 23. He has been mentioned, c. 13, *ad fin.* He studied
under Aldhelm at Malmesbury (*v. infra*).

[2] The greatest scholar of his time and the man of widest influence
as a teacher. He was a West Saxon, of royal blood, born about 639;
he studied first under Hadrian in the School of Canterbury, then
under Maildufus (*v. infra*), was ordained priest by Bishop Hlothere
(Leutherius, *v.* III, 7), and about the year 675 became Abbot of
Malmesbury, which under his rule grew to be a place of importance
and attracted crowds of students. On one occasion he went by
invitation of Pope Sergius to Rome. He became Bishop of Sherborne, when in 705 the West Saxon diocese was divided (*v. infra*).
He died in 709 in the little church of Doulting in Somerset and was
buried in St. Michael's Church at Malmesbury. He greatly
strengthened the Church in Wessex by his influence with King Ini
and his zeal in building churches and monasteries in various
places. His widespread influence, as well as his generous use of
it, is shown by his letter to Wilfrid's clergy after the Council of
Estrefeld, exhorting them to remain faithful to their bishop (*v.*
Haddan and Stubbs, III, 254).

[3] In 705. The bishopric of the West Saxons was the only one
which Theodore did not subdivide. The delay may have been due
to the political disturbances of the time, and these had come to an
end under the rule of Ini. Haedde's death removed a further
difficulty. He seems to have resisted Bertwald's attempt to divide
the diocese, for we find in 704 a council threatening the West
Saxons with excommunication if the division is not carried out.
Hampshire, Surrey, and, for a time, Sussex, were assigned to
Winchester; Berkshire, Wiltshire, Dorsetshire, and Somersetshire
to Sherborne (Haddan and Stubbs, III, 276), but the authorities
differ on this point. After the Conquest, the combined bishoprics
of Sherborne and Ramsbury (founded in 909 for Wiltshire) had their
see established at Old Sarum.

Daniel,[1] which he governs to this day; the other to Aldhelm, wherein he presided most vigorously four years;
both of them were fully instructed, as well in matters
touching the Church as in the knowledge of the Scriptures. Aldhelm, when he was as yet only a priest and
abbot of the monastery which is called the city of Maildufus,[2] by order of a synod of his own nation, wrote a
notable book[3] against the error of the Britons, in not
celebrating Easter at the due time, and in doing divers
other things contrary to the purity of doctrine and the
peace of the church; and through the reading of this
book many of the Britons, who were subject to the West
Saxons, were led by him to adopt the Catholic celebration of our Lord's Paschal Feast. He likewise wrote
a famous book on Virginity,[4] which, after the example of
Sedulius,[5] he composed in twofold form, in hexameters
and in prose. He wrote some other books, being a man
most instructed in all respects, for he had a polished style,[6]
and was, as I have said, of marvellous learning both in
liberal and ecclesiastical studies. On his death, Forthere[7]

[1] Cf. Preface, p. 3, and note, and IV, 16. In 744 he resigned
his see and died in 745. It appears from a letter of Boniface to him
that he became blind in his old age.

[2] Malmesbury. It was founded by an Irish monk and scholar,
Maildufus (Irish " Maelduib "), as a small settlement living under
monastic rule (v.s. note on Aldhelm).

[3] His letter to Geraint or Gerontius, king of Dumnonia (Devon
and Cornwall). A West Saxon synod in 705 appointed Aldhelm to
write a book, "quo maligna haeresis Britonum destrueretur"
(Faricius, Life of Aldhelm). He appears to have influenced only
those Britons who were subject to the West Saxons. Devon and
Cornwall did not finally conform to the Catholic Easter till early
in the tenth century.

[4] Cf. IV, 10 (note on Hildilid).

[5] A poet of the fifth century (circ. 450), author of a poem called
" Carmen Paschale." He translated it into prose and called it
" Opus Paschale." Aldhelm wrote his prose work first.

[6] His style is turgid and grandiloquent, and, owing to the high
estimation in which he was held, his influence in this respect on
contemporary writing was harmful.

[7] Cf. infra c. 23. A letter to him from Archbishop Bertwald is
extant. We do not know how long he lived. We have his signature
to a charter of 739.

was made bishop in his stead, and is living at this time, being likewise a man very learned in the Holy Scriptures.

Whilst they administered the bishopric, it was determined by a synodal decree, that the province of the South Saxons, which till that time belonged to the diocese of the city of Winchester, where Daniel then presided, should itself have an episcopal see, and a bishop of its own.[1] Eadbert, at that time abbot of the monastery of Bishop Wilfrid, of blessed memory, called Selaeseu,[2] was consecrated their first bishop. On his death, Eolla succeeded to the office of bishop. He also died some years ago, and the bishopric has been vacant to this day.[3]

CHAP. XIX. *How Coinred, king of the Mercians, and Offa, king of the East Saxons, ended their days at Rome, in the monastic habit; and of the life and death of Bishop Wilfrid.* [709 A.D.]

IN the fourth year of the reign of Osred,[4] Coenred,[5] who had for some time nobly governed the kingdom of the Mercians, much more nobly quitted the sceptre of his kingdom. For he went to Rome, and there receiving the tonsure and becoming a monk, when Constantine[6] was pope, he continued to his last hour in prayer and fasting and alms-deeds at the threshold of the Apostles.

[1] Cf. IV, 15. The see was established at Selsey. The date of this event is not known (Matthew of Westminster is the only authority for 711). Bede indicates it very vaguely ("quibus administrantibus"), and does not make it clear to whose administration he alludes. The more obvious reference is surely to Daniel and Aldhelm, the passage about Forthere being parenthetical, but the other view has the authority of Haddan and Stubbs (III, 296), viz., that he means Daniel and Forthere, and that thus the date is fixed to some time after Aldhelm's death (709).

[2] Selsey, cf. IV, 13, 14.

[3] The vacancy was filled in 733 by the appointment of Sigfrid (*v.* Continuation).

[4] Cf. c. 18, *ad init.* His fourth year was 709.

[5] C. 13 and *infra* c. 19 *ad fin.*, and c. 24. For a similar action, cf. Caedwalla and Ini (*v.s.* c. 7) and (*infra*) Offa.

[6] Constantine I, 708-715.

He was succeeded in the throne by Ceolred,[1] the son of
Ethelred, who had governed the kingdom before Coenred.
With him went the son of Sighere,[2] the king of the East
Saxons whom we mentioned before, by name Offa, a
youth of a most pleasing age and comeliness, and greatly
desired by all his nation to have and to hold the sceptre
of the kingdom. He, with like devotion, quitted wife,
and lands, and kindred and country, for Christ and for
the Gospel, that he might "receive an hundred-fold in
this life, and in the world to come life everlasting."[3] He
also, when they came to the holy places at Rome, received the tonsure, and ending his life in the monastic
habit, attained to the vision of the blessed Apostles in
Heaven, as he had long desired.

The same year that they departed from Britain, the
great bishop, Wilfrid, ended his days in the province
called Inundalum,[4] after he had been bishop forty-five
years.[5] His body, being laid in a coffin, was carried to
his monastery, which is called Inhrypum,[6] and buried in
the church of the blessed Apostle Peter, with the honour
due to so great a prelate. Concerning whose manner of

[1] 709-716. St. Boniface (Letter to Ethelbald) gives Ceolred a very
bad character, and says that he died impenitent at a banquet, seized
with sudden madness. He alludes to him and Osred of Northumbria
as the first kings who tampered with the privileges of the Church.
[2] III, 30, and IV, 6. Sighere reigned jointly with Sebbi. They
were succeeded by Sebbi's sons, Sighard and Swefred (IV, 11).
Offa probably succeeded them just before this time (709); William
of Malmesbury says he reigned for a short time. He was succeeded by Selred (d. 746).
[3] St. Matt., xix, 29; St. Mark, x, 30; St. Luke, xviii, 30.
[4] Oundle in Northamptonshire, where he had a monastery on
land given him by Wulfhere of Mercia. For the form of the name,
cf. infra, "in provincia Undalum." Here the preposition is prefixed as often; v. II, 14, note. Wilfrid died on a Thursday in
October: there is some uncertainty about the day of the month.
[5] Cf. the epitaph (infra) and c. 24, where Bede places his consecration in 664. This is supported by William of Malmesbury, but
Eddius says he was bishop for forty-six years.
[6] Ripon, v. infra, p. 56. In the tenth century, Odo, Archbishop of
Canterbury, removed certain relics to Canterbury, believing them
to be the body of Wilfrid. At Ripon it was maintained that the
relics were those of Wilfrid II.

life, let us now turn back, and briefly make mention of
the things which were done.[1] Being a boy of a good disposition, and virtuous beyond his years, he conducted
himself so modestly and discreetly in all points, that he
was deservedly beloved, respected, and cherished by his
elders as one of themselves.[2] At fourteen years of age he
chose rather the monastic than the secular life; which,
when he had signified to his father, for his mother was
dead, he readily consented to his godly wishes and
desires, and advised him to persist in that wholesome
purpose. Wherefore he came to the isle of Lindisfarne,
and there giving himself to the service of the monks, he
strove diligently to learn and to practise those things
which belong to monastic purity and piety; and being of
a ready wit, he speedily learned the psalms and some
other books, having not yet received the tonsure, but
being in no small measure marked by those virtues of
humility and obedience which are more important than
the tonsure; for which reason he was justly loved by his
elders and his equals. Having served God some years in
that monastery, and being a youth of a good understanding, he perceived that the way of virtue delivered
by the Scots was in no wise perfect, and he resolved to
go to Rome, to see what ecclesiastical or monastic rites
were in use at the Apostolic see. When he told the
brethren, they commended his design, and advised him
to carry out that which he purposed. He forthwith
went to Queen Eanfled, for he was known to her, and it
was by her counsel and support that he had been admitted into the aforesaid monastery, and he told her of
his desire to visit the threshold of the blessed Apostles.
She, being pleased with the youth's good purpose, sent

---

[1] Our main authority for the life of Wilfrid is Eddius (v. IV, 2).
Bede's account is remarkable for its omissions, though it gives a
few facts which Eddius omits.

[2] His birth must be placed in 634 (cf. *infra,* his consecration at
the age of thirty). His father was a Northumbrian thegn. He is
said to have had an unkind stepmother. He was sent by his father
to the court of Oswy, thence, by Eanfled (cf. II, 9, 20; III, 15, 24,
et saep.) to Lindisfarne, at that time under the rule of Aidan.

him into Kent, to King Earconbert,[1] who was her uncle's
son, requesting that he would send him to Rome in an
honourable manner. At that time, Honorius,[2] one of the
disciples of the blessed Pope Gregory, a man very highly
instructed in ecclesiastical learning, was archbishop
there. When he had tarried there for a space, and,
being a youth of an active spirit, was diligently applying
himself to learn those things which came under his
notice, another youth, called Biscop, surnamed Benedict,[3]
of the English nobility, arrived there, being likewise
desirous to go to Rome, of whom we have before made
mention.

The king gave him Wilfrid for a companion, and bade
Wilfrid conduct him to Rome. When they came to
Lyons, Wilfrid was detained there by Dalfinus,[4] the
bishop of that city; but Benedict hastened on to Rome.
For the bishop was delighted with the youth's prudent
discourse, the grace of his comely countenance, his eager
activity, and the consistency and maturity of his thoughts;
for which reason he plentifully supplied him and his
companions with all necessaries, as long as they stayed
with him; and further offered, if he would have it, to
commit to him the government of no small part of Gaul,
to give him a maiden daughter of his own brother[5] to
wife, and to regard him always as his adopted son. But
Wilfrid thanked him for the loving-kindness which he was
pleased to show to a stranger, and answered, that he
had resolved upon another course of life, and for that
reason had left his country and set out for Rome.

Hereupon the bishop sent him to Rome, furnishing
him with a guide and supplying plenty of all things
requisite for his journey, earnestly requesting that he
would come that way, when he returned into his own

[1] III, 8. He was the son of Eadbald (II, 5, 6, 9, *et saep.*).
Eanfled's mother was the sister of Eadbald, the Kentish princess
Ethelberg ("Tata"), wife of Edwin (II, 9, 11, 20).
[2] II, 18 *et saep.*   [3] IV, 18, and note.
[4] Cf. III, 25. Annemundus was the name of the Archbishop.
Dalfinus, Count of Lyons, was his brother. Eddius makes the same
mistake.
[5] A daughter of the Count.

country. Wilfrid arriving at Rome, and daily giving himself with all earnestness to prayer and the study of ecclesiastical matters, as he had purposed in his mind, gained the friendship of the most holy and learned Boniface, the archdeacon,[1] who was also counsellor to the Apostolic Pope, by whose instruction he learned in their order the four Gospels, and the true computation of Easter; and many other things appertaining to ecclesiastical discipline, which he could not learn in his own country, he acquired from the teaching of that same master. When he had spent some months there, in successful study, he returned into Gaul, to Dalfinus;[2] and having stayed with him three years, received from him the tonsure, and Dalfinus esteemed him so highly in love that he had thoughts of making him his heir; but this was prevented by the bishop's cruel death, and Wilfrid was reserved to be a bishop of his own, that is, the English, nation. For Queen Baldhild[3] sent soldiers with orders to put the bishop to death; whom Wilfrid, as his clerk, attended to the place where he was to be beheaded, being very desirous, though the bishop strongly opposed it, to die with him; but the executioners, understanding that he was a stranger, and of the English nation, spared him, and would not put him to death with his bishop.

[1] He presented Wilfrid to the Pope, Eugenius I. A leaden "bulla" with the name of Boniface, Archdeacon, inscribed upon it was found at Whitby not long ago.

[2] *I.e.*, to Annemundus.

[3] This seems to be another mistake in which Bede follows Eddius. It was probably Ebroin (*v.* IV, 1, note), Mayor of the Palace to her infant son Clothaire III, who put Annemundus to death. Baldhild was, however, regent at the time. Eddius calls her a Jezebel, but all that we know of her shows her to have been a most pious and charitable lady, and she has been canonized by the Church. She was especially active in her efforts to stop the traffic in slaves. She herself, though she is said to have been of noble English birth, had been sold as a slave into Gaul. She was married first to Ercinwald, Mayor of the Palace, the predecessor of Ebroin (*v.* III, 19), and afterwards to Clovis II, King of Neustria and Burgundy, 638-656. Baldhild ended her life in the monastery of Chelles (*v.* III, 8, and note).

Returning to Britain, he won the friendship of King Alchfrid,[1] who had learnt to follow always and love the catholic rules of the Church; and therefore finding him to be a Catholic, he gave him presently land of ten families at the place called Stanford;[2] and not long after, the monastery, with land of thirty families, at the place called Inhrypum;[3] which place he had formerly given to those that followed the doctrine of the Scots, to build a monastery there. But, forasmuch as they afterwards, being given the choice, had rather quit the place than adopt the Catholic Easter and other canonical rites, according to the custom of the Roman Apostolic Church, he gave the same to him whom he found to be instructed in better discipline and better customs.

At the same time, by the said king's command, he was ordained priest in the same monastery, by Agilbert,[4] bishop of the Gewissae above-mentioned, the king being desirous that a man of so much learning and piety should attend him constantly as his special priest and teacher; and not long after, when the Scottish sect had been exposed and banished,[5] as was said above, he, with the advice and consent of his father Oswy, sent him into Gaul, to be consecrated as his bishop,[6] when he was about thirty years of age, the same Agilbert being then bishop of the city of Paris. Eleven other bishops met at the consecration of the new bishop, and that function was most honourably performed. Whilst he yet tarried beyond the sea, the holy man,

[1] III, 14, 21, 24, 25, 28. He was a friend of Coinwalch of Wessex, from whom, as Eddius says, he learned to love the Roman rules.

[2] Possibly Stamford, in Lincolnshire; more probably, since the land belonged to Alchfrid, Stamford Bridge, on the Derwent, in Yorkshire.

[3] Cf. III, 25, where the extent is given as forty families, i.e., "hides."

[4] Cf. III, 7, 25, 28; IV, 1, 12. For the Gewissae, v. II, 5 and note.

[5] At the synod of Whitby, 664 (III, 25).

[6] Tuda (III, 26) had died of the plague of 664. For Wilfrid's consecration, v. III, 28, ad init., and note. Agilbert was not Bishop of Paris till 666 (cf. III, 25, p. 194, note).

Ceadda,[1] was consecrated bishop of York[2] by command of King Oswy, as has been said above; and having nobly ruled that church three years, he retired to take charge of his monastery of Laestingaeu, and Wilfrid was made bishop of all the province of the Northumbrians.

Afterwards, in the reign of Egfrid, he was expelled from his bishopric, and others were consecrated bishops in his stead, of whom mention has been made above.[3] Designing to go to Rome, to plead his cause before the Apostolic Pope, he took ship, and was driven by a west wind into Frisland,[4] and honourably received by that barbarous people and their King Aldgils, to whom he preached Christ, and he instructed many thousands of them in the Word of truth, washing them from the defilement of their sins in the Saviour's font. Thus he began there the work of the Gospel which was afterwards finished with great devotion by the most reverend bishop of Christ, Wilbrord.[5] Having spent the winter there successfully among this new people of God, he set out again on his way to Rome,[6] where his cause being

---

[1] Cf. III, 28, and note. Wilfrid did not return to Britain till 666. Bede omits the story of his shipwreck on the coast of Sussex, and says nothing of the three years spent as Abbot of Ripon, whither he retired on finding Ceadda installed in his place. During this time he acted occasionally as Bishop for Mercia, where the see was vacant by the death of Jaruman in 667, and for Kent, during part of the vacancy between the death of Deusdedit in 664 and Theodore's arrival in 669.

[2] The same Witan which elected Wilfrid decided to transfer the Northumbrian see from Lindisfarne back to York, where Paulinus had originally established it.

[3] In 678, v. IV, 12, and note. Bede passes over nine years of ceaseless activity in the diocese. It was during this time that Wilfrid built his great churches.

[4] Eddius says that he went there by his own wish. This is not the occasion referred to in III, 13 (v. note, ad loc.). Ebroin, from motives of private enmity (Wilfrid had helped his enemy, Dagobert II of Austrasia), attempted to bribe Aldgils to kill or surrender Wilfrid, but his offer was indignantly rejected.

[5] Cc. 10, 11; cf. III, 13.

[6] On the way he visited Dagobert II of Austrasia, and Perctarit king of the Lombards.

tried before Pope Agatho and many bishops,[1] he was by
the judgement of them all acquitted of all blame, and
declared worthy of his bishopric.

At the same time, the said Pope Agatho assembling a
synod at Rome, of one hundred and twenty-five bishops,
against those who asserted that there was only one will
and operation in our Lord and Saviour,[2] ordered Wilfrid
also to be summoned, and, sitting among the bishops, to
declare his own faith and the faith of the province or
island whence he came; and he and his people being found
orthodox in their faith, it was thought fit to record the
same among the acts of that synod, which was done in
in this manner: "Wilfrid, the beloved of God, bishop of
the city of York, appealing to the Apostolic see, and
being by that authority acquitted of every thing, whether
specified against him or not, and being appointed to sit
in judgement with one hundred and twenty-five other
bishops in the synod, made confession of the true and
catholic faith, and confirmed the same with his subscription in the name of all the northern part of Britain and
Ireland, and the islands inhabited by the nations of the
English and Britons, as also by the Scots and Picts."

After this, returning into Britain,[3] he converted the
province of the South Saxons from their idolatrous

[1] At a council of fifty bishops held in the Lateran in 679. Theodore had sent documents stating his side of the case in charge of
a monk named Coenwald. For Agatho, v. IV, 18. The decision
was that Wilfrid should be reinstated in his bishopric and the
intruding bishops removed, but that afterwards he should appoint
coadjutors who should be consecrated by the Archbishop.

[2] This council was held in 680 in preparation for the Council at
Constantinople in 680-681, against the Monothelites (cf. IV, 17, 18,
and notes).

[3] In 680. Here Bede strangely omits important events. On
Wilfrid's return to Northumbria he was accused of having procured his acquittal by bribery and was imprisoned for nine months,
first at Bromnis (unidentified) and then at Dunbar. Being released
at the request of Aebba, Abbess of Coldingham (v. IV, 19, 25), who
was Egfrid's aunt, he went first to Mercia and then to Wessex,
but was expelled from both provinces. Egfrid's sister Osthryth
was the wife of Ethelred of Mercia, and in Wessex the king,
Centwine, had married a sister of the Northumbrian queen,
Eormenburg.

worship to the faith of Christ.[1] He also sent ministers of the Word to the Isle of Wight;[2] and in the second year of Aldfrid, who reigned after Egfrid, was restored to his see and bishopric by that king's invitation.[3] Nevertheless, five years after, being again accused, he was deprived of his bishopric by the same king and certain bishops.[4] Coming to Rome,[5] he was allowed to make his defence in the presence of his accusers, before a number of bishops and the Apostolic Pope John.[6] It was shown by the judgement of them all, that his accusers had in part laid false accusations to his charge; and the aforesaid Pope wrote to the kings of the English, Ethelred

[1] IV, 13.

[2] IV, 13, 16. His connection with Caedwalla of Wessex is to be placed here (IV, 16).

[3] In 686 he was restored to the bishopric of York and the monastery of Ripon. The diocese over which he was now placed was greatly circumscribed. Lindsey and Abercorn, besides having been detached by the subdivision, had both ceased to belong to Northumbria; Lindisfarne and Hexham were separate bishoprics and were merely administered by Wilfrid till the appointment of Eadbert to Lindisfarne and of John to Hexham. The restoration of Wilfrid was brought about by Theodore who had become reconciled to him and induced Aldfrid to allow him to be reinstated.

[4] This was his second expulsion, in 691. Dissensions had arisen about various matters. The most important were the attempt, resisted by Wilfrid, to form Ripon into a separate see, and the requirement that he should accept the decrees of Theodore of 678. To accept these would have been equivalent to a rejection of the Pope's judgement in his case.

[5] Bede omits here Wilfrid's second sojourn in Mercia (eleven years), when he acted temporarily as Bishop of the Middle English (he alludes to it in IV, 23), and the great Council, representative of the whole English Church, summoned by Aldfrid in 702 and held at a place in Northumbria (unidentified; possibly Austerfield in the West Riding of Yorkshire) called by Eddius "Ouestraefelda" and "Aetswinapathe" (supposed to mean "at the swine's path," or "Edwinspath"). At this Council Wilfrid was excommunicated and deprived of all his possessions except the monastery of Ripon. He appealed again to the Apostolic see and returned to Mercia. Probably in the following year he set out for Rome, visiting Wilbrord in Frisia by the way (cf. III, 13).

[6] John VI, 701-705. Bertwald had sent envoys to represent Wilfrid's opponents. The investigation took four months, during which seventy sittings of the Council were held.

A A

and Aldfrid, to cause him to be restored to his bishopric, because he had been unjustly condemned.[1]

His acquittal was much forwarded by the reading of the acts of the synod of Pope Agatho,[2] of blessed memory, which had been formerly held, when Wilfrid was in Rome and sat in council among the bishops, as has been said before. For the acts of that synod being, as the case required, read, by order of the Apostolic Pope, before the nobility and a great number of the people for some days, they came to the place where it was written, " Wilfrid, the beloved of God, bishop of the city of York, appealing to the Apostolic see, and being by that authority acquitted of everything, whether specified against him or not," and the rest as above stated. This being read, the hearers were amazed, and the reader ceasing, they began to ask of one another, who that Bishop Wilfrid was. Then Boniface, the Pope's counsellor,[3] and many others, who had seen him there in the days of Pope Agatho, said that he was the same bishop that lately came to Rome, to be tried by the Apostolic see, being accused by his people, and "who, said they, having long since come here upon the like accusation, the cause and contention of both parties being heard and examined, was proved by Pope Agatho, of blessed memory, to have been wrongfully expelled from his bishopric, and was held in such honour by him, that he commanded him to sit in the council of bishops which he had assembled, as a man of untainted faith and an upright mind." This being heard, the Pope and all the rest said, that a man of so great authority, who had held the office of a bishop for nearly forty years, ought by no means to be condemned, but being altogether cleared of the faults laid to his charge, should return home with honour.

When he came to Gaul, on his way back to Britain, on a sudden he fell sick, and the sickness increasing, he was so weighed down by it, that he could not ride, but was

---

[1] Bertwald was admonished to hold a synod and come to an agreement with Wilfrid. In the event of failure, both parties were to appear in Rome. The letter is cautious and conciliatory in tone.
[2] Cf. *supra*, p. 352.   [3] Cf. *supra*, p. 349.

carried in his bed by the hands of his servants. Being thus come to the city of Maeldum,[1] in Gaul, he lay four days and nights, as if he had been dead, and only by his faint breathing showed that he had any life in him. Having continued thus four days, without meat or drink, without speech or hearing, at length, on the fifth day, at daybreak, as it were awakening out of a deep sleep, he raised himself and sat up, and opening his eyes, saw round about him a company of brethren singing psalms and weeping. Sighing gently, he asked where Acca,[2] the priest, was. This man, straightway being called, came in, and seeing him somewhat recovered and able to speak, knelt down, and gave thanks to God, with all the brethren there present. When they had sat awhile and begun to discourse, with great awe, of the judgements of heaven, the bishop bade the rest go out for a time, and spoke to the priest, Acca, after this manner:

"A dread vision has even now appeared to me, which I would have you hear and keep secret, till I know what God will please to do with me. There stood by me a certain one, glorious in white raiment, and he told me that he was Michael, the Archangel, and said, "I am sent to call you back from death: for the Lord has granted you life, through the prayers and tears of your disciples and brethren, and the intercession of His Blessed Mother Mary, of perpetual virginity; wherefore I tell you, that you shall now recover from this sickness; but be ready, for I will return and visit you at the end of four years. And when you come into your country, you shall recover the greater part of the possessions that have been taken from you, and shall end your days in peace and quiet.'" The bishop accordingly recovered, whereat all men rejoiced and gave thanks to God, and setting forward on his journey, he arrived n Britain.

Having read the letters which he brought from the Apostolic Pope, Bertwald, the archbishop, and Ethelred,[3]

---

[1] Meaux, cf. IV, 1 (Meldi).
[2] III, 13, and note; *infra* c. 20.
[3] Ethelred of Mercia had resigned his throne and was now Abbot of Bardney; cf. III, 11, and IV, 12, p. 241, note.

sometime king, but then abbot, readily took his part; for the said Ethelred, calling to him Coenred,[1] whom he had made king in his own stead, begged him to be friends with Wilfrid, in which request he prevailed; nevertheless Aldfrid, king of the Northumbrians, disdained to receive him. But he died soon after,[2] and so it came to pass that, during the reign of his son Osred,[3] when a synod was assembled before long by the river Nidd,[4] after some contention on both sides, at length, by the consent of all, he was restored to the government of his own church;[5] and thus he lived in peace four years, till the day of his death. He died in his monastery, which he had in the province of Undalum,[6] under the government of the Abbot Cuthbald;[7] and by the ministry of the brethren, he was carried to his first monastery which is called Inhrypum,[8] and buried in the church of the blessed Apostle Peter, hard by the altar on the south side, as has been mentioned above, and this epitaph was written over him:

"Here rests the body of the great Bishop Wilfrid, who, for love of piety, built these courts and consecrated them with the noble name of Peter, to whom Christ, the Judge of all the earth, gave the keys of Heaven. And devoutly he clothed them with gold and Tyrian purple; yea, and he placed here the trophy of the Cross, of shining ore, uplifted high; moreover he caused the four

[1] Cc. 13 and 19, *ad init.*; cf. c. 24.
[2] Cf. c. 18, *ad init.* He received his envoys courteously, but refused to alter his decision for any "alleged writings from the Apostolic see." But Eddius says he repented on his deathbed.
[3] *Ibid.*
[4] In 705. It was a Northumbrian council, not, like Estrefeld, representative of the whole Church. Bertwald was present and adopted a conciliatory line.
[5] He was restored only to Hexham and to his monastery at Ripon. Bishop John, on the death of Bosa about this time, was transferred to York; *v.s.* c. 3, *ad init.*
[6] Oundle, *v.s.* p. 346, note 4.
[7] Or Cudwald. A Cuthbald succeeded Sexwulf (IV, 6) as Abbot at Medeshamstead. He is, perhaps, identical with the Abbot of Oundle.
[8] Cf. *supra*, p. 346, and III, 25.

books of the Gospel to be written in gold in their order, and he gave a case meet for them of ruddy gold. And he also brought the holy season of Easter, returning in its course, to accord with the true teaching of the catholic rule which the Fathers fixed, and, banishing all doubt and error, gave his nation sure guidance in their worship. And in this place he gathered a great throng of monks, and with all diligence safeguarded the precepts which the Fathers' rule enjoined. And long time sore vexed by many a peril at home and abroad, when he had held the office of a bishop forty-five years, he passed away and with joy departed to the heavenly kingdom. Grant, O Jesus, that the flock may follow in the path of the shepherd."

CHAP. XX. *How Albinus succeeded to the godly Abbot Hadrian, and Acca to Bishop Wilfrid.* [709 A.D.]

THE next year after the death of the aforesaid father,[1] which was the fifth year of King Osred, the most reverend father, Abbot Hadrian,[2] fellow labourer in the Word of God with Bishop Theodore[3] of blessed memory, died, and was buried in the church of the Blessed Mother of God, in his own monastery,[4] this being the forty-first year after he was sent by Pope Vitalian with Theodore, and the thirty-ninth after his arrival in England. Among other proofs of his learning, as well as Theodore's, there is this testimony, that Albinus,[5] his disciple, who succeeded him in the government of his monastery, was so well instructed in literary studies, that he had no small knowledge of the Greek tongue, and knew the Latin as well as the English, which was his native language.

Acca,[6] his priest, succeeded Wilfrid in the bishopric of

---

[1] *I.e.* 710. But Hadrian left Rome in 668 (*v.* IV, 1), and Bede says he died forty-one years after that event. This would be in 709.
[2] Cf. Preface and IV, 1.   [3] *Ibid.*
[4] St. Augustine's, Canterbury; cf. IV, 1, *ad fin.*
[5] Cf. Preface and note.   [6] III, 13, and note

the church of Hagustald, being likewise a man of zeal
and great in noble works in the sight of God and man.
He enriched the structure of his church, which is dedicated in honour of the blessed Apostle Andrew with
manifold adornments and marvellous workmanship. For
he gave all diligence, as he does to this day, to procure
relics of the blessed Apostles and martyrs of Christ from
all parts, and to raise altars in their honour in separate
side-chapels built for the purpose within the walls of the
same church. Besides which, he industriously gathered
the histories of their martyrdom, together with other
ecclesiastical writings, and erected there a large and
noble library. He likewise carefully provided holy vessels,
lamps, and other such things as appertain to the adorning of the house of God. He in like manner invited to
him a notable singer called Maban,[1] who had been
taught to sing by the successors of the disciples of the
blessed Pope Gregory in Kent, to instruct himself and
his clergy, and kept him twelve years, to the end that he
might teach such Church music as they did not know,
and by his teaching restore to its former state that which
was corrupted either by long use, or through neglect.
For Bishop Acca himself was a most skilful singer, as
well as most learned in Holy Writ, sound in the confession of the catholic faith, and well versed in the rules of
ecclesiastical custom; nor does he cease to walk after
this manner, till he receive the rewards of his pious devotion. For he was brought up from boyhood and instructed among the clergy of the most holy and beloved
of God, Bosa, bishop of York.[2] Afterwards, coming to
Bishop Wilfrid in the hope of a better plan of life, he
spent the rest of his days in attendance on him till that
bishop's death, and going with him to Rome, learned
there many profitable things concerning the ordinances
of the Holy Church, which he could not have learned in
his own country.

[1] A.S. version: Mafa. For the Roman style of Church music,
cf. II, 20, *ad fin.*
[2] IV, 12, 23; V, 3.

CHAP. XXI. *How the Abbot Ceolfrid sent master-builders to the King of the Picts to build a church, and with them an epistle concerning the Catholic Easter and the Tonsure.* [710 A.D.]

AT that time,[1] Naiton, King of the Picts, who inhabit the northern parts of Britain, taught by frequent meditation on the ecclesiastical writings, renounced the error whereby he and his nation had been holden till then, touching the observance of Easter, and brought himself and all his people to celebrate the catholic time of our Lord's Resurrection. To the end that he might bring this to pass with the more ease and greater authority, he sought aid from the English, whom he knew to have long since framed their religion after the example of the holy Roman Apostolic Church. Accordingly, he sent messengers to the venerable Ceolfrid,[2] abbot of the monastery of the blessed Apostles, Peter and Paul, which stands at the mouth of the river Wear, and near the river Tyne, at the place called Ingyruum,[3] which he gloriously governed after Benedict,[4] of whom we have before spoken; desiring, that he would send him a letter of exhortation, by the help of which he might the better confute those that presumed to keep Easter out of the due time; as also concerning the form and manner of tonsure whereby the clergy should be distinguished,[5] notwithstanding that he himself had no small knowledge of these things. He also prayed to have master-builders sent him to build a church of stone in his nation after

¹ In 710. Naiton, or Nechtan mac Derili, succeeded in 706. The northern Picts had received Christianity through Columba (III, 4). Naiton is said to have been converted to Roman usages by a missionary named Boniface, who was probably an Irishman, St. Cuiritin. Naiton did not succeed in forcing all his people to adopt them, but in 717 he expelled the Columban clergy who refused to conform.
² IV, 18 and note.
³ Wearmouth (*ibid.*) and Jarrow, Bede's own monastery (*v. infra,* c. 24). Though they were some distance apart, Wearmouth and Jarrow formed together one monastery.
⁴ IV, 18.   ⁵ II, 2, p. 85, note.

the Roman manner,[1] promising to dedicate the same in honour of the blessed chief of the Apostles. Moreover, he and all his people, he said, would always follow the custom of the holy Roman Apostolic Church, in so far as men so distant from the speech and nation of the Romans could learn it. The most reverend Abbot Ceolfrid favourably receiving his godly desires and requests, sent the builders he desired, and likewise the following letter:[2]

" *To the most excellent lord, and glorious King Naiton, Abbot Ceolfrid, greeting in the Lord.* We most readily and willingly endeavour, according to your desire, tc make known to you the catholic observance of holy Easter, according to what we have learned of the Apostolic see, even as you, most devout king, in your godly zeal, have requested of us. For we know, that whensoever the lords of this world labour to learn, and to teach and to guard the truth, it is a gift of God to his Holy Church. For a certain profane writer[3] has most truly said, that the world would be most happy if either kings were philosophers, or philosophers were kings. Now if a man of this world could judge truly of the philosophy of this world, and form a right choice concerning the state of this world, how much more is it to be desired, and most earnestly to be prayed for by such as are citizens of the heavenly country, and strangers and pilgrims in this world, that the more powerful any are in the world the more they may strive to hearken to the commands of Him who is the Supreme Judge, and by their example and authority may teach those that are committed to their charge, to keep the same, together with themselves.

"There are then three rules given in the Sacred Writings, whereby the time of keeping Easter has been appointed for us and may in no wise be changed by any authority of man; two whereof are divinely established

---

[1] Wood being the usual material, cf. III, 4, "Candida Casa." The locality of the church is not known. Rosemarkie, on the Moray Frith, and, more probably, Restennet, near Forfar, have been suggested.

[2] The letter has been supposed to have been written by Bede himself.   [3] Plato, Rep. 473, D.

in the law of Moses; the third is added in the Gospel by reason of the Passion and Resurrection of our Lord. For the law enjoined, that the Passover should be kept in the first month of the year, and the third week of that month, that is, from the fifteenth day to the one-and-twentieth. It is added, by Apostolic institution, from the Gospel, that we are to wait for the Lord's day in that third week, and to keep the beginning of the Paschal season on the same. Which threefold rule whosoever shall rightly observe, will never err in fixing the Paschal feast. But if you desire to be more plainly and fully informed in all these particulars, it is written in Exodus, where the people of Israel, being about to be delivered out of Egypt, are commanded to keep the first Passover,[1] that the Lord spake unto Moses and Aaron, saying, 'This month shall be unto you the beginning of months; it shall be the first month of the year to you. Speak ye unto all the congregation of Israel, saying, In the tenth day of this month they shall take to them every man a lamb, according to the house of their fathers, a lamb for an house.' And a little after,[2] 'And ye shall keep it up until the fourteenth day of the same month; and the whole assembly of the congregation of Israel shall kill it in the evening.' By which words it most plainly appears, that in the Paschal observance, though mention is made of the fourteenth day, yet it is not commanded that the Passover be kept on that day; but on the evening of the fourteenth day, that is, when the fifteenth moon, which is the beginning of the third week, appears in the sky, it is commanded that the lamb be killed; and that it was the night of the fifteenth moon, when the Egyptians were smitten and Israel was redeemed from long captivity. He says,[3] 'Seven days shall ye eat unleavened bread.' By which words all the third week of that same first month is appointed to be a solemn feast. But lest we should think that those same seven days were to be reckoned from the fourteenth to the twentieth, He forth-

---

[1] Exod., xii, 1-3. (The quotations are from the Vulgate.)
[2] Exod., xii, 6.   [3] *Ibid.*, xii, 15.

with adds,[1] 'Even the first day ye shall put away leaven
out of your houses; for whosoever eateth leavened bread,
from the first day until the seventh day, that soul shall
be cut off from Israel;' and so on, till he says,[2] 'For in
this selfsame day I will bring your army out of the
land of Egypt.'

"Thus he calls that the first day of unleavened bread,
in which he was to bring their army out of Egypt. Now
it is evident, that they were not brought out of Egypt
on the fourteenth day, in the evening whereof the lamb
was killed, and which is properly called the Passover or
Phase, but on the fifteenth day, as is most plainly written
in the book of Numbers:[3] 'and they departed from
Rameses on the fifteenth day of the first month, on the
morrow after the Passover the Israelites went out with
an high hand.' Thus the seven days of unleavened bread,
on the first whereof the people of the Lord were brought
out of Egypt, are to be reckoned from the beginning of
the third week, as has been said, that is, from the fifteenth
day of the first month, till the end of the one-and-twentieth of the same month. But the fourteenth day is named
apart from this number, by the title of the Passover, as
is plainly shown by that which follows in Exodus:[4]
where, after it is said, 'For in this self-same day I will
bring your army out of the land of Egypt;' it is forthwith added, 'And ye shall observe this day in your generations by an ordinance for ever. In the first month,
on the fourteenth day of the month, ye shall eat unleavened bread, until the one-and-twentieth day of the
month at even. Seven days shall there be no leaven
found in your houses.' Now, who is there that does not
perceive, that there are not only seven days, but rather
eight, from the fourteenth to the one-and-twentieth, if
the fourteenth be also reckoned in the number? But if,
as appears by diligent study of the truth of the Scriptures, we reckon from the evening of the fourteenth day
to the evening of the one-and-twentieth, we shall cer-

[1] Exod., xii, 15.
[3] Numbers, xxxiii, 13.
[2] *Ibid.*, xii, 17.
[4] Exod., xii, 17-19.

tainly find, that, while the Paschal feast begins on the evening of the fourteenth day, yet the whole sacred solemnity contains no more than only seven nights and as many days. Wherefore the rule which we laid down is proved to be true, when we said that the Paschal season is to be celebrated in the first month of the year, and the third week of the same. For it is in truth the third week, because it begins on the evening of the fourteenth day, and ends on the evening of the one-and-twentieth.

" But since Christ our Passover is sacrificed,[1] and has made the Lord's day, which among the ancients was called the first day of the week, a solemn day to us for the joy of His Resurrection, the Apostolic tradition has included it in the Paschal festival; yet has decreed that the time of the legal Passover be in no wise anticipated or diminished; but rather ordains, that according to the precept of the law, that same first month of the year, and the fourteenth day of the same, and the evening thereof be awaited. And when this day should chance to fall on a Saturday, every man should take to him a lamb, according to the house of his fathers, a lamb for an house, and he should kill it in the evening, that is, that all the Churches throughout the world, making one Catholic Church, should provide Bread and Wine for the Mystery of the Flesh and Blood of the spotless Lamb ' that hath taken away the sins of the world;'[2] and after a fitting solemn service of lessons and prayers and Paschal ceremonies, they should offer up these to the Lord, in hope of redemption to come. For this is that same night in which the people of Israel were delivered out of Egypt by the blood of the lamb; this is the same in which all the people of God were, by Christ's Resurrection, set free from eternal death. Then, in the morning, when the Lord's day dawns, they should celebrate the first day of the Paschal festival; for that is the day on which our Lord made known the glory of His Resurrection to His disciples, to their manifold joy at the merciful revelation.

[1] 1 Cor., v, 7.   [2] St. John, i, 29.

The same is the first day of unleavened bread, concerning which it is plainly written in Leviticus,[1] 'In the fourteenth day of the first month, at even, is the Lord's Passover. And on the fifteenth day of the same month is the feast of unleavened bread unto the Lord; seven days ye must eat unleavened bread. In the first day ye shall have an holy convocation.'

"If therefore it could be that the Lord's day should always happen on the fifteenth day of the first month, that is, on the fifteenth moon, we might always celebrate the Passover at one and the same time with the ancient people of God, though the nature of the mystery be different, as we do it with one and the same faith. But inasmuch as the day of the week does not keep pace exactly with the moon, the Apostolic tradition, which was preached at Rome by the blessed Peter, and confirmed at Alexandria by Mark the Evangelist,[2] his interpreter, appointed that when the first month was come, and in it the evening of the fourteenth day, we should also wait for the Lord's day, between the fifteenth and the one-and-twentieth day of the same month. For on whichever of those days it shall fall, Easter will be rightly kept on the same; seeing that it is one of those seven days on which the feast of unleavened bread is commanded to be kept. Thus it comes to pass that our Easter never falls either before or after the third week of the first month, but has for its observance either the whole of it, to wit, the seven days of unleavened bread appointed by the law, or at least some of them. For though it comprises but one of them, that is, the seventh, which the Scripture so highly commends, saying,[3] 'But the seventh day shall be a more holy convocation, ye shall do no servile work therein,' none can lay it to our charge, that we do not rightly keep Easter Sunday, which we re-

[1] Levit., xxiii, 5-7.
[2] Cf. Bede's "Expositio in Marci Evangelium" (Opp. X, 2), where he says that St. Mark founded the Church in Alexandria, and taught the canonical observance of Easter; and Opp. VI, 235 (De Temp. Rat.).
[3] Levit., xxiii, 8.

ceived from the Gospel, in the third week of the first month, as the Law prescribes.

"The catholic reason of this observance being thus explained, the unreasonable error, on the other hand, of those who, without any necessity, presume either to anticipate, or to go beyond the term appointed in the Law, is manifest. For they that think Easter Sunday is to be observed from the fourteenth day of the first month till the twentieth moon, anticipate the time prescribed in the law, without any necessary reason; for when they begin to celebrate the vigil of the holy night from the evening of the thirteenth day, it is plain that they make that day the beginning of their Easter, whereof they find no mention in the commandment of the Law; and when they avoid celebrating our Lord's Easter on the one-and-twentieth day of the month, it is surely manifest that they wholly exclude that day from their solemnity, which the Law many times commends to be observed as a greater festival than the rest; and thus, perverting the proper order, they sometimes keep Easter Day entirely in the second week, and never place it on the seventh day of the third week. And again, they who think that Easter is to be kept from the sixteenth day of the said month till the two-and-twentieth [1] no less erroneously, though on the other side, deviate from the right way of truth, and as it were avoiding shipwreck on Scylla, they fall into the whirpool of Charybdis to be drowned. For when they teach that Easter is to be begun at the rising of the sixteenth moon of the first month, that is, from the evening of the fifteenth day, it is certain that they altogether exclude from their solemnity the fourteenth day of the same month, which the Law first and chiefly commends; so that they scarce touch the evening of the fifteenth day, on which the people of God were redeemed from Egyptian bondage, and on which our Lord, by His Blood,

---

[1] This was an error of the Latins in the fifth century. The object was to make it possible for Good Friday to fall on the fourteenth of the month Nisan, which they believed to be the actual day of the Crucifixion, and to keep Easter Day entirely clear of the Jewish festival.

rescued the world from the darkness of sin, and on which
being also buried, He gave us the hope of a blessed rest
after death.

"And these men, receiving in themselves the recompense of their error, when they place Easter Sunday on
the twenty-second day of the month, openly transgress
and do violence to the term of Easter appointed by the
Law, seeing that they begin Easter on the evening of
that day in which the Law commanded it to be completed and brought to an end; and appoint that to be
the first day of Easter, whereof no mention is any where
found in the Law, to wit, the first of the fourth week.
And both sorts are mistaken, not only in fixing and com-
puting the moon's age, but also sometimes in finding the
first month; but this controversy is longer than can be
or ought to be contained in this letter. I will only say
thus much, that by the vernal equinox, it may always be
found, without the chance of an error, which must be
the first month of the year, according to the lunar computation, and which the last. But the equinox, according to the opinion of all the Eastern nations, and particularly of the Egyptians,[1] who surpass all other learned
men in calculation, falls on the twenty-first day of March,
as we also prove by horological observation. Whatsoever moon therefore is at the full before the equinox,
being on the fourteenth or fifteenth day, the same belongs to the last month of the foregoing year, and consequently is not meet for the celebration of Easter; but
that moon which is full after the equinox, or at the very
time of the equinox, belongs to the first month, and on
that day, without a doubt, we must understand that the
ancients were wont to celebrate the Passover; and that
we also ought to keep Easter when the Sunday comes.
And that this must be so, there is this cogent reason.
It is written in Genesis,[2] 'And God made two great
lights; the greater light to rule the day, and the lesser
light to rule the night.' Or, as another edition[3] has it,
'The greater light to begin the day, and the lesser to

[1] *I.e.* Alexandrians.   [2] Gen., i, 16.   [3] The Itala.

begin the night.' As, therefore, the sun, coming forth from the midst of the east, fixed the vernal equinox by his rising, and afterwards the moon at the full, when the sun set in the evening, followed from the midst of the east; so every year the same first lunar month must be observed in the like order, so that its full moon must not be before the equinox; but either on the very day of the equinox, as it was in the beginning, or after it is past. But if the full moon shall happen to be but one day before the time of the equinox, the aforesaid reason proves that such moon is not to be assigned to the first month of the new year, but rather to the last of the preceding, and that it is therefore not meet for the celebration of the Paschal festival.

"Now if it please you likewise to hear the mystical reason in this matter, we are commanded to keep Easter in the first month of the year, which is also called the month of new things, because we ought to celebrate the mysteries of our Lord's Resurrection and our deliverance, with the spirit of our minds renewed to the love of heavenly things. We are commanded to keep it in the third week of the same month, because Christ Himself, who had been promised before the Law, and under the Law, came with grace, in the third age of the world, to be sacrificed as our Passover; and because rising from the dead the third day after the offering of His Passion, He wished this to be called the Lord's day, and the Paschal feast of His Resurrection to be yearly celebrated on the same; because, also, we do then only truly celebrate His solemn festival, if we endeavour with Him to keep the Passover, that is, the passing from this world to the Father, by faith, hope, and charity. We are commanded to observe the full moon of the Paschal month after the vernal equinox, to the end, that the sun may first make the day longer than the night, and then the moon may show to the world her full orb of light; inasmuch as first 'the Sun of righteousness, with healing in His wings,'[1] that is, our Lord Jesus, by the triumph of His Resurrec-

---

[1] Mal., iv, 2.

tion, dispelled all the darkness of death, and so ascending into Heaven, filled His Church, which is often signified by the name of the moon, with the light of inward grace, by sending down upon her His Spirit. Which order of our salvation the prophet had in his mind, when he said 'The sun was exalted and the moon stood in her order.'[1]

" He, therefore, who shall contend that the full Paschal moon can happen before the equinox, disagrees with the doctrine of the Holy Scriptures, in the celebration of the greatest mysteries, and agrees with those who trust that they may be saved without the grace of Christ preventing them,[2] and who presume to teach that they might have attained to perfect righteousness, though the true Light had never by death and resurrection vanquished the darkness of the world. Thus, after the rising of the sun at the equinox, and after the full moon of the first month following in her order, that is, after the end of the fourteenth day of the same month, all which we have received by the Law to be observed, we still, as we are taught in the Gospel, wait in the third week for the Lord's day; and so, at length, we celebrate the offering of our Easter solemnity, to show that we are not, with the ancients, doing honour to the casting off of the yoke of Egyptian bondage; but that, with devout faith and love, we worship the Redemption of the whole world, which having been prefigured in the deliverance of the ancient people of God, was fulfilled in Christ's Resurrection, and that we may signify that we rejoice in the sure and certain hope of our own resurrection, which we believe will likewise happen on the Lord's day.

" Now this computation of Easter, which we set forth to you to be followed, is contained in a cycle of nineteen years, which began long since to be observed in the Church, to wit, even in the time of the Apostles, especially at Rome and in Egypt, as has been said above.'[3]

[1] Habak., iii, 11 (from the Itala).
[2] The Pelagians; I, 10, and note; cf. I, 17.
[3] The reference must be to p. 364, "the apostolic tradition." For the nineteen years' cycle, cf. III, 3 (Anatolius).

But by the industry of Eusebius,[1] who took his surname
from the blessed martyr Pamphilus,[2] it was reduced to a
plainer system; insomuch that what till then used to be
enjoined every year throughout all the Churches by the
Bishop of Alexandria, might, from that time forward, be
most easily known by all men, the occurrence of the fourteenth moon being regularly set forth in its course. This
Paschal computation, Theophilus,[3] Bishop of Alexandria,
made for the Emperor Theodosius, for a hundred years
to come. Cyril[4] also, his successor, comprised a series
of ninety-five years in five cycles of nineteen years. After
whom, Dionysius Exiguus[5] added as many more, in
order, after the same manner, reaching down to our own
time. The expiration of these is now drawing near, but
there is at the present day so great a number of calcu-
lators, that even in our Churches throughout Britain,
there are many who, having learned the ancient rules of
the Egyptians, can with great ease carry on the Paschal
cycles for any length of time, even to five hundred and

[1] The celebrated Bishop of Caesarea, called also Eusebius
Pamphili, a name which he adopted from devotion to his friend,
Pamphilus. How much he had to do with the nineteen years' cycle
seems altogether uncertain. He took a leading part in the Council
of Nicaea (325 A.D.), but there is no proof that the Council formally
adopted the cycle, as has been supposed. It had been in use long
before, but it may have received authoritative sanction at Nicaea.
Eusebius wrote a treatise on Easter, of which a fragment is extant.

[2] A presbyter of Caesarea, the founder of the famous library in
that place. He was martyred in 309 A.D. Eusebius wrote his life,
but the work is lost.

[3] Archbishop of Alexandria, 385-412. He made a cycle of 418
years (19 × 22) for Theodosius, and reckoned the days on which
Easter would fall for 100 years from the first year of the consulate
of Theodosius (380 A.D.).

[4] The great Archbishop of Alexandria, 412-444. He shortened
the cycle of Theophilus, making a cycle of ninety-five years (19 × 5),
for the sake of convenience. Part of his "Computus Paschalis"
remains.

[5] A monk of the Western Church in the sixth century. The
surname, "Exiguus," refers, not to his stature, but to his humble-
ness of heart. Our method of dating from the Birth of Christ was
begun by him. He revived the cycle of Victorius (or Victorinus)
of Aquitaine (463 A.D.), hence called Dionysian. It was a cycle of
532 years, i.e. the lunar cycle of 19 × the solar cycle of 28.

thirty-two years,[1] if they will; after the expiration of
which, all that appertains to the succession of sun and
moon, month and week, returns in the same order as
before. We therefore forbear to send you these same
cycles of the times to come, because, desiring only to be
instructed respecting the reason for the Paschal time,
you show that you have enough of those catholic cycles
concerning Easter.

"But having said thus much briefly and succinctly, as
you required, concerning Easter, I also exhort you to
take heed that the tonsure, concerning which likewise
you desired me to write to you, be in accordance with
the use of the Church and the Christian Faith. And we
know indeed that the Apostles were not all shorn after
the same manner, nor does the Catholic Church now, as
it agrees in one faith, hope, and charity towards God,
use one and the same form of tonsure throughout the
world. Moreover, to look back to former times, to wit,
the times of the patriarchs, Job, the pattern of patience,
when tribulation came upon him, shaved his head,[2] and
thus made it appear that he had used, in time of prosperity, to let his hair grow. But concerning Joseph, who
more than other men practised and taught chastity,
humility, piety, and the other virtues, we read that he
was shorn when he was to be delivered from bondage,[3]
by which it appears, that during the time of his bondage,
he was in the prison with unshorn hair. Behold then
how each of these men of God differed in the manner of
their appearance abroad, though their inward consciences
agreed in a like grace of virtue. But though we may be
free to confess, that the difference of tonsure is not
hurtful to those whose faith is pure towards God, and
their charity sincere towards their neighbour, especially
since we do not read that there was ever any controversy
among the Catholic fathers about the difference of tonsure, as there has been a contention about the diversity
in keeping Easter, and in matters of faith; nevertheless,
among all the forms of tonsure that are to be found in

[1] Cf. p. 369, note 5.   [2] Job, i, 20.   [3] Gen., xli, 14.

the Church, or among mankind at large, I think none
more meet to be followed and received by us than that
which that disciple wore on his head, to whom, after his
confession of Himself, our Lord said,[1] 'Thou art Peter,
and upon this rock I will build My Church, and the gates
of Hell shall not prevail against it, and I will give unto
thee the keys of the kingdom of Heaven.' Nor do I think
that any is more rightly to be abhorred and detested
by all the faithful, than that which that man used, to
whom that same Peter, when he would have bought the
grace of the Holy Ghost, said,[2] 'Thy money perish with
thee, because thou hast thought that the gift of God
may be purchased with money. Thou hast neither part
nor lot in this word.' Nor do we shave ourselves in the
form of a crown only because Peter was so shorn; but
because Peter was so shorn in memory of the Passion of
our Lord, therefore we also, who desire to be saved by
the same Passion, do with him bear the sign of the same
Passion on the top of our head, which is the highest part
of our body. For as all the Church, because it was made
a Church by the death of Him that gave it life, is wont
to bear the sign of His Holy Cross on the forehead, to
the end, that it may, by the constant protection of His
banner, be defended from the assaults of evil spirits, and
by the frequent admonition of the same be taught, in
like manner, to crucify the flesh with its affections and
lusts;[3] so also it behoves those, who having either taken
the vows of a monk, or having the degree of a clerk, must
needs curb themselves the more strictly by continence,
for the Lord's sake, to bear each one of them on his
head, by the tonsure, the form of the crown of thorns
which He bore on His head in His Passion, that He
might bear the thorns and thistles of our sins, that is,
that he might bear them away and take them from us;
to the end that they may show on their foreheads that
they also willingly, and readily, endure all scoffing and

[1] St. Matt., xvi, 18.
[2] Acts, viii, 20 (Vulgate). The origin of this form of tonsure was
attributed to Simon Magus.
[3] Gal., v, 24.

reproach for his sake; and that they may signify that
they await always 'the crown of eternal life, which God
hath promised to them that love him,'[1] and that for the
sake of attaining thereto they despise both the evil and
the good of this world. But as for the tonsure which
Simon Magus is said to have used, who is there of the
faithful, I ask you, who does not straightway detest and
reject it at the first sight of it, together with his magic?
Above the forehead it does seem indeed to resemble a
crown; but when you come to look at the neck, you will
find the crown cut short which you thought you saw;
so that you may perceive that such a use properly belongs not to Christians but to Simoniacs, such as were
indeed in this life by erring men thought worthy of the
glory of an everlasting crown; but in that which is to
follow this life are not only deprived of all hope of a
crown, but are moreover condemned to eternal punishment.

"But do not think that I have said thus much, as
though I judged them worthy to be condemned who use
this tonsure, if they uphold the catholic unity by their
faith and works; nay, I confidently declare, that many
of them have been holy men and worthy servants of
God. Of which number is Adamnan,[2] the notable abbot
and priest of the followers of Columba, who, when sent
on a mission by his nation to King Aldfrid, desired to
see our monastery, and forasmuch as he showed wonderful wisdom, humility, and piety in his words and behaviour, I said to him among other things, when I talked
with him, ' I beseech you, holy brother, how is it that
you, who believe that you are advancing to the crown of
life, which knows no end, wear on your head, after a
fashion ill-suited to your belief, the likeness of a crown
that has an end? And if you seek the fellowship of the
blessed Peter, why do you imitate the likeness of the
tonsure of him whom St. Peter anathematized? and why
do you not rather even now show that you choose with

[1] St. James, i, 12.
[2] Cf. c. 15 and notes. It is uncertain whether this incident is to
be connected with Adamnan's first or second visit to King Aldfrid.

all your heart the fashion of him with whom you desire to live in bliss for ever.' He answered, 'Be assured, my dear brother, that though I wear the tonsure of Simon, according to the custom of my country, yet I detest and abhor with all my soul the heresy of Simon; and I desire, as far as lies in my small power, to follow the footsteps of the most blessed chief of the Apostles.' I replied, ' I verily believe it; nevertheless it is a token that you embrace in your inmost heart whatever is of Peter the Apostle, if you also observe in outward form that which you know to be his. For I think your wisdom easily discerns that it is much better to estrange from your countenance, already dedicated to God, the fashion of his countenance whom with all your heart you abhor, and of whose hideous face you would shun the sight; and, on the other hand, that it beseems you to imitate the manner of his appearance, whom you seek to have for your advocate before God, even as you desire to follow his actions and his teaching.'

" This I said at that time to Adamnan, who indeed showed how much he had profited by seeing the ordinances of our Churches, when, returning into Scotland,[1] he afterwards by his preaching led great numbers of that nation to the catholic observance of the Paschal time; though he was not yet able to bring back to the way of the better ordinance the monks that lived in the island of Hii over whom he presided with the special authority of a superior. He would also have been mindful to amend the tonsure, if his influence had availed so far.

" But I now also admonish your wisdom, O king, that together with the nation, over which the King of kings, and Lord of lords, has placed you, you strive to observe in all points those things which are in accord with the unity of the Catholic and Apostolic Church; for so it will come to pass, that after you have held sway in a temporal kingdom, the blessed chief of the Apostles will also willingly open to you and yours with all the elect the entrance into the heavenly kingdom. The grace of

---

[1] *I.e.*, Ireland; cf. c. 15.

the eternal King preserve you in safety, long reigning
for the peace of us all, my dearly beloved son in Christ."

This letter having been read in the presence of King
Naiton and many learned men, and carefully interpreted
into his own language by those who could understand
it, he is said to have much rejoiced at the exhortation thereof; insomuch that, rising from among his
nobles that sat about him, he knelt on the ground,
giving thanks to God that he had been found worthy to
receive such a gift from the land of the English. "And
indeed," he said, " I knew before, that this was the true
celebration of Easter, but now I so fully learn the reason
for observing this time, that I seem in all points to have
known but little before concerning these matters. Therefore I publicly declare and protest to you that are here
present, that I will for ever observe this time of Easter,
together with all my nation; and I do decree that this
tonsure, which we have heard to be reasonable, shall be
received by all clerks in my kingdom." Without delay
he accomplished by his royal authority what he had said.
For straightway the Paschal cycles of nineteen years were
sent by command of the State throughout all the provinces
of the Picts to be transcribed, learned, and observed, the
erroneous cycles of eighty-four years being everywhere
blotted out.[1] All the ministers of the altar and monks
were shorn after the fashion of the crown; and the
nation thus reformed, rejoiced, as being newly put under
the guidance of Peter, the most blessed chief of the
Apostles, and committed to his protection.

CHAP. XXII. *How the monks of Hii, and the monasteries
subject to them, began to celebrate the canonical Easter
at the preaching of Egbert.* [716 A.D.]

NOT long after, those monks also of the Scottish nation,
who lived in the isle of Hii, with the other monasteries that
were subject to them, were by the Lord's doing brought

[1] Cf. *supra*, p. 359, note 1.

to the canonical observance with regard to Easter, and
the tonsure. For in the year of our Lord 716, when
Osred[1] was slain, and Coenred[2] took upon him the
government of the kingdom of the Northumbrians, the
father and priest,[3] Egbert, beloved of God, and worthy
to be named with all honour, whom we have before
often mentioned, came to them from Ireland, and was
honourably and joyfully received. Being a most gracious
teacher, and most devout in practising those things
which he taught, and being willingly heard by all, by
his pious and diligent exhortations, he converted them
from that deep-rooted tradition of their fathers, of whom
may be said those words of the Apostle, "That they
had a zeal of God, but not according to knowledge."[4]
He taught them to celebrate the principal solemnity
after the catholic and apostolic manner, as has been
said, wearing on their heads the figure of an unending
crown.[5] It is manifest that this came to pass by a
wonderful dispensation of the Divine goodness; to the
end, that the same nation which had willingly, and
without grudging, taken heed to impart to the English
people that learning which it had in the knowledge of
God, should afterwards, by means of the English nation,
be brought, in those things which it had not, to a perfect
rule of life. Even as, contrariwise, the Britons, who

---

[1] Cf. c. 18 and note; cc. 19, 20, 24. He was killed in battle, but
neither the locality nor the war is known.

[2] He reigned two years, v. *infra* c. 23. He belonged to a
younger branch of the royal house of Northumbria. His father's
name was Cuthwine, and Ceolwulf, who succeeded Osric (c. 23),
was his brother.

[3] Or, perhaps, "bishop,' cf. III, 4, note. For the circumstances
which led Egbert to undertake his work among the Columban
monasteries, *v.s.* c. 9. As the events narrated there were prior to
690 (Wilbrord's mission to Frisia), we may, perhaps, assume
that he had been labouring during this long interval among the
Columban monasteries in Ireland. In III, 4, Bede places Egbert's
arrival in Iona a year earlier.

[4] Rom., x, 2.

[5] Cf. p. 372. This seems to be the meaning of the somewhat
obscure sentence, ". . . celebrationem, ut diximus, praecipuae
solemnitatis sub figura coronae perpetis agere perdocuit."

would not reveal to the English the knowledge which they had of the Christian faith, now, when the English people believe, and are in all points instructed in the rule of the Catholic faith, still persist in their errors, halting and turned aside from the true path, expose their heads without a crown, and keep the Feast of Christ apart from the fellowship of the Church of Christ.[1]

The monks of Hii, at the teaching of Egbert, adopted the catholic manner of conversation, under Abbot Dunchad, about eighty years after they had sent Bishop Aidan to preach to the English nation.[2] The man of God, Egbert, remained thirteen years in the aforesaid island, which he had thus consecrated to Christ, as it were, by a new ray of the grace of fellowship and peace in the Church; and in the year of our Lord 729, in which Easter was celebrated on the 24th of April, when he had celebrated the solemnity of the Mass, in memory of the Resurrection of our Lord, that same day he departed to the Lord and thus finished, or rather never ceases endlessly to celebrate, with our Lord, and the Apostles, and the other citizens of heaven, the joy of that greatest festival, which he had begun with the brethren, whom he had converted to the grace of unity. And it was a wonderful dispensation of the Divine Providence, that the venerable man passed from this world to the Father, not only at Easter, but also when Easter was celebrated on that day,[3] on which it had never been wont to be celebrated in those parts. The brethren rejoiced in the sure and catholic knowledge of the time of Easter, and were glad in that their father, by whom they had been brought into the right way, passing hence to the Lord should plead for them. He also gave thanks that he had so long continued in the flesh, till he saw his hearers accept and

---

[1] For the conversion of the Britons to Roman usages, v. cc. 15 and 18, notes.

[2] This is accurate enough in round numbers. Aidan's mission (v. III, 3) was probably in 635.

[3] I.e., 24th April. According to the Celtic rule, Easter Day could never have been so late, 21st April being the latest possible day, while the Romans might celebrate as late as 25th April.

keep with him as Easter that day which they had ever before avoided. Thus the most reverend father being assured of their amendment, rejoiced to see the day of the Lord, and he saw it and was glad.

CHAP. XXIII. *Of the present state of the English nation, or of all Britain.* [725-731 A.D.]

IN the year of our Lord 725, being the seventh year of Osric,[1] king of the Northumbrians, who had succeeded Coenred, Wictred,[2] the son of Egbert, king of Kent, died on the 23rd of April, and left his three sons, Ethelbert, Eadbert, and Alric,[3] heirs of that kingdom, which he had governed thirty-four years and a half. The next year Tobias,[4] bishop of the church of Rochester, died, a most learned man, as has been said before; for he was disciple to those masters of blessed memory, Theodore, the archbishop, and Abbot Hadrian, wherefore, as has been said, besides having a great knowledge of letters both ecclesiastical and general, he learned both the Greek and Latin tongues to such perfection, that they were as well known and familiar to him as his native language. He was buried in the chapel of St. Paul the

[1] Osric had succeeded in 718. Simeon of Durham says he was a son of King "Alfrid." It has been suggested (Dr. Stubbs, in Dict. of Christian Biog.) that this may mean Alchfrid, son of Oswy (III, 14, *et saep.*), further, that this Osric is to be identified with the Hwiccian sub-king, mentioned in IV, 23, who may have found a refuge in Mercia, when Alchfrid was disinherited. Against this it has been maintained that the statement of Simeon of Durham may, with greater probability, be referred to Aldfrid, the successor of Egfrid and father of Osred.

[2] Cf. IV, 26, and V, 8.

[3] From Bede we should infer that they all succeeded in 725, and the evidence of charters goes to show that Eadbert and Ethelbert began to reign jointly in that year. Florence of Worcester makes Eadbert and Ethelbert reign successively, and William of Malmesbury gives successive reigns of considerable length to all three brothers. This prolongs Alric's life beyond probability, and as his reign rests on no early evidence, Dr. Stubbs is inclined to set it aside altogether.

[4] Cf. c. 8.

Apostle, which he had built within the church of St. Andrew [1] for his own place of burial. After him Aldwulf [2] took upon him the office of bishop, having been consecrated by Archbishop Bertwald.

In the year of our Lord 729, two comets appeared about the sun, to the great terror of the beholders. One of them went before the sun in the morning at his rising, the other followed him when he set in the evening, as it were presaging dire disaster to both east and west; or without doubt one was the forerunner of the day, and the other of the night, to signify that mortals were threatened with calamities at both times. They carried their flaming brands towards the north, as it were ready to kindle a conflagration. They appeared in January, and continued nearly a fortnight. At which time a grievous blight fell upon Gaul, in that it was laid waste by the Saracens with cruel bloodshed; but not long after in that country they received the due reward of their unbelief. [3] In that year the holy man of God, Egbert, departed to the Lord, as has been said above, on Easter day; [4] and immediately after Easter, that is, on the 9th of May, Osric, [5] king of the Northumbrians, departed this life, after he had reigned eleven years, and appointed Ceolwulf, [6] brother to Coenred, [7] who had reigned before him, his successor; the beginning and progress of whose reign have been so filled with many and great commotions and conflicts, that it cannot yet be known what is to be said concerning them, or what end they will have.

In the year of our Lord 731, Archbishop Bertwald died of old age, on the 13th of January, having held his

[1] Cf. II, 3 and note; III, 14.
[2] Consecrated in 727 (Saxon Chronicle) and died in 739 (Simeon of Durham).
[3] This must refer to the battle of Tours in 732, in which Charles Martel defeated the Saracens. As the Ecclesiastical History was finished in 731, this passage must be regarded as a later insertion. For Bede's view with regard to the Saracens, v. his theological works *passim*. He believed them to be the descendants of Ishmael.
[4] In 729; *v.s.* c. 22.   [5] Cf. *supra*, this chapter, *ad init.*
[6] Cf. Preface, note 1, and the Continuation.
[7] Cf. c. 22, *ad init* and note.

see thirty-seven years, six months and fourteen days.[1] In his stead, the same year, Tatwine,[2] of the province of the Mercians, was made archbishop, having been a priest in the monastery called Briudun.[3] He was consecrated in the city of Canterbury by the venerable men, Daniel,[4] bishop of Winchester, Ingwald of London,[5] Aldwin of Lichfield,[6] and Aldwulf of Rochester,[7] on Sunday, the 10th of June, being a man renowned for piety and wisdom, and of notable learning in Holy Scripture.

Thus at the present time,[8] the bishops Tatwine and

[1] *I.e.*, since 29th June, 693; *v.s.* c. 8, *ad fin.*
[2] He received the pall in 733 and died in 734; cf. Continuation.
[3] Bredon in Worcestershire.
[4] Cf. Preface; IV, 16; V, 18.
[5] *I.e.*, of the East Saxons. He died in 745; *v.* Continuation.
[6] Called also Worr. In the Act of the Council of Clovesho in 716 he signs as Bishop of Lichfield (to which at this time Leicester was united) along with his predecessor, Hedda, but the authenticity of the Act is not fully established, and it is generally supposed that he succeeded in 721. At his death in 737 (Simeon of Durham) Leicester was finally separated from Lichfield.
[7] Cf. *supra*, p. 378.
[8] The following list of the English bishoprics at the time when Bede closed his history [731 A.D.], will enable the reader to recognize those which belonged to each separate kingdom:

KINGDOMS.	SEES.	PRELATES.
Kent	Canterbury	Tatwine.
	Rochester	Aldwulf.
East Saxons .	London	Ingwald.
East Angles .	Dunwich	Aldbert.
	Elmham	Hadulac.
West Saxons .	Winchester	Daniel.
	Sherborne	Forthere.
Mercia . . .	Lichfield (to which Leicester had been reunited in 705, cf. Haddan and Stubbs, III, 129)	
		Aldwin.
	Hereford	Walhstod.
	Worcester	Wilfrid.
	Lindsey (Sidnacester) . .	Cynibert.
South Saxons .	Selsey	Vacant.
Northumbria .	York	Wilfrid II.
	Lindisfarne	Ethelwald.
	Hexham	Acca.
	Whitern	Pechthelm.

Aldwulf preside in the churches of Kent; Ingwald is bishop in the province of the East Saxons. In the province of the East Angles, the bishops are Aldbert and Hadulac;[1] in the province of the West Saxons, Daniel and Forthere;[2] in the province of the Mercians, Aldwin.[3] Among those peoples who dwell beyond the river Severn to the westward,[4] Walhstod is bishop; in the province of the Hwiccas, Wilfrid;[5] in the province of Lindsey, Bishop Cynibert[6] presides; the bishopric of the Isle of Wight[7] belongs to Daniel, bishop of the city of Winchester. The province of the South Saxons,[8] having now continued some years without a bishop, receives episcopal ministrations from the prelate of the West Saxons. All these provinces, and the other southern provinces, as far as the boundary formed by the river Humber, with their several kings, are subject to King Ethelbald.[9]

[1] Aldbert was Bishop of Dunwich, Hadulac of Elmham.
[2] Cf. c. 18.   [3] Cf. *supra*, p. 379, note 6.
[4] *I.e.*, in Herefordshire. It is not certain when the see of Hereford was founded. Besides Putta (*v.* IV, 2, and note), Florence of Worcester mentions Tyrhtel and Torthere as predecessors of Walhstod.
[5] This is Wilfrid, Bishop of Worcester, contemporary with Wilfrid II of York (*v.* IV, 23; V, 6). He succeeded St. Egwin, whom Bede strangely omits to mention, the successor of Oftfor (IV, 23). For the Hwiccas, *v.* II, 2, p. 84, and for the see of Worcester, IV, 23, p. 273, note 7.
[6] Cf. Preface, p. 4, and IV, 12. For Lindsey as a separate bishopric, *ibid.*
[7] Cf. IV, 16.   [8] Cf. c. 18, *ad fin.*, and notes.
[9] He was a son of Penda's brother, Alweo. He had lived at one time in retirement near the hermitage of St. Guthlac, flying from the enmity of Ceolred, but on the death of the latter in 716, he succeeded to the throne. Though he is not included in Bede's list of Bretwaldas (II, 5), he established the supremacy of Mercia for twenty years over all England south of the Humber, till in 754 Wessex freed itself in the battle of Burford. For his wars with Wessex and Northumbria, *v.* Continuation, *sub* 740 and 750. There is a charter of his dated 749 in which he grants certain ecclesiastical privileges, "pro expiatione delictorum suorum." His oppression of the Church and his private life are rebuked in the letter of Boniface and five German bishops addressed to him (*v.* Haddan and Stubbs, III, 350).

But in the province of the Northumbrians, where King Ceolwulf reigns, four bishops now preside; Wilfrid[1] in the church of York, Ethelwald[2] in that of Lindisfarne, Acca[3] in that of Hagustald, Pecthelm[4] in that which is called the White House, which, as the number of the faithful has increased, has lately become an episcopal see, and has him for its first prelate. The Pictish people also at this time are at peace with the English nation, and rejoice in having their part in Catholic peace and truth with the universal Church. The Scots[5] that inhabit Britain, content with their own territories, devise no plots nor hostilities against the English nation. The Britons,[6] though they, for the most part, as a nation hate and oppose the English nation, and wrongfully, and from wicked lewdness, set themselves against the appointed Easter of the whole Catholic Church; yet, inasmuch as both Divine and human power withstand them, they can in neither purpose prevail as they desire; for though in part they are their own masters, yet part of them are brought under subjection to the English. In these favourable times of peace and calm,[7] many of the Northumbrians, as well of the nobility as private persons, laying aside their weapons, and receiving the tonsure, desire rather both for themselves and their children to take upon them monastic vows, than to practise the pursuit of war. What will be the end hereof, the next age will see. This is for the present the state

[1] Wilfrid II, v. IV, 23, and note; cf. V. 6.
[2] Cf. c. 12, p. 331, and note.
[3] III, 13, and note; cf. IV, 14; V, 20.
[4] Cf. cc. 13, 18. For the "White House" (Whitern), v. III, 4, and note. About this time (the exact date is not known) it became an Anglian see, a fact which indicates that in spite of the defeat of Egfrid in 685, which freed the Northern Picts, the Picts of Galloway were still subject to Northumbria. The bishopric came to an end about the close of the century, when the Northumbrian power had fallen into decay.
[5] The Scots of Dalriada (I, 1). They had recovered their liberty after the defeat and death of Egfrid; cf. IV, 26.
[6] Cf. *ibid.*, and p. 376, note 1.
[7] External peace apparently. For the internal state of Northumbria, *v.s.* p. 378.

In the year 605, Gregory died. [II, 1.]

In the year 616, Ethelbert, king of Kent died. [II, 5.]

In the year 625, Paulinus was ordained bishop of the Northumbrians by Archbishop Justus. [II, 9.]

In the year 626, Eanfled, daughter of King Edwin, was baptized with twelve others, on the eve of Whitsunday. [Ib.]

In the year 627, King Edwin was baptized, with his nation, at Easter. [II, 14.]

In the year 633, King Edwin being killed, Paulinus returned to Kent. [II, 20.]

In the year 640, Eadbald, king of Kent, died. [III, 8.]

In the year 642, King Oswald was slain. [III, 9.]

In the year 644, Paulinus, formerly bishop of York, but then of the city of Rochester, departed to the Lord. [III, 14.]

In the year 651, King Oswin was killed, and Bishop Aidan died. [Ibid.]

In the year 653, the Middle Angles, under their prince, Peada, were admitted to the mysteries of the faith. [III, 21.]

In the year 655, Penda was slain, and the Mercians became Christians. [III, 24.]

In the year 664, an eclipse came to pass; Earconbert, king of Kent, died; and Colman with the Scots returned to his people; a pestilence arose; Ceadda and Wilfrid were ordained bishops of the Northumbrians. [III, 26-28, IV, 1.]

In the year 668, Theodore was ordained bishop. [IV, 1.]

In the year 670, Oswy, king of the Northumbrians, died. [IV, 5.]

In the year 673, Egbert, king of Kent, died; and a synod was held at Hertford, in the presence of King Egfrid, Archbishop Theodore presiding: the synod was of great profit, and its decrees are contained in ten articles. [Ibid.]

In the year 675,[1] Wulfhere, king of the Mercians,

---

[1] Wulfhere's death is not mentioned in the narrative.

when he had reigned seventeen years, died and left the government to his brother Ethelred.

In the year 676, Ethelred ravaged Kent. [IV, 12.]

In the year 678, a comet appeared; Bishop Wilfrid was driven from his see by King Egfrid; and Bosa, Eata, and Eadhaed were consecrated bishops in his stead. [*Ibid.*; V, 19.]

In the year 679, Aelfwine was killed. [IV, 21.]

In the year 680, a synod was held in the plain of Haethfelth, concerning the Catholic faith, Archbishop Theodore presiding; John, the Roman abbot, was also present. The same year also the Abbess Hilda died at Streanaeshalch. [IV, 17, 18, 23.]

In the year 685, Egfrid, king of the Northumbrians, was slain. The same year Hlothere, king of Kent, died. [IV, 26.]

In the year 688, Caedwald, king of the West Saxons, went to Rome from Britain. [V, 7.]

In the year 690, Archbishop Theodore died. [V, 8.]

In the year 697, Queen Osthryth was murdered by her own nobles, to wit, the nobles of the Mercians.[1]

In the year 698, Berctred, an ealdorman of the king of the Northumbrians, was slain by the Picts.[2]

In the year 704, Ethelred, after he had reigned thirty-one years over the nation of the Mercians, became a monk, and gave up the kingdom to Coenred. [V, 19.][3]

In the year 705, Aldfrid, king of the Northumbrians, died. [V. 18.]

In the year 709, Coenred, king of the Mercians, having reigned five years, went to Rome. [V, 19.]

In the year 711, the commander Bertfrid fought with the Picts.[4]

[1] This is not in the narrative. For Osthryth cf. III, 11; IV, 21.

[2] Not in the narrative. Berctred is probably to be identified with Berct in IV, 26 *ad init.* (Ulster Annals: " Brectrid"; Sax. Chron.: "Briht."

[3] Above it is said that he succeeded in 675, making his reign twenty-nine years, and this agrees with the Saxon Chronicle. Wilfrid, on his return to England in 705, found him already an abbot. (V, 19.)

[4] Not in the narrative. Bertfrid was Osred's chief ealdorman,

In the year 716, Osred, king of the Northumbrians, was killed; and Ceolred, king of the Mercians, died; and the man of God, Egbert, brought the monks of Hii to observe the Catholic Easter and the ecclesiastical tonsure. [V, 22.]

In the year 725, Wictred, king of Kent, died. [V, 23.]

In the year 729, comets appeared; the holy Egbert passed away; and Osric died. [*Ibid.*]

In the year 731, Archbishop Bertwald died. [*Ibid.*]

The same year Tatwine was consecrated ninth archbishop of the church of Canterbury, in the fifteenth year of the reign of Ethelbald, king of the Mercians. [*Ibid.*]

THUS much of the Ecclesiastical History of Britain, and more especially of the English nation, as far as I could learn either from the writings of the ancients, or the tradition of our forefathers, or of my own knowledge, with the help of the Lord, I, Bede,[1] the servant of Christ, and priest of the monastery of the blessed Apostles, Peter and Paul, which is at Wearmouth and Jarrow,[2] have set forth. Having been born in the territory of that same monastery, I was given, by the care of kinsmen, at seven years of age, to be educated by the most reverend Abbot Benedict,[3] and afterwards by Ceolfrid,[4] and spending all the remaining time of my life a dweller in that monastery, I wholly applied myself to the study of Scripture; and amidst the observance of monastic rule, and the daily charge of singing in the church, I always took delight in learning, or teaching, or writing. In the nineteenth year of my age, I received deacon's orders; in the thirtieth, those of the priesthood, both of them by the ministry of the most reverend Bishop John,[5] and at

and was besieged with him in Bamborough by the usurper Eadwulf; cf. p. 342, note 2. We find him acting as spokesman in the Council on the Nidd (V, 19, p. 356) in demanding to have the Papal letters translated into English.

[1] For Bede's life, *v.* Introduction.
[2] IV, 18, p. 257, note 3.   [3] *Ibid.*
[4] *Ibid.*, note 4, cf. V, 21.
[5] John of Beverley, IV, 23; V, 2-6.

the bidding of the Abbot Ceolfrid. From the time when I received priest's orders, till the fifty-ninth year of my age, I have made it my business, for my own needs and those of my brethren, to compile out of the works of the venerable Fathers, the following brief notes on the Holy Scriptures, and also to make some additions after the manner of the meaning and interpretation given by them:[1]

On the Beginning of Genesis, to the birth of Isaac and the casting out of Ishmael, four books.

Concerning the Tabernacle and its Vessels, and of the Vestments of the Priests, three books.

On the first part of Samuel, to the Death of Saul, three books.

Concerning the Building of the Temple, of Allegorical Exposition, and other matters, two books.

Likewise on the Book of Kings, thirty Questions.[2]

On the Proverbs of Solomon, three books.

On the Song of Songs, seven books.

On Isaiah, Daniel, the twelve Prophets, and Part of Jeremiah, Divisions of Chapters, collected from the Treatise of the blessed Jerome.

On Ezra and Nehemiah, three books.

On the song of Habakkuk, one book.

On the Book of the blessed Father Tobias, one Book of Allegorical Explanation concerning Christ and the Church.

Also, Chapters of Readings on the Pentateuch of Moses, Joshua, and Judges;

---

[1] For a full account of Bede's works, v. Plummer, vol. I, Introduction, or Dictionary of Christian Biography, s.v. "Beda." Besides the works mentioned in this list, the following are certainly genuine:
The short "Epistola ad Albinum" (sent with a copy of the Ecclesiastical History).
"Retractationes in Acta."
"Epistola ad Egberctum."
"De locis Sanctis" (to which Bede alludes in V. 17). A number of other works, some certainly, others probably spurious, and a few possibly genuine, have been attributed to him.

[2] An answer to questions put to him by Nothelm (v. Preface, p. 2, note 4, and Continuation, sub 735).

On the Books of Kings and Chronicles;
On the Book of the blessed Father Job;
On the Proverbs,[1] Ecclesiastes, and the Song of Songs;
On the Prophets Isaiah, Ezra, and Nehemiah.
On the Gospel of Mark, four books.
On the Gospel of Luke, six books.
Of Homilies on the Gospel, two books.
On the Apostle,[2] whatsoever I have found in the works
of St. Augustine I have taken heed to transcribe in order.
On the Acts of the Apostles, two books.
On the seven Catholic Epistles, a book on each.
On the Revelation of St. John, three books.
Likewise, Chapters of Lessons on all the New Testament, except the Gospel.
Likewise a book of Epistles to divers Persons, of which one is of the Six Ages of the world; one of the Halting-places of the Children of Israel; one on the words of Isaiah, "And they shall be shut up in the prison, and after many days shall they be visited";[3] one of the Reason of Leap-Year, and one of the Equinox, according to Anatolius.[4]
Likewise concerning the Histories of Saints: I translated the Book of the Life and Passion of St. Felix, Confessor,[5] from the metrical work of Paulinus, into prose; the Book of the Life and Passion of St. Anastasius,[6] which was ill translated from the Greek, and worse amended by some ignorant person, I have corrected as to the sense as far as I could; I have written the Life of

---

[1] "Parabolae" = comparisons. "Parabolae Salomonis" are the first words of the Book of Proverbs in the Vulgate.
[2] *I.e.*, St. Paul.   [3] Isa., xxiv, 22.
[4] III, 3, note; cf. III, 25, p. 198.
[5] A priest of Nola in Campania. He was of Syrian extraction, but born at Nola, and ordained priest *circ.* 250 A.D. He was persecuted under Decius, and again under Valerian, but escaped. His history is told in the poems of Paulinus, Bishop of Nola (409-431).
[6] This work is not known to exist. Probably the saint is Anastasius the Younger, Patriarch of Antioch, killed in 610 by the Jews in a sedition on 21st December, and in the Roman martyrology honoured on that day as a martyr (*v.* Butler, "Lives of the Saints").

the Holy Father Cuthbert, who was both monk and bishop, first in heroic verse, and afterwards in prose.

The History of the Abbots of this monastery, in which I rejoice to serve the Divine Goodness, to wit, Benedict, Ceolfrid, and Huaetbert,[2] in two books.

The Ecclesiastical History of our Island and Nation, in five books.

The Martyrology of the Festivals of the Holy Martyrs, in which I have carefully endeavoured to set down all whom I could find, and not only on what day, but also by what sort of combat, and under what judge they overcame the world.

A Book of Hymns in divers sorts of metre, or rhythm.

A Book of Epigrams in heroic or elegiac verse.

Of the Nature of Things, and of the Times, one book of each; likewise, of the Times, one larger book.

A book of Orthography arranged in Alphabetical Order.

Likewise a Book of the Art of Poetry, and to it I have added another little Book of Figures of Speech or Tropes; that is, of the Figures and Modes of Speech in which the Holy Scriptures are written.

And I beseech Thee, good Jesus, that to whom Thou hast graciously granted sweetly to drink in the words of Thy knowledge, Thou wilt also vouchsafe in Thy lovingkindness that he may one day come to Thee, the Fountain of all wisdom, and appear for ever before Thy face.

---

[1] Cf. IV, 26-32.
[2] For Benedict and Ceolfrid, v. IV, 18. Huaetbert belonged to the monastery of Wearmouth and Jarrow from his earliest childhood, and succeeded Ceolfrid as abbot in 716. He survived Bede. The latter dedicated his commentary on the Apocalypse and the De temp. Rat. to him under his name of Eusebius given him for his piety (v. Bede's Hist. Abb. and Anon., Hist. Abb.).

The Continuation of Bede.[1]

IN the year 731 King Ceolwulf was taken prisoner, and tonsured, and sent back to his kingdom; Bishop Acca was driven from his see.

In the year 732, Egbert[2] was made Bishop of York, in the room of Wilfrid.

[Cynibert Bishop of Lindsey died.]

[In the year of our Lord 733, Archbishop Tatwine, having received the pall by Apostolic authority, ordained Alwic[3] and Sigfrid,[4] bishops.]

In the year 733, there was an eclipse of the sun on the 14th day of August about the third hour, in such wise that the whole orb of the sun seemed to be covered with a black and gloomy shield.

In the year 734, the moon, on the 31st of January, about the time of cock-crowing, was, for about a whole hour, coloured blood-red, after which a blackness followed, and she regained her wonted light.

In the year from the Incarnation of Christ, 734, bishop Tatwine died.

In the year 735, Nothelm was ordained archbishop; and bishop Egbert, having received the pall from the Apostolic see, was the first to be established as arch-

---

[1] (Only names which have not occurred in the narrative are annotated; references for those already mentioned will be found in the Index.) The Continuation is by a later hand. But Mr. Plummer considers that the entries under the years 731, 732, 733 and 734 may have been added by Bede himself. They appear in the great Moore MS., and those for 733 and 734 also in another eighth century MS. The entries enclosed in square brackets are found in a fifteenth century MS.

[2] He succeeded Wilfrid II, and two years later became Archbishop of York (*v. infra* under 735). It was to him that Bede addressed the "Epist. ad Egberctum."

[3] Bishop of Lindsey.

[4] Bishop of Selsey.

bishop[1] after Paulinus, and he ordained Frithbert,[2] and Frithwald[3] bishops; and the priest Bede died.[4]

In the year 737, an excessive drought rendered the land unfruitful; and Ceolwulf, voluntarily receiving the tonsure, left the kingdom to Eadbert.[5]

In the year 739, Edilhart,[6] king of the West-Saxons, died, as did Archbishop Nothelm.

In the year 740, Cuthbert[7] was consecrated in Nothelm's stead. Ethelbald, king of the Mercians, cruelly and wrongfully wasted part of Northumbria, their king, Eadbert, with his army, being employed against the Picts. Bishop Ethelwald died also, and Conwulf,[8] was consecrated in his stead. Arnwin[9] and Eadbert[10] were slain.

In the year 741, a great drought came upon the country. Charles,[11] king of the Franks, died; and his sons, Caroloman and Pippin,[12] reigned in his stead.

In the year 745, Bishop Wilfrid and Ingwald, Bishop of London, departed to the Lord.

In the year 747, the man of God, Herefrid,[13] died.

In the year 750, Cuthred, king of the West Saxons, rose up against king Ethelbald and Oengus; Theudor

---

[1] *I.e.*, of York.   [2] Bishop of Hexham.

[3] Bishop of Whitern.

[4] The early authorities differ as to the year, but this is the traditional date, and is usually accepted.

[5] King of Northumbria 737-758 (*v. infra*); died in 768. He was a son of Eata, called by Nennius, Eata "Glinmaur," a descendant of Ida, and was the brother of Archbishop Egbert. Under him the Northumbrian power revived for a period.

[6] He was the kinsman and predecessor of Cuthred (*v. infra*).

[7] Archbishop of Canterbury in succession to Nothelm. The first archbishop not buried in St. Augustine's, *v.* II, 3, p. 90, note.

[8] Bishop of Lindisfarne in succession to Ethelwald (V, 12, *ad fin.*, note).

[9] Probably a son of that Eadwulf who usurped the throne of Northumbria at Aldfrid's death (V, 18); cf. Simeon of Durham, II, 38 (Rolls Series), "Arwine filius Eadulfi."

[10] Not known.   [11] Charles Martel.

[12] Pippin the Short. Carloman resigned in 747, and became a monk.

[13] There is a letter of Boniface (*v.* Haddan and Stubbs III, 358) to a priest, Herefrid, who is supposed to be the man mentioned here.

and Eanred died; Eadbert added the plain of Kyle and other places to his dominions.[1]

In the year 753, in the fifth year of King Eadbert, on the 9th of January,[2] an eclipse of the sun came to pass; afterwards, in the same year and month, on the 24th day of January, the moon suffered an eclipse, being covered with a gloomy, black shield, in like manner as was the sun a little while before.

In the year 754, Boniface,[3] called also Winfrid, Bishop of the Franks, received the crown of martyrdom, together with fifty-three others; and Redger was consecrated archbishop in his stead, by pope Stephen.

In the year 757, Ethelbald, king of the Mercians, was treacherously and miserably murdered, in the night, by his own guards; Beornred[4] began his reign; Cyniwulf,[5] king of the West Saxons, died; and the same year, Offa, having put Beornred to flight, sought to gain the kingdom of the Mercians by bloodshed.

In the year 758, Eadbert, king of the Northumbrians,

---

[1] This seems confused and obscure. The West Saxons under Cuthred threw off the Mercian yoke in the insurrection which culminated in the battle of Burford (v. V. 23, p. 380, note 9). Oengus or Angus (the Brythonic form is Ungust), son of Fergus, was a Pictish king who crushed the Dalriadic Scots, and, in alliance with Eadbert of Northumbria, conquered the Britons of Strathclyde. But this does not explain the strange statement which brings him into connection with Ethelbald of Mercia. Nor is it told who Eanred was. Theudor was a king of the Britons of Strathclyde. Kyle is a district in Ayrshire.

[2] Adopting the emendation "quinto Idus" (Hussey). The date is thus right for the eclipses, but the year is the sixteenth of Eadbert. Probably the numeral (XVI) has fallen out, and the passage ought to run: "anno regni Eadbercti XVI, quinto Id. Ian."

[3] The great missionary bishop of Germany, a West Saxon by birth. He crossed to the Continent *circ.* 716, and, supported by Charles Martel and his sons, evangelized Central Europe, became Archbishop of Mainz, and founded sees throughout Germany. Finally he was martyred in Frisland. Lul, a West Saxon, was his successor, not Redger, but it has been suggested that this may be another name for him. The pope is Stephen III.

[4] He is said by William of Malmesbury to have been the murderer of Ethelbald. After a year of anarchy Offa succeeded, and retrieved the position of Mercia.

[5] He was killed in an insurrection in 784. (Sax. Chron.)

receiving St. Peter's tonsure for the love of God, and to the end that he might take the heavenly country by force,[1] left the kingdom to his son Oswulf.

In the year 755, Oswulf was wickedly murdered by his own thegns; and Ethelwald, being chosen the same year by his people, entered upon the kingdom; in whose second year there was great tribulation by reason of pestilence, which continued almost two years, divers grievous sicknesses raging, but more especially the disease of dysentery.

In the year 761, Oengus,[2] king of the Picts, died; who, from the beginning to the end of his reign, continued to be a blood-stained and tyrannical butcher; Oswin[3] was also slain.

In the year 765, King Aluchred came to the throne.[4]

In the year 766 A.D., Archbishop Egbert, of the royal race, and endued with divine knowledge, as also Frithbert, both of them truly faithful bishops, departed to the Lord.

---

[1] St. Matt. xi, 12. After Eadbert, Northumbria fell into a state of anarchy, obscure kings contending for the throne.

[2] Cf. *supra, sub* 750.

[3] An aetheling killed by Moll, king of Northumbria, at a place called Edwin's Cliff (Sax. Chron.).

[4] Of Northumbria.

INDEX

Aaron, British Martyr, 18.

Aaron, High Priest, 361.

"Abbots, Anonymous History of the," editorial references to, xxxv, 257 n., 389 n.; *and see* Bede.

Abercorn or Aebbercurnig, Monastery of, xxix, 286.

Abraham's Oak, 342.

Abraham's Tomb, 341.

Acca, friend of Bede, afterwards Bishop of Hexham, in succession to Wilfrid, xxx, 161, 248, 357, 358, 379 n., 381; his attachment to Wilfrid, 161, 355, 358; driven from his see, 161, 390; his good works, musical gifts and learning, 358; educated by Bosa, 358.

Acha, sister of Edwin, wife of Ethelfrid, and mother of Oswald, 147, 383 n.

Acts of the Apostles, quoted, 11, 197, 304, 335, 371.

"Adalbert, Life of," editorial reference to, 143 n.

Adam, 130, 341 n.; his tomb, 341.

Adamnan, Abbot of Iona, 140 n., 285 n.; his work on the Holy Places ("De Locis Sanctis"), xxii, xxx, 337, 338; his "Life of St. Columba," 336 n.; his missions to King Aldfrid, 336, 372; converts the Irish to the Catholic Easter and ecclesiastical tonsure, 336, 337, 372, 373; his

death, 337; receives Arculf, 338; return to Ireland, 373.

Adamnan, Monk of Coldingham, foretells the burning of Coldingham Monastery, xxix, 283, 284; his vision, 281, 283, 284; his penitence, 282, 283; his austerity, 281, 282, 283.

Ad Barvae, or At the Wood, Monastery of, 219, 231.

Adda, Northumbrian priest, xxvii, 180, 181.

Addi, a thegn, 308.

Adeodatus, 179 n.

Adgefrin, *see* Yeavering.

Adtuifyrdi, *see* Twyford.

Adulwald, *see* Eadbald.

Aebba, Abbess of Coldingham, half-sister of Oswy, 260, 283, 284; account of, 260 n.; her name, 260 n.; founds the monasteries of Ebchester and Coldingham, 260 n.; her friendship for Cuthbert, 260 n.; intercedes for Wilfrid, 260 n., 352 n.; her death, 284.

Aebbercurnig, *see* Abercorn.

Aecci, Bishop of Dunwich, 231.

Aedan, King of Scots, defeated by Ethelfrid, 73, 74.

Aedgils, fellow priest of Bede, 284.

Aelfric ("Grammaticus") editorial reference to, 288 n.

Aelfric, father of Osric, 134, 164 n.

Aelfwine, brother of Egfrid, 267, 385.

395

D D

Eumer, attempts to murder Edwin, 103, 104.

Euphemia, St., 265.

Europe, 5.

Eusebius Pamphili, Bishop of Caesarea, 369.

Eusebius, name in religion given to Huaetbert, 389 n.

Eutropius, quoted, xxii, 19.

Eutyches, founder of Eutychianism, 78 n., 254 n., 256.

Eutychius, heretic patriarch of Constantinople, 78.

Eve, 266.

Excommunication, 184.

"Excursus on Paschal Controversy," see Plummer.

"Exodus," quoted, 361, 362.

Exorcism of Evil Spirits, 311 n.

"Ezekiel, Commentary on," by Gregory, 79.

"Ezra," 387, 388.

Fainéant, Roi, see Clotaire III.

Famines, 26, 27, 28.

Fara, or Burgundofara, foundress of the Monastery of Brige, 151, 215 n.

Faremoûtier-en-Brie, or Farae Monasterium in Brige, see Brige.

Farne, Isle of, or House Island, xxix, 168, 288, 295, 301, 302.

Faro, or Burgundofarus, Bishop of Meaux, 215.

Fasting, 145, 151, 206, 282, 307 n.

Feliskirk, Yorkshire, 121 n.

Felix, St., 388.

Felix III, Pope, 75.

Felix IV, Pope, 75.

Felix, Bishop of Dunwich, xxv, 121, 122, 193; his school, 172; death, 122, 178.

Felixstowe, 121 n.

Fen Country, The, 179 n.

Fergus, father of Oengus, 392 n.

Field-of-Oaks, see Dearmach.

Fina, mother of Aldfrid, 287.

Finan, Bishop of Lindisfarne, after Aidan, 169, 201, 204; baptizes Peada, 180; ordains Diuma, 181; baptizes Sigbert, 182; ordains Cedd, 183; builds a church at Lindisfarne, 192; his controversy with Ronan on the Easter question, 193; death, 193.

Finchale, 204 n.

Fire, future punishment by, 175.

Fire of London, 240 n.

Fish of Britain, 5.

Fiskerton, 123 n.

Flintshire, 86 n.

Florence of Worcester, editorial references to, 191 n., 218 n., 231 n., 241 n., 244 n., 272 n., 273, 274, 301 n., 377 n., 380 n.

Foillan, see Fullan.

Folcard, his Life of St. John of Beverley, editorial references to, 303 n., 305 n.

Fontaines, Monastery of, 92 n.

Forfar, 285 n., 360 n.

Forth, the, or Sea of Giudan, 23 n., 24 n., 142 n., 285 n., 286 n.

Forthere, Bishop of Sherborne after Aldhelm, 344, 345, 379 n., 380.

Forthhere, Edwin's thegn, 104.

Fortunatus, Venantius, Bishop of Poitiers, 14, 265 n.; his "Praise of Virgins" quoted, 15.

Fosite, the god, son of Balder, 323 n.

Fosse, monastery of, 177 n.

Fosse, Abbot of, see Ultan.

France, 5.

Franks, the, 13, 22, 92 n.; their language, 45 n.; Church of, 51, 54, 55; and see Gaul.

Franks, King of the, see Carloman, Charles Martel, Charibert, Childebert, Chilperic, Clothaire III, Clovis, Dagobert, Pippin, Theodebert, Theoderic.

Franks, Duke of the, see Pippin of Heristal.

Freeman's "Norman Conquest," editorial references to, 32, 246 n.

E E

Millfield (perhaps Maelmin), 120 n.

Miracles, xxix, xxxix, 232, 233, 237, 238, 268, 269, 270, 325; of Aidan, 167; of Augustine, 81, 83; of Cedd, 187; of Cuthbert, 291, 292, 297, 300; of Earcongota, 152, 153; of Earconwald, 232; of Ethelthryth, 262, 263; of Ethelwald, 301, 302; of Haedde, 343; of the Hewalds, 322; of John of Beverley, 302-311; of Oswald, xxvi, 136, 137, 138, 154-160, 162, 163, 248, 249, 250; of Paulinus, 122; of Sebbi, 240.

Miracles, Gregory on, 68, 69.

"Mission of St. Augustine," see Mason.

Moberly, his edition of the "Ecclesiastical History," xx.

Moinenn, name for Ninias, 141 n.

Moll, King of Northumbria, 393.

Monasteries, in England, xxvi, 151; in Gaul, xxvi, 151; double or mixed, 151 n., 177 n., 190, 233, 260 n., 273, 283, 284; rules for, 229; constitution of, 142 n.; hereditary succession in, 306 n.

"Monasticon," see Dugdale.

Monk, an ungodly, his wicked life and miserable death, 334, 335; his visions of hell, 335.

Monophysite Heresy, the, 254 n.

Monothelitism, xxix, 214 n., 254 n., 258, 352.

"Monumenta Historica Britannica," xx.

Moore, Bishop, his MS. of the "Ecclesiastical History," xix, xx.

Moray Frith, 360 n.

Mopsuestia, Bishop of, see Theodore.

Morgan, see Pelagius.

Morini, The, 5, 9.

Mosaic Law, 196, 198, 361.

Mount of Olives, 340, 341.

Mount Sion, 340.

Muigeo, see Mayo.

Mul, usurper in Kent, 287 n.

Music, Church, 133, 217, 218, 258, 265 n., 358, 386; supernatural, 221.

Naiton, or Nechtan mac Derili, King of the Picts, xxx, xxxi; adopts Catholic usages, 359, 360, 374; asks Ceolfrid for advice and builders, 359; builds a stone church, 359; expels the Columban clergy, 359 n.; receives Ceolfrid's letter, 374.

Namur MS. of the "Ecclesiastical History," xix.

Naples, 214.

Nativity of our Lord, see Christmas.

Nechtan mac Derili, see Naiton.

Nechtansmere, or Dunnechtan, battle of, 285.

Nendrum, or Inishmahee, Bishop of, see Cromanus.

Nennius, editorial references to, 23 n., 147 n., 188 n., 189 n., 391 n.

Nero, Emperor, 11, 14.

Nestorius, Bishop of Constantinople, his heresy, 255 n., 256.

Neustria, King of, see Chilperic, Clothaire III, Clovis II.

Neustrians defeated by Pippin, 320 n.

Newark, 123 n.

Newcastle, 180 n.

Nicaea, Council of, 19, 128, 198, 227 n., 255, 369 n.

Nicene Creed, 256 n.

Nidd, Synod of the, 356, 385 n.

Ninian, Ninias or Moinenn, Bishop of Whitern, 48 n., 141; his mission to the Southern Picts, 141.

Niridanum, monastery of, 214.

Nisan, the month, 84 n., 365 n.

Nivelles, monastery of, 177 n.

Nola, Campania, 388 n.

Nola, Bishop of, see Paulinus.

Norfolk, Bishopric of, 231 n.

"Norman Conquest, The," see Freeman.

Northamptonshire, 179 n., 180, 268 n., 346 n.
North Burton, 308.
North Pole, the, 6.
Northumberland, 4 n., 292 n.
Northumbria, Bede's acquaintance with its history, xxii, xxiii; history of, xxiv, xxv, xxvii, xxix, 82 n., 122 n., 127 n., 131, 164, 168, 185, 190 n., 195, 204, 226 n., 286, 325, 352 n., 380 n., 393 n.; establishment of Christianity in, xxiv, xxv, 102, 104, 117, 118, 119, 120, 132, 133, 139, 381; diocese of, xxvii, xxix, 3, 4, 137 n., 219, 242, 351 n., 379 n., 381.
Northumbria, King of, see Aldfrid, "Alfrid," Aluchred, Ceolwulf, Coenred, Eadbert, Eadwulf, Edwin, Egfrid, Ethelfrid, Ethelwald, Moll, Osred, Osric, Oswald, Oswulf, Oswy.
Northumbria, Bishop of, 143 n.; and see Bishops of Lindisfarne and York.
Northumbrians, 30.
North Wales, 86 n.
Norwich, the diocese of, 122 n., 231 n.
Nothelm, Archbishop of Canterbury, xxii, 2, 390; his research, xxii, 2; his questions to Bede answered, 387 n.; death, 391.
Nottinghamshire, 115 n.
Numbers, quoted, 362.

Oak, the (possibly Augustine's Ác), 84 n.
Octa, grandfather of Ethelbert, King of Kent, 95.
Oder, the river, 317 n.
Odo, Archbishop of Canterbury, 346 n.
Oecumenical Councils, see Councils.
Oengus, Angus or Ungust, King of the Picts, son of Fergus, 392 n., 393.
Oeric, Oisc, son of Hengist, 95.

Offa, King of Essex, son of Sighere, his abdication and pilgrimage to Rome, xxx, 345 n., 346.
Offa, King of Mercia, 18 n., 219 n., 392.
Offerings at the Altar, divisions of, 49, 50.
Oftfor, Bishop of Worcester, 273, 274, 380 n.
Oiddi, a priest of Wilfrid's, 245.
Oidilwald, sub-king of Deira, see Ethelwald.
Oil calms a storm, 167.
Oisc, see Oeric.
Oiscings, the, 94.
Olivet, Mount, see Mount of Olives.
Old Saxons, The, 317, 320, 321, 322.
Old Sarum, 343 n.
Opus Paschale, see Sedulius.
Orcades, The, see Orkneys.
Ordination of bishops, 49, 50, 53, 54.
Orkneys, The, 5, 11, 142 n., 382.
Orosius, xxii, 5 n., 25 n.
Orthography, 389.
Osfrid, son of Edwin, baptized, 119; slain in battle, 131; his son, 132.
Osred, King of Northumbria, after Aldfrid, xxx, 342, 345, 346 n., 356, 357, 377 n., 385 n., besieged in Bamborough by Eadwulf, 385 n.; killed in battle, 375, 386.
Osric, sub-king of the Hwiccas, 273 n.
Osric, King of Deira after Edwin, son of Aelfric, 134, 135, 164.
Osric, King of Northumbria after Coenred, xxxi, 1 n., 273 n., 375 n., 377; his parentage, 377 n.; death, 378, 386.
Osthryth, daughter of Oswy, wife of Ethelred, King of Mercia, 157, 267, 352 n.; her love for Bardney Monastery, 157, 158; murdered by her nobles, 385.

F F

Tynemouth, Abbot of, *see* Herebald.
Tyrhtel, Bishop of Hereford,
380 n.
Tytilus, father of Redwald, King
of East Anglia, 121.

Ulster, 8 n.
"Ulster, the Annals of," editorial
references to, 225 n., 385 n.
Ultan, a hermit, Abbot of Fosse and
Péronne, brother of Fursa, 177.
Undalum, *see* Oundle.
Urbs Giudi, 23 n.
Urbs Iudeu, 23 n.
Utrecht, 320 n., 324 n.
Utrecht, Archbishop of, *see* Wil-
brord.
Utta, Abbot of Gateshead, 166,
180; sent to fetch Eanfled from
Kent, 166, 167; calms a storm
with oil, 167.
Uuffa, grandfather of Redwald,
King of East Anglia, 121.
Uuffings, *i.e.*, Kings of East
Anglia, 121.
Uurtigern, *see* Vortigern.

Vaeclingacaestir, *see* St. Albans.
Valens, Emperor, 20.
Valentinian II, Emperor, 20; ex-
pelled from Italy, 20; restored,
20; kills Maximus, 20.
Valentinian III, Emperor, 29, 383;
murders Aetius, 27 n., 41; mur-
dered, 41.
Valerian, Emperor, 388 n.
Vandals, the, 22.
Vecta, 30.
Venantius Fortunatus, *see* Fortun-
atus.
Venta, *see* Winchester.
Vergil, quoted, 113, 118, 159, 286,
327.
Vergilius, Archbishop of Arles,
49 n., 54, 55, 63, 64.
Verlamacaestir, or Verulam, *see*
St. Albans.
Vespasian conquers the Isle of
Wight, 11.

Vestments, Ecclesiastical, 65.
Viaticum, the, 249 n., 275, 280.
Victgilsus, Father of Hengist and
Horsa, 30.
Victorinus, St., 99 n.
Victorius, or Victorinus of Aquitaine, his Paschal Cycle, 369 n.
Vienne, 22.
Vines in Britain, 5; in Ireland, 9.
Virgil, *see* Vergil.
Virginity, poem in honour of, 264,
265, 266, 267; Aldhelm's work
on, 237 n., 344.
Visions, xxx, 248, 249, 250, 332,
333, 334, 335, 336; seen by Adamnan, 281, 282, 283, 284; by Begu,
275, 276; by a nun at Whitby,
277; by Bregusuid, 274; by
Caedmon, 278, 279; by Drythelm, 325-331; at Barking, 232-
237; by Earcongota, 152, 153;
by Edwin, 112, 113, 114; by a
disciple of Boisil, 224, 317, 318,
319; by Fursa, 173-177; by Sebbi, 239; by Theodore, 314; by
Tilmon, 322; by Wilfrid, 355.
Vitalian, Pope, xxvii, 2 n., 216;
his letter to Oswy, 208, 209, 210,
211; seeks a suitable Archbishop for Canterbury, 213, 214;
ordains Theodore, 215; sends
Theodore and Hadrian to Britain, 357.
Vitta, 30.
Voyage Provision, *i.e.*, the Viaticum, 249, 275.
Vortigern, or Uurtigern, King of
Britain, calls in the Saxons, 29,
95.
Vulgate, the, quoted, 80, 107, 174,
209, 282, 361-372.

Wagele, perhaps Whalley, 204 n.
Wahlstod, Bishop of Hereford,
379 n., 380.
Walbottle, 180 n.
Waldhere, Bishop of London,
239.
Wales, 33 n.
Wall, At the, 180, 182.

CPSIA information can be obtained
at www.ICGtesting.com
Printed in the USA
LVHW080307070123
736630LV00005B/280